Environmental Economics for Sustainable Growth

A Handbook for Practitioners

Anil Markandya

*Professor of Economics, University of Bath, UK, and
Lead Economist, World Bank, USA*

Patrice Harou

*Senior Environmental Economist, World Bank, USA, and
Visiting Professor, ENGREF, Nancy, France*

Lorenzo Giovanni Bellù

*Economist, and Policy Support Officer, Food and Agriculture
Organization of the United Nations, Rome, Italy*

Vito Cistulli

*Senior Economist at the Blue Plan, a regional activity centre
of the Mediterranean Action Plan of the United Nations
Environment Programme (UNEP), Sophia Antipolis, France*

IN ASSOCIATION WITH THE INTERNATIONAL BANK FOR
RECONSTRUCTION AND DEVELOPMENT/THE WORLD BANK

Edward Elgar

Cheltenham, UK • Northampton, MA, USA

Published by
Edward Elgar Publishing Limited
Glensanda House
Montpellier Parade
Cheltenham
Glos GL50 1UA
UK

Edward Elgar Publishing, Inc.
136 West Street
Suite 202
Northampton
Massachusetts 01060
USA

A catalogue record for this book is available from the British Library

Library of Congress Cataloguing in Publication Data
Environmental economics for sustainable growth: a handbook for practitioners /
Anil Markandya ... [et al.]
    p. cm.
    "In association with the International Bank for Reconstruction and Development/
The World Bank."
    Includes bibliographical references and index.
1. Environmental policy—Economic aspects—Handbooks, manuals, etc. 2. Sustainable
development—Handbooks, manuals, etc. I. Markandya, Anil, 1945–

HC79.E5 E57726 2002
338.9'27—dc21   2001053213

ISBN 1 84064 306 4 (cased)
ISBN 1 84064 812 0 (paperback)

Printed and bound in Great Britain by Biddles Ltd, *www.biddles.co.uk*

Environmental Economics for Sustainable Growth

Contents

Figures

ix

Tables

Boxes

Foreword

Environmental issues are not a luxury for the rich. Most often the poor who depend directly on natural resources and environmental goods and services for their livelihoods, suffer most the consequences from environmental degradation. The costs of such degradation in developing countries can easily reach several percentage points of GDP. Environmental problems threaten the natural resource base: soils, water, fisheries and forests. It can hurt the health of the poor through water and air pollution and through their increased vulnerability to natural disasters such as flooding and desertification. Environmental degradation reaches across borders and impacts both the regional and global commons.

The new World Bank strategy sets three related objectives to respond to these challenges: improving the quality of life, improving the quality of growth, and protecting the global commons. To improve the quality of life, it seeks to help protect the long term productivity and resilience of natural resources on which so many poor people depend, to reduce environmental health risks by reducing water and air pollution, and to reduce the vulnerability of the poor to environmental hazards such as those caused by desertification and climate change. The quality of growth will be improved by the sustainable management of environmental and natural resources through policy, regulatory and institutional reforms fully involving the private sector in the process. Finally, the global commons will be protected through new financing mechanisms to compensate countries for the incremental costs of protection.

Economic tools are important to set the priorities among all these possible actions and to properly mainstream the issues of the environment into policy and decision-making processes at the macro, sector and program/project levels. This book presents many of the key tools necessary for achieving these goals and provides examples of their applications. It has evolved over many years of training by the authors and others in the 'Political Economy of the Environment' program of the World Bank Institute. The program has the double objectives of empowering national professionals to do the analysis required to mainstream the environment in the policy and decision-making processes and of creating regional epistemic communities, or communities of practice, which through their analytical work and advocacy can move economic policies towards more sustainable outcomes.

The global development community is facing a grave challenge to transform the environments and the quality of life of the rural and urban poor, help them build communities and improve their living conditions, strengthen their ability to integrate into a rapidly interconnected world and, at the same time, maintain their resources base and a sense of community and place. Not only does this challenge need to be met, but also it must be within our life times. Only with the sharing of knowledge through programs of communities of practice and the use of training materials such as this book provides, will we be able to rise to the professionals and those they advise on mainstreaming the environment in economic development and sector strategies, and in programs and projects.

Frannie A. Leautier
Vice President
The World Bank

Acknowledgements

This book was prepared initially as part of a contract between the World Bank Institute (WBI), formerly the Economic Development Institute (EDI), and the Commission of the European Union (DGVIII). Subsequent support for this venture was provided by the governments of the Netherlands, Italy and the United Kingdom. This book has been developed over some years, with parts of the final material having been presented at various training workshops all over the world. Many different resource persons contributed to the final product and their contribution is gratefully acknowledged. Chapter 6 in particular draws heavily on the contribution of Benoit Laplante. Special thanks go to Nancy Agwu, Manolo Clar Massanet, Joelle Dehasse, Fadi Doumani, Rama Jammi, Julian Lampietti and Lawrence Markowitz, of EDI/WBI environmental economics and policy team; and to Tim Taylor, Nick Dale, Ibon Galarraga, Alistair Hunt, Pamela Mason and Alison Poole of the University of Bath. Tim Taylor has been particularly important in ensuring the delivery of the final manuscript. Patrice Harou acknowledges with thanks the kind hospitality of "L'Ecole Nationale du Génie Rural, des Eaux et des Forêts" (ENGREF), Nancy, France and of Dr. Jean-Luc Peyron, Head of the Forestry Economics unit, during the finalisation of the book. Comments from European Union staff in DGVIII have also been useful in shaping the final product. All errors and omissions are of course the responsibility of the authors. Patrice Harou was co-author of all modules and helped ensure a balanced presentation. The overall editorship was undertaken by Anil Markandya. In writing the book, primary responsibility for revising Chapters 1 to 8 was with Anil Markandya. Chapters 9 to 15 were primarily the result of a joint effort of Lorenzo Giovanni Bellù and Vito Cistulli. Lorenzo Giovanni Bellù focused more on analytical sections and numerical applications; Vito Cistulli focused more on the methodological sections and discussions.

the data included in this publication and accepts no responsibility whatsoever for any consequences of their use. The boundaries, colours, denominations, and other information shown on any map in this volume does not imply on the part of the World Bank Group any judgement on the legal status of any territory or the endorsement or acceptance of such boundaries.

1.   Introduction and structure

OBJECTIVE

To present the objectives and the structure of the book.

SUMMARY

The framework used to organize the chapters of the book is presented. The first part of the book presents economy-wide policies and their potential impacts on the environment. The second part analyses the environmental impact of projects in economic terms. As a whole, the aim of the book is to integrate the economy-wide policies presented in Part I with the analytical tools for monetary valuation of environmental impacts of Part II. This is achieved by focusing on the valuation of environmental effects. The chapters are listed together with their objectives.

1.1 INTRODUCTION

This book is designed primarily for trainers and practitioners, but also for government advisors involved in formulating and implementing environmental policies in developing countries and economies in transition. The overall objective is to train, using material based on state-of-the art tools of environmental–economic analysis combined with extensive practical experience, national professionals to contract or implement environmental economic studies themselves so as to identify policies and investments that will ensure sustainable development in their respective countries. It is *not* a book on environmental economics in the pure sense,[1] but rather a book that shows how the tools of environmental economics can be used in a policy-making context particularly in developing countries and economies in transition.

The broad context within which policies are to be analysed is that of sustainable development. This term was brought into common use by the World Commission on Environment and Development (the Brundtland Commission) in 1987. The Brundtland Commission report, *Our Common Future*, calls for development that meets the needs of the present generation without compromising the needs of future generations and highlights the need to simultaneously address developmental and environmental imperatives.

Since 1987, substantial efforts have drawn out the operational implications of the concept of sustainable development. This was the main theme, for example, of the World Bank's 1992 World Development Report. The discussion of this concept in this book is not designed to generate a general theory of sustainability, but rather to focus on key conceptual issues with potentially important operational implications.

This book offers three perspectives that are essential to any successful economic policy that has claims to meeting the goals of sustainable development:

- *Economists'* methods, which seek to maximize human welfare within the constraints of existing resources and technologies. In this context, economists are relearning the importance of natural capital and attempting to value it. Economic valuation is at the core of this book.
- *Ecologists*, who stress preserving the integrity of ecological subsystems, which are critical for the overall stability of the global ecosystem. Some argue for the preservation of all ecosystems, but a less extreme view would maintain the resiliency and dynamic adaptability of natural life-support systems. The ecological accounting units are physical, not monetary, and the prevailing ecological disciplines are biology, geology, chemistry and the natural sciences. Many policy makers argue that there is a need to value these accounting units.

- *Sociologists*, who emphasize the human nature of key actors and patterns of social organization which are crucial in devising viable means of attaining sustainable development. In fact, evidence is mounting that a failure to pay sufficient attention to social factors, including institutional and governance aspects, in the development process is seriously jeopardizing the effectiveness of various development programmes and projects aiming at economic growth. This element should be integrated in the policy and project analyses.

Although this book considers all three viewpoints, as well as other dimensions relevant to the quality of growth such as the institutional and governance aspects of development (Thomas et al. 2000), its focus is on the use of the economist's tools to address policy issues of sustainable development.

1.2   OBJECTIVES OF THE BOOK

The overall objective of the first part of the book, 'Economy-wide Policies and the Environment', is to link economy-wide policies, both macroeconomic and sectoral, with the environment. A range of economy-wide policies is used to address macroeconomic problems and sectoral issues. Although they are not intended to influence the quality of the natural environment, these policies can affect it both positively and negatively.

After placing the environment in the perspective of a vision for sustainable development, five sub-objectives are covered in Part I:

- to link macroeconomic policy variables with environmental impacts;
- to link sectoral economic policy variables with environmental impacts;
- to determine appropriate policies and instruments for the implementation of the national environmental strategies;
- to determine the appropriate legal and institutional changes necessary for the implementation of the strategies; and
- to link economy-wide policies with project and programme analyses duly integrating environmental assessment.

The objective of Part II, 'Environmetal Valuation Methods for Policies and Projects', is to provide the basic principles of valuation, and to show how they can be used for decision-making at the project as well as policy level. At the core of the book is the issue of the proper pricing and valuation of environmental impacts. The starting point for good environmental management is recognizing the costs of environmental damage and the benefits of good environmental management and introducing them into the decision-making process.

This should systematize priorities setting. Faced with a complex array of environmental dangers but possessing limited resources, where should a government start? This book provides some economic tools that can help answer this question in a broad political context.

The following are the five sub-objectives to Part II:

- to integrate environmental assessment (EA) early in the decision making process;
- to integrate EA in the physical input–output of the economic analysis of policies and projects;
- to value non-priced inputs and outputs, especially those added by the EA;
- to consider non-economic indicators in the project decision; and
- to provide case studies showing how valuation methods for environmental impacts can be used in a cost-benefit analysis context to select and monitor projects and policies.

In the quest to enable developing countries and transition economies to undertake macroeconomic, sectoral and investment policies that consider the environmental dimension, this book follows analyses that have been developed by a number of development agencies and governments. Figure 1.1 presents a general framework that organizes the chapters. The framework is general enough and flexible. Deletions and additions can be made to the material to cope with the very different macroeconomic, sectoral and project settings that one is actually likely to experience. The interrelationship of such analyses and their interconnections are also represented schematically in Figure 1.1. The book begins by setting out the 'vision' of sustainable development, and how it influences the way in which we look at the interface between the environment and the economy (Chapter 2). The next chapter is devoted to the policy framework, macroeconomic as well as sectoral. Policy reforms aimed at restructuring an entire economy are undertaken to integrate better the national economy into the world market by adjusting the exchange rate, liberalizing trade, or phasing out different subsidies. These reforms will generally have a direct impact on the growth of the different sectors of the economy as well as on the environment (Chapter 3). An impact on a particular sector is further analysed in a specific sector study and in other studies directly related to that sector (Chapter 4). In order to develop adequate policies, we need to understand how economic incentives work in the area of the environment, and how they can be used in the efficient regulation of natural resources and pollution problems (Chapter 5). Environmental policy cannot, however, be made solely with regard to economic instruments. Arguably, legal and institutional tools are at least as important (Chapter 6).

The environmental impact of national and sectoral economic policies, but also other policies, such as population and education, is addressed across sectors

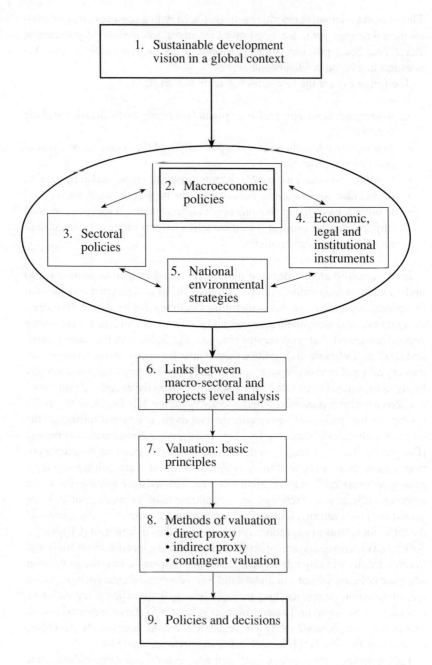

Figure 1.1   Schematic representation of chapters

in a national environmental action plan, which proposes an overall national strategy to protect the country's environment (Chapter 7). The consideration of both environmental and economic dimensions in designing appropriate policies and investment programmes is a complex undertaking. The macro aspects of sustainable development can be distinguished as including country economic studies (CEMs), sector studies (SSs), national environmental action plans (NEAPs), or environmental strategies (ESs), public expenditure review (PERs) and country development strategies (CDSs). The budgeting exercise should reflect these macro, sectoral and environmental policies, and expenditures should be monitored to see if the budget is being effectively implemented as planned. These environmental action plans, or similar environmental strategies, should provide a framework for integrating environmental and natural capital considerations into a nation's economic and social development plan. Recently the World Bank has adopted the Comprehensive Development Framework with its client countries as a strategy to design and evaluate its activities through the ultimate criteria of poverty reduction (Wold Bank 1999). This framework encourages countries to pursue economic development duly considering its human, social, natural and physical dimensions.

All the above represent a macroeconomic and sectoral perspective to the problem. Much of the detailed evaluation, however, has to take place at the project or microeconomic level. But before we can do that, we need to understand the conceptual basis for such an evaluation, and how the microeconomic aspects are related to the macroeconomic ones (Chapter 8). This completes Part I of the book.

Part II is devoted to the valuation of environmental impacts, and the use of such valuations in project appraisal and policy formulation. Before describing the techniques of valuation, it is important to understand the basis of the methodologies used (Chapter 9). There are a number of techniques that can be used for the valuation of environmental impacts. These range from approaches based on assessing changes in the physical environment and then valuing the changes – the so-called productivity approach (Chapter 10); to inferring the values from behaviour in related markets (the travel cost and hedonic approaches) (Chapter 11); to soliciting the values by questionnaire methods (the contingent valuation approach) (Chapter 12). All these methods can and have been applied in project appraisal exercises in developing countries and examples are given as case studies (Chapters 13, 14 and 15).

1.3 DESCRIPTION OF THE CHAPTERS

Box 1.1 provides a brief description of the chapters given the objectives outlined above. To meet these objectives, 14 training chapters have been prepared. Each chapter is associated with elements of the framework given in Figure 1.1 and explained in the previous section. A brief description of each chapter and its link with the elements of the framework follows. The chapters are divided into two parts. Part I, Economy-wide Policies and the Environment, is linked to the first six boxes of the framework. Part II, Analysis of Projects with Environmental Impacts, is linked to the remaining boxes of the framework, which all relate to the project cycle.

BOX 1.1   DESCRIPTION OF THE CHAPTERS

Part I   Economy-wide Policies and the Environment

Chapter 2: Sustainable development in a global context (Box 1, Figure1.1)

In the spirit of the Rio Summit, a vision of global context, backed by a national strategy, is an important precondition to implementing successful policies for sustainable development. The strategy itself must be translated into a plan of action. The plan should be flexible and adaptable to new circumstances over time. This chapter places the training on political economy of the environment in the broader perspective of sustainable development as envisaged at the Earth Summit in Rio and enunciated in Agenda 21.

Chapter 3: Macroeconomic policies and the environment (Box 2, Figure 1.1)

Macroeconomic policies are implemented by manipulating mechanisms such as exchange rates, interest rates, wage policies, trade and privatization. The impacts on and linkages of these mechanisms to the natural environment and social fabric are unique to each country. The 'green accounts' discuss the integration of environmental impacts into national accounts.

Chapter 4: Sectoral policies and the environment (Box 3, Figure 1.1)

Sectoral policies involve a broad range of specific policy variables, such as pricing, economic and regulatory instruments. In this chapter the emphasis is placed on having the price 'right'. Sectoral policies can be analysed with an aggregate supply–demand framework for different natural resources and sink functions. Examples illustrate sector policy and environmental linkages for the green (water, forestry and land use) and brown (energy) issues.

Chapter 5: Policies, instruments and the environment (Box 4, Figure 1.1)

Once a vision of sustainable development and the appropriate macroeconomic and sectoral policies has been established, environmental policy priorities are set above and among sectors. An approach which includes economic considerations should be used to determine priorities among direct public and private investments and indirect public investments, such as environmental incentives programmes, and social, institutional and legal actions. This chapter deals with the economic aspects of the decision-making process.

Chapter 6: Laws, regulations and institutions (Box 4, Figure 1.1)

The other dimension of policy making in the environmental domain is the provision of a proper legislative and institutional framework for decision making. A participatory processes is a crucial element for establishing priorities within this framework. This chapter deals with the laws, regulations and institutions necessary for the implementation of sustainable development policies.

Chapter 7: National environmental strategies (Box 5, Figure 1.1)

A strategy needs to be put in place for all the economic policies to incorporate the environmental and social aspects. The strategy should respond to national and international aspirations. This chapter provides a discussion of the experiences in setting up national environmental strategies and the tools used in their development.

Chapter 8: Economy-wide policies and the valuation of environment impacts (Box 6, Figure 1.1)

This chapter links economy-wide policies with the project level by looking at the sequencing of the investment/policy decisions and by integrating environmental assessment into project analysis.

Part II   Environmental Valuation Methods for Policies and Projects

Chapter 9: Economic principles and an overview of valuation methods (Box 7, Figure 1.1)

This chapter provides an outline of the basic principles of valuation and its use in environmental economics. This provides concepts of total economic value, use value and non-use value. It discusses the issues arising in the measurement of willingness to pay (WTP) and willingness to accept (WTA) and relates them to the demand curve. Valuation techniques help project analysts integrate EA information in the with/without economic analysis. They help value some of the non-priced inputs and outputs of the project, especially those identified in the EA.

Chapter 10: Revealed preferences: direct proxy methods (Box 8, Figure 1.1)
This chapter describes two techniques used in environmental economics: the productivity change method (PCM) and the substitute cost method (SCM).

Chapter 11: Revealed preferences: indirect proxy methods (Box 8, Figure 1.1)
This chapter describes two of the indirect methods of valuing environmental impacts. These include the use of travel cost data and property price data as sources of indirect information on environmental values.

Chapter 12: Stated preference: contingent valuation methods (Box 8, Figure 1.1)
This chapter provides a discussion of the use of questionnaire methods in valuing environmental impacts (contingent valuation method).

Chapter 13: Use of monetary values of environmental and natural resources for benefit–cost analysis: an application to a soil moisture conservation project in Tunisia (Box 9, Figure 1.1)
A case study based on the use of monetary values of environmental and natural resources in the framework of cost–benefit analysis of project is provided with an application to the soil moisture conservation project in Tunisia.

Chapter 14: Use of monetary values of environmental and natural resources in the framework of national accounts: an application to Costa Rica (Box 9, Figure 1.1)
A case study based on the use of monetary values for the construction of environmental accounts for Costa Rica is presented.

Chapter 15: Valuing health impact: a case study of air pollution in New Delhi, India (Box 9, Figure 1.1)
A case study of the application of the different methods of valuation and their use in the valuation of health impacts in Delhi is presented.

A very important part of the handbook is the set of exercises, which are provided at the end of most of the chapters. Not only do these illustrate the techniques and complement the explanation of the methods in the main text of the chapter; they also provide 'hands-on' training to the reader in how the method can actually be applied in practice. This is particularly true of the exercises for the valuation chapters (10–12), and for the case studies at the end (Chapters 13–15). Hence they must be seen as a requirement for any course for which the workbook is used. To facilitate the delivery of training, all step-wise exercises of Part II are available on spreadsheet accompanied by a set of slides in electronic format, which summarize the contents of the different chapters.

NOTE

1. There are many good books on the market that fulfil that role. See, for example, Hanley et al. (1997) or Tietenberg (1996).

CITED BIBLIOGRAPHY

Hanley N., Shogren J.F. and B. White (1997), *Environmental Economics – In Theory and Practice*, London: Macmillan.
Thomas, V., M. Dailami, A. Dhareshwar, D. Kaufman, N. Kishor, R. Lopez and Y. Wang (2000), *The Quality of Growth*, Oxford: Oxford University Press for the World Bank.
Tietenberg, T. (1996), *Environmental and Natural Resource Economics*, New York: Harper Collins.
Wold Bank (1999), 'A proposal for a comprehensive development framework', Washington, DC, Mimeo.
World Bank (1992), *World Development Report 1992*, Executive Summary, Washington DC: World Bank.
World Bank (1994), *Making Development Sustainable: From Concepts to Action*, Environmentally Sustainable Development Occasional Paper Series No. 2. Washington, DC: World Bank.
World Commission on Environment and Development (Brundtland Commission) (1987), *Our Common Future*, Oxford: Oxford University Press.

PART I

Economy-wide Policies and the Environment

2. Sustainable development vision in a global context

OBJECTIVE

1. To introduce the notion of sustainable development and its operationalization in the formulation of environmental, economic and social policies.
2. To present the tools and processes necessary to develop a sustainable development strategy, as proposed in Chapters 8, 38 and 39 of Agenda 21 of the Rio Declaration on Environment and Development.

SUMMARY

There is a considerable body of literature on sustainable development, how it can be measured and what it implies for economic, social and environmental policies. This chapter provides an introduction to that literature. At the same time there has been a growth of interest at the political level in sustainable development and in the institutional reforms necessary to bring it about. Agenda 21 is the basis on which a sustainable development vision and strategy can be built in a global context. General lessons learned from environmental strategies are summarized in this chapter. Chapter 8 of Agenda 21 encourages countries to integrate the environment in economic development plans. In addition, Chapters 38 and 39 provide the global perspective into which the national strategies fit. This chapter concludes by discussing how the analytical tools and the politically driven institutional changes can be integrated in procedures that will promote sustainable development.

2.1   THE EARLIEST DEFINITION OF SUSTAINABLE DEVELOPMENT[1]

The term 'sustainable development' has its origins in the International Union for the Conservation of Nature and Natural Resources (IUCN) 1980 World Conservation Strategy report, but it was with the World Commission on Environment and Development's *Our Common Future* (1987) that the term gained broad currency.[2] The Commission defined sustainable development as 'development that meets the needs for the present without compromising the ability of future generations to meet their own needs'. This definition, while useful in drawing attention to the concern with the long-term implications of present-day development, asks as many questions as it answers. What constitutes 'needs', and how will these change over time? What reductions in the options available to future generations are acceptable and what are not? The operational aspects of sustainable development were not answered by the Brundtland Commission, although the Report itself gave strong hints that the environmental degradation resulting from today's economic policies was a major source of concern from a sustainability viewpoint. The recent World Bank *World Development Report* (2000) emphasizes the quality of growth and its distribution taking poverty alleviation over time as the ultimate criterion of sustainable development.

The first attempts to make the concept more precise were theoretical rather than practical. They focused on the economic and the environmental dimensions of the debate. From the economic perspective, some of the earlier contributions (Pearce et al. 1990) suggested sustainable development should imply that *no generation* in the future would be worse of than the present generation. In other words society should not allow welfare to fall over time.

Recent work has sought to analyse sustainable development more broadly; in terms of its economic, social and environmental dimensions. Indeed one commentator (Munasinghe 1993, 2000) has argued that implementing sustainable development will need a new science of 'sustainomics', in which a transdisciplinary approach has to be followed. Figure 2.1, taken from Munasinghe (1993), summarizes this vision. Each dimension requires a mixture of skills and disciplines, from ecology, economics and sociology; sustainomics also draws on related areas like anthropology, biotechnology, botany, chemistry, demography, engineering, ethics, geography, information technology, law, philosophy, physics, psychology, zoology and so on. Methods that bridge the economy–society–environment interfaces are especially important, including environmental and resource economics, ecological economics, conservation ecology, energetics and energy economics, economics of sociology, environmental sociology, environmental ethics and so on. While building on such earlier work, sustainomics projects a more neutral image which focuses attention explicitly on sustainable development, and avoids the implication of any disciplinary bias or hegemony.

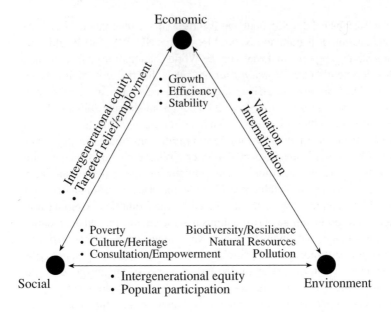

Source: Munasinghe (1993).

Figure 2.1   A vision of sustainable development

2.2   ECONOMIC DIMENSION OF SUSTAINABLE DEVELOPMENT

2.2.1   Optimality in Economic Development and Sustainability

The basic question in designing an optimal development strategy for a country is the following: if a society is to maximize the welfare of all generations, present and future, how should it allocate resources over time? The models that have been used for this analysis are sophisticated and complex, and it is not appropriate to go into detail about them here. However, one or two aspects about them are worth noting. First, the models maximize *discounted welfare*. This means that the welfare of future generations is given a lower weight than that of present generations. Why is that? Again the reasons are complex but essentially boil down to saying that people attach progressively less value to utility as it moves further into the future. They do so because the future is more uncertain, and because future generations will have access to more technology and capital than the present generations. The discount rate measures the rate at which utility becomes less important as it moves further away in time. The social planner derives the optimal solution by maximizing the welfare function subject to a budget constraint of the form:

Investment = Output – Consumption.

The budget constraint means that the cost of postponing consumption by investing in capital is offset by the return on capital, which permits higher consumption in the future.

The first formal analysis of this problem in a framework that included both man-made capital and non-renewable natural resources was carried out by Dasgupta and Heal (1974). They demonstrated that with a low initial man-made capital stock and a high initial resource stock the optimal path for per capita consumption may look as shown in Figure 2.2, with consumption rising initially and then falling. In other words it is possible, with a non-renewable resource stock and a man-made capital stock for the optimal path to decline towards zero over time. This is a direct result of the fact that a positive (and constant) utility discount rate means that the cost of low levels of utility far into the future is outweighed by the benefit of higher levels of utility in the near future.

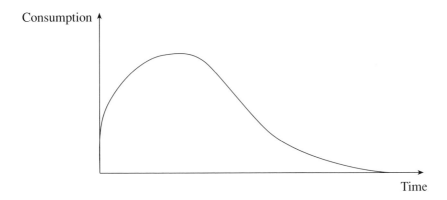

Figure 2.2   The path of consumption in Dasgupta and Heal's model

2.2.2   Sustainability and Natural Resource Use

The above shows that a classical economic analysis of growth can result in a strategy that does not fit in with the common-sense interpretation of what is sustainable. The question that follows then is, how can one modify such strategies to make them more sustainable? One interpretation, as noted above, is that welfare should not decline over time. In this context that would mean consumption should not decline. What in turn does this imply for the use of natural resources? Since sustainable extraction of a non-renewable resource is, for practical purposes, impossible, sustainable resource *use* can be defined as maintaining a *capacity* to provide the benefit in question, for example by investing in a substitute for the non-renewable resource or, if the resource is exported, in an alternative revenue-generating asset. This corresponds to Solow's (1991, p. 3) definition of sustainability as leaving to the future 'the option or the capacity to be as well off as we are'.

The best-known rule for sustainability in the presence of non-renewable resource extraction is the Hartwick rule (Hartwick 1977). Hartwick showed that if the objective is to achieve the highest *constant* per capita consumption then society should invest in man-made capital an amount equal to the rents from the depletion of the natural resource. Hence, Hartwick's rule has become known as the 'invest resource rents for sustainability' rule. This rule holds under a wide variety of conditions and applies to both renewable and non-renewable resources. By resource rents we mean the change in the value of the stock as it is used. Typically the use of a resource results in a decline in the value of what is left. The Hartwick rule requires that society invest an amount equal to this decline.

2.3   ENVIRONMENTAL SUSTAINABILITY

This discussion of sustainability has considered only sustainability of consumption, and the contribution of natural resources to production. Sustainability of consumption, however, is only one definition of economic sustainability. Economic sustainability requires that the more fundamental services provided by the environment be sustained at or above some minimum levels over time. This can be described as environmental sustainability.

The most conspicuous services that the natural environment provides are food and inputs to production, including energy, metals and timber. Energy and metals are non-renewable resources, while timber is a renewable resource. We have just seen how these resources can be used sustainably in terms of maximizing the level of sustainable consumption that their owners can afford. In addition, the environment provides utility directly via, for instance, aesthetic and recreational values.

The natural environment also provides more fundamental services, without which human life on earth would not be possible. These are known as global life-support services, since they provide the basic necessities to allow human life such as food and shelter, and the maintenance of suitable climatic and atmospheric conditions. There is often a trade-off between using natural ecosystems to provide inputs to production, even if this use is sustainable, and preserving them in their natural condition to maintain life-support services. The opportunity cost of preservation is the value that could be obtained from harvesting ecosystems, and from converting the land to an alternative use.

Ecosystems, whether natural or managed, are required to capture the sun's energy and to produce food and raw materials. They regulate the hydrological cycle, which is a direct service to agricultural production. They create and maintain fertile soils, and they break down both natural and man-made waste into nutrients, maintaining soil productivity. Some of these ecosystem services are summarized in Figure 2.3.

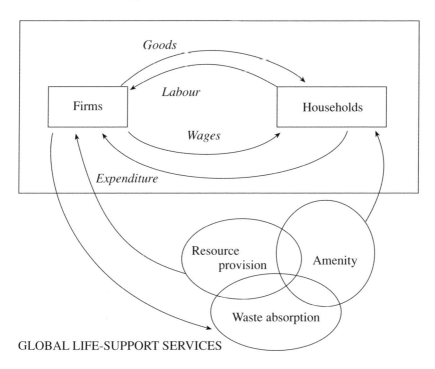

Figure 2.3   The ecological services of the natural environment

A key life-support service provided by natural ecosystems is climate regulation, both on a local and on a global scale. As noted, ecosystems are necessary at a local level for regulation of the hydrological cycle. On a global scale, they are necessary to maintain the composition of the world's atmosphere and therefore its system of climate regulation. The mitigation of global warming is the best-known example of this ecological service. A major issue for global environmental sustainability is how far ecosystems can be depleted, and pollutants allowed to accumulate in the atmosphere, without threatening global life-support services. One of the problems in analysing this issue is that scientific knowledge of ecosystem structure is far from complete. This results to a certain extent from the immense complexity and interdependence of species and systems. It is very difficult, therefore, to predict the effect that removing or reducing a population of one species will have on the rest of the species in a community, or on the viability of the ecosystem.

Figure 2.3 highlights three important facts. First, the environment provides a wide variety of services that improve human welfare, both directly and indirectly. Second, the use of the environment for some services, for example, waste absorption, reduces its capacity to provide other services, for example, amenity or resource inputs. Third, the services of the environment can be thought of as representing 'natural capital'. Stocks of natural resources, including the capacity to perform global life-support services, can be used unsustainably over time, reducing their capacity to deliver the same services in the future.

The implication of the second factor is that economic growth should be limited so that the positive contributions of economic growth to welfare are not outweighed by its negative environmental effects. This is the point that Daly (1991) makes in complaining that while in microeconomics, the optimal scale of an economic activity is clearly defined, with further growth uneconomic past the point at which the costs of growth outweigh the benefits, there is no corresponding recognition of an optimum scale of the macro economy. The question for environmental macroeconomics is, therefore, to what extent should economic growth be allowed to destroy environmental assets?

It has been suggested that this is not an issue, since people become richer with economic growth and demand a cleaner environment. This hypothesis is encapsulated in the environmental Kuznets curve debate. The environmental Kuznets curve represents an empirically observed phenomenon, namely the fact that some environmental problems have become less severe as income levels rise. This is shown in Figure 2.4. This phenomenon has been used to argue that economic growth is in fact good for the environment, and that the argument that there are limits to the contribution that economic growth can make to human well-being is false. However, it is not clear that this is the case. This is mainly because the effect is not observed for all types of pollutant. For energy use, greenhouse gases (GHGs) and waste, for instance, the relationship between emissions and income is linear and increasing, rather than following the pattern depicted in the figure. The available empirical evidence is therefore insufficient to draw any general conclusions regarding the existence of an environmental Kuznets curve effect.

A separate issue is the third fact mentioned above, namely that the essential services provided by natural capital stocks may be run down unsustainably over

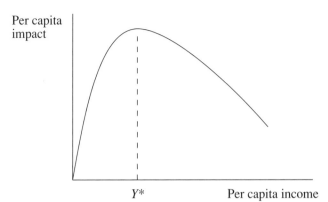

Figure 2.4   An example of an environmental Kuznets curve

time. If we accept that the market cannot reflect all of the values of the services provided by the natural environment, this implies that environmental sustainability places a constraint on economic growth. The current section has underlined that natural ecosystems perform fundamental life-support functions without which human life would not be possible. However, because these services are not traded in markets, they are not reflected in the value of conserving natural resource stocks. Therefore, it is possible that when a natural resource stock is depleted efficiently in terms of maximizing its net present value, crucial life-support services could be lost.

An example of this conflict could be in the use of forest resources. Many of the world's forests are being depleted, since this is the economically optimal strategy for their owners. These forests, however, also perform global ecosystem services. First, they absorb carbon dioxide and therefore reduce the effects of global warming. Second, they contain much of the world's biodiversity. Therefore, global environmental sustainability, which is a prerequisite for economic sustainability, might require that limits be placed on the depletion of natural resource stocks, even if it appears that this means sacrificing some of the monetary value of these stocks. A practical way to ensure that is to create a market for these ecological services and functions. This would show in fact that there is no monetary sacrifice.

2.4   SOCIAL SUSTAINABILITY

The discussion so far has focused on two dimensions of sustainability: the economic and the environmental. In the last few years, the discussion of sustainability has extended to the social dimension. Economic and environmental factors alone fail to explain substantial differences in the level of economic development achieved by the countries with similar endowments of human, natural and physical capital and in the outcomes of the similar sets of policies (for example, structural adjustment) applied to the countries with similar characteristics. This suggests that the three types of capital determine only partially the process of economic growth, overlooking the way in which the economic actors interact and organize themselves to generate growth and development. The missing link is seen as social capital (World Bank 1997, 2000).

There are many competing definitions of social capital but most of them incorporate the following features: relations of trust, reciprocity and exchanges between individuals which facilitates cooperation, common rules, norms and sanctions mutually agreed or handed down within societies, networks and groups including access to wider institutions. In the last years the debate over social capital has mostly been focused on the following issues (DFID 1999):

- the role of different forms of social capital in achieving sustainable development;
- the distinction between forms of social capital;
- how social capital can be assessed and whether it can be measured;
- whether social capital can be created through externally catalysed processes; and
- the role of social capital in ensuring good governance and strong civil society.

There is little disagreement about the relevance of social capital for sustainable development in general. However, there is no consensus on which aspects of interaction and organization it defines, nor about the validity of the term capital to describe this.[3] Least progress has been made in measuring social capital and in determining empirically its contribution to economic growth and development (World Bank 1997).

2.4.1 Definitions of Social Capital

The concept of social capital comes from two major intellectual streams. One lies in economic literature, and is based on the utilitarian doctrine that people who bond in recognized and comfortable groupings, based on trust, reciprocity and agreed norms of behaviour, will conduct business more expediently, and with less chance of failure (O'Riordan 1999). The other is sociological. It sees the actor as socialized and governed by social norms, rules and obligations. It describes action in a social context. According to this tradition a more coherent and supportive social setting will be more conducive to effective participatory democracy.

At the general level, the term 'social capital' is based on the idea that social bonds and social norms are important for sustainable development. However, different authors have emphasized different aspects of this idea.

The narrowest view of social capital regards it as a set of *horizontal associations* between people: social networks and associated norms that influence productivity and well-being of a community. This view is associated with the work of Robert Putnam, who puts emphasis on civic participation. He argues that strong traditions of civic engagement are the hallmarks of social cohesion and, in turn, economic progress. Initially it was believed that social networks can increase productivity by reducing the costs of doing business. However, some groups can have negative impacts as well, working at cross-purposes to society's collective interests (the Mafia, drug cartels and so on). The key feature of social capital here is that it facilitates coordination and cooperation for the mutual benefit of the society. However, it represents a difficulty for the empirical measurement of the capital, as some judgement has to be established regarding what is 'beneficial' for the society.

A broader and perhaps the most commonly cited definition is that of Coleman (1990). It includes *vertical* as well as *horizontal* associations between people and the behaviour within and among organizations (for example, firms). Social capital is defined in terms of the features of social organization such as trust, norms of reciprocity and networks of civil engagement. Horizontal ties give communities sense of identity and common purpose, but they can become a basis for the pursuit of narrow interests and preclude access to information and material resources without 'bridging' ties that transcend various social divides (religion, ethnicity, socioeconomic status).

The broadest view of social capital includes the *social and political environment*, which enables norms to develop and shapes social structures. It extends social capital to the most formalized institutional relationships and structures, such as government, the political regime, the rule of law, the court system, and civil and political liberties. It recognizes that capacity of various social groups to act in their interest depends upon the support (or the lack) that they receive from the state and private sectors. Similarly, the state depends on social stability and popular support.

2.5 MEASURES OF STRONG AND WEAK SUSTAINABILITY

It is clear from the discussion so far that there are various different types of capital stock that contribute to human well-being. These include man-made capital, such as factories and machinery. Human capital is also a productive stock that can be invested in, and allowed to deteriorate. An intangible type of capital is social capital, discussed above. Finally there is natural capital, which performs many different functions. The fact that there are different types of capital stock that contribute to well-being has led to a distinction between weak sustainability and strong sustainability, as discussed by Rennings and Wiggering (1997). Weak sustainability can be defined as the maintenance of the value of the aggregated stock of capital. This implies two things: first, that different capital stocks can be expressed in common terms, namely in terms of monetary value; second, that different types of capital stock can substitute for each other in a sustainable solution. A definition of weak sustainability might be:

$$\dot{K} + \dot{H} + \dot{SC} + \dot{N} \geq 0$$

where K is manmade capital, H is human capital, SC is social capital and N is natural capital. As long as these capital stocks can be expressed in money terms, then under a policy of weak sustainable development, depletion of the stock of natural capital may be compensated for by investment of the same or greater value in, for instance, man-made capital.

Strong sustainability, on the other hand, requires that each type of capital stock be maintained in its own right, at least above some minimum level. Therefore a strong sustainability constraint can be expressed as follows:

$$\dot{K} \geq 0, \dot{H} \geq 0, \dot{SC} \geq 0, \dot{N} \geq 0.$$

In the case of natural capital, the minimum level of different types of natural capital stock might be determined by safe minimum standards and the precautionary principle. Under a policy of strong sustainability, depletion of the world's forests might be limited so that the remaining stock is sufficient to maintain biodiversity at safe levels, to sustain timber supplies at adequate levels, and to absorb carbon dioxide emissions. In the rest of this section we look at the measurement of strong and weak sustainability at the macro and micro levels. Much of the literature has been devoted to such measures and they are most closely tied to the conceptual basis outlined above.

2.5.1   Daly's Rules for Strong Sustainability

Herman Daly's (1990) criteria for sustainability provide an example of a suggested programme for strong sustainable development. Daly's criteria are as follows:

1. Renewable resources must be harvested at or below the growth rate for some predetermined level of resource stock.

2. As non-renewable resources are depleted, renewable substitutes must be developed so as to maintain the flow of services over time.
3. Pollution emissions should be limited to the assimilative capacity of the environment.

In another paper, Daly (1995) answers Beckerman's criticisms of the concept of strong sustainable development, saying that it does not mean, as Beckerman (1994) maintains, that every species must be preserved and that no non-renewable resource can ever be extracted. Rather it involves acknowledging, in contrast to the weak sustainability paradigm, that natural resources are basically complements to man-made capital in production and that decreased availability of natural resources can be compensated only to a limited extent by increased man-made capital. Therefore Daly does agree with Beckerman that the concept of weak sustainability is illogical, since it assumes that man-made capital can substitute for natural capital, an assumption which Daly says is not borne out empirically. The concept of weak/strong sustainability has a bearing on the shadow pricing of environmental goods and services (Harou et al. 1994).

2.5.2　Indicator of weak sustainability: Genuine Savings

An example of an indicator of weak sustainability is provided by Atkinson and Pearce's (1993) measure of 'genuine savings'. This indicator takes a country's savings, and deducts from it the value of the depreciation on its man-made capital, and the value of the depreciation on its natural capital. This allows a judgement to be made as to a country's sustainability, since if the genuine savings measure is positive then the country is weakly sustainable. The genuine savings measure is the following:

$$Z = \frac{S}{Y} - \frac{\delta M}{Y} - \frac{\delta N}{Y}$$

where Z is genuine savings, Y is income, S is savings, δ is the depreciation on M, the country's stock of manmade capital and on N, the country's stock of natural resources. The World Bank has constructed estimates of this variable, which summarizes the evidence of the last two decades (see Figure 2.5). It shows that many countries in Sub-Saharan Africa have had negative genuine savings and are therefore not on a sustainable path. Indeed there are striking differences in average genuine saving rates among various regions in the world, with East Asia and the Pacific experiencing a positive rate throughout the period in question, while the Latin America and Caribbean region exhibited a mixed rate, reflecting the 'lost decade' of the 1980s, but experienced positive growth rates from the mid-1980s. For Sub-Saharan Africa, the genuine saving rate was negative from the late 1970s to 1993. Broadly similar conclusions can also be derived from country-specific estimates prepared by Atkinson and Pearce, which are reported in Table 2.1.

Percentage of GNP

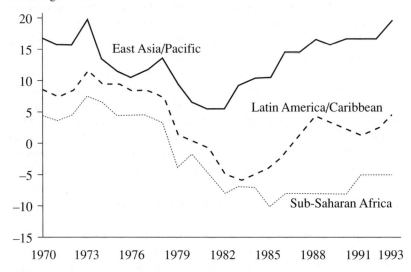

Source: World Bank calculations.

Figure 2.5   Genuine saving rates by region

These estimates have been criticized for the same reason that Daly criticized the concept of weak sustainable development, that is, it is illogical to suppose that maintaining the overall level of capital stock, with increases in man-made capital substituting for decreases in natural capital, can constitute a policy of sustainable development. Moreover, countries such as Japan, which deplete very few natural resources, can count most of their investment, net of man-made capital depreciation, as genuine savings. However, their production is dependent on natural resource imports, which may well derive from unsustainable extraction elsewhere. Therefore, the high sustainability rating for such countries may be misleading. Atkinson and Pearce's position is that a positive measure of genuine savings does not necessarily mean that a country is sustainable, but rather that if a country does not pass even such a weak test of sustainability as this, this is a clear sign of *un*sustainability.

Table 2.1   Measures of genuine savings for selected countries

	$\dfrac{S}{Y}$	$-\dfrac{\delta M}{Y}$	$-\dfrac{\delta N}{Y}$	Z
Sustainable economies				
Brazil	20	7	10	+3
Costa Rica	26	3	8	+15
Czechoslovakia	30	10	7	+13
Finland	28	15	2	+11
Germany	26	12	4	+10
Hungary	26	10	5	+11
Japan	33	14	2	+17
Netherlands	25	10	1	+14
Poland	30	11	3	+10
USA	18	12	3	+3
Zimbabwe	24	10	5	+9
Marginally sustainable economies				
Mexico	24	12	12	0
Philippines	15	11	4	0
United Kingdom	18	12	6	0
Unsustainable economies				
Burkina Faso	2	1	10	−9
Indonesia	20	5	17	−2
Madagascar	8	1	16	−9
Nigeria	15	3	17	−5
Papua New Guinea	15	9	7	−1

Source: World Bank (1997).

2.5.3   Rule for Strong Sustainability: the Shadow Project Constraint

Another rule for strong sustainability, suggested by Pearce et al. (1990), is the shadow project constraint. This is based on the idea that strong sustainability can be interpreted to mean that the stock of natural capital, including ecosystems, must not decrease over time. This is quite a stringent criterion since it implies that no new land may be developed. This could mean that a development project with large economic benefits might have to be forgone because it involves some environmental damage. The shadow project constraint presents a way to avoid this problem. The standard cost–benefit criterion, including environmental costs and benefits is:

$$\sum_{t=0}^{T} B_t \theta_t - \sum_{t=0}^{T} C_t \theta_t - \sum_{t=0}^{T} E_t \theta_t > 0,$$

where T is the time period over which the costs and benefits of a project are analysed, θ is the discount factor in each period, B is monetary benefits of the project, C is its monetary costs, and E is its environmental costs. Therefore the standard cost–benefit criterion is that the net present value of the benefits of a project must outweigh the net present value of its costs, including the environmental costs. The shadow project constraint allows for any ecosystem destruction to be compensated by a shadow project which increases environmental quality elsewhere. Given this, as well as the standard cost–benefit criterion, the project must satisfy:

$$\sum_{t=0}^{T} \sum_{i=1}^{n} E_{it} \theta_t \le \sum_{t=0}^{T} \sum_{j=1}^{m} a_{jt} \theta_t,$$

where there are i sites at which environmental damage is caused, and a denotes the j shadow projects that create environmental benefits. Therefore this condition states that the net present value of environmental damage over the relevant time period must be negative. This is a weak version of the shadow project constraint. A strong version would be that the environmental damage in each time period must be negative.

2.5.4   Rule for Strong Sustainability: Safe Minimum Standards

Another rule which is associated with land use and non-declining natural capital stock is the safe minimum standards (SMS) approach. This was developed by Ciriacy-Wantrup (1952) and Bishop (1978). It stems from a concern that the type of calculation carried out under cost–benefit analysis cannot be used to plan for sustainability, because the valuation of damage to ecosystems cannot reflect sustainability principles. In the absence of a reliable calculation, it is suggested that ecosystem damage be limited so that the remaining stocks are above safe minimum levels, usually calculated as the minimum levels required for the ecosystem to remain viable.

The SMS rule, therefore is 'prevent reductions in the natural capital stock below the safe minimum standard identified for each component of this stock unless the social opportunity costs of doing so are "unacceptably" large' (Hanley et al. 1997, p. 430). This implies, for example, that pollution emissions and biodiversity loss should be kept below identified safe levels. The indicator of sustainability implied by this criterion is then whether or not the SMS is breached for any class of resource. An example of the possible application of the SMS is given in Harou (1983) with regard to the conservation of genetic resources.

2.6 SUSTAINABLE DEVELOPMENT VISION IN A POLITICAL CONTEXT

2.6.1 Introduction

The discussion so far has summarized the intellectual debate on sustainable development and ways in which the concept can be made operational. Parallel to this, there has been an explosion of interest in sustainable development at the political level. This section discusses the political context to sustainable development, especially with reference to the proposals for sustainability outlined at the Rio Conference on Environment and Development in 1992 (the Earth Summit) in Agenda 21.

2.6.2 Earth Summit

The Rio Declaration on Environment and Development includes 27 principles that form the basis of the 40 chapters of Agenda 21. These principles are listed in United Nations (1993). Boxes 2.1 and 2.2 provide some essential ingredients to a thoughtful sustainable development strategy through mentioning some of the key elements in Agenda 21.

Agenda 21 emphasizes the importance of national strategies and international cooperation. Chapter 8 proposes integrating environment and development in decision making. These strategies aim to operationalize the concept of sustainable development and so propose accompanying action plans. Because many initiatives (see Box 2.1) to establish different sectoral strategies and plans have already begun, it is argued that they should be incorporated into a sustainable development strategy in a global context.

Chapter 38 addresses the need for intergovernmental and inter-UN agency coordination as well as overall implementation of Agenda 21. Chapter 39 deals with the international law-making process, related problems and the necessary reforms. It emphasizes the importance of the involvement of country governments in developing international instruments. As a result, there is a need to strengthen domestic institutional and regulatory capacities in order to implement international legal instruments. With the growth of the importance of global environmental problems such as climate change, the depletion of the stratospheric ozone layer and the loss of biodiversity, the importance of internationally agreed solutions to such environmental problems is even greater than it was in 1992 when Agenda 21 was drafted.

BOX 2.1   AGENDA 21 ON NATIONAL STRATEGIES

Preamble

'Its [Agenda 21's] successful implementation is first and foremost the responsibility of governments. National strategies, plans, policies and processes are crucial in achieving this. International cooperation should support and supplement such national efforts'.

Chapter 8

'Governments, in cooperation, where appropriate, with international organizations, should adopt a national strategy for sustainable development based on, *inter alia*, the implementation of decisions taken at the Conference, particularly in respect of Agenda 21. This strategy should build upon and harmonize the various sectoral economic, social, and environmental policies and plans that are operational in the country. The experience gained through existing planning exercises such as national reports for the Conference, national conservation strategies and environment action plans should be fully used and incorporated into a country-driven sustainable development strategy. Its goals should be to ensure socially responsible economic development while protecting the resource base and the environment for the benefit of future generations. It should be developed through the widest possible participation. It should be a thorough assessment of the current situation and initiatives.'

Source: Excerpts from Agenda 21 (UNCED 1992).

A sustainable development strategy at the national and regional levels should provide a framework for analysis and a focus for debating sustainable development issues. It helps identify important development and environmental issues, establish priority actions and plan their implementation. Sustainable development strategy in a global context provides the opportunity to project collectively a vision for the country and, in so doing, encourage participation in the implementation of the action plan linked to the strategies. As noted at the beginning of this chapter, implementing a sustainable development strategy requires an interdisciplinary approach, focusing on the structure of development and not only on the rate of economic growth, as conventionally measured. These issues are elaborated below.

BOX 2.2   AGENDA 21 ON INTERNATIONAL INSTITUTIONAL ARRANGEMENTS AND INTERNATIONAL LEGAL INSTRUMENTS AND MECHANISMS

Chapter 38

'All agencies of the United Nations system have a key role to play in the implementation of Agenda 21 within their respective competence. To ensure proper coordination and avoid duplication in the implementation of Agenda 21, there should be an effective division of labour between various parts of the United Nations system based on their terms of reference and comparative advantages. Member States, through relevant governing bodies, are in a position to ensure that these tasks are carried out properly. In order to facilitate evaluation of agencies' performance and promote knowledge of their activities, all bodies of the United Nations system should be required to elaborate and publish reports of their activities on the implementation of Agenda 21 on a regular basis. Serious and continuous reviews of their policies, programmes, budgets and activities will also be required.'

Chapter 39

'At the global level, the participation and contribution of all countries, including developing countries, in treaty making in the field of international law on sustainable development is of essential importance. Many of the existing international legal instruments and agreements in the field of the environment have been developed without adequate participation and contribution of developing countries, and thus may require review in order to reflect the concerns and interests of developing countries and to ensure a balanced governance of such instruments and agreements.'

'Developing countries should also be provided with technical assistance in their attempts to enhance their national legislative capabilities in the field of sustainable development.'

Source: Excerpts from Agenda 21 (UNCED 1992).

2.7   INTEGRATING ENVIRONMENT AND DEVELOPMENT

How can one bring the tools of analysis discussed in the first part of this chapter to bear on the political processes that have been initiated under Agenda 21? The following are some of the key implications.

1. The Hartwick rule of investing resource rents provides an indicator of sustainable development with respect to the use of natural resources.
2. Environmental sustainability requires policy makers to develop measures of critical natural capital and to ensure that the minimum levels are respected. These should, however, be informed by considerations of how the economies will develop over time (for example, the Kuznets curve). Equally, economic tools, such as cost–benefit analysis can be modified to take account of minimum conservations requirements.
3. Social sustainability is an integral part of the sustainability concept and development policies need to be assessed against indicators relating to social as well as environmental and economic criteria.
4. The concepts of genuine savings and other measures of weak sustainability are useful guides to the economic dimension of sustainability, although we should interpret the latter to include measuring environmental and social impacts in economic terms.

In other words, the day-to-day implementation of sustainable development requires an integration of economic, environmental and social tools of analysis. Much of this book provides a detailed description of these tools, which are largely economics based, although they attempt to integrate all three dimensions. While such methods have been quite successful they have also had their critics, who have rightfully pointed to their limitations. The difficulty in using economic-based methods is that the benefits of certain actions are difficult to measure (see Common (1995) for a discussion of these). Consequently standards will often be set on political grounds even if trade-offs have determined benefits/costs. Because pollution cannot be reduced to a zero level, targets for pollution reduction or environmental improvements are often established through a political process. As we discuss in Chapter 5, this process can be successful if the lessons of recent projects are learned. The setting of standards needs to be participatory, according to Principle 10 of the Rio Declaration. The targets can then be translated into policy measures aimed at institutional reforms, such as the establishment of property rights and/or improvement of the function of markets, particularly by internalizing environmental costs (Principle 16).

The national strategy should also be seen in a global context for trade (Principle 12).

Each government needs to define its own policy approach to decision making with regard to sustainable development at the national level. Chapter 8 of Agenda 21 provides a guide to such decision making, a comprehensive plan for action in integrating environment and development in making decisions at the macro, sectoral and project levels. This plan contains four programme areas:

1. Integrating environment and development at the policy, planning, and management levels.
2. Providing an effective legal and regulatory framework.
3. Making effective use of economic instruments and the market, and other incentives.
4. Establishing systems for integrated environmental and economic accounting.

These issues are taken up in Chapters 3 to 6 of this book.

Concerning the integration of environment and development at the policy level, Agenda 21 advocates improving the decision making process in several areas, including:

- integrating economic, social and environmental considerations at all levels and in all ministries;
- greater coherence of different policies;
- monitoring and evaluation;
- transparency of and accountability for the environmental implications of economic and sectoral policies;
- access to information and effective participation; and
- improving planning and management systems, including through environmental impact assessments (8.4–8.5).

Agenda 21 suggests that the means for implementing these measures should include, among others:

- researching environment and development interactions with a view to assisting policy decisions (8.9);
- promoting public awareness (8.11); and
- strengthening national institutional capacity (8.12).

A legal and regulatory framework, reviewed in Chapter 6, should be established to implement environmental policies. In doing so, it is important to make sure that it is in compliance with the international legal instruments referred to in Chapter 39 of Agenda 21. This second programme, also proposed in

Chapter 8 of Agenda 21, contains a number of recommendations for appropriate legal and regulatory policies, instruments and enforcement mechanisms.
For this approach to be successful it is essential to develop and implement
integrated, enforceable and effective laws and regulations based upon sound,
scientific principles (8.14).

The use of economic instruments, which are reviewed in Chapter 5 of this
book, is part of the third programme area proposed in Chapter 8 (8.1) of Agenda
21. It recognizes that environmental laws and regulations are important but
alone cannot be expected to deal with environment and development. In some
cases, market-based instruments provide cost-effective solutions. Agenda 21
suggests that a policy based on the use of market-based instruments would
allow governments to institute the following reforms:

- establish a policy framework that encourages the creation of new markets
  in pollution control and environmentally sounder resource management;
- reform or recast existing structures of economic and fiscal incentives to
  meet environmental and developmental goals;
- establish effective combinations of economic, regulatory and voluntary
  (self-regulatory) approaches;
- remove or reduce subsidies that do not comply with sustainable development objectives; and
- establish policies based on greater reliance on resource pricing.

Establishing systems of integrated environmental and economic accounting
is a fourth area discussed in Chapter 8 of Agenda 21 and briefly reviewed in
Chapter 3 of this book. This programme area concerns developing national
systems of integrated environmental and economic accounting (IEEA). Because
sustainable development cuts across social, economic and environmental issues,
it is important that national accounts are not restricted to measuring the
production of goods and services according to conventional measures. Changes
in the stock of natural resources should also be recorded. At the present time,
national accounts record changes in welfare only when they occur on the market.
For example, if a natural resource is depleted to provide exports, a country
seems to grow richer, even if the reduced natural resource base is not replen-
ished and the environment degraded. This must be corrected: if a country's
natural resource base is reduced, the national account should reflect this.

Agenda 21 is an important document indicating broad-based agreement
among nations on all aspects of the environment related to social and economic
growth, including the need to reduce poverty. However, there is not always
consensus on methods for internalizing environmental costs. The topic is at the
'cutting edge' of research and debate in the international community. This book
covers some of the economic methods and techniques that could be used or

have been used in development lending. It also points out optimal practices whenever possible.

2.8   STRATEGIES AND POLITICAL ECONOMY

As the title indicates, this book is concerned with the political economy of the environment. As such it seeks to look for ways in which the tools for environmental analysis can be embedded in political and social institutions that are responsible for environmental policies. In this chapter we have described some of the key messages that the technical literature on sustainable development provides to those responsible for policy. At the same time there are details of how policies should be designed and implemented, which can only be answered at the 'hands on' practical level.

Agenda 21 outlines the key issues that need to be included in policy making at the more practical level. This is discussed further when national environmental strategy (NES) is presented in Chapter 7. It is important to note, however, that environmental policy formulation is essentially a political process in which not only government but also the private sector and civil society play a role. By definition, interests that have evolved over time and become a strategy should simply be considered an environmental management instrument, which is subject to change. Decisions that shape a country's future environmental situation are made every day.

The rest of the book stresses the methods and tools useful for making daily decisions that affect the environment. Decision analyses need to be extended to ensure that environmental considerations are given a higher priority at the macroeconomic, sectoral and project levels by policy makers. Environmental considerations should permeate the debate on the political economy of development.

Although this book has been designed with trainers in mind, it can be used by professionals and decision makers. The hope remains that the trainees' influence on decision makers will soon be reflected in improved policy decisions for sustainable development. Yet, one should be made aware that research findings and information provided to policy makers do not automatically produce optimal strategy, policy or programme choices. What we know about the relationship between the information generated by research, and changes in policy and policy implementation can be summarized as follows:

- Changes in policy and policy implementation rarely result from a linear process of generating research, outlining policy options, choosing between alternatives, and evaluating the implementation of the selected choice.

- Rather, changes come about through a process of iterative interactions among three 'streams' of activity: defining the problem, suggesting solutions and obtaining political consensus.
- Changes occur when these streams converge, presenting a 'window of opportunity' to the vigilant reformer.
- Advocacy plays an important role in these three streams. Indeed, policy champions are often required to place a problem on the agenda, bring a solution to the attention of decision makers, and galvanize political consensus. Advocacy implies a more dynamic approach to the presentation of information. To make a difference, not only does information need to be disseminated, but advocates – using this information – must argue for change with those who can actually influence policies and their implementation.
- Information is often more acceptable and, thus, more useful for advocacy when produced internally and not imported.

NOTES

1. This section draws heavily on Markandya et al. forthcoming.
2. This is more popularly known as the Brundtland Report, after the Chairman of the Commission. For a state-of-the-art discussion of sustainable development in an economic/ecological context, see Arrow et al (1996) and for a survey of the debate, see Munasinghe, (1993).
3. The relationship between social capital and development is not always oriented towards material gain. Benefits from the social capital include enhanced spiritual well-being, a sense of identity and belonging, social status, honour and prestige (DFID 1999).

CITED BIBLIOGRAPHY

Arrow, K., B. Bolin, R. Costanza, P. Dasgupta, C. Folke, C.S. Holling, B.-O. Jansson, S. Levin, K.-G. Maler, C. Perrings and D. Pimentel (1996) 'Economic growth, carrying capacity, and the environment', *Environment and Development Economics*, Vol. 1, Part 1, pp. 104–10.

Atkinson, G. and D.W. Pearce (1993), 'Measuring sustainable development', *The Globe*, No. 13, June, UK GER Office, Swindon.

Beckerman, W. (1994), 'Sustainable development: is it a useful concept', *Environmental Values*, **3** (3), 191–209.

Bishop, R.C. (1978), 'Endangered species and uncertainty: the economics of a safe minimum standard', *American Journal of Agricultural Economics*, **60**, 10–18.

Ciriacy-Wantrup, S.V. (1952), *Resource Conservation: Economics and Policies*, Berkeley and Los Angeles, CA: University of California Press.

Coleman, J. (1990), *Foundations of Social Theory*, Cambridge, MA: The Belknap Press of Harvard University Press.

Common, M. (1995), *Sustainability and Policy: Limits to Economics*, Cambridge: Cambridge University Press.

Daly, H.E. (1990), 'Toward some operational principles of sustainable development', *Ecological Economics*, **2** 1–6.

Daly, H.E. (1991), 'Towards an environmental macroeconomics', *Land Economics*, **67** (2), 255–9.

Daly, H.E. (1995), 'On Wilfred Beckerman's critique of sustainable development', *Environmental Values*, **4**, 49–55.

Dasgupta, P.S. and G. Heal (1974), 'The Optimal depletion of exhaustible resources', in *Review of Economic Studies* Symposium, Economics of Exhaustible Resources, pp. 3–28.

Hanley, N.D., J.F. Shogren and B. White (1997), *Environmental Economics in Theory and Practice*, Basingstoke, UK: Macmillan.

Harou, P.A. (1983), 'The economics of biosphere reserves and the conservation of genetic resources', *Agriculture Administration*, **13**, 219–37.

Harou, P.A., H. Daly and R. Goodland (1994), 'Environmental sustainability and project appraisal', Environment Divisional Working Paper No. 1994–48, Washington DC: World Bank.

Hartwick, J.M. (1977), 'Intergenerational equity and the investing of rents from exhaustible resources', *American Economic Review*, **67** (5), 972–4.

IUCN (1980) *World Conservation Strategy: Living Resource Conservation for Sustainable Development*, International Union for Conservation of Nature and Natural Resources, Gland.

Markandya, A., K. Halsnaes, P. Mason and A. Olhoff (forthcoming), 'Sustainable development and climate change: a conceptual approach', in Markandya, A. and K. Halsnaes (eds), *Climate Change and Sustainable Development*, Earthscan: London.

Munasinghe, M. (1993), *Environmental Economics and Sustainable Development*, Washington, DC: World Bank.

Munasinghe, M. (2000), 'Sustainable development and climate change – applying the sustainomics transdisciplinary metaframework', *International Journal of Global Environmental Issues*, **1**, 3–48.

O'Riordan, T. (1999), 'Social capital, civic science and deliberative dialogue', Centre for Social and Economic Research on the Global Environment (CSERGE), University of East Anglia, UK, http://sdri.ubc.ca/GBFP/soc cap.html.

Pearce, D.W., E.W. Barbier and A. Markandya (1990), *Sustainable Development*, London: Earthscan.

Rennings, K. and H. Wiggering (1997) 'Steps towards indicators of sustainable development: linking economic and ecological concepts', *Ecological Economics*, **20** (1), 25–36.

Solow, R. (1991), 'Sustainability: an economist's perspective', 18th J. Seward Johnson Lecture.

UK Department for International Development (D.F.I.D.) (1999), 'Social capital: overview of the debate', www.oneworld.org/odi/keysheets/.

United Nations (1993), *Agenda 21: Programme of Action for Sustainable Development and Rio Declaration*, New York: United Nations.

World Bank (1997), *Expanding the Measure of Wealth: Indicators of Environmentally Sustainable Development*, Washington, DC: World Bank.

World Bank (2000), *World Development Report 1999/2000: Entering the 21st Century*, Washington, DC: World Bank.

World Commission on Environment and Development (Brundtland Commission) (1987), *Our Common Future*, Oxford: Oxford University Press.

3. Macroeconomic policies and the environment

OBJECTIVE

To link macroeconomic policies and changes in these policies (stabilization and structural adjustment) with the environment.

SUMMARY

Many macroeconomic policies have an indirect impact on the environment. Stabilization and structural adjustment programmes aim for a stable economy over the long run. In turn, this should help bring about more appropriate environmental policies that are integrated in economic development plans. A country's system of national account should accurately indicate a depleted natural capital base to highlight the costs of inaction in the face of environmental degradation. In the short run, the negative impacts of proper national economic policies should be remedied at the sector, programme, and project levels. If debt gets out of control, it could affect the environment negatively. Environment and poverty are related in various ways.

3.1 INTRODUCTION

Macroeconomic policies have a widespread impact on the use of a country's resources and ecological services. The economic reforms change patterns and levels of public expenditures as well as causing relative price shifts. The policies change economic signals throughout the economy, influencing decisions on which and how much of a resource or service will be used. Macroeconomic policies, whether or not successful in generating economic growth, also indirectly impact the environment due to changes in income, taxes, subsidies, public revenues and innovative capacity.

Frequently countries in economic transition had to undertake major macro-economic reforms in order to transform their economies to compete globally. Many studies have analysed the effects of stabilization and structural adjustment on the environment (Markandya 1994; Munasinghe and Cruz 1995; Munasinghe 1996; Reed 1996; Lopez et al. 1998; and Munasinghe et al. 2000). The issues that are of interest here are: (a) how can one assess these impacts and (b) what actions if any need to be taken to correct any negative environmental effects.

The chapter is organized as follows. The next section (Section 3.2) describes the major macroeconomic reforms and their likely effects on the environment. Section 3.3 describes the tools that are available for the analysis of such impacts and their respective strengths and weaknesses, and Section 3.4 presents some conclusions as to the possible conflicts between macroeconomic policy objectives and the state of the environment, and presents some techniques that may be applied to reconcile these issues. The whole discussion of the environmental impacts of macroeconomic policies and the correction mechanisms suffers, however, from the fact that the basic information on macroeconomic indicators, such as GDP, is approximate. It is imprecise because it does not account for the loss of natural capital and damages done to the environment in the process of generating economic growth. Hence a major area of research in recent years has been that of integrated economic–environment accounting. The major results of this work are reported in Section 3.3. The chapter concludes with three case studies (Annexes 3A1–3), which set the debate in the context of actual problems – two are studies where macroeconomic policies have been in potential conflict with environmental objectives, and one is a discussion exercise raising some of the issues that arise in environmental accounting.

The precise impact of macroeconomic policies on the environment is difficult to determine because of the vagueness of environmental indicators. But even a qualitative assessment of the potential environmental impact of policies designed to modify aggregate demand, counter fiscal deficits, or address balance of payments problems will suggest minor adjustments to these policies to limit environmental damage. However, it would be difficult to convince policy makers that the exchange rate policy, which defines an economy's broad framework, should be modified because specific sectors may suffer certain environmental impacts. Nor is it appropriate that an economy-wide variable should be used for such sector-specific goals. Instead, additional environmental policy instruments should be designed to mitigate potential environmental impacts due to a new exchange rate policy. Similarly, the economic benefits of trade liberalization will often outweigh concerns about particular environmental problems. To address the latter, specific environmental policy instruments are generally required. Some of these are mentioned in this chapter and are further discussed in Chapter 4.

3.2   MACROECONOMIC POLICIES AND THE ENVIRONMENT

Most macroeconomic reform programmes have two distinguishable time horizons. In the short term, the focus is on the stabilization programme aimed at rapid restoration of macroeconomic balance through demand management policies. In the longer term, the goal is to improve efficiency and economic growth through liberalization of trade and domestic pricing policies, and to initiate institutional reform through the structural adjustment and sectoral adjustment loans. The components and policy tools comprising a typical adjustment programme are reviewed below. Any potential conflicts between the short- and long-term goals are highlighted.

3.2.1   Short-term Stabilization Programmes

This is a short-term programme (12–18 months) to achieve *rapid* internal and external balance of payments via adoption of policies to reduce both the level and composition of aggregate demand.

Measures to achieve rapid balance of payments relief would primarily address any imbalance on the current account. A deficit on the current account implies that domestic absorption of goods and services exceeds domestic production. In the short term, the analysis underlying the formulation of such programmes assumes productive capacity to be fixed. Hence, the stabilization programme focuses on demand-reducing and expenditure-switching polices.

A number of policy options are available to reduce domestic absorption and typically might include all or a combination of the following:

1. *Fiscal policy.*   Large budget deficits have been a primary source of external disequilibria and macroeconomic instability. A major objective of the stabilization programme has therefore been to reduce the budget deficit via

both reductions in government spending and increases in tax revenue. Government spending may be cut on recurrent expenditures (for example, reductions in public sector wages, food subsidies) and/or public sector investment and lending to the private sector.

2. *Monetary policy.* In its simplest form, the rate of domestic credit expansion has been the primary monetary policy instrument of the short-term stabilization programme. The desired effect is to reduce domestic absorption via reductions in private consumption and investment. The rate of domestic expansion can be controlled through direct regulation of the money supply, as well as through indirect measures such as rationing credit, regulating the banking system and controlling interest rates.

3. *Exchange rate policy.* These fiscal and monetary instruments are *demand reducing* but do not necessarily ensure that simultaneous balance is achieved on both the government budget deficit and the balance of payments. To ensure this, an additional instrument – exchange rate modification, usually devaluation – is needed. This acts to change the composition of demand from foreign to domestic goods and to increase incentives for production of exports and/or import-substituting goods. Balancing the government budget is sometimes referred to as *internal balance* and balancing the external budget account is referred to as *external balance*.

   Managing both external and internal balance involves adjustments to the different instruments and is difficult to achieve, even in developed countries. Moreover, it entails costs, at least over the short run, in the form of reductions in real income for certain sectors of society. Partly to mitigate these, and partly to protect special interest groups, import/export controls are sometimes employed as additional instruments. However, their use is generally not supported by the international financial institutions as they tend to be discriminatory in their impact and result in inefficient resource use.

In summary, the stabilization programme would therefore typically target reductions in fiscal deficits, money and credit restrictions and real exchange rate devaluation. The emphasis is on achieving rapid reductions and switching in the composition of aggregate demand to achieve internal and external balance. The success of such a programme in the short term is very much dependent on political and social acceptability and the ability of the economy to respond to this new set of price incentives. In any transitional phase, during which time the balance of payments may even worsen (depending on the elasticities of imports and exports), the impacts may be cushioned by the provision of conditional funds under the stabilization programme.

It is also important to stress that these contractionary policies will *not* ensure *long term* balance of payments stability or increase the capacity of the economy to respond to external shocks. The medium-term structural and sectoral adjustment packages address these issues.

3.2.2   Medium-term Structural and Sectoral Adjustment Programmes (SALs and SECALs)

The stabilization programme focuses on reducing *demand* whereas the medium-term strategy focuses on relaxing *supply*-side constraints. The programme aims at both increasing output from existing capacity and increasing the rate of growth of capacity by prescribing a greater role for prices, markets and the private sector in the development process.

The market-based argument for *improving efficiency* is to reduce distortions that drive a wedge between prices and marginal costs. To encourage *growth of existing capacity* the SAL conditionality will target policies that increase the rate of and return to investment.

The array of policy instruments to achieve these ends is varied and country specific. Some of the major instruments are highlighted below:

1. *Trade liberalization.*   Those countries that adopted the import substitution development path popularized in the 1950s and 1960s now have a legacy in the form of a comprehensive package of import and export taxes. Such protectionist policies are now regarded as a major source of trade distortions and as a constraint on efficiency and growth. The gradual dismantling of import and export taxes is thus a central component of both SALs and SECALs.
2. *Domestic pricing policies.*   Price controls and subsidies have frequently been used in developing countries both to stabilize markets and to achieve income support for the poorer groups in society. They are, however, also regarded as a major domestic distortion and source of economic rigidity. Agricultural input and food subsidies have been particularly popular in many countries but are now being dismantled as a central part of their structural adjustment programme.
3. *Non-price incentives.*   'Getting the prices right' via trade and domestic pricing reforms often has to be combined with non-price measures to obtain the desired supply response. Therefore, in addition to pricing policies, the medium-term strategy may also identify the need for reforms and developments in other areas such as institutional reforms (for example, land tenure, credit, marketing and distribution, research and extension); infrastructural developments (transport, education); stimulation of technological innovation (high-yielding crop varieties, irrigation); and expansion of education and manpower training programmes.

3.2.3　Conflicts Between the Short-term and Long-term Strategies

Conflicts between the short-term objectives of stabilization and the long-term objectives of structural adjustment can arise. Where the pressure for an increase in foreign exchange earnings is very strong, in order to finance the purchase of imports as inputs for continued growth and development or to finance debt overhangs, for instance, it can take precedence over all other considerations. This can lead to a non-sustainable use of the natural resource base and the acceptance of environmental standards that are so low as to cause lasting damage to the absorptive capacity of the local environment. Examples of the former might be the mining of forest resources and the export of wild animals and animal products. Examples of the latter are the environmental damage caused in some places by tourism and the uncontrolled discharges of industrial effluent into water and land bodies from industrial activities. In any attempt to foster a sustainable economic policy in a developing country it is precisely this conflict between the short- and long-term objectives that has to be resolved.

Inappropriate macroeconomic policies could also undermine the success of sector-based environmental policies. For example, when the Ghanaian government introduced a system of royalties in forestry aimed at improving the efficiency of logging, the overvalued exchange rate rendered the stumpage prices negligible, almost a free good, and trees continued to be felled at the same rate.

The exact impact of macroeconomic policies on the environment is difficult to generalize and depends on specific factors concerning each country's institutions, existing environmental policies, market organizations and natural capital. The remainder of this chapter illustrates some specific examples of impacts. Here we address the impacts of the most important macroeconomic policies on the environment.

3.2.4　General Environmental Impacts of the Macroeconomic Policies

A summary of the linkages discussed above is provided in Box 3.1. The same box also summarizes the major environmental linkages. These are described below. Where adverse impacts are clearly present a (–) sign has been inserted and where they are clearly beneficial a (+) has been put in. Where the impacts are unclear a (+/–) has been used. Further discussion of these issues can be found in Reed (1992, 1996).

Short-term stabilization programmes
The policy instruments of short-term stabilization programmes are aimed at a short sharp reduction and, if necessary, a change in the composition of aggregate demand. Such policies have been criticized on the grounds that the burden of

---

BOX 3.1 EFFECTS OF STRUCTURAL ADJUSTMENT ON THE ENVIRONMENT

Type	Target	Variable	Anticipated impact	Examine impacts through
		Government expenditure	+/−	Drought relief, food aid, agricultural extension, public infrastructure (including roads), environmental management
	Fiscal	Taxes	+/−	Changed demand for resources, environmental charges
Short-term macro	Monetary	Subsidies	+/−	Input effects: machinery, fertilizers, pesticides, water
		Credit	+/−	Reduced credit for inputs, e.g. fertilizers, and for investments, e.g. irrigation or machinery
		Interest rates	+/−	Reduced investment and resource demand
	Exchange rate	Devaluation	+/−	Import effects: increased prices of imported inputs – energy, fertilizers. Export effects: increased crops, natural resources
	Trade	Import/export controls	+/−	Removal of protectionist taxes has similar effects as devaluation but for specific commodities
		Trade controls	+/−	Similar effects as trade taxes. Possibility of technological lock-in
	Pricing policy	Price controls	+/−	Impacts of price changes depend on crop characteristics, farming practices
Medium to long term macro		Reduce subsidies	+/−	Reduced use of pesticides, fertilisers, credit, irrigation, energy, machinery
		Increased taxes	+	Indirect impacts through reduced demand
	Institutional reform	Land	+	More on farm investments and sustainable resource management
		Financial	+	Improved credit may promote sustainability
		Research & extension	+	Improved services promote sustainable resource management
	Investment policies	Training	+	Investment in human capital through agricultural extension, wildlife and resource management
		Valuation	+	Project evaluation to include environmental costs and benefits
Investment policies		Technology	+	Industrial pollution abatement technologies and new agricultural technologies impact on environment
		Public infrastructure	+/−	May increase access to natural resources and encourage exploitation. May also have an impact on the price responsiveness of producers

adjustment has often fallen on those sectors of the population that are least able to bear it (Cornia et al. 1987). Three main areas of policy that have important direct impacts on the environment are: public sector expenditures, taxation and exchange rate adjustments.

Reductions in public sector spending. The economic rationale behind reductions in public spending is to relieve possible deficits on both the internal and external accounts. Exactly which areas of public spending will suffer is the subject for negotiation, but there is considerable evidence to suggest that special environmental programmes, food relief, agriculture extension services, welfare and similar programmes tend to get cut. This could have short-term negative effects on both the poor and the environment. Investments in infrastructure, education, health and reforestation are also likely to suffer in the short term. Over the long run, however, following a change in the relative price of resources, resource use may become more efficient, and projects that impact the environment negatively, such as inappropriate irrigation schemes, could become unprofitable. Thus, the impact of each of these scenarios is country and site specific. The following are some examples of possible impacts.

- Reductions in drought relief, food aid, subsidies and general welfare programmes may *intensify* unsustainable resource management and farming of marginal lands (–). Analysis of the incentive effects of the removal of various subsidies is reviewed in greater depth under the domestic pricing section of sectoral policies in Chapter 4.
- Reductions in agricultural extension services and environmental and resource management programmes will probably have a direct and adverse environmental impact (–). In many countries there have been major cutbacks in extension staff, which undoubtedly will affect the adoption of improved practices and land conservation methods if no institutional measures are put in place or the private sector fills the void.

Changes in taxation. Taxes and subsidies affect relative prices of resources. If subsidies encourage the use of resources, their dimunition will force their more parsimonious use (OECD 1998). An important case where a subsidy reduction leads to a positive environmental impact is that of subsidies on energy. Complex linkages exist between subsidy levels and environmental damage. OECD (1998) identifies three main mediating factors on the level of damage resulting from subsidies: the impact of the subsidy on the level and composition of output (+/–), environmental policies in place to mitigate damage resulting from the subsidy (+) and the assimilative capacity of the environment (+).

If eco-taxes are levied, they should diminish the source of pollution (+) (OECD 1999). Examples of eco-taxes include taxes on waste, emissions and other environmentally damaging products or byproducts of industry. Other changes in taxes cannot be generalized, though the environmental impacts may be estimated through the use of complex general equilibrium modelling processes.

Exchange rate devaluation.   Exchange rate devaluation directs expenditure away from foreign imports and encourages exports by increasing the domestic price for both exports and imports. This new set of price incentives will affect the economy across the board and can indirectly affect natural resource management. Increased export prices may favour the export of cash crops. If property rights are well established and the export crops are perennials, the effects for soil conservation purposes are neutral to positive (+). In the case of timber, which is often produced on public lands, environmental effects will depend on the strength of the government institutions to control logging and the land tenure arrangement. A crop's price increase will cause higher land values, which may induce conservation practices, but, again, only if property rights are well established. Increasing the cost of fertilizer and pesticides by, for example, reducing subsidies, reduces their use and improves the quality of the environment (+).

Monetary policies.   Monetary policies aimed at increasing the cost of capital, that is, the real rate of interest, directly impact the management of natural resources by enforcing rapid use rather than a conservation approach. However, because attention is given to the long-term interest rate, long-term stability is more important than a short-term interest rate change in a stabilization programme. In this respect, inflation caused by bad monetary policies does not help. An increase in inflation raises nominal rates immediately as well as raising long-term expected interest rates. Targeted credit affects the resource in a similar way to a subsidy and is discussed under sectoral policies in Chapter 4. Environmental impacts from monetary policies cannot be generalized but depend on the sector and the particular circumstances of land tenures, informal availability of credit and other factors.

Sectoral policies.   Various sectoral policies are associated with macroeconomic reform. These include reductions in subsidies to energy, agriculture and so forth. They are discussed further in Chapter 4.

Structural adjustment and trade liberalization
Trade-related measures have been discussed briefly above. This section looks more closely at the possible effects of trade liberalization, as they are the subject of considerable debate.
   Stabilization techniques focus on reducing demand, whereas structural adjustment (SA) programmes, over the medium term, relax supply-side con-

straints, which increases efficiency over the long run. By prescribing a greater role for prices, markets and the private sector, while improving the institutional framework, SA aims both at increasing existing output capacity and increasing the capacity's rate of growth. SA policies attempt to establish the right price through trade liberalization and domestic pricing policies. Domestic pricing will be discussed at the sectoral level later (Chapter 4). However, trade liberalization through a floating exchange rate is a major force behind domestic prices across the economy. Removing protectionist quotas and tariffs, and export taxes and incentives are discussed here with regard to their potential impact on the state of the environment.

Trade liberalization's macroeconomic objective is to open the economy to foreign competition and technology, to encourage foreign exchange earning capacity, and so to move towards a more sustainable balance of payments. Trade instruments are often a central component of fiscal and industrial policy. Trade levies account for a substantial portion of government revenue in developing economies and play a role in the promotion of certain industries. If these levies are removed, alternative sources of taxes have to be found. The relative price changes within sectors in which protection or incentives are removed and between sectors will affect resource use. If trade liberalization occurs in conjunction with sound environmental and macroeconomic and sectoral policies, it can contribute to sustainable development.

Import barriers (tariffs and quotas) increase the price of goods and services in an economy but more particularly in a specific sector. These barriers often reduce the general level of economic activity, increase producer surplus, but decrease consumers' welfare. Producers are protected, often in terms of the infant industry argument. Given a monopolistic situation, less may be produced decreasing pressure on the environment, but producers can be more inefficient users of resource inputs, which makes the net impact on the environment uncertain. Tariffs can be levied against the import of old, polluting technologies, improving a country's environment. The environmental impact of import barriers is similar to that of devaluation discussed earlier. These impacts cannot be predicted on a general level and depend on the economy's structure and institutional capabilities. In the agricultural and natural resource sectors, the environmental impact of import barriers depends heavily on the property rights system.

Trade liberalization can help or hurt the environment depending on which sectors expand or contract, on the effectiveness of the country's environmental policies and institutions, and on the extent to which increases in income are spent on improving environmental quality. Trade liberalization, by letting the economy use its comparative advantage, tends to expand the export sector, while causing the import-competing formerly protected sector to contract, a sector composition effect. The environmental impact of the composition effect depends on the country-specific conditions, that is, whether the industries that expand following liberalization are more environmentally damaging than those that contract. In many developing countries the export industries, for example, tree crops and labour-intensive light manufacturing, are relatively 'clean' industries, in particular when compared to import-competing heavy industry. In the Philippines, for example, trade liberalization could have reduced soil erosion and consequent water pollution by shifting resources away from import-competing annual crops like upland rice to export-oriented tree crops, where soil erosion rates are lower by a factor of between five and ten. In many African countries export crops such as tree crops grown with grass cover in West Africa cause much less erosion than food crops such as cassava.

Global agricultural liberalization is likely to be environmentally beneficial since much of the agricultural industry that has developed behind high protective barriers in developed countries has become very intensive in the use of chemicals and pesticides because high producer prices create incentives to increase yields, and these chemicals are often subsidized. Agricultural liberal-ization of the type begun under the Uruguay Round of the General Agreement on Tariffs and Trade (GATT) will reduce worldwide pollution by reducing the artificial stimulus to agricultural production more often in developed countries. This will come about as world prices are raised when overproduction in developed countries is reduced, and output in the developing countries, where fertilizer use per hectare is frequently less than in the highly protected countries, is increased (Anderson 1992).

Where environmental policies are inadequate, trade liberalization can have an adverse impact on the environment in the short run. However, a dynamic positive effect of trade liberalization can also occur for two reasons (Grossman and Krueger 1993). First, trade liberalization leads in the long run to an increase in income that is vitally important both for reducing poverty and for improving environmental quality. Higher economic growth is likely to increase the political demands for a cleaner environment. Second, foreign producers may transfer modern technologies to the local economy when restrictions on foreign investment are relaxed. Industries in developing countries with open trade regimes have been found to be cleaner than in countries with closed trade regimes (Lucas et al. 1992).

Trade liberalization causes a scale effect by expanding economic activity, and if the nature of that activity remains unchanged, the total amount of pollution generated must increase. To the extent that economic growth gives rise to an increase in the demand for energy, generated by the same means as before, output of harmful pollutants will increase. Furthermore, if expanded trade results in increased demand for transportation services without any change in trans-portation practices, increased trade can contribute to a deterioration in environmental quality.

The key to ensuring that trade liberalization improves the environment as well as raising real incomes is to implement sound environmental policies at the same time. The environment has to be mainstreamed in all SA reforms. These policies need to deal with the externalities that are at the root of most environmental problems. Key policy reforms needed in developing countries include the establishment of secure land tenure to encourage sustainable use of land and resources such as forests and fisheries, and the introduction of policies based on the polluter pays principle (PPP), which implies that the polluter should pay for the environmental damage caused, that is, internalize the negative environmental externalities.

If they are to be used at all, trade restrictions should only be used with caution in support of environmental goals. In general, trade policies are not the best policy measures for environmental objectives. Even if trade policies are environmentally beneficial, they will generally be inferior to policies targeted directly at an environmental problem. Where consumption of the good causes pollution, an import barrier reduces consumption, but will also create a distortion that favours domestic production of that good. By contrast, a consumption tax will reduce consumption without creating an incentive to expand domestic production of that good.

Export barriers (taxes) are often levied to raise revenue and finance price stabilization and marketing activities. Exchange rate devaluation is equivalent to an export tax removal. Again, the environmental impact of export barriers is sector specific. A priori, it is difficult to say whether the long-run response to export taxes will beneficially or adversely affect the environment. The arguments that apply to import tariff liberalization also apply to export taxes.

Debt

The severity of the debt problem cannot be measured by the absolute level of the debt burden. Debts are only problematic when repayments become difficult due to poor economic performance and foreign exchange constraints. It is for this reason that they are often regarded as a symptom rather than a cause of economic mismanagement or structural imbalance. For example, the newly industrialized countries in South East Asia incurred significant levels of external debt in the 1970s when funds were readily available and interest rates were low. They have not run into the same financial difficulties as many countries in Africa and Latin America. Their success has partly been due to restructuring and diversification of their economies together with higher growth rates and greater access to foreign exchange via expansion in exports.

Once a country moves into a financial crisis situation, it is possible that the financial distress induces an economic response that may be in direct conflict with longer-term economic and environmental objectives. In such circumstances, debt itself becomes the source of further economic and environmental stress as it actually changes economic behaviour. Both bankers and their debtors may give priority to their survival over other long-term objectives, including profitability.

The empirical evidence on this issue is unclear. In a cross-section of 45 countries over the period from 1967 to 1985, Capistrano and Kier (1990) showed that there was a significant relationship between the rate of industrial logging and the debt service ratio, the real rate of devaluation and the export price of agricultural crops. Although these studies do not establish any causality between these variables, the evidence cannot be ignored as indicative of a possible relationship between debt and the environment.

Debt for environmental projects or sustainable development policies swaps could be a win–win proposition if the relief is used both as a stabilization and a structural adjustment tool. The underlying principle is that a portion of a country's external debt is bought at a discount on the secondary loan market. The market value of the debt is likely to be considerably below the face value, depending on the risk of default attached to the debt. The local currency equivalent of the debt is then set aside for investment in environmental projects or to undertake policy reforms beneficial to the economy and the environment. Such projects have been successfully implemented, although their overall impact has not been well studied.

3.2.5   Poverty, Population and Environmental Degradation

The previous section examined specific macroeconomic policy variables and their possible environmental impacts. In this section we focus on a specific set of issues that are important in designing macroeconomic policy – the linkages between poverty and environmental degradation and population change and the environment. These are important because many macroeconomic policies will impact directly on one or more of these issues. If we know the relationships between them we are able to trace through the longer-term and deeper effects of macroeconomic reforms on poverty, population and the environment.

The poverty-environment nexus

Many macroeconomic policies have an impact on poverty and thereby, it is claimed, on the environment. This section looks at some of the evidence on this issue. Poverty and environmental degradation can be studied by looking at how the two are correlated over time, as well as how they are correlated across society at a given point in time. For the latter, there are few serious cross-section studies. In one of the earlier efforts in this area, Jaganathan (1989) reports on a study between rates of deforestation and the level of poverty in West Java, which finds little evidence that poverty was a driving force in the deforestation of that region. Likewise, the main factors driving land-use change in two regions in Nigeria were infrastructure projects such as roads, market incentives, such as increased producer prices for food, and institutional factors that determined access to land (Jaganathan 1989). Poverty *as such* appears to have played little part.

There are studies that point to the role of agricultural expansion by (generally) poor farmers as the cause of deforestation and other environmentally damaging land-use changes (Southgate 1988; Mink 1993). The argument is that poor farmers tend to occupy fragile lands. If there is any increase in the number of such farmers, or if peasants are displaced from other occupations, they will occupy more of such lands. But there is not much empirical evidence to suggest that it is an increase in the level of poverty per household that is the determining factor. Rather, it is because of an increase in the number of poor households, either through population increase, or through policies that increase landlessness, that the problem may arise.

Researchers in this area stress the importance of the policy context in determining the nature of the agricultural expansion and its environmental impacts. Land that is cleared for agriculture can be managed in a sustainable way, or it can be 'mined' and then abandoned in a degraded state. What happens depends on the property management regimes that are in place and whether they provide the right incentives for proper land management. These could be through secure private property rights, but could also be through common management systems (Bromley 1991; Dasgupta and Mäler 1991). Where the management regime is secure the impacts on the environment are not necessarily negative and may even be positive. One study from Nigeria (Mortimore 1989) shows how poor farmers there adopted sustainable management strategies on new but secure land even when the short-term costs of doing so were high.

A more equitable distribution of land, as a poverty alleviation policy, might be associated with environmental improvement. If poor farmers must use marginal land because owners occupy the good soil, inequitable land distribution could drive deforestation (Ekbom and Bojo 1999). Ravallion et al. (1997) estimated a large positive coefficient between carbon dioxide emissions per capita and the Gini coefficient of income inequality for a sample of 42 countries. This study suggests that reducing income inequality and poverty could lead to a decline in pollution.

The population–environment nexus
As with poverty, for a fuller appreciation of macro policy impacts it is important to look at the linkages between population and the environment. There is a widespread perception that high population density and high rates of population growth are a direct cause of environmental degradation. Some of the poorest countries in the world are also densely populated. Statistics on rates of fertility and mortality indicate rapid growth in human populations over the coming

decades, especially in the developing countries. High rates of population growth imply increasing demand for employment, education, health and many other public services. Population growth also implies an increasing demand for natural resources. The question arises, can the environment bear the strain of ever increasing human pressures?

There is little doubt that increases in population exacerbate the pressure on natural resources. The latter are fixed and as more people make demands on them, the quality and possibly the volume of the resources declines. Hence policies that reduce the rate of population growth will, *ceteris paribus*, reduce the pressure on the natural resource base. As far as macroeconomic policy is concerned, the key issue is to ensure that resources are efficiently devoted to reducing fertility, especially where it is having a detrimental environmental effect. In this context, there is considerable evidence to suggest that education (particularly of women), the level of agricultural employment and level of nutrition and the extent of civil liberty all act to reduce the levels of total fertility (Sen 1994; Dasgupta 1995). Policies, therefore, that act to improve these factors can be expected to reduce total fertility and, thereby, pressure on the natural resource base. Macroeconomic adjustment measures should therefore be sensitive to these links.

In addition, general economic growth has been negatively associated with population growth and it has been argued that the former will act to reduce population pressures over time. The problem with this argument, however, is that while *average* population growth rates may decline with per capita GDP, sections of the community that depend on natural resources may find themselves locked into a cycle of poverty in which high fertility rates are maintained and that, in turn, exacerbate the pressure on the natural environment. Dasgupta (1995) has argued that this cycle could work in the following way. As common resource management systems break down, so individuals are more able and willing to make family size decisions that do not take full account of the social costs of child rearing, with the use of common resources treated as a free good. Over time, the natural resource base is increasingly depleted and the family unit requires more members to achieve the same level of welfare. Thus a cycle of increasing degradation is established. The theory has some plausibility but clearly needs to be tested with real data.

The population–environment and poverty–environment nexuses are partial views and we can conclude that the three factors are interlinked (Cleaver and Schreiber, 1994). The type of linkage will vary with a host of factors, including existing institutions and laws (Lopez 1998).

The dynamics of institutional change

At the heart of the poverty–environment relationship is the question of what management systems operate for natural resources and how they evolve over time. There is some evidence that in pre-industrial societies, natural resources have been managed with some degree of sustainability in cohesive communities. With the onset of major social and political changes in the post-war period, these systems have, for many communities, broken down. Different reasons are offered for this. One is the process of privatization, which reduced the common land available and destroyed existing systems (Dasgupta 1996). Another is nationalization of common lands (particularly forests) where the government took responsibility for the lands but was not able to control its exploitation (Bromley 1991). A third is agricultural expansion for large-scale production, as in the case of Brazil, Kenya and other countries (Panayotou 1993). A fourth is simply the pressure of population increase, which may result from families following traditional norms for family size even when mortality rates have declined. In all these cases, the argument runs, traditional systems have broken down and common resources have been overexploited.

The situation is, however, dynamic and one would expect institutions to reform themselves where it is in the common interest to do so. There is some evidence that this happens, albeit over a medium to long time frame. Taking data from Western India, Chopra and Gulati (1996) have shown that property rights have evolved in such a way so as to reduce out-migration and improve the management of common resources. Institutional issues are discussed further in Chapter 5.

3.3   TOOLS AND METHODS OF MACROECONOMIC ANALYSIS

The preceding chapters pointed to the need to mainstream the environment in economy-wide policy changes. The issue of how all these possible links between macroeconomic policy variables and the environment can be presented to facilitate the decision-making process and lead to improvements in the design of environmental mitigation measures is discussed in the following section.

3.3.1   Action Impact Matrices

In analysing the macroeconomic/environmental linkages we now have a number of tools at our disposal. Some of these are quite complex and demand a high level of technical expertise. Before going into the details of such models, it is useful for the analyst to draw up a summary of likely impacts that might follow from the policies being considered. A general organizational tool used to do this is the action impact matrix (AIM) (Munasinghe 1996). The AIM is a tool for policy dialogue and coordination. It helps identify important environmental problems and the link with a change in macroeconomic and sectoral policy variables resulting from economy-wide policy reforms. It is a qualitative tool but, since it is broad, the link between policy change and environmental impact can be explored in a wider context and in a way that is easily understood by all.

Economic and environmental analyses and policies may be used more effectively to achieve sustainable development goals, by linking and articulating these activities explicitly. Implementation of such an approach would be facilitated by constructing an AIM – a simple example is shown in Table 3.1, although an actual AIM would be very much larger and more detailed. Such a matrix helps to promote an integrated view, meshing development decisions on key macroeconomic variables with priority economic, environmental and social impacts. The left-most column of the table lists examples of the main development interventions (both policy variables and projects), while the top row indicates some of the main sustainable development issues. Thus the elements of cells in the matrix help to: (a) explicitly identify the key linkages; (b) focus attention on valuation and other methods of analysing the most important impacts; and (c) suggest action priorities. At the same time, the organization of the overall matrix facilitates the tracing of impacts, as well as the coherent articulation of the links between a range of development actions – that is, policies and projects.

A stepwise procedure, starting with readily available data, has been used effectively to develop the AIM in several recent country studies including Ghana and Sri Lanka. This process has helped to harmonize views among those involved (economists, environmental specialists and others), in the country concerned and the Bank, thereby improving the prospects for successful implementation. First, data from national environmental action plans (NEAPs), environmental assessments (EAs) and so forth may be organized into an environmental issues table that prioritizes these problems, provides quantitative or qualitative indicators of damage, and helps identify underlying economic causes. Second, using information readily available from country economic and sector work, the main economy-wide policies (current and intended) are set out in a second table, together with a brief review of the basic economic issues that they address and potential environmental linkages. The information from these two tables is then combined to develop a preliminary AIM (for examples, see Munasinghe and Cruz 1995), which first present the main environmental issues, then describe various economy-wide policy reforms, and finally combine these two building blocks to produce an illustrative AIM.

As noted above, one of the early objectives of the AIM-based process is to help in the problem identification – by preparing a preliminary matrix that identifies broad relationships, without necessarily being able to specify with any accuracy, the magnitudes of the impacts or their relative priorities. For

Table 3.1 *Simple example of an action impact matrix (AIM)*[1]

Activity/Policy	Main objective	Impacts on key sustainable development issues			
		Land degradation	Air pollution	Resettlement	Other
1. Macroeconomic & sectoral policies • Exchange rate • Energy pricing • Other	Macroeconomic and sectoral improvements • Improve trade balance and economic growth • Improve economic and energy use efficiency	Positive impacts due to removal of distortions Negative impacts mainly due to remaining constraints (–H) (deforest open-access areas)	(+M) (energy efficiency)		
2. Complementary Measures[2] • Market based • Non-market based	Specific/Local social and environmental gains • Reverse negative impacts of market failures, policy distortions and institutional constraints	Enhance positive impacts and mitigate negative impacts (above) of broader macroeconomic and sectoral policies (+H) (property rights)	(+M) (pollution tax) (+M) (public sector accountability)		
3. Investment projects • Project 1 (Hydro dam) • Project 2 (Re-afforest and relocate)	Improve efficiency of investments • Use of project evaluation (cost benefit analysis, environmental assessment, multi-criteria analysis, etc.)	Investment decision made more consistent with broader policy and institutional framework (–H) (inundate forests) (+H) (replant forests)	(+M) (displace fossil fuel use)	(–M) (displace people) (+M) (relocate people)	

Notes:

1. A few examples of typical policies and projects as well as key environmental and social issues are shown. Some illustrative but qualitative impact assessments are also indicated: thus + and – signify beneficial and harmful impacts, while H and M indicate high and moderate intensity. The AIM process helps to focus on the highest priority environmental issues and related environmental and social concerns.

2. Commonly used market-based measures include effluent charges, tradable emission permits, emission taxes or subsidies, bubbles and offsets (emission banking), stumpage fees, royalties, user fees, deposit-refund schemes, performance bonds, and taxes on products (such as fuel taxes). Non-market-based measures comprise regulations and laws specifying environmental standards (such as ambient standards, emission standards and technology standards) which permit or limit certain actions ('dos' and 'don'ts').

Source: Munasinghe (1993).

example, in Table 3.1, a currency devaluation may make timber exports more profitable and lead to deforestation of open access forest. The appropriate remedy might be to strengthen property rights or restrict access to the forest areas. A second example might involve increasing energy prices towards marginal costs to improve energy efficiency and decrease pollution. Adding pollution taxes to marginal energy costs will further reduce pollution. Increasing public sector accountability will reinforce favourable responses to these price incentives, by reducing the ability of inefficient firms to pass on cost increases to consumers or to transfer their losses to the government. In the same vein, a major hydroelectric project is shown in Table 3.1 as having two adverse impacts – inundation of forested areas and villages, as well as one positive impact – the replacement of thermal power generation (thereby reducing air pollution). A reforestation project coupled with adequate resettlement efforts may help address the negative impacts. The matrix-based approach therefore encourages the systematic articulation and coordination of policies and projects to achieve sustainable development goals. Based on readily available data, it would be possible to develop such an initial matrix for many countries. Furthermore, a range of social impacts could be incorporated into the AIM, using the same approach.

This process may be developed further to assist in analysis and remediation. For example, more detailed analyses may be carried out for the subset of main economy-wide policies and environmental impact links identified in the cells of the preliminary matrix. This, in turn, would lead to a more refined final matrix, which would help to quantify impacts and formulate additional measures to enhance positive linkages and mitigate negative ones. The more detailed analyses which could help to determine the final matrix would depend on planning goals and available data and resources. They may range from the application of conventional sectoral economic analysis methods (appropriately modified in scope to incorporate environmental impacts, see Chapter 4), to fairly comprehensive system or multisector modelling efforts and green accounting. The methods and tools for these analyses are described in the following sections.

3.3.2   Methods of Macroeconomic-Environment Modelling

The analysis of environment–economy linkages is carried out using techniques essentially developed for a better understanding of the relationships between different sectors of the economy. Broadly speaking these fall into three groups: those using intersectoral input–output models, those developing less restrictive general equilibrium models and those based on more limited macroeconomic models.

Input–output analysis[1]

Input–output analysis (I/O) focuses on the relationships existing between different sectors in a complex economy. The overall objective of I/O analysis is to determine the total output required to meet the total demand. The total demand is made up of the intermediate consumption and the final demand. It is possible to incorporate environmental impacts into the I/O model,[2] as shown in Table 3.2. The economy is described as a table of transactions. The horizontal rows are the outputs produced by the sectors and the vertical columns are the inputs received. Each cell gives the physical quantity of each input required by a specific sector.

Table 3.2   Integrating pollution into an I/O model

Outputs from producing sector	Inputs to purchasing sector				
	Sector 1 (Agriculture)	Sector 2 (Industry)	Sector 3 (Water pollution)	Final demand	Total production
Sector 1 (Agriculture)	25	20	0	55	100
Sector 2 (Industry)	14	6	0	30	50
Sector 3 (Water pollution)	50	10	0	0	60

In the last row and third column (sector 3) an environmental resource is considered as a sector which provides inputs (row 3) for agricultural and industrial activities, but does not require agricultural and/or industrial inputs for its production. It is important to notice that the total output of each sector includes both the intermediate and the final demand of each sector in the economy. This model can be used to calculate the quantities of environmental resources necessary for satisfying human activities, including both productive activities and final consumption. A further advantage is that the model allows for the inclusion of prices and an analysis of the cost of mitigation measures.

An important recent application of I/O analysis has been to forecast the emissions of greenhouse gases (GHGs). A model has been developed for Russia (Golub and Strukova 2000), which took the existing I/O matrix and, given projections of changes in final output, estimated the requirement of all inputs, including energy inputs. From these, the emissions of GHGs could be calculated. The model allowed for changes in technology over time by assuming that new investment in each sector will be based on technologies that are appropriate in the year in which they are undertaken. That in turn will depend, *inter alia*, on the prices of different types of energy. The result is a model that gives projections of GHGs under different energy pricing assumptions.

Other questions that I/O models can be used to answer include the following.

- What are the implications of alternative growth paths on the demand for key commodities such as energy and key factors such as labour, and environmental goods and services including the amount of pollution co-produced?
- What are the regional implications of alternative development policies?
- If resources are likely to be limited for investment, which sectors are the 'priority' ones to give the greatest benefit in terms of economic growth? The same applies if key commodities are also in short supply, such as oil. I/O models have been used to identify the key bottlenecks in the economy that need to be cleared for maximum efficiency to be obtained from a given supply.

The difficulty with this approach is essentially the lack of good recent data. I/O tables exist for most developing countries but they are often out of date and there are rarely enough data on the environmental flows, in the comprehensive and systematic manner required, for them to be usable within this modelling framework. The rigidity of the technique does not allow use of incomplete information easily. However, short-cut, approximate I/O multipliers useful for sizing economic and environmental impacts can be estimated (Zheng and Harou 1988).

General equilibrium models

I/O models incorporate a number of restrictive assumptions about technology that are sometimes considered to lead to invalid conclusions to the sorts of questions raised above. The development of non-linear modelling techniques with a more flexible structure with regard to the number of sectors and the relationships between them has been developed over the last 20 years. Such models (referred to as computable general equilibrium models (CGEs)) have reached the stage of being easily applicable with relatively limited computing equipment.

General equilibrium models take, as their point of departure, the data on the demands and supplies of all the goods and services in the economy to the different agents. This information is summarized, partly in the I/O tables referred to above, and in the 'social accounting matrices' (SAMs), which give a breakdown of how the inputs and outputs in an economy are distributed across different groups of individuals in society. The modeller then constructs aggregate demand and supply functions for the different outputs (for example, manufacturing, services and agriculture) and inputs (labour, capital and raw materials).

Each aggregate demand and supply can be made up of components (for example, domestic demand and exports and domestic supply and imports), and is a function of relative prices of all inputs and outputs, as well as income and other economic factors. The model solves for the prices that equate supply and demand in all the markets. Some of the prices can be determined outside the system (for example, world prices for traded commodities). The model can be 'dynamic' in the sense that it solves for prices over time, with the prices in one period determining the levels of some inputs such as capital in the next period.[3]

For environmental problems specific advances have been made in the use of CGE models in recent years. Examples of their use are presented in one of the case studies at the end of this chapter (Annex 3A2). Although such models represent an important tool, we should be aware of their limitations. The key problem is that there are many parameters of the models that cannot be determined empirically with accuracy. Hence values have to be assigned to them on a somewhat arbitrary basis and the results of using them are subject to considerable uncertainty. This can be avoided to some extent by looking for the sensitivity of the policy conclusions to the values of key parameters. Nevertheless a broad area of uncertainty can remain. Another difficulty is that given their complex structure, it is hard to see why certain impacts arise when taxes or other parameters are changed. This makes it unconvincing when explaining the results to a policy maker.

Macroeconomic models

The most frequently used models for economic management are the short-term macroeconomic models linking the key aggregates such as income, consumption and investment. Such models are frequently used for forecasting short-term movements in the economy, as well as in analysing the implications of alternative fiscal and monetary policies. Such models are formally structured, with equations relating the movements of key variables, and the latter divided into two groups: those whose values are determined within the model (endogenous variables) and those whose values are to be fed into the model from outside (exogenous variables).

More recently, however, the policy analysis of alternative policies has been carried out in a less formal modelling framework. Finance ministries in developing countries have adopted 'intersectoral' accounting models to look at the key questions relating to the impacts of alternative policies on different sectors. These can usually be set up in a spreadsheet, and would consist of projected national accounts for the economy by production sector, and sectoral accounts for the government budget, the external account, the private account and the monetary sector. Further sectors can be added as appropriate. For example, if we are analysing the impacts of investments in the energy sector, an energy sector as well as a set of accounts for the key entities in that sector could be appended. The 'model' consists of tracing the flow of funds between the sectors and ensuring consistency in the values of the variables. In terms of predicting future values of these variables, the distinction between the endogenous and exogenous variables remains, except that the endogenous variables are now those determined by the accounting framework in the model and the exogenous ones are those determined outside the framework, including any that are forecast from other macroeconomic models.

Could such models be used for the analysis of environmental questions? Given their flexibility the answer is almost certainly yes, partly in terms of the environmental impact of economic policy but more effectively in terms of the economic implications of environmental regulation. The former may be illustrated with the example of the forestry sector. One could develop a physical accounting framework for such a sector relating stocks and flows of different timbers and a link between the level of harvesting and the economic incentives for doing so. Every time there was a change in a policy instrument, such as export taxes or the exchange rate, its implications could then be worked out for this sector.

The more useful applications of such models, however, lie in dealing with the second linkage between the economy and the environment, namely the economic impacts of environmental regulation. If taxes and charges are imposed on certain sectors of the economy for environmental reasons, the framework allows one to trace through their implications on the government budget account, the external account and the private sector.

3.3.3   Integrated Environmental–Economic Accounts

The integration of environmental and economic objectives, which is the goal of sustainable development, and mainstreaming the environment in economy-wide policies requires information at the macro level, which includes both economic and environmental variables. This is the goal of integrated environmental–economic accounts, or 'environmental accounting' as it is commonly known. The development of such accounts is a major development in many countries. The need for consistent data, which allow international comparisons, has prompted the Statistical Office of the United Nations to prepare a set of guidelines on the preparation of such accounts. These are known as the System of Environmental Economic Accounting (SEEA).

Different systems of environmental accounts
There are a large variety of approaches in the design of statistical systems describing the interrelationships between the natural environment and the economy (UNECE 1991). Two extreme positions can be identified. One extreme is the statistical description that focuses on the natural environment. Environ-

mental–economic linkages are described with regard to impacts on the environment. Much of the statistical framework is concentrated on the spatial description of the natural environment, involving the use, for instance, of maps of particular regions (ecosystems or eco-zones). The information is normally presented in physical units. At the other extreme, some statistical frameworks focus on the economy and take environmental–economic linkages into account only in so far as they are connected with actual economic transactions (for example, environmental protection expenditures and actual damage costs). These data systems are more closely related to the conventional national accounts, as they present monetary data on actual transactions in market values. In Box 3.2 these two concepts – physical data collection and monetary accounting – are indicated in boxes 1 and 6. Approaches that are located between these two extremes could be classified with regard to the extent to which they incorporate monetary values.

Systems that mainly use physical units could extend the description of the natural environment to include information on the physical flows between the environment and the economy (use of natural resources, flow of residual products). The existing systems of natural resource accounting and environment statistics comprise such data (Box 3.2, boxes 1 and 2). This description in physical terms could be further extended to include information on transformation processes within the economy. Material/energy balances comprise a physical description of the use of natural resources, their transformation by production and consumption activities and the flow of residuals back to the natural environment (Box 3.2, boxes 2 and 3). Natural resource accounting and material/energy balances overlap, especially with regard to flows between the economy and the environment (Box 3.2, box 2).

The description of economic activities in monetary terms has been extended in the case of the SEEA to the valuation of the use of natural environment. Different methods are discussed below. The comprehensive measurement of costs and benefits of economic activities and their environmental impacts is the purpose of such calculations (Box 3.2, boxes 5 and 6) (see, for example, Bartelmus et al. 1991). Such valuation not only facilitates the incorporation of environmental concerns into economic analysis but also creates a common scale of measurement that allows the compilation of environmental–economic aggregates, such as green GNP.

The SEEA thus covers in principle both *national accounts* describing economic activities and *environmental accounts* including all monetary and physical flows that describe the interrelationship between the environment and the economy (Box 3.2, boxes 1, 2, 3, 5 and 6). This ideal concept cannot be fully realized at present, since comprehensive data systems for describing the natural environment and its interaction with the economy are still missing. Some ambitious approaches have been advanced in several developed countries, but no overall description of the natural environment has been realized so far.

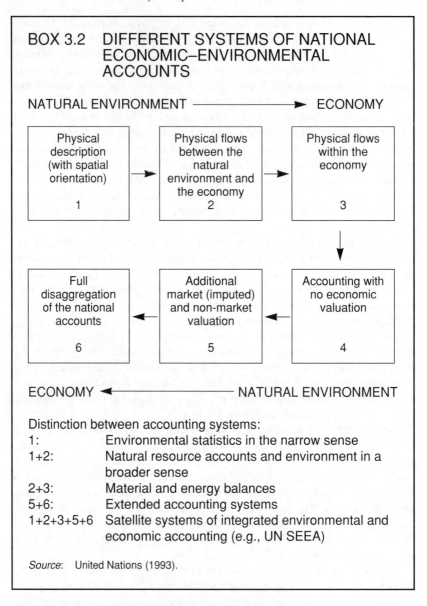

BOX 3.2   DIFFERENT SYSTEMS OF NATIONAL
           ECONOMIC–ENVIRONMENTAL
           ACCOUNTS

NATURAL ENVIRONMENT ──────────────► ECONOMY

| Physical description (with spatial orientation) 1 | Physical flows between the natural environment and the economy 2 | Physical flows within the economy 3 |

| Full disaggregation of the national accounts 6 | Additional market (imputed) and non-market valuation 5 | Accounting with no economic valuation 4 |

ECONOMY ◄────────────── NATURAL ENVIRONMENT

Distinction between accounting systems:
1:              Environmental statistics in the narrow sense
1+2:   Natural resource accounts and environment in a
                broader sense
2+3:   Material and energy balances
5+6:   Extended accounting systems
1+2+3+5+6   Satellite systems of integrated environmental and
                economic accounting (e.g., UN SEEA)

Source: United Nations (1993).

3.3.4   Monetary Accounting of the Environment

While there is no general agreement on the monetization of the environmental accounts, there are some accepted principles and some areas of controversy that need to be considered if such accounts are constructed. These are described below.

First, a clear distinction is made between stock and flow accounts. Value measures of stocks of natural resources and other forms of wealth form one method of accounting, which brings together the economic and environmental components. The flow accounts deduct the depletion of natural resources from the value of output, to arrive at a net income figure. Both are useful and relevant types of accounts.

The components of a stock calculation of capital require adjustments to be made for changes in the quality and quantity of natural assets along with changes in man-made capital and changes in human capital. The sum of all such assets is the total wealth of the economy, rough measures of which have been attempted (World Bank 1997). Methods of valuing the natural resource components are discussed further below. By themselves they are not very informative, but *changes in the wealth* over time are. If total wealth is declining then the country is passing on a declining asset base, which is inconsistent with the goal of sustainability. As we noted in the last chapter, one definition of sustainability is precisely that the total asset base should not decline over time in value terms (one definition of weak sustainability). The data presented in the previous chapter showed striking differences in genuine savings rates, with the African countries demonstrating the highest negative genuine savings.

In the flow accounts, we are interested in a measure of 'sustainable income'. This is the income that the present asset base could provide indefinitely.[4] Hence the idea is closely tied to that of total wealth. To obtain a measure of sustainable income we have to subtract, from the value of gross output, depletion in all forms of capital. We should also make some adjustment for damages in the form of environmental pollution and, possibly, an allowance for the fact that some expenditures in the economy are for 'defensive' purposes – that is, they are undertaken to protect individuals and society from the harmful consequences of environmental pollution and degradation. There is not, however, the same degree of agreement on whether these last two items should be deducted from the value of output.

Methods of estimating the depletion of natural capital vary and there is no agreement on precisely which method should be used. For a discussion of the issues, see Lutz (1993). In the case of renewable assets, such as water, forests and fish, it is the economic loss from unsustainable exploitation that is relevant. In the case of exhaustible resources it is the scarcity value or user cost (see Chapter 4) – the fact that a part of the wealth extracted has to be saved if future generations are not to be disadvantaged as result of the extraction – that is being sought.

Pollution damages are valued using a variety of methods, which are discussed in detail in Part II of this book. As far as defensive expenditures are concerned, several countries are attempting to estimate what is required to maintain a safe and sustainable environment. Some economists argue that these expenditures should be subtracted from the net national product to estimate true national income. They include expenditures for environmental protection as well as the alleviation of congestion, clean-up from accidents, reparations for crime victims, and health costs incurred due to an unhealthy environment. The main difficulty with defensive expenditures, however, is identifying them in the various accounting data available to statistical offices.

While it remains the case that no one country has addressed all the above issues, a number of developing countries have prepared integrated environmental and economic accounts as described in the UN handbook. In developing countries, these include Mexico, Papua New Guinea and Thailand. In Mexico, resource depletion reduced national income by 5.7 per cent for the year studied; including degradation the reduction was 13 per cent (Bartelmus et al. 1991 and van Tongerent et al 1993).

3.4   CONCLUSIONS

The discussion so far has shown that the kind of macroeconomic policies often pursued in structural adjustment programmes can have a detrimental effect on the environment, especially in the short run. They can also have many positive effects, as reforms bring about economic stability and prosperity. Of course, such prosperity will bring with it new and different environmental problems, but no one seriously suggests that growth should be curtailed on the grounds that such problems will occur.

Where there are conflicts between macroeconomic policies and environmental goals, how should they be resolved? While it is important to know what the environmental consequences of major macroeconomic policy reforms are, it is almost impossible to think of arresting such reforms on the grounds that they have unfavourable environmental consequences. The imperative for such reforms is simply too great – it is the need to ensure national survival and long-term economic development.

Hence the only ways in which the environmental objectives can be reconciled with the macroeconomic objectives is to introduce *more* instruments to mitigate negative environmental impacts or sustained positive ones. Following the rules of the theory of planning as set out by Tinbergen, one needs as many instruments as there are objectives. With the environment, one has added a further objective – or set of objectives – which have to be met at the same time as the environmental reforms are taking place. What form should such instruments take? They could include economic measures such as environmental charges and taxes, or legal measures, such as pollution licences, property reforms and so on. The general choice of instruments is discussed in Chapter 5, but a few general propositions can be advanced here.

First, when further instruments are introduced one cannot generally 'assign' instruments to objectives. The classical case is when policy makers assign monetary policy to control inflation and fiscal policy to control unemployment. Both policies of course interact and affect both inflation and unemployment. In the case of the environment, devaluation could result in increased deforestation and a possible additional instrument would be export controls on forest products. The levels of such controls have to be taken in conjunction with the level of devaluation, as both have an effect on the natural resource sector and the gains from devaluation. A total ban on forest products, for example, could reduce the benefits of the devaluation by restricting the export of products made with domestic wood. That said, the goal is to find instruments that are able to be set more or less independently of the macroeconomic instruments, simply because it is too difficult to get the macroeconomic policy makers to adjust their instruments on the grounds of the environmental objectives.

Second, in setting the environmental instruments one should try not to introduce other distortions in the economy. Taking the same example as above, an export tax on logs will make domestic prices different from world prices and thereby create inefficiencies in the economy. A better instrument would be to ensure that forest loggers pay the full social cost of their actions. Then there would be no need to regulate exports. The latter is called a 'second-best' policy, because it introduces further distortions while solving one set of problems. Where second-best policies have to be followed one has to analyse the gains and losses to different sectors rather carefully. There are, however, some general rules. One is in relation to trade. Here the theory of the second best establishes that there almost always exists a domestic economic instrument, the use of which will be superior to the implementation of a tariff or other trade restriction. Thus, for example, if the manufacturing sector is unionized and wages are above marginal costs, taxes on labour or subsidies on capital are generally preferable to export subsidies or import tariffs. Similarly with a production externality a production tax is preferred to trade interventions (Bhagwati 1984). This powerful result implies that, *where alternative instruments are available*, environmental impacts should be dealt with through the use of domestic economic instruments. What are the instruments available for environmental regulation that would be preferable to the use of trade restrictions? There is a substantial literature, which shows how environmental costs can be internalized through the use of economic and non-economic instruments (Tietenberg 1996). These are discussed further in Chapter 5.

The third general proposition relates to way in which economic growth can eventually resolve the environmental problems of a country, and that some degradation is the inevitable cost of the pursuit of such growth through the various macroeconomic policies discussed above. We touched on this in Chapter 2, and we elaborate on it here.

There is a strand of literature (Grossman and Krueger 1993; World Bank 1992), which suggests that the relationship between GDP and the quality of the environment is 'U-shaped' – that is, the quality of the environment deteriorates initially as GDP per capita increases, and then improves after a certain critical value of per capita GDP has been reached. This critical value varies with the pollutant, and indeed for some pollutants such as Volatile Organic Compounds (VOCs) there is no 'turning point'. Furthermore some recent work, which has analysed the general sustainability of conventional growth (Munasinghe et al. 2000) casts doubt on the validity of the using the simple 'U' shape to conclude that the environment will in general improve with growth.

This model (also referred to as the 'environmental Kuznets curve') can be looked at in conjunction with the original Kuznets curve, which postulated a deterioration in income distribution in the early stages of economic growth, followed by an improvement later. Taking the two together one would conclude that a declining environmental quality and increasing income inequality go hand in hand as part of the 'development process'. In the end it will all work out fine, with improvements in both these indicators of human welfare.

Such a sanguine view is inappropriate and misleading from a policy viewpoint. First, some of the environmental degradation being observed, and sometimes being caused by extreme poverty, is irreversible and will never be recovered. Second, what is a long-term time-series relationship is being inferred from cross-section intercountry data. There is no reason why a particular country should follow the path characterized by a cross-section of countries. Indeed the aim should be to follow a policy based on a comparison of domestic costs and benefits of different options, taking account of their impacts on all aspects of welfare, including poverty/inequality, environmental quality, GDP and other indicators such as those used by the United Nations Development Programme in its human development reports. The existence of the Kuznets curve is of little relevance in determining such a set of policies.

NOTES

1. This section draws on Costa and Marangoni (1995).
2. For an early example of the I/O technique to the issue of economy–environment linkages, see Leontief (1970).
3. The total value of supplies and demands must be equal by the way in which they are defined. Hence the supplies and demand are not independent. This is known as Walras Law and its implication is that only relative prices can be determined by the CGE model. Usually the full set of prices is then calculated by selecting one of the prices from their current levels.
4. This concept is attributed to the English economist, John Hicks.

CITED BIBLIOGRAPHY

Anderson, K. (1992), 'Effects on the environment and welfare of liberalizing world trade: the cases of coal and food', in K. Anderson and R. Blackhurst (eds), *The Greening of World Trade Issues*, London: Harvester Wheatsheaf, pp. 145–72.

Bartelmus, P. C. Stahmer and J. van Tongeren (1991), 'Integrated environmental and economic accounting: framework for a SNA satellite system', *Review of Income and Wealth*, ser.37, No. 2, 111–48.

Bhagwati, J.N. (1987), 'The generalized theory of distortions and welfare', in J.N. Bhagwati (ed.), *International Trade: Selected Readings*, 2nd edn, Cambridge, MA: MIT Press, pp. 265–86.

Bromley, D.W. (1991), *Environment and Economy: Property Rights and Public Policy*, Cambridge, MA: Basil Blackwell.

Capistrano, A.D. and C.F. Kier (1990), *Global Economic Influences on Tropical Closed Broadleaved Forest Depletion, 1967–1975*, Tampa, FL: Food Resources Department, University of Florida Press.

Chopra, K. and S.C. Gulati (1996), 'Environmental degradation and population movements: the role of property rights', *Environmental and Resource Economics*, **9** (4), 383–408.

Cleaver, K.M. and A.G. Schreiber (1994), Reversing the Spiral: The Population, Agriculture and Environment Nexus in Sub-Saharan Africa, Washington DC: The World Bank.

Cornia G., R. Jolly and F. Stewart (1987), *Adjustment with a Human Face*, Oxford: Oxford University Press.

Costa P. and G. Marangoni (1995), *Economia delle interdipendenze produttive*, Padua: CEDAM.

Dasgupta, P. (1995), 'The population problem: theory and evidence', *Journal of Economic Literature*, **33**, 1879–902.

Dasgupta, P. (1996), 'The economics of the environment', *Environment and Development*, **1**, 387–428.

Dasgupta, P. and K.-G. Mäler (1991), 'The environment and emerging development issues', in *Proceedings of the Annual Bank Conference on Development Economics, 1990*, Supplement to *World Bank Economic Review*, 101–32.

Elibom, A. and J. Bojo (1999), Poverty and Environment: Evidence of Links and Integration into the Country Assistance Strategy Process, Discussion Paper 4, Environment Group, Africa Region, Washington DC: The World Bank.

Golub, A. and E. Strukova (2000), 'Study on Russian national strategy of greenhouse gas emission reduction', mimeo, Washington, DC: World Bank.

Grossman, G.M. and A.B. Krueger (1993), 'Environmental impacts of a North American free trade agreement', in P.M. Garber (ed.), *The Mexico–U.S. Free Trade Agreement*, Cambridge, MA: MIT Press, pp. 13–56.

Jaganathan, V.N. (1989), 'Poverty, public policies and the environment', Environment Working Paper No. 24, Washington, DC: World Bank.

Leontief W. (1970), 'Environmental repercussions and the economic structure: an input–output approach', *Review of Economics and Statistics*, **52**, 262–71.

Lopez, R. (1998), 'Where development can or cannot go: the role of poverty-environment linkages', in B. Pleskovic and J. Stiglitz, (eds), Annual Bank Conference on Development Economics 1997, Washington DC: The World Bank Press.

Lopez, R., V. Thomas and Y. Wang (1998), 'Addressing the education puzzle – the distribution of education and economic reforms', World Bank Policy Research Paper 2031, The World Bank, Washington DC.

Lucas, R.E.B., D. Wheeler and H. Hettige (1992), 'Economic development, environmental regulation and the international migration of toxic industrial pollution: 1960–88', in P. Low (ed.), *International Trade and the Environment*, World Bank Discussion Paper No. 159, Washington, DC: World Bank, pp. 67–86.

Lutz, E. (ed.) (1993), *Toward Improved Accounting for the Environment*, Washington, DC: World Bank.

Markandya, A. (1994), *Essays in Sustainable Development*, Rome: Food and Agriculture Organization.

Mink, S.D. (1993), 'Poverty, population and the environment', Environment Working Paper No, 189, Washington, DC: World Bank.

Mortimore, M. (1989), 'The causes, nature and rate of soil degradation in the northernmost states of Nigeria and an assessment of the role of fertilizer in counteracting the process of degradation', Environment Working Paper No. 17, Washington, DC: World Bank.

Munasinghe, M. (1993), Environmental Economics and Sustainable Development, World Bank Discussion Paper No. 3, Washington, DC: World Bank.

Munasinghe, M. (1996), *Environmental Impacts of Macroeconomic and Sectoral Policies*, Washington, DC: ISEE, UNEP and World Bank.

Munasinghe, M. and W. Cruz (1995), 'Economy-wide policies and the environment', Environment Working Paper No. 10. Washington, DC: World Bank.

Munasinghe, M., O. Sunkel and C. de Miguel (2000), *The Sustainability of Long-Term Growth*, Cheltenham, UK and Northampton, MA, USA: Edward Elgar.

OECD (1998), Improving the Environment Through Reducing Subsidies: Parts I–III, Paris: OECD.

OECD (1999), Environmental Taxes: Recent Developments in China and OECD Countries, Paris: OECD.

Panayotou, T. (1993), *Green Markets: The Economics of Sustainable Development*, San Francisco, CA: Institute for Contemporary Studies Press.

Ravaillon, M., M. Heil and J. Halan (1998), 'Carbon emissions and income inequality', World Bank Discussion Paper, Washington DC: World Bank.

Reed, D. (ed.) (1992), *Structural Adjustment and the Environment*, London: Earthscan.

Reed, D. (ed.) (1996), *Structural Adjustment, the Environment, and Sustainable Development*, London: Earthscan.

Sen, A. (1994), 'Population: delusion and reality', *New York Review of Books*, **41** (15), 62–71.

Southgate, D. (1988), 'The economics of land degradation in the Third World', Environment Working Paper No. 2, Washington, DC: World Bank.

Tietenberg, T. (1996), *Environmental and Natural Resource Economics*, New York: Harper Collins.

United Nations (1993), *Integrated Environmental and Economic Accounting*, Interim Version, Studies and Methods, Series F, No. 61, Handbook of National Accounting, New York: United Nations.

United Nations, Economic Commission for Europe (UNECE) (1991), *Revised System of National Accounts*, New York: UNECE.

van Tongeren, J., S. Schweinfest, E. Lutz, M. Gomez Luna and F. Guillen Martin (1993), 'Integrated economic and environmental accounting: a case study for Mexico', in M.

Munasinghe (ed.) *Environmental Economics and Natural Resource Management in Developing Countries*, Washington, DC: World Bank, pp. 257–89.

World Bank (1992), *World Development Report*, New York: Oxford University Press.

World Bank (1997), *Expanding the Measure of Wealth: Indicators of Environmentally Sustainable Development*, Environmentally Sustainable Development Studies and Monographs No. 17, Washington, DC: World Bank.

Zheng, C. and P. Harou (1988), 'A method to estimate input–output multipliers for the forestry sector without an I/O table', *Forest Science*, **34** (4): pp. 882–93.

ANNEX 3A1   CASE STUDY 1: STRUCTURAL
            ADJUSTMENT AND SUSTAINABLE
            DEVELOPMENT IN ZAMBIA: A STUDY OF
            THE IMPACT OF MACROECONOMIC
            POLICIES ON THE ENVIRONMENT

Background Information[1]

Zambia is one of Africa's last great 'frontier' territories. It has numerous species
of wild animals, with 45 per cent of the country set aside for wildlife such as
in the national parks and game management area. Since population density is
10 per square km, with half of the population living in mining towns on the
Copperbelt, land pressure is not an issue, and only 3.5 per cent of cultivable
land is currently cropped. The climate is good for a wide range of cash crops
including maize, wheat, sugar, cattle, tobacco and cotton as well as small grains,
legumes and cassava. Forty-five per cent of all southern Africa's water resources
are within Zambia's frontiers, including part of the largest man-made lake in
the world, Lake Kariba, which is a major source of hydro-electric power.
Zambia also has massive mineral resources; it is the fourth largest producer of
copper in the world, as well as mining lead, zinc and coal.

In the last 20 years or so the country has seen a major decline in its living
standards. There are several reasons for this, one being a fall in the value of its
largest and most valuable export, copper. Production fell by one-third between
1975 and 1990, due to declining world prices, but poor management and
unreliable external transport also contributed to this fall.

There have also been other problems. The hydro-electric capacity of Zambia
has been characterized by poor maintenance, frequent breakdowns and low
capacity utilization. Agriculture has been bedevilled by inefficient state supply
of inputs and marketing, low prices, and insecure land tenure arrangements,
which have created problems of overcultivation in some areas.

The economic and social impacts of this decline have been severe.
Government deficits equivalent to 20 per cent of GDP became the norm during
the late 1970s and early 1980s; foreign debt rose to 300 per cent of GDP at its
peak; inflation ran to three-digit levels; and economic growth was negative for
a number of years (at the same time as population was increasing at 3 per cent
per year). Moreover, the distribution of income has remained a problem and
inequality has always been high. As early as 1970, the top 7 per cent of the
population received nearly 25 per cent of all income. Poverty has been a rural
as well as an urban phenomenon with 50 to 60 per cent of the total population
living below the poverty line.

Zambia did not anticipate the global collapse in copper prices in 1974–75 and subsequently failed to diversify away from copper and to run an effective government budget. The United National Independence Party (UNIP), which ruled from Independence until 1991, instead used the state machinery to control economic activity, to create jobs, and to act as a source of political patronage. Furthermore the country's massive debt burden confounded policy initiatives for restoring macroeconomic balance and growth. Implementation of a donor-funded structural adjustment programme (SAP) started in 1983 and has continued intermittently to the present time, with a break between 1987 and 1989. In 1991 there were multi-party elections for the first time in 19 years and the winners, the Movement for Multi-Party Democracy (MMD), have stated that implementing the SAP is a priority.

Structural Adjustment

Zambia has had a mixed relationship with its international donors. It first received International Monetary Fund (IMF) support in 1975 but, until 1983, compliance to donor conditions was poor. Between 1983 and 1987 Zambia made significant headway with economic deregulation, although relations with the IMF were broken in May 1987 and a New Economic Recovery Programme was initiated, on the theme of 'Growth From Own Resources'. This was similar to the SAP in its objectives but its strategy was a return to central economic control. It also involved a unilateral limitation on debt repayments to 10 per cent of export earnings. Relations with the IMF resumed in July 1989 (running the economy had been made virtually impossible by the suspension of external aid), and since then structural adjustment has continued – albeit with a period of policy volatility preceding the 1991 multi-party elections.

The overall aim of Zambia's structural adjustment programme has been to restore macroeconomic balance and growth by:

- reducing state control of the economy;
- reducing food subsidies in order to control the budget deficit and encourage a return to the land, to increase agricultural production and exports;
- reducing import dependence (especially the overdependence on imported capital equipment of much of the industrial sector); and
- diversifying exports away from copper.

Privatization of the 80 per cent of the economy controlled by the government has been slow, but external and internal trade has been fully liberalized. The final steps towards complete liberalization of agricultural marketing were taken in 1993. This caused considerable disruption as private traders failed to move into all areas.

Food subsidies were finally removed in late 1991, as one of the incoming MMD government's election pledges. Earlier attempts in 1986 and 1990 had resulted in riots and been retracted. A move in the mid-1980s from universal price subsidies to the distribution of maize coupons to the urban poor was widely held responsible for the increase in malnutrition recorded in the late 1980s (maize meal prices increased by 160 per cent in the 12 months to July 1989). There was no significant move back to the land.

The real appreciation of the kwacha has contributed to a flood of cheap imports, particularly consumer goods, with which local agriculture and manufacturing cannot compete. This, together with civil service retrenchment since the MMD came to power, has produced a reduction in the share of formal sector employment from 27 to 9 per cent between 1974 and 1990.

Export diversification has been insignificant, partly because of the difficulties facing domestic agriculture and manufacturing. At the same time, copper exports have fallen substantially, due to a reduction in production caused by poor maintenance and the exhaustion of some reserves.

At the macro level, foreign exchange liberalization has contributed to domestic inflation and the continuation of a large balance of payments deficit, as well as making control of the budget deficit more difficult. The MMD introduced cash-based budgeting into the government system at the beginning of the 1993 financial year, and this severe step appears finally to have stamped out the deficit.

Economic performance was hampered by a critical drought which destroyed Zambia's 1992 harvest and necessitated massive food imports. Thus economic growth remained negative for most of the 1980s and early 1990s and real per capita GDP also fell. This resulted in an increase in poverty and inequality, which moved Zambia from middle-income to least-developed country status, sliding between 1987 and 1992 from 39th to 15th poorest country in per capita GDP terms. That in turn had a knock-on effect on social indicators, pushing Zambia – according to UNICEF statistics – from 47th to 17th highest under-five mortality rate between 1990 and 1992. The year 1993 was the first year for which a positive rate of growth of GDP was recorded.

Environmental Dimensions

For many years, there was no real consideration of environmental issues in policy planning because of the perception of Zambia as a frontier territory. Serious conflicts over resource use only began to emerge when the economy deteriorated in the late 1970s. During the UNIP era the economic strategy of widespread state control meant that, for many resources, the same institution was responsible for both exploitation and control (for example, Zambia Consolidated Copper Mines for minerals, the Forest Department for timber). In addition, UNIP's policy of humanism (roughly, human-centred socialism) meant that it was politically difficult to enforce some environmental regulations, for example, removal of squatters from protected areas.

As a result of this neglect, and other factors to be discussed in this case study, environmental problems have emerged, including: deforestation; loss of wildlife (poaching for trophies has pushed the rhino population to the brink of extinction and reduced elephant numbers by 90 per cent since 1960); water pollution in urban areas; and loss of soil fertility.

In recognition of the growing problem, and following the lead of the World Conservation Union (IUCN), a National Conservation Strategy (NCS) was completed in 1985 and became the accepted basis of environmental policy in Zambia. It resulted in a new act for environmental protection, a new Ministry of the Environment and Natural Resources (MENR), and a National Environmental Council. The NCS was recently updated to form Zambia's National Environmental Action Plan, which was ratified in 1994. Despite this, serious conflicts still occur between the MENR and other ministries concerning the implementation of environmental policy. For example, following a recent appeal by the MENR to remove squatters from Zambia's forest reserves, the minister for the Copperbelt area refused to comply, stating 'I cannot see any forest here. All I can see are cassava, groundnuts and cabbage forests'.

The following subsections describe the economy–environment linkages that were established in the research carried out.

Wildlife

The reduction in big game has accelerated in the SAP period. For example, elephant numbers fell by about 3 per cent a year from 1960 to 1975 (from 270,000 to 75,000). In the period between 1985 and 1993 they fell to 22,000, a rate of decline of 9 per cent per annum.

The decline is attributed to several causes, prominent among which is poaching for trophies. This has been exacerbated by the SAP, as urban unemployment has risen and farm incomes have fallen. The SAP was also responsible for cuts in the government budget, which have affected the enforcement of anti-poaching laws. The budget for the National Parks and Wildlife Service fell by 65 per cent in real terms between 1975 and 1990, and now accounts for 0.4 per cent of the total government budget.

Deforestation

Deforestation has been taking place at an increasing rate. Forty-five per cent of the country is covered by dry evergreen forest, but this has been lost at a rate of 900,000 ha, or 2.6 per cent a year throughout the 1980s.

The main factor responsible for this fall was land clearance for agriculture (over 90 per cent). Between 1980 and 1990 clearing land for permanent agriculture and for shifting cultivation were equally responsible for the loss of wooded land. The increased demand for land for agricultural use arose because of the growth in population, limited employment opportunities outside agriculture and limited ability to increase output through intensive farming. At the same time the expansion was exacerbated by a slow rate of conversion of Trust Land into small plots for farmers (there are 43 million ha or 58 per cent of the total land that could be used for small farm plots), and by the fact that the forest land that is being cleared has no well-defined and enforced property rights.

The SAP has contributed to accelerated deforestation through increased urban unemployment, which has added to the pressure on rural lands as people return to rural areas. However, this impact is complex; while it may increase the demand for permanent agricultural land, it does not necessarily increase the demand for shifting cultivation clearance. When population densities increase above 2.4 persons/km^2, studies have observed a decrease in the frequency of land clearance for shifting cultivation.

One factor that could have played a part in deforestation was the decline in SAP-induced fertilizer subsidies, the argument being that as the price of fertilizer rose, so application would fall, agricultural productivity would fall, and more land would be needed to provide a given amount of output. However, the studies on the linkages did not show any such impact. Applications with the subsidy were small in any event, and the poor soils that cover much of Zambia require extensive fallowing even with regular applications of chemical fertilizer.

Finally charcoal production also contributes to deforestation, especially in peri-urban areas. With 45,000 persons employed in this activity it is becoming a major source of demand for wood. The demand for wood is also growing due to the removal of energy subsidies, the fall in real income and the increase in price of commercial beer. Home beer brewing requires a lot of fuelwood and is becoming increasingly popular.

Urban water pollution
Effluent discharge into water bodies has increased considerably in recent years. The composition of that effluent has also changed with mining pollution declining and industrial and household effluent increasing.

The percentage of households connected to piped water and a sewerage system declined in the early years of the SAP (1985–88), but has picked up since then. However, although a large number of households are connected to these facilities, they still face long periods without running water and the sewerage treatment plants are unable to cope with the volume of effluent. As a result, increases in the rate of waterborne diseases are being observed. For example, cholera epidemics are now an annual occurrence.

The SAP has contributed to this problem with the decline in funding for the Department of Water Affairs. In the mid-1980s the decline in its budget was about 5 per cent a year; but between 1983 and 1990 the real decline doubled to 10 per cent per annum. The other factor that has contributed to the problem is the growth in the urban population. About 60 per cent of Zambia's population is urban dwelling and this share is increasing.

Approach Used and Data Collected

In analysing the links between macroeconomic policies and the environment, two things are paramount. First, a model needs to be developed, showing how both the economic variables (GDP, per capita consumption and so on) and the ecological variables (rates of deforestation, levels of pollution and so on) are affected by the policy parameters that are being altered (government budgets, subsidies, investment and so on). Second, the analyst has to look at the environmental impacts *with* the policy changes and *without* the policy changes. Only then can s/he see what effects the policies have. Too often the results of macroeconomic policy on the environment are reported with only the 'with policy' options having been considered.

The kinds of models available range from the sophisticated computable general equilibrium (CGE) type to the simpler sectoral ones where macroeconomic policy is traced through to the agricultural, industrial and other sectors without modelling the links between the sectors in any detail. The arguments for and against the different models are not discussed here. Ideally, the more sophisticated models enable one to make a better evaluation of the linkages between macroeconomic policy and sectoral impacts than do the simpler sectoral or aggregate macroeconomic models. On the other hand such models are more difficult to construct, and need more information, not only about the level of activity in the different sectors but also about the responsiveness of these sectors to policy parameters such as tax rates, exchange rates and the like. In the absence of good information on this kind of policy responsiveness, the models may be seen by policy makers as speculative and therefore less valid.

The kinds of links between the macroeconomic policy variables and the environment are demonstrated in Box 3.1 of the chapter. These distinguish between short-run and long-run factors; and between sectoral policies (such as land reform) and economy-wide policies (such as devaluation). In any actual analysis it is extremely difficult to model all, or even a large part of these linkages. What the modeller has to do is to select the important linkages for the country being analysed, and then make sure these are accounted for in the modelling.

In the Zambian case, a complex CGE model was developed and used to analyse SAP policy changes and their impacts on the environment (Reed 1996). This model is too complex to present here, but a simplified macroeconomic model is presented which focuses on the main environmental factors analysed within the CGE framework. The level of complexity in the modelling process clearly impacts on the quality of results, but for illustrative purposes and to provide an estimation of the main environmental impacts, the simplified spread-sheet-based macroeconomic model is adequate. The simplified model allows the use of the model to demonstrate the impacts of policy changes and allows the estimation of the impacts of different policy options.

The main assumptions in the model are:

1. *Economic variables*

    i.   Gross domestic product (GDP) is a function of investment.[2]

    ii.   Investment is divided into public and private. Public investment is exogenous and entirely financed from official external assistance. Private investment responds positively to economic growth and declining inflation.

    iii. Non-investment government expenditure is exogenous.

    iv. Exports respond partially to devaluation with a lag of 12–18 months. Service exports in the form of tourism earnings decline if wildlife numbers are reduced. A one per cent reduction in wildlife numbers is estimated to reduce service exports by 0.3 per cent.

    v.   Imports are a function of domestic output but also respond to devaluation/trade liberalization with a lag.

    vi. Government tax revenues are mainly exogenous, but there is a small component that responds to increased non-agricultural output changes.

    vii. Official transfers from abroad cover public investment, and may cover some public sector consumption. In the case of an SAP, additional transfers for public consumption are introduced.

   viii. Subsidies from the government budget are exogenous but are reduced when a SAP is introduced.

2. *Employment and population*

    ix. Urban 'employment' is a function of the urban population. It is acknowledged that much of this may be underemployed. The formal sector employs only about 9 per cent of the total urban labour force.

    x.   The urban population increases through natural growth plus migration. Migration is a function of the changing structure of output; if the share of agriculture in output falls, there is out-migration.

    xi   Population growth at 3 per cent per annum is exogenous. This assumption may be changed.

3. *Social indicators*

    xii.   The population below the poverty line is a function of per capita rural and urban incomes. If either or both fall, the number in poverty increases.

   xiii.   Per capita rural and urban incomes are calculated from the GDP and the total population in each sector.

   xiv.   Inflation responds with a lag to changes in the government budget deficit.

4. *Ecological variables*

    xv.   Wildlife numbers decline with: (a) falls in the budget of the national parks service; (b) increases in rural populations; and (c) declines in rural per capita incomes. If wildlife numbers fall, this affects the 'export' of tourism services, as visitors decline.

   xvi.   Forest clearance for agriculture is a function of per capita rural incomes and the rural population.

  xvii.   Forest cover loss from fuelwood is a function of: (a) subsidies on energy, with falling subsidies increasing fuelwood demand; (b) increases in rural and urban populations; and (c) decreases in per capita urban and rural incomes.

 xviii.   The number of cases of waterborne diseases in urban areas increases with increases in the urban population but declines with increased investment in waste water treatment.

   xix.   The elasticity with respect to government expenditure assumes that the expenditure structure remains unchanged. Thus a one per cent fall in government expenditure is assumed to cause a one per cent fall in expenditure on national parks, and subsidies for energy and wastewater treatment. Again, this assumption may be changed.

The basic 'elasticities' between the ecological variables and macroeconomic policy variables are given in Table 3A1.1. The interpretation of the numbers can be illustrated by taking the value in the top left-hand corner (-0.3). This means that if government expenditure on national parks falls by one per cent, wildlife numbers will decline by 0.3 per cent per annum. Analogous interpretations apply to the other numbers. In addition, it is also assumed (see iv above) that a fall in wildlife numbers of one per cent will cause a fall in visitors to Zambia of 0.3 per cent.

It is important to emphasize that this simple model has been developed and is used here for illustrative purposes. A more complex model has been developed, using the CGE framework, to better inform policy makers of the impacts of policy reform. CGE modelling should be used where possible in order to more fully represent impacts on the economy and, consequently, the environment. However, the links to the ecological variables are unlikely to be much more sophisticated than those modelled here, the reason being that little is known about them and the modelling of such links tends to be quite crude.

Table 3A1.1   Elasticities linking economic and ecological variables

	Government expenditure reduction	Urban population increase	Rural population increase	Urban per capita income Increase	Rural per capita income increase
Wildlife nos	−0.3	0.0	1.0	0.0	−1.0
Land clearance	0.0	0.0	0.6	0.0	−0.3
Fuelwood forest cover	0.1	−0.1	−0.1	0.1	0.1
Waterborne diseases	1.0	1.2	0.0	0.0	0.0

The model described above was calibrated to approximate the structure of the Zambian economy in 1990, with values of the main economic indicators corresponding to that period of time. The model was then run for five years under the assumption of no SAP and the results are given in Table 3A1.2 below.

The results of the model with the no-SAP scenario can be summarized as follows:

1. Both public and private investment decline by approximately 11 per cent per annum over the five years.
2. Tax revenues remain at 12 per cent of GDP and government non-investment expenditure falls slightly in real terms.
3. Official transfers decline with the decline in public sector investment but by more than the fall in public investment.
4. The share of agriculture in total output falls by about 2 per cent over the five years.
5. The economy grows very slowly and at a declining rate. In year 1 the rate is 1.5 per cent; by the end of the five years it is about 0.14 per cent.
6. The trade deficit increases a small amount in real terms.
7. Export earnings from services (principally tourism) fall by about 1 per cent per annum.

Table 3A1.2   Structural adjustment and sustainable development in Zambia economic and social projections with no SAP

	Units	Year 1	Year 2	Year 3	Year 4	Year 5
National economic indicators						
GDP	Index (*)	100.00	101.50	102.19	102.70	102.90
Consumption	Index (*)	87.00	89.60	90.61	91.90	94.74
Investment	Index (*)	14.00	11.50	11.00	10.00	8.50
Public	Index (*)	6.00	4.50	4.00	4.00	3.50
Private	Index (*)	8.00	7.00	7.00	6.00	5.00
Non-investment government						
expenditure	Index (*)	16.00	16.00	15.50	15.00	14.00
exports	Index (*)	32.00	32.00	31.95	31.88	31.82
Goods	Index (*)	28.00	28.00	28.00	28.00	28.00
Services	Index (*)	4.00	4.00	3.95	3.88	3.82
Imports	Index (*)	40.00	40.60	40.88	41.08	41.16
Trade deficit	Index (*)	−8.00	−8.60	−8.93	−9.20	−9.34
Government account						
Government tax revenue	Index (*)	12.00	12.18	12.29	12.39	12.47
Official transfers from overseas	Index (*)	13.00	11.00	9.00	8.00	7.00
Development expenditure	Index (*)	6.00	4.50	4.00	4.00	3.50
Other expenditure	Index (*)	29.00	29.00	28.50	28.00	27.00
Subsidies	Index (*)	13.00	13.00	13.00	13.00	13.00
Repayment of debt	Index (*)	4.00	4.00	3.00	3.00	2.00
Net deficit	Index (*)	−14.00	−14.32	−14.21	−14.61	−13.03
Employment						
Urban employment		1.21	1.24	1.25	1.27	1.28
Formal sector	Million	0.11	0.11	0.11	0.11	0.12
Informal sector	Million	1.10	1.13	1.14	1.16	1.17
Social indicators						
Population	Million	8.10	8.34	8.59	8.85	9.12
Urban population	Million	4.86	5.04	5.23	5.43	5.64
Rural population	Million	3.24	3.31	3.36	3.42	3.48
Percentage below official						
poverty line (OPL) (%)	%	50.00	51.08	52.65	54.32	56.18
Per capita urban income	Index (*)	14.40	14.20	13.87	13.53	13.14
Per capita rural income	Index (*)	9.26	9.06	8.81	8.55	8.28
Summary indicators						
Growth in GDP (%)	%p.a.	n.a	1.50	0.68	0.50	0.19
Growth in per capita GDP (%)	%p.a	n.a	−1.50	−2.32	−2.50	−2.81
Tax revenue as % of GDP	%	12.00	12.00	12.03	12.07	12.12
Gov. deficit as % of GDP	%	−14.00	−14.11	−13.90	−14.22	−12.66
Investment as % of GDP	%	14.00	11.33	10.76	9.74	8.26
Share of agriculture in GDP (%)	%	30.00	29.50	29.00	28.50	28.00
Rate of inflation (%)	%p.a	50.00	50.11	49.90	50.22	48.66
Population growth (%)	%p.a	3.00	3.00	3.00	3.00	3.00
Ecological impacts						
Decline in major wildlife specie	%p.a	n.a	4.18	5.51	5.66	6.99
Forest land clearance for agriculture	%p.a	n.a	2.66	2.61	2.62	2.62
Forest cover loss for fuelwood	%p.a	n.a	0.92	1.21	1.26	1.70
Water pollution cases	000 p.a	145.80	152.20	164.05	177.01	197.82

Notes:
(*)   The index is in constant prices.
The model is calibrated to match approximately the structure of the economy in 1990.
The values are indexed to match approximately the structure of the economy in 1990.
n.a. = not available.

8. Per capita rural and urban incomes decline by approximately 2.5 per cent per annum.
9. Urban population grows by nearly 4 per cent per annum while rural populations only increase at 1.8 per cent per annum.
10. The poverty percentage increases by around 3 per cent per annum.
11. Wildlife numbers continue to decline, and the rate of decline increases from 5 per cent per annum in year 1 to 7 per cent in year 5.
12. Forest clearance remains steady at 2.6 per cent of total area.
13. Loss of forest cover due to fuelwood collection continues and rises from 1 to 2 per cent per annum.
14. The number of cases of waterborne diseases increase, as urban populations rise and investment in waste water treatment does not keep pace.

These assumptions reflect the likely developments in the absence of a SAP. Availability of external assistance would decline as would the climate for private investment. Agricultural output is static or declining, and the absence of investment as well as expansion into agricultural land could be expected to continue this trend.

Problem Set

Using the model developed in the case study, you are asked to estimate the impact of a SAP on the social and environmental indicators for the country. The SAP can be characterized by the following agreement:

1. The government agrees to reduce subsidies in each year as shown in Table 3A1.3 below.
2. The government agrees to a one-off real devaluation in year 1 of 20 per cent (that is, 20 per cent more than the difference between the national rate of inflation and that of countries with which it trades).
3. Official assistance increases by the amounts in each year as shown in Table 3A1.3 below.
4. The SAP opens the door to substantial increased investment in the public sector, with investment increasing by about 14 per cent per annum over the five years. Private investment is also stimulated and grows at around 8 per cent per annum. In addition, the economy benefits from the increased efficiency of measures such as privatization. These factors are assumed to increase GDP by a small amount (1–1.5 per cent a year for 3–4 years).
5. The share of agriculture in total output increases by about 2 per cent over the five years. This is the opposite of the case with 'no SAP' where agriculture's share declines by 2 per cent. The assumption is that investment in agriculture is substantially increased as a result of the SAP.
6. The reductions in subsidies result in an increase in public investment (30 per cent of the reduction goes into investment). The rest goes to reduce the budget deficit.

On the basis of the information given to you, complete Table 3A1.4, giving indicators for the economy and the environment for years 1–5, with a SAP in place. You are encouraged to use the data given in Tables 3A1.1–2, as well as the description of the economy, as presented in the previous section. Table 3A1.2 will provide you with a benchmark of what the impacts are in the absence of a SAP.

Table 3A1.3   Agreement under the SAP

	Year 1	Year 2	Year 3	Year 4	Year 5
Reduction in subsidy % over no SAP	8	23	31	38	46
Increase in official assistance % over no SAP	0	36	78	100	130
Real devaluation %	20	0	0	0	0

Table 3A1.4   Estimates of impacts of SAP to be worked out

	1	2	3	4	5
Growth in per capita GDP					
Percentage below OPL					
Per capita rural income					
Per capita urban income					
Decline in major wildlife species (%)					
Increase in land clearance for agriculture (%)					
Loss in forest cover loss for fuelwood (%)					
Cases of waterborne diseases (000)					

Solution to Problem Set

The solution to the problem is shown in Table 3A1.5. With the SAP in place the country benefits from some increased investment but has to undertake substantial reductions in the government budget deficit, and liberalize the economy with increased privatization and more openness to trade. The main SAP scenarios can be summarized as follows:

1. The economy grows slowly at the start but the rate picks up. In year 1 it is just 2.1 per cent; by the end of the five years it is about 5.7 per cent.
2. The trade deficit is reduced as imports are reduced and exports increased. The fall in imports is less than the devaluation would lead one to expect because the growth in GDP increases demand for imports. By year 5, however, the deficit is 15 per cent smaller than in the no-SAP case.
3. Export earnings from services no longer fall, but remain more or less constant.
4. Per capita urban and rural incomes rise by approximately 0.5 and 1.4 per cent per annum, respectively.
5. Urban population grows by only 2.0 per cent per annum while the rural population increases at 3.0 per cent per annum.
6. The percentage below the poverty line decreases by about 3 per cent over the five years.
7. Wildlife numbers continue to decline, but the rate of decline is much less than in the no-SAP case.
8. Forest clearance increases very slightly compared to the no-SAP case.
9. Loss of forest cover due to fuelwood collection declines and is in fact reversed by year 3.
10. The number of cases of waterborne diseases remain constant but are much less, amounting to about 50,000 cases less, than in the no-SAP case.

Table 3A1.5   Structural adjustment and sustainable development in Zambia economic, social and environmental projections with SAP

	Units	Year 1	Year 2	Year 3	Year 4	Year 5
National economic indicators						
GDP	Index (*)	100.0	102.16	105.98	111.03	116.63
Private consumption	Index (*)	85.96	83.90	85.92	91.07	98.77
Investment	Index (*)	14.52	18.50	22.02	23.47	24.60
Public	Index (*)	6.52	9.50	12.02	12.47	12.60
Private	Index (*)	8.00	9.00	10.00	11.00	12.00
Non-investment government						
expenditure	Index (*)	16.52	17.50	18.02	18.47	18.60
Exports	Index (*)	32.00	33.28	34.60	34.58	34.57
Goods	Index (*)	28.00	29.12	30.28	30.28	30.28
Services	Index (*)	4.00	4.16	4.31	4.30	4.29
Imports	Index (*)	40.00	40.05	41.55	43.56	45.81
Trade deficit	Index (*)	−8.00	−6.77	−6.95	−8.98	−11.24
Government account						
Government tax revenue	Index (*)	12.00	12.12	12.36	12.70	13.07
Official transfers from overseas	Index (*)	13.00	14.96	16.02	16.00	16.10
Development expenditure	Index (*)	6.00	8.00	10.00	10.00	10.00
Other expenditure	Index (*)	28.48	27.51	26.99	26.53	26.40
Subsidies	Index (*)	11.96	10.01	8.97	8.06	7.80
Repayment of debt	Index (*)	4.00	4.00	3.00	3.00	2.00
Net deficit	Index (*)	−13.48	−12.43	−11.61	−10.83	−9.23
Employment						
Urban employment		1.21	1.23	1.26	1.31	1.37
Formal sector	Million	0.11	0.11	0.12	0.13	0.14
Informal sector	Million	1.10	1.11	1.14	1.19	1.24
Social indicators						
Population	Million	8.10	8.34	8.59	8.85	9.12
Urban population	Million	4.86	5.00	5.12	5.24	5.36
Rural population	Million	3.24	3.35	3.47	3.61	3.75
Percentage below official						
poverty line (OPL)	%	50.00	50.24	49.61	48.43	47.11
Per capita urban income	Index (*)	14.40	14.21	14.28	14.51	14.79
per capita rural income	Index (*)	9.26	9.31	9.47	9.69	9.94
Summary indicators						
Growth in GDP (%)	% p.a.	n.a.	2.16	3.74	4.76	5.05
Growth in per capita GDP (%)	% p.a.	n.a.	−0.84	0.74	1.76	2.05
Tax revenue as % of GDP	%	12.00	11.86	11.66	11.44	11.21
Gov. deficit as % of GDP	%	−13.48	−12.17	−10.95	−9.76	−7.91
Investment as % of GDP	%	14.52	18.10	20.77	21.14	21.09
Share of agriculture in GDP (%)	%	30.00	30.50	31.00	31.50	32.00
Rate of inflation (%)	% p.a.	50.00	48.69	47.47	46.28	44.43
Population growth (%)	% p.a.	3.00	3.00	3.00	3.00	3.00
Ecological impacts						
Decline in major wildlife species	% p.a.	n.a.	1.02	1.21	0.89	1.24
Forest land clearance for agriculture	% p.a.	n.a.	3.09	3.23	3.29	3.25
forest cover loss for fuelwood	% p.a.	n.a.	0.13	−0.25	−0.41	−0.29
Water pollution cases	p.a.	145.80	142.61	142.79	143.26	146.20

Notes:
(*)   The index is in constant prices.
The model is calibrated to match approximately the structure of the economy in 1990.
The values are indexed to match approximately the structure of the economy in 1990.
n.a. = not available.

Questions for Discussion

The reasons why the SAP scenario does so well are: (a) it generates growth which increases real incomes, and (b) it makes more resources available for investment and government expenditure, so that the environmental investments can be made and expenditures supported. Some critics might say that SAP programmes increase poverty much more than has been allowed for. Currently SAPs are more conscious of that problem, but one can easily change the underlying assumptions.

The model and solution described above presents the SAP scenario as more beneficial to the environment than the 'no-SAP' case. If we had looked only at the SAP scenario this would not have been observed. This shows the importance of the with and without policy comparison, as it is for proper project analysis also (see Part II of this book).

The conclusions in favour of the SAP scenario depend on specific assumptions. Moreover, there are a number of factors that influence the environment but that cannot be modelled in the framework presented here. In this section, the reader is asked to consider a number of questions regarding the conclusions.

1. The impact of macroeconomic policy on wildlife depends on: (a) expenditures on the national parks, (b) rural real incomes and (c) the rural population.
   a. What other factors related to macroeconomic policy could influence wildlife numbers?
   b. How could the impacts of the SAP on wildlife be reduced?
   c. What measures can the authorities take to reduce the impact of a fall in wildlife numbers on earnings from tourism?
2. The impact of macroeconomic policy on clearance of agricultural land depends on: (a) the rural population and (b) rural real income.
   a. What other factors related to macroeconomic policy could influence deforestation by this source?
   b. How could the impacts of the SAP on deforestation be reduced without reducing the other benefits of the SAP?
3. The impact of macroeconomic policy on fuelwood depends on: (a) population growth, (b) per capita incomes and (c) subsidies to other energy sources.
   a. What other factors related to macroeconomic policy could influence deforestation by this source?
   b. How could the negative impacts of reducing subsidies on the demand for fuelwood be reduced without reducing the other benefits of the SAP?

4. The impact of macroeconomic policy on waterborne diseases depends on: (a) urban population growth, (b) investment in water treatment, (c) subsidies in water treatment. How could the government make up the negative impacts of losses in subsidies on the number of waterborne diseases?

Sample Answers to Questions

Some brief answers to the questions posed are presented below. These are intended to stimulate discussion.

Question 1

a. Increased profitability of exports increases the demand for poaching.
b. Some factors that reduce the impacts of a SAP are: (i) barriers to trade in wildlife products (for example, CITES), (ii) mobilization of increased revenues through a tax on visitors or through the sale of limited hunting licences (iii) not allowing expenditure in this area to fall when the government cuts other expenditures.
c. Visitor numbers may be maintained by spending more on specific places where tourists visit frequently, and making wildlife more accessible to visitors. There are several activities relating to wildlife management that could be discussed in this context.

Question 2

a. As with wildlife, it is possible for increased pressure for deforestation to come about with devaluation, trade liberalization and so on. It is not an issue in Zambia but could be elsewhere.
b. As the text makes clear there are many factors influencing land clearance. Tenure changes, increased release of trust lands and so on could all help reduce deforestation without losing the other benefits of a SAP.

Question 3

a. The model may not give enough weight to the possible impacts of an increase in poverty on the demand for fuelwood.
b. Reducing energy subsidies makes fuelwood more attractive. This could be accompanied by increasing incentives for fuelwood plantations, which would then reduce the more damaging collection from forest areas. Another measure which has been tried in some areas is to tax deliveries into urban areas, but this has not been successful.

Question 4

This example of environment–economy linkages is perhaps the least convincing of the four. If subsidies for wastewater treatment are reduced, fewer households will be able to afford the service. This has *not* been built into the model, but it can still be discussed. Possible ways to make up the negative impacts of reduced subsidies include: (i) using increasing block tariffs, so that poor households could receive the basic service at a low cost, (ii) where treated water improves recreational facilities, placing a small betterment fee for that improvement. There may be other possibilities.

Notes

1. The discussion of the country background and the history of structural adjustment is taken from C. Mupimpila, V. Seshamani, A. Mwanza, E. Chidumayo, I. Mwanawina and E. Cromwell, 'Structural adjustment and sustainable development in Zambia', Working Paper, London: Overseas Development Institute (ODI); and from a summary of that working paper prepared by the ODI. The numerical data in the examples, and the reported links between economic and environmental variables, are only partly based on observed relationships. In order to make the examples more useful from a pedagogic viewpoint, quantitative relationships have been assumed in several cases, based on what researchers broadly believe to be true. Hence the analysis carried out here, or the underlying model, should *not* be interpreted as representing the actual situation in Zambia.
2. The basic model – a simple accelerator model – is not selected for its realism but for illustrative purposes, as explained in the text.

ANNEX 3A2 CASE STUDY 2: A GENERAL EQUILIBRIUM MODEL OF THE BOTSWANA ECONOMY, INCLUDING THE LIVESTOCK SECTOR

Introduction

This case study focuses on the key economic aspects of the preferential treatment that the European Union market gives to Botswana beef imports under the Lomé Convention. This is known as the Beef Protocol. In particular, it examines the impacts of changes in the Protocol, namely the discontinuation of the beef subsidy, on the cattle sector in Botswana. Changes in cattle stocks are of environmental importance due to their impact on rangeland degradation. A model of the cattle sector has been constructed, using data from 1966 to 1994, which quantifies the responses of the cattle suppliers and the consumers of beef and other cattle products, so that the impacts of a change in the subsidy can be analysed. Following a report of the results of the model, the case study goes on to discuss the results of other models, and to arrive at a consensus on the impacts of changes in beef prices on the cattle sector, on cattle holdings and the environment.

Cattle are an important part of the Botswana economy and society and have been so for a long time. In relative economic terms, however, the sector is declining in importance. Between 1966 and 1994, agriculture (which is dominated by livestock) as a whole has fallen from 42 per cent of GDP to 6 per cent. Nevertheless, it remains an important sector, providing income and livelihood to a wide range of income groups.

The number of cattle rose nearly threefold between 1967 and 1979, when they reached 3 million. Numbers were steady in the early 1980s but declined in 1983 and 1986 (as a result of drought); and then again in 1993, following the 1992 drought. Unofficial estimates of numbers for 1996 indicate that the stock was about 2.4 million cattle in that year. The Beef Protocol was initiated in 1975, by which time the stock had already increased from 1.1 to 2 million. It is difficult to see what impact the Protocol had on the stock, without carrying out an analysis, which requires a model of the supply and demand for cattle and for beef to be constructed. This case study looks at the development of such a model to answer some of the 'as if' questions that are being asked about the Protocol.

In this section, a CGE model is presented, based on the social accounting matrix, to show the impacts of the Protocol on the Botswana economy. An alternative methodology, using a partial equilibrium framework, is presented in Chapter 4 for the same case.

Computable General Equilibrium Analysis: Background to Model

In a paper analysing the role of community-based wildlife in Botswana, Tyler (1996)[1] has constructed a CGE model of the economy, using the social accounting matrix[2] (SAM) of the country for 1992/93. The underlying model has 15 production activities, including the cattle sector, the 'hunting and gathering sector' and the hotel and restaurants sectors. The last two sectors pick up the major impacts of wildlife-related activities in the country. There are seven categories of labour and three of capital. Households are classified as urban (wage earning, self-employed), rural (wage earning and self-employed) and non-citizens.

The model builds demand and supply functions for each of the categories of production, labour and capital. Demand for goods comes either from the domestic sectors or from the rest of the world. Both categories of demand are assumed to be price elastic, although the paper does not report all the assumed elasticities. Unlike the partial equilibrium model developed in Chapter 4, the exports from domestic production do not assume a perfectly elastic export demand for Botswana goods; the paper reports that the demand for 'non-mining' goods is taken to have an elasticity of 3 and that for 'mining' goods it is taken as 1. The imports of final goods and intermediate goods into the Botswana economy are assumed to be supplied at world prices and to be direct substitutes for the same goods produced at home. Domestic and export production are treated as a single sector, with domestic suppliers being indifferent between supplying the two parts of the market. The model takes world prices, the exchange rate and the level of investment as exogenous and determines the domestic prices to clear all markets, with the exception of unskilled labour. For this market the wages are taken as fixed and the level of employment is determined by the model. This last assumption allows for unemployment in that category, which is an observed feature of the economy.

The advantage of a general equilibrium model over the partial equilibrium model presented in Chapter 4 is that it allows for interactions between the different sectors, in response to changes in the exogenous variables. As noted in the chapter, the difficulty with such models is that many of the underlying parameters are unknown and therefore guesses have to be made. This makes the results less credible, although some sensitivity analyses can help in that regard. The other problem is in understanding the results that emerge, so that policy makers are not confronted with a 'black box' in which plausible linkages of causality cannot be established and one is only able to say that something 'happens' because the model says it happens.

In spite of these reservations, the model constructed by Tyler is useful and important in the context of changes in the Beef Protocol aims, especially as he has looked at the possible impacts of a change in the export price of beef. This model was run with a reduction in the price of beef of 48 per cent, (estimated by the partial equilibrium analysis reported in Chapter 4 as the fall in price following the elimination of the Beef Protocol). Taking the values for 1992/93 as the base case, the results of these simulations, as well as those for a 20 per cent fall in the export price of beef are reported for the different sectors of the economy in Table 3A2.1. The following impacts should be noted for the 48 per cent decline in price of beef:

1. A decline in the export of beef products of 85.7 per cent. This figure compares with the partial equilibrium model estimate of an 80–85 per cent loss of export markets and is remarkably similar.
2. A decline in output from the beef sector of 21 per cent. The partial equilibrium model predicts a sharper decline to begin with (36 per cent); however, as the domestic market adjusts, the decline in output after eight years is reduced to 25 per cent, which is not dissimilar to that from the Tyler model.
3. A decline in the 'cattle output' of 9.35 per cent. This is taken to mean a decline in cattle numbers. In 1991 (the year of calibration of the model) the cattle numbers were about 2.8 million. A fall of 9.35 per cent would mean a figure of about 2.5 million, which is also similar to the partial equilibrium model's predicted long-term stock.
4. A decline in unskilled formal employment of about 3.2 per cent and a decline in total informal employment of 7.8 per cent.
5. A decline in GDP of 1.36 per cent.

Although the figures from the Tyler paper can only be approximately compared with the partial equilibrium model, the closeness of the two is an encouraging guide to what is likely to happen with a removal of the subsidy. The paper is also useful in providing some information on the likely fall in employment as a result of the removal of the beef subsidy.

As Tyler notes, these results show some significant negative effects on the economy, which will impact negatively on low-income households. He goes on to consider what changes in the hotels and hunting sectors would be needed to compensate, in economic terms, for these losses. He looks at increases in exports from the two wildlife-related sectors of 28 million pula each, which translate into increases in output for the two sectors of 16.5 and 26.3 per cent respectively. *If* such increased demand can be generated, he shows that total export revenue and GDP are more or less restored to their 'pre-beef price fall' level, but unskilled employment is still 2.4 per cent lower than with no fall in beef prices. The serious impact of the fall in the beef price on low-income households is also something predicted in the partial equilibrium model.

Table 3A2.1   Selected results from Tyler's model of a fall in the export price of beef

	Base solution (pula m.)	Percentage change in beef price from base solution	
		20% drop	48% drop
Real GDP at factor cost	8,291.3	–0.77	–1.36
Export revenue	3,902.1	–1.75	–3.09
Import payments	3,444.4	–1.21	–2.14
Current account surplus	480.5	–3.73	–6.58
Net indirect taxes	1,057.4	–1.25	–2.22
Income taxes	1,356.3	–0.64	–1.12
Government income	5,467.1	–0.70	–1.24
Government real consumption	2,596.0	–0.15	–0.27
Government savings	1,731.0	–0.70	–1.24
Cattle output	274.0	–5.30	–9.35
Cattle value added	262.1	–5.27	–9.35
Agric., beef, other process (output)	840.4	–11.84	–21.0
Agric., beef, other process (value added)	191.1	–11.83	–21.0
Agric., beef, other process (exports)	153.7	–48.5	–85.7
Hunting, gathering, etc. (output)	104.8	–1.72	–3.05
Hunting, gathering, etc. (value added)	99.0	–1.72	–3.04
Hunting, gathering, etc. (exports)	1.4	0	0
Hotels and restaurants (output)	178.2	0.84	1.57
Hotels and restaurants (value added)	100.8	0.89	1.59
Hotels and restaurants (exports)	147.3	1.29	2.38
Employment (skilled citizens)	745.2	–1.34	–2.38
Employment (unskilled citizens)	479.3	–1.80	–3.19
Employment (informal (total))	549.5	–4.40	–7.81
Employment (informal (cattle))	262.1	–5.27	–9.35
Employment (informal (agric. etc.))	48.9	–12.5	–22.1
Employment (informal (hunting etc.))	20.9	–1.91	–2.87
Real consumption:			
Rural waged households	901.1	–1.29	–2.28
Rural other households	758.5	–1.93	–3.42

An Earlier General Equilibrium Model of the Botswana Economy

Unemo (1993)[3] has also constructed a CGE model of the Botswana economy, based on the 1985/86 social accounting matrix. She models Botswana as a small open economy. Like Tyler's model it is a one-period model despite the fact that environmental degradation is a highly dynamic phenomenon. There is, however, a lack of data as to when and to what extent livestock productivity responds to deteriorating range conditions, which therefore would render difficult a dynamic approach.

The model has the following inputs: capital, skilled labour, unskilled labour, land and cattle holdings (treated as a separate form of capital). On the output side there are the following sectors: mining, manufacturing, meat processing, livestock, crops, infrastructure and services. For all the sectors except livestock, output is a function of the amount of the above inputs used in that sector. For the livestock sector output for each cattle owner depends positively on the amount of labour and 'livestock capital', and negatively on the *total stock* of cattle. The argument for the last assumption is that as total cattle numbers increase, so the amount of grazing available to any one farmer decreases. In each sector, output is determined to maximize profit.

The model distinguishes between the exports and domestic consumption of the outputs, and treats both imports and exports as imperfect substitutes for their domestically produced equivalents. Households are divided into urban and rural and the model makes the demands for the different goods and factors a function of the prices of these items and of household income. It finds a solution where demand and supply are equal in each of the markets, implying, *inter alia*, that all factors such as labour and capital are fully employed.

As in the case of Tyler's model, a complex CGE such as this requires several parameters to be estimated. For some of them, external estimates are available. For others guesses based on reasonable values in other studies were taken. For one or two of the undetermined parameters, values were selected so that the model generated the correct sectoral output and input values for the base year. This 'calibration' was done for 1986/87. The model was used to investigate the impacts of the following external changes:

1. a decline in the price of diamonds by 5 per cent;
2. a decline in the terms of trade so that both beef and diamond prices fall by 5 per cent;
3. a lower import tariff on crops, from a base value of 13.8 per cent down to zero;
4. a constraint on unskilled labour whereby the amount was decreased by 10 per cent; and
5. an increase in foreign capital of $100 million, equivalent to 16 per cent of total savings.

For each of these the model focused on the holding of cattle and the stocking rate – the number of hectares of grazing land per animal.

The model's main findings are:

1. A 5 per cent decline in the price of diamonds results in a large fall (12 per cent) in the stocking rate. This is primarily attributed to a relative fall in the rate of return on capital in that sector.
2. A 5 per cent decline in the prices of all exports (principally beef and diamonds) also increases cattle holding and causes a small (3 per cent) rise in the stocking rate, attributed to the reduced attractiveness of beef production. However, rural household incomes fall by 5 per cent.
3. Lowering the import tariff on crops has very little impact on the stocking rate, but is primarily the result of the assumption that land for crops is fixed and cannot be increased, at the expense of land for cattle, for example.
4. Reducing the amount of unskilled labour by 10 per cent results in a con-
   traction of the livestock sector by 1 per cent. The crop sector, however, which is more labour intensive, declines by nearly 8 per cent.
5. A sudden capital inflow of $100 million has an effect on the exchange rate, which appreciates, resulting in the contraction of most tradable sectors (imports are more attractive relative to domestic production). However, although meat processing declines, the holding of livestock does not, and in fact increases slightly. This is explained by the movement of labour into this sector, as it is shifted out of the other tradable sectors.

The Unemo model was not run for only a change in the price of beef. From the results obtained, however, we can make some estimate of what effects such a price change would have. The difference between scenario runs (1) and (2) would suggest that when beef and diamond prices both fall, the stocking rate rises slightly (by 3 per cent) and when only diamond prices fall the stocking rate *falls* by 12 per cent. Hence the impact of the fall in the price of beef on the stocking rate is considerable; adding the two impacts (which is not really valid but will give an idea of the size of the effect) results in the conclusion that the 5 per cent beef price fall results in a decline in the stocking rate of about 15 per cent. From the stock levels of 1986 (the year of calibration) this would imply a reduction in the stock from 2.3 million to 1.96 million. With a fall in the price of 48 per cent, which is what we are assuming, there would be a very big impact on the stock of cattle.

It should be noted that Unemo's analysis may be misleading about the impact of the change in the price. The model basically assumes that cattle holding is based on profit maximization from livestock production and does not take account of the fact that cattle holding is also a form of wealth for the rancher or herdsman. Hence the model generates very substantial reductions in response to falls in price that are unrealistic. A second assumption that distinguishes this model from the Tyler model is the assumption of full employment of all classes of labour. With the present high levels of unskilled unemployment this assumption is particularly suspect, and tends to make the model more responsive to price changes than the economy really is.

Conclusions on the Possible Economic Effects of a Phase-out of the Beef Subsidy

The analysis of the impacts of a phase-out of the beef subsidy, based on the partial equilibrium model of Chapter 4, suggests that the real price of cattle will fall by about 48 per cent and that cattle numbers will stabilize at about 2 million in the absence of a subsidy, and then rise slightly as domestic demand grows with growth in per capita income and growth in population.

Tyler's general equilibrium model predicts a decline in the stock based on a fall in the price of 20 per cent. Based on a rough linear projection from that fall in price the projected stock of cattle is 2.03 million, which is almost the same as the partial equilibrium model estimate. Tyler also predicts a decline in employment of about 10 per cent following the fall in beef prices, which is a serious issue, given the level of overall unemployment of 40 per cent.

Unemo's general equilibrium model makes somewhat different predictions. Her paper predicts a major fall in cattle numbers following a decline in the international price received for beef. These high estimates are the result of modelling cattle as a purely economic activity, in which owners maximize profits from livestock production. The fact that cattle are held as a form of wealth and have important social considerations needs to be taken into account. Furthermore the assumption of full employment of labour which she makes is not valid. The econometric work allows for an asset-holding approach to cattle, and for farmers' reactions to changes in prices that are not necessarily fully economically rational.

If, following the phase-out of the beef subsidy, the stock stabilizes at 2 million, the corresponding off-take will become about 30,000 tons a year, compared to about 53,000 tons at present. As a percentage of the stock the off-take rate has varied from 7 to 13 per cent, if we exclude 1993, which was an exceptional year. The predicted off-take rate after the phase-out is 7.8 per cent, which is consistent with the rates observed in the period prior to the Lomé Agreement. Thus, the major conclusion from these studies is that the elimination of the beef subsidy will not result in a major decline in cattle numbers. Therefore, impacts on rangeland degradation may also be small.

Questions for Discussion

1. Given the results for the three models, what additional information would you seek to arrive at a firmer conclusion on the impacts of the phase-out of the Beef Protocol?
2. What do the models and the discussions of the results tell us about the measures needed to mitigate the effects of a phase-out?

Some Suggested Answers

Question 1
The key areas for which more information is required are:

1. Supply responsiveness of cattle holdings to prices of cattle and other assets. The estimates in the model are quite crude.
2. What other factors (social and economic) determine the holding of cattle?
3. What other factors influence the off-take? The model does not look at veterinary costs, improved health and so on.
4. The factors determining death rates for cattle. This equation is poorly determined.

Question 2
The following measures should be considered:

1. Providing alternative financial assets that 'mimic' the asset characteristics of cattle.
2. Increasing the off-take rate from a given stock of cattle.
3. The availability of alternative source of employment and income, which could replace cattle and how they could be developed.

Notes

1. Tyler, G.J. (1996), *The Contribution of Community Based Wildlife to Tourism in Botswana*, prepared for IFAD, Rome, University of Oxford, 1996.
2. The SAM embodies the information normally included in national accounts but it is organized in a different way.
3. Unemo, L. (1993), *Environmental Impact of Government Policies and External Shocks in Botswana – A CGE Model Approach*, Beijer Institute Working Paper No. 26, Stockholm.

ANNEX 3A3   CASE STUDY 3: SYSTEM OF NATIONAL ACCOUNTS AND THE ENVIRONMENT

Background

To illustrate the distortions inherent in the existing system of national accounts (SNA), we can use the example of an accidental oilspill. Suppose that a super-tanker that is owned by country A runs aground as it leaves one of the country's harbours with a full cargo of oil that has been drilled domestically. The resulting oilspill causes massive ecological damage in the form of oil contamination of sea mammals, birds and ecosystems, loss of marine productivity in general, damage to tourist beaches and so on. The following questions ask you to think about how each aspect of the accident will impact on country A's national accounts.

Questions

1. How will the cost of transporting the oil affect GNP?
2. How will GNP be affected by the fact that the country's oil stocks are lower by the amount of oil that the tanker was carrying?
3. How will the costs of the labour and equipment used to clean up the environmental effects of the oilspill affect GNP?
4. To what extent will the environmental damage caused by the oilspill be reflected in GNP? (In answering this question you should think of the effects on fish and other marine populations and ecosystems, some of which are commercially exploited while others are not, and of damage to beaches, which are visited by holidaymakers as well as local people.)
5. How is GNP affected by the loss of, or damage to, the tanker?

Sample answers are provided overleaf.

Answers

Question 1
Assuming that the oil company does not pay the tanker company for the unsuccessful voyage, the accident results in GNP being lower by the amount of the revenue lost.

Question 2
The decrease in value of oil stocks due to depletion is not reflected in GNP. Therefore the loss of the oil has no effect on GNP from this point of view.

Under the revised system of national accounts with environmental satellite accounts, the value of depleted oil stocks is calculated as an item to be deducted from net national product (NNP) as part of the depreciation of the economy's assets. However, in both cases, the fact that the oil is lost at sea does not affect national accounts.

Question 3
The answer to this question depends on whether or not labour and other resources are fully employed. The need for environmental work created by the oilspill increases the demand for labour, creating new employment. If there is unemployment, the labour used for the work was previously unproductive, and the wages and other costs paid to finance the work are fully reflected as an increase in GNP. However, if resources are currently fully employed, their transfer to environmental work will mean less output in their current use. The net effect on GNP will then be much lower, although it is unlikely to be negative.

Question 4
The environmental damage to marine productivity will be reflected by GNP in so far as it results in lower harvest of commercially exploited species. Thus, for example, lower catches from commercial fisheries will result in lower GNP. However, damage to ecosystems that are not commercially exploited is not reflected in the national accounts.

The damage to beaches that attract tourists may result in reduced revenue to the local tourist industry, although if the tourists simply move to other resorts within the country this will not affect GNP. However, if the alternative destinations chosen by tourists are abroad, then revenue would be lost to the national tourist industry and this would be reflected in lower GNP. It should be noted that even in this case, not all of the value of the damage to beaches will be reflected in the lost revenue. For instance, local people enjoy the local scenery without having to pay for it. The fact that this enjoyment is not possible for as long as the damage remains is not reflected in any decrease in expenditure, and thus is not reflected in GNP.

Question 5
The loss of or damage to the tanker is likely to result in an increase in GNP if, as in the answer to (3), labour and other resources are not fully employed. That is, the extra work created in repairing the tanker, or in building a replacement, will count as increased final expenditure, and thus will increase GNP. However, while the tanker is out of commission, the tanker company may be able to undertake less work than previously. This loss of revenue would result in a decrease in GNP.

Discussion

The above description of the effects of the various aspects of the oilspill on the country's GNP has illustrated that these effects work in different directions. Moreover, whether or not the effects of the oilspill are reflected in GNP depends on whether they result in alterations in commercial activity (such as a slow-down in the tourist trade) that are not offset by compensating factors elsewhere in the economy (such as an increase in tourism). The main point to note is that it is quite possible that the net effect of the accident on the country's GNP could be positive, due for example to the employment effects of the environmental clean-up work created. This seemingly counterintuitive result stems from the fact that the standard SNA does not differentiate between expenditure to increase well-being and expenditure to decrease the negative side-effects of economic activity, and does not reflect the welfare lost due to environmental damage.

4. Sectoral policies and the environment

OBJECTIVE

The objective of this chapter is to introduce an environmental dimension to sector analysis by examining how market failures affect the price of natural resources in each sector. The chapter examines suitable sectoral policy measures, which ensure more appropriate pricing, incorporate environmental concerns and assist in determining the values of non-marketed goods and services.

SUMMARY

Sectoral analysis requires an assessment of the resources, inputs and outputs, demands, problems and opportunities for individual sectors within the economy.

This chapter addresses the problems associated with market prices that do not include the external costs and benefits of the goods or services in question. Market sector (partial) equilibrium is reached when goods and services establish market-clearing prices, through the interaction of supply and demand. However, market failures, particularly with respect to environmental issues, can mean that the social marginal value is not fully reflected in the price. The equilibrium price may need correcting in order to ensure that resources are allocated optimally throughout the sector. Such price corrections can be beneficial to the environment by providing more accurate signals of the relative scarcity of goods and services with respect to the environment.

The chapter also looks at policy and institutional failures – that is, government actions that result in inefficient use of natural resources. Measures to correct such failures are considered.

Five guiding principles for incorporating environmental concerns into decision making are discussed: the polluter pays principle; the user pays principle; the precautionary principle; the subsidiarity principle; and intergenerational equity. These principles can be used to tailor environmental instruments and to raise funds to finance environmental public investments planned in the sectoral or overall budget.

4.1 INTRODUCTION

Formulating sectoral policies involves the analysis of outputs, inputs, production processes, opportunities, problems and natural resource uses of individual sectors within the economy. The goals of sectoral analysis[1] are:

- To propose policies and strategies to enhance the sector's contribution to the country's sustainable development.
- To determine investment priorities for the sector.
- To contribute and assist in planning macroeconomic policies and strategies.
- To evaluate instruments, including laws and institutions, in the sector as a framework for implementing policies, programmes and projects consistent with the goal of sustainable development.

Environmental issues relating to individual sectors should be integrated within the processes undertaken to meet these goals (Harou et al, 1998).

Implementation of specific sectoral policies can influence the macroeconomic system, particularly if the sector involved is central to the national economy. Concomitantly, macroeconomic variables, such as exchange rates, the public deficit, external debts, interest rates, wage rates, inflation levels and so on can affect the performance of sectors such as energy and agriculture. As we saw in the previous chapter, the relationship between specific sectoral policies and macroeconomic variables can impact significantly on environmental factors. For example, devaluation can result in increased exploitation of forestry and fisheries, but the size of the effect and the amount of damage associated with it will depend on what sectoral policies are in place to protect the sector and to ensure sustainable management.

The existence of these interactions between: (a) a specific sector and the environment, (b) a specific sector and the rest of the economy, and (c) individual sectors with other sectors in the economy, has led to the development of several tools for sectoral analysis which can be adapted by the analyst according to the relationship between the sector and the economy. These tools are summarized at the end of this chapter. The most important sectoral policy is the pricing of resources within each sector, and therefore the primary objective of this chapter is to introduce the concept of market failures which result in the incorrect pricing of resources.

4.2 PARTIAL OR SECTORAL MARKET EQUILIBRIUM

A market is in equilibrium when the quantity of a good or service demanded equals the quantity supplied. The equilibrium price is the price at which the quantity of a good that buyers demand is equal to the quantity that sellers supply. The price clears the market, and at this level there is no gap between supply and demand. Figure 4.1 derives demand for timber in sawn-wood production and the supply and demand for sawn wood.

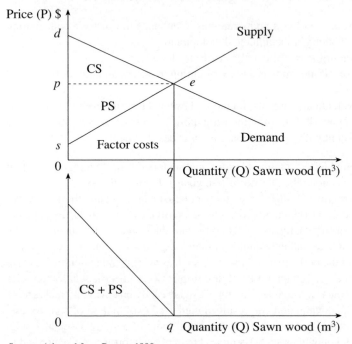

Source: Adapted from Pearse, 1990

Figure 4.1   Demand and supply for sawn wood

Information given in the supply and demand curve for a good is useful in determining the *social value* of that good to consumers. With a downward-sloping demand curve, the market price reflects only the willingness to pay for the marginal unit purchased. As will be discussed in Part II of this handbook, willingness to pay for a good is assumed to be a measure of the *monetary value* of the good. If a market is competitive, the market price indicates the aggregate marginal willingness to pay for the marginal unit of the good, that is, the additional unit at the margin. For all units of the good except the unit at the margin, consumers are willing to pay more than the market price. In effect, the market price underestimates the total value to the consumers of purchasing the good or service. The amount of additional benefits that the consumer acquires when purchasing the good or service is called the *consumer surplus*. The consumer surplus is represented for a particular commodity (sawn wood) in

Figure 4.1 by the triangle *dpe*, and is always found above the price line (*pe*) and under the demand curve (*de*). The total revenue of suppliers is represented by the rectangle 0*peq*. The factor costs, 0*seq*, are less than the suppliers' total revenue. The difference between the total revenue and the factor costs is the triangle, *spe*, which is called the producers' surplus. The total net value of sawn-wood production in the figure is the gross value, 0*deq*, minus the factor costs 0*seq*, or put another way it is the sum of the producer and consumer surpluses.

4.3   CONSUMER AND PRODUCER SURPLUS

4.3.1   Demand/Supply Own-price Elasticity

Supply and demand curves can be difficult and time consuming to derive. Fortunately, for many products, coefficients reflecting the link between the quantity demanded (supplied) and the price, called the own-price elasticities, have been calculated in a range of empirical studies. The demand own-price elasticity is defined as the percentage change in the quantity demanded (Q) due to a unit percentage change in its price (P). When this coefficient is numerically less than one (the actual demand elasticity is negative), the demand is said to be inelastic; if it is greater than one, it is elastic. Analogous considerations hold for the elasticity of supply. When the numerical value of the elasticity is equal to one, total expenditure remains unchanged as the price increases. If the elasticity is numerically greater than one, expenditure decreases as price goes up and if it is less than one the reverse is true.

The shape of the demand curve of a good is influenced by the prices of substitutes and complements. The demand curve will shift upwards following an increase in the price of substitutes or downwards following an increase in the price of complementary goods. The reverse holds for price decreases. Shifts in the demand curves can also occur when consumer incomes or tastes change. Similarly, the supply curve for a commodity shifts according to changes in the prices of inputs and factors such as natural resources, land, labour and capital. If the price of an input or a factor increases, it is likely that its use will decrease. Conversely, if the price of an input decreases it is likely that the use of that input will increase. For example, if fertilizers are suddenly subsidized by the national government the producer effectively experiences a price reduction, and will probably use more fertilizers in the future, for a given output price. In turn this is likely to contribute to an increase in levels of water pollution.

For all practical purposes, the importance of consumer and producer surpluses depends upon the elasticities of the supply and demand curves. Supply and demand information for social valuation becomes less relevant as the elasticity of demand and supply curves increases. Consumer and producer surpluses are important when analysing more large-scale or strategically important sectoral policies that may influence many programmes and actions simultaneously. Analysis of surpluses is also particularly relevant if the environmental goods and services offered are unique and therefore face no competitive market.

4.3.2   Pricing Natural Resources

Determining the demand for natural resources can be a complex process. The demand for a primary natural resource is often derived from the demand for a final product made from that resource, for example, the demand for timber is derived from many other timber-based products such as newspaper, plywood or particle board. Furthermore, natural resources can be used in a wide range of goods and services where often there is not a specific market. For example, forests provide direct benefits such as timber and fuelwood, but can also be used as a place of recreation and can provide biodiversity benefits (for use by present or future generations). There is not a market where demand for enjoyment of the countryside and biodiversity can be bought at a price, and therefore, the benefits of recreational use and ecological functions are difficult to value. Observed prices do not always reflect the economic value of goods and services, and these differences are often due to market failures. The next section addresses the issue of market failures by analysing their main sources and methods for adjusting market failures to close the gap between the distorted market price and the social value of a good and service.

The most important sectoral policy is the pricing of resources within each sector: fisheries, energy, mining, timber, water and so on. The objective should be to price resources efficiently so that the prices cover the *full cost* of the resource. The supply and demand model can be modified to illustrate the policy of efficient pricing.

Figure 4.2 shows how market failures can be removed by shifts in the supply curve. The proper price of a resource includes the private costs of production, the cost of various policies (in this case a subsidy), the cost of external effects (market failures) and the cost of failures due to institutional deficiency (institutional failures, notably, a lack of institutions acting on behalf of future generations) and the cost of external effects (externalities).

To conclude, pricing of natural resources should reflect:

- The costs of extraction or harvesting, as measured by the marginal private cost (MPC), which is the private cost of taking out one extra unit of the resource. On the graph, the marginal private cost curve (MPC_1) includes a subsidy, which is added in MPC, correcting for a possible policy failure. MPC_2 corrects the supply schedule for institutional failures.
- The environmental costs involved in extraction or harvesting and use, as measured by the marginal external cost (MEC), which is the value of the

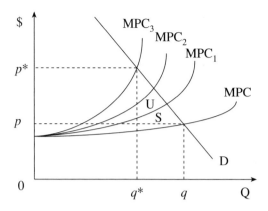

Key:
D   = Demand
MPC   = Marginal private cost
MPC_1 = MPC + Subsidy (policy failures)
MPC_2 = MPC_1 + External costs (market failures)
MPC_3 = MPC_2 + User costs (institutional failures)
p = MPC market price
p^* = MPC – Subsidy + MUC + MEC
          = MPC_3 = social or shadow price
          = Equilibrium Price under optimal conditions
U   = Marginal user cost (MUC)
E   = Marginal External Cost (MEC)
S   = Subsidy.

Figure 4.2   Supply and demand corrected for policy, market and institutional failures

additional damage that the extra unit of the harvested and used resource caused. MPC_2 adds the external cost (E) to rectify any market failures caused by negative externalities generated by the use of that resource.

• The forgone future benefits caused by the use of the resource today, measured by the marginal user costs or depletion premiums (MUC). The MUC is the cost of replacing the resources that future generations will have to bear, as required by the intergenerational equity principle. MPC_3 adds the marginal user cost to the other marginal costs.

The resulting quantity produced and the full cost pricing result in a new equilibrium price (p^*) which reflects the real value of the resource. This price would exist only if policies to use only full cost pricing were adopted. This full cost is also referred to as the social cost and full cost pricing is also called social cost pricing or shadow pricing.

The price of a natural resource in an 'efficient market' (that is, one with no monopoly and low transactions and information costs) reflects the private cost of its extraction or harvest and scarcity rent. However, resource extraction and harvesting may give rise to external costs. Timber exploitation may contribute to soil erosion and affect farmers downstream. This is not accounted for in the market. Moreover, as we noted above, if property rights are not clearly defined and enforced, resources may be underpriced. In such a case, market prices will convey misleading information about resource scarcity and provide inadequate incentives for efficient resource use, and investments for the future.

4.4 MARKET FAILURES

Market failures occur when a market is not able to set an equilibrium price of a good/service that equals the social marginal cost, that is, the value that society places on the last unit of the good/service exchanged. The main sources of market failures which are particularly relevant to an analysis of environmental resources are:

1. externalities;
2. unpriced assets and missing markets;
3. public goods;
4. transaction costs;
5. undefined/unenforced property rights;
6. ignorance and uncertainty;
7. short-sightedness; and
8. irreversibility.

4.4.1 Externalities

Externalities arise because of the non-existence of markets, that is, there are no markets in clean air or peace and quiet. An externality arises when a mutually beneficial transaction between two or more parties results in a third-party effect where someone not a party to the transaction is either better off or worse off. For example, a brewery situated downstream from a chemical plant, which pumps effluents into the stream will find that the cost of producing beer depends on its choice of output levels and input combinations, and on the amount of effluents which have to be removed from the water before it can be used in beer production. These effluents then constitute an externality (Gravelle and Rees 1992). In the forest sector, timber exploitation may contribute to soil erosion and affect farmers downstream.

In some cases externalities can be positive, that is, there can be gains for both the affected parties and the generators of externalities. A quantitative analysis of externalities would require that both parties can be precisely identified and that the externalities can be valued in monetary terms. In many situations, however, such an analysis of externalities is too difficult. This could be due to a lack of information, specifically, an inability to define the monetary value of the external effects, or to establish which firms or industries are generating the externalities and who the affected people are. In order for market prices to reflect the true social value of the good or service, these externalities should be internalized. To internalize an externality one or other of the affected parties has to have control over the relevant resource.[2] For example, if the pollution from an electricity plant damages agriculture, then either the farmers should be able to decide how much pollution is acceptable or the polluter should be able to decide how much pollution to generate. In the latter case, the victims would have to 'buy' reductions from the polluter. In the former case they would 'sell' increases to the polluter. Externalities can occur over time, and affect future generations (intertemporal externalities). Invariably, intertemporal externalities are only partly internalised because the rights of future generations cannot be fully reflected in present resource use decisions. Table 4.1 summarizes the impact of externalities.

Table 4.1   A summary of the impact of externalities

	Negative externality	Positive externality
Quantity produced	Greater than optimal	Lower than optimal
Social costs/benefits	Social costs greater than socially optimal	Social benefits less than socially optimal
Price	Too low	Too high
Stimulus to innovate	Little incentive to reduce social costs	Little incentive to expand social benefits

4.4.2   Unpriced Assets and Missing Markets

As discussed previously, markets often do not exist, or are incomplete for many environmental goods and services, that is, clean air, landscape quality, biodiversity, and for open access resources such as firewood, berries, fish stocks and game. There are no incentives for individuals, firms, industry and so on to incur costs to protect and maintain these resources which, in the absence of other arrangements for managing the resource efficiently (see Chapter 2), leads to a situation of overuse and environmental degradation. The best instrument to internalize externalities in these cases is to create markets for these environmental goods and services as discussed in Chapter 5.

4.4.3   Public Goods

Public goods/bads are characterized by non-rivalry in consumption and by non-excludability. Non-rivalry implies that consumption by one person does not reduce the quantity available for others, for example, watching a television programme or the view in a park. Non-excludability means that individuals living in an area cannot be excluded from the good or bad effects of the environmental benefits or costs. Air pollution is an example of a public bad. There would be non-rivalry in consumption because the entry of another person into the polluted area does not change the impact of pollution on any other individual living within the area. It is also non-excludable because it is impossible for individuals living in the area to be excluded from the effects of pollution.

4.4.4   Transaction Costs

Transaction costs (costs incurred gathering information, in formal and informal negotiations and monitoring) may be high, and prevent environmentally beneficial exchanges between generators and affected parties because the transaction costs exceed the gains of the transaction or trade.

4.4.5   Property Rights

The definition and enforcement of clear property rights is an essential criterion for ensuring that markets exist. Land and property problems are often resulting from institutional failures (see 4.5). Clearly, it is only possible to sell goods that are owned and it is only worth buying goods if the property right is also transferred. In the absence of a market there will not be a market-clearing price, that is, communal grazing grounds, communal forests and coral reefs are not owned and do not have a market-clearing price. To prevent overuse and environmental degradation, owners of environmental resources should have clearly defined property rights so that any losses, profits and rents from managing resources would serve as an incentive to maintain (or sell onwards) the resource. Such rights need not be individual, as is the case in most developed countries, but could be collective. As long as they are well defined and able to be enforced, sustainable use of the resource is possible.

Figure 4.3 shows how a lack of property rights can result in socially non-optimal use of natural resources. To fix ideas think of the resource as a fishery, in which access to the resource is open to all. The cost to each fisherman of removing one more fish is given by the individual marginal private cost. However, by removing this one fish, the costs to all other fishermen are increased, and so the marginal cost to the sector corresponding to the individual is the social marginal cost resulting from the institutional failure to manage properly the fishery 'commons'. With open access individuals will continue to fish until the additional cost to them is equal to the price. This is at q. At this point, however, the resource is socially overused. The appropriate level of exploitation is q^*. To achieve optimality, either property rights have to be defined, so that access is not open, or alternative instruments introduced to increase the private costs of exploitation.

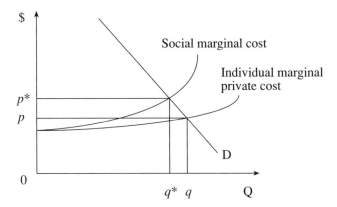

Figure 4.3   Supply and demand corrected for open access

Another example, which shows how property rights matter is in forestry. If those responsible for the exploitation of forest land do not have full rights of ownership (including the right to sell the land), they will seek to obtain the maximum return in the time over which they do have the rights. This will make long-term investments in afforestation and conservation unattractive, in a way that makes their behaviour consistent with a high discount rate (see short-sightedness, below).

4.4.6   Ignorance and Uncertainty

Ignorance and uncertainty may prevent clear and accurate understanding of environmental processes. Therefore changes in the availability of natural resources may not be perceived in time for price changes to effectively impact upon the demand and supply of the resource. Individuals or societies are often ignorant about the results of their activities, which may occur gradually or far into the future. Consequently, it is unlikely that they will adjust their behaviour. Increasing the range and depth of information about environmental processes can increase understanding and awareness among consumers and producers and hence can play an important role in sustainable development by internalizing many environmental externalities.

4.4.7   Short-sightedness

Individuals and politicians are not used to (or not able or willing to) account for, or to consider, the long-run impacts of their current policies and actions. This emphasis on policies, which will produce changes in the short-term leads to high discount rates which outweigh the future stream of benefits that may be realized in the long run. Society, however, usually has a much longer time horizon, and cannot discount future benefits in the same way that an individual does. For example, short-sighted individuals will rarely invest in the forestry sector, where returns on investment occur after several decades, whereas society (or the government on behalf of society) often decides to invest in forests to ensure their availability for future generations.

4.4.8   Irreversibility

Irreversibility refers to a situation of uncertainty about possible future development options. For example, the extinction of pharmaceutical plants due to deforestation in the Amazon might prevent pharmaceutical firms developing new drugs in the future, which could be used by future generations. In such cases, market prices may not reflect the value, which future generations would attach to the loss and hence there could be a need to correct the undervaluation.

4.5   POLICY AND INSTITUTIONAL FAILURES

Governments usually formulate policies which attempt to close the gap between rich and poor or to address some sectoral issues. However, government interventions in some sectors of the economy may be imperfect and thus lead to further distortions[3] in the rest of the economy. The literature calls these additional, government-led sectoral failures 'policy failures'. Examples of documented policy failures (OECD, 1995) which have exacerbated market distortions with respect to environmental resources are: lowering the price of irrigation water, subsidizing energy, subsidizing pesticides and fertilizers, tax incentives and credit subsidies on ranching, bureaucratic obstacles to land titling, low logging royalties and nationalization of forests without the resources to control and manage them.

Removing or phasing out costly subsidies that distort the economy and cause environmental damage is one of the most cost-effective means for achieving the twin goals of environmental protection and economic development (Markandya 1994; Panayotou 1996). Areas where such subsidies are significant include: the consumption of fossil fuels, electricity, water, pesticides, logging, land clearing and construction. Panayotou (1996), reports estimates of subsidies world-wide as follows: energy (US$300–400bn); agriculture (US$350–380bn); transport (US$100–200bn); water (US$10–20bn) and extractive industries (up to US$240bn). This amounts to about $1 trillion world-wide, or about 5 per cent of the world's GNP. If such subsidies were removed, the benefits would take the form of reduced environmental damage, which has a real economic value, as well as the more efficient use of natural and other scarce national resources. Panayotou contends that removing one dollar of subsidies generates 24 cents of reduction in environmental damages. Hence the overall environmental benefit of removing the subsidies above would be about $240 billion. In addition to this, the reductions in subsidies have a macroeconomic benefit, in that they reduce the fiscal deficits and make the process of structural adjustment more thorough.

Although the above figures are indicative only of orders of magnitude, they point to the extent of savings available if the subsidies are removed. The case for removing or sharply reducing such subsidies is very strong, both on economic and on environmental grounds (a win–win situation). The arguments against such action are often on the social and political side. From a sustainable development viewpoint, removing such subsidies should preferably precede the imposition of taxes on inputs or outputs, as subsidies are merely negative taxes.

However, some subsidies are not environmentally harmful, and indeed could benefit the environment. A case in point is subsidy to the use of liquified petroleum gas (LPG) or kerosene, which can lead to a switch away from more damaging fuels, or from fuelwood consumption in fragile ecosystems such as the Sahel. Another, more complex case is that of fertilizer subsidies. If these are removed, farmers could reduce their use, which in turn would reduce any adverse environmental affects. However, if agricultural production decreases, and demand is inelastic, farmers may decide to expand agricultural activities on marginal lands. Such 'benefits' are a definite 'second best' in the sense that the environmental benefits can be obtained without the high cost associated with a general subsidy on the fuel throughout the economy. There are also serious concerns about misuse of the subsidy. In some cases, subsidy removal has to be accompanied by appropriate secondary measures to prevent possible negative environmental impacts.

Another common policy failure is the inefficient taxation of economic rent or pricing of resources. In many instances the persons or organizations exploiting natural resources do not bear the full social cost of that exploitation; in particular they do not have to take account of the environmental damages they cause. By changing institutions and laws, the market mechanism can be made to work more effectively, so that resources are not underpriced in this way. The problems are specially severe when existing management systems for resource use have broken down, so that the resource is of the 'open access' type. The breakdown can occur because traditional systems of management no longer operate, or because the government, as the owner of the resource, is incapable of managing it effectively. Such underpricing is prevalent for forest and fishery resources in many developing countries (Panayotou 1995).

Changes in fiscal instruments such as royalties, licences and so on, to increase prices for the exploitation of natural resources, will only work if the necessary legal changes can be made and enforced. For privately owned land, internalizing the environmental costs may be better done through requirements for remediation, replanting and so on, rather than through a tax or fiscal instrument.[4] In other cases, where local management can be restored by making the appropriate legal changes, that may prove to be more effective than staying with government ownership and implementing a taxation system that is difficult to enforce. Where government ownership of the resources is necessary and desirable, different types of licences will suit different situations and cultures. With limited competition, it may be appropriate to have long-term agreements with the exploiters, making them responsible for the environmental protection as well as the exploitation. In other cases, auctions may be the preferred instrument. Another issue to be addressed is that of proper documentation. To ensure that stumpage prices for timber grown on public lands are adequate, an extensive and updated database, which includes all the factors necessary to calculate timber residual values, is needed. If non-timber values and sustainability constraints are not well documented, stumpage prices will be underestimated.

Changing resource prices through the phasing out of subsidies or eco-taxes requires political will and good institutions (see Chapters 5 and 6). Competitiveness of an industry, sector or even the entire economy may change. Before the policy can be implemented, the regulator needs to know who will benefit from the new policy and who will lose. The difficulty with many economic instruments for environmental protection is that the beneficiaries are frequently a large number of people who each suffer mildly from the pollution and the payment of the subsidy. The individual benefits are small for any one marginal policy change. On the other side, the losers, typically the enterprises or farmers, are now required to bear the social costs of their actions. Their losses could be substantial and they will put up a great deal of resistance to the measure.

4.6 SHADOW PRICING

From the above it is clear that when appraising projects that involve natural resources and environmental goods and services, there will frequently be a deviation between the market price of a resource and its true social cost. In order to base the appraisal of new policies and investments on their true social costs one has to adjust the market prices. One has to shadow price these environmental goods and services.

Classical economic analysis of projects often attempts to rectify imperfect, 'failed' market prices by estimating shadow prices. Shadow prices are formed by hypothetically removing the market failures from the project's prices. Here additional shadow pricing is made to internalize externalities. Details of valuation techniques are presented in Part II of this book. At the risk of over-simplification, the following adjustments are often made in shadow pricing:

1. Traded goods are priced with reference to international, or border, prices.[5]
2. Transfer payments such as taxes and subsidies are excluded.
3. Shadow pricing of domestic non-traded inputs and outputs is based on estimates of their opportunity cost. The opportunity cost of non-traded inputs and outputs can be calculated indirectly by estimating the costs of producing them using inputs valued at their true costs, or by observing what people are actually paying in informal markets (that is, water supply costs can be based on payments made to water vendors); through estimates of time and labour inputs; or directly by estimating the willingness to pay for the forgone goods and services.
4. Interest or discount rates are determined to reflect social rates of time preference and will generally be below those in the private capital markets.
5. External effects will be valued using the techniques discussed in Part II of this handbook.

The shadow price should also, in situations of irreversibility, include the user costs as shown in Figure 4.2, above, that is, the cost of future use forgone. The marginal user or depletion cost may be estimated as the present value of the cost of replacing the depleted asset at some future date. For resources such as water and electricity, where natural monopolies exist in their supply, the prices need to reflect long-run marginal cost pricing, duly taking into consideration higher future production costs if appropriate.

Such adjustments of market prices, that is, shadow pricing, are especially critical in making an economic appraisal of policies and projects with environmental impacts. The case studies presented in Part II of this handbook show how such shadow pricing is actually carried out.

4.7 ENVIRONMENTAL MANAGEMENT PRINCIPLES

Once sectoral analyses have been completed and the important sectoral environmental issues identified, suitable policy measures and investment projects/programmes should be devised and an action plan defined and implemented at the national level through both the economic and command and control instruments. Environmental instruments to implement these policy measures are discussed in detail in Chapters 5 and 6. At this point the following five useful environmental management guiding principles should be considered when designing environmental instruments:

1. polluter pays principle (PPP);
2. user pays principle (UPP) (or resource pricing principle);
3. precautionary principle (PP);
4. subsidiarity principle (SP); and
5. intergenerational equity principle (IEP).

4.7.1   Polluter Pays Principle

The PPP stipulates that the polluter has to bear the cost of complying with environmental standards, which are predetermined by public authorities. Theoretically, if the polluters have to pay for the costs of any pollution they cause, market forces will then encourage them to change their behaviour either by introducing new pollution control techniques or by switching to more efficient production processes. The two objectives of the PPP when encouraging a switch to more efficient production processes are: (i) to promote economic efficiency in the implementation of pollution control policies; and (ii) to minimize potential trade distortions arising from environmental policies. When the concept was agreed by the OECD in 1970, the justification was partly based on equity considerations (the polluter *should* pay the cost of any mitigation measures), and partly to ensure that countries do not provide a competitive advantage for their producers by subsidizing the pollution abatement measures.

It is important to note that the PPP is not necessary to achieve an efficient solution to an environmental problem. That can also be achieved if the victim or the government 'pays', as long as the payments are related to pollution reduction and the polluter responds to the incentive offered by the payment. Second, it should be noted that the PPP does not require pollution to recede to zero levels, nor does it require reductions to an optimal level, although this is not excluded. It requires only that the environment is in an acceptable state, which will evolve from a political process requiring inputs from the local, national and international levels. In establishing norms, development and environmental considerations need to be balanced. Hence, standards may vary from one country to another, and within a country, depending on environmental variables, such as ecosystem capacities to assimilate waste, population densities, degrees of industrialization, and the willingness of certain countries to pay for higher environmental standards or to tolerate environmental risks.

4.7.2 User Pays Principle

The UPP states that the beneficiaries should pay for the full cost of using the resources and its related services, together with the cost of losses for future generations following the IEP, which is known as 'future uses forgone' or 'users costs'. As mentioned earlier, 'resource pricing' often raises resource prices for the users, forcing them to reduce their use of the service or of the natural resources. The critical question when adopting the UPP is to determine who actually is the user of the good or service.

In some respect both the PPP and UPP principles can be considered as equitable and both offer the prospect of achieving efficiency. The following example illustrates how they may be applied:

(i)   There are 20 dischargers of waste into a river, with total annual discharges of 100,000 M^3 of wastewater.
(ii) The cost of operating a treatment facility for the wastewater is $ 10 million per annum.
(iii) There are 10,000 households receiving water from the river, with each getting 500 M^3 per annum.

On a PPP basis a charge of $20 per cubic metre ($10 million/20* 1,000,000) would be applied on the dischargers, and on a UPP basis, a charge of $2 per cubic metre (($10 million/10,000*500) would be levied as a water treatment charge on the households. Of course, the polluters and the households could be partly the same people. For example, one or more of the discharges could be of household wastewater.

The choice between these will depend on political and institutional considerations, as well the possible impacts of the measures on employment poverty and so on. It is by no means clear that the PPP will be the most desirable policy. If, however, the users pay, then some form of incentive to the polluters will be needed. This could take the form of a subsidy based on each unit of discharge reduced.

4.7.3 Precautionary Principle

The PP emphasizes that standards and regulations should be based on sound science but that in cases where there is a serious risk of irreversible environmental damage, insufficient scientific evidence should not be used as a reason to postpone action. This principle seeks to present and ease environmental stress before conclusive evidence of damage exists and adapts policy when raw scientific evidence becomes available. It requires decisions based on wise judgement in order to balance the magnitude of the potential damage and the risk of occurrence against the cost of preventing it. Unfortunately, 'operationalizing' the precautionary principle is not straightforward. Because it says nothing of the costs of pre-emptive action, it leaves the policy maker to decide what is affordable and how increased expenditure trades off against reduced risk.

4.7.4　Subsidiarity Principle

The SP, was not originally designed as an environmental principle, but provides useful guidance when applying the UPP, the PPP and the PP. It states that political decisions should be taken at the lowest possible level of public authority consistent with effective action. Setting standards and interpreting risk are essentially a political process. The subsidiarity principle urges that these decisions are made by the authorities that are closest to the population concerned.

The Brundtland Report (WCED 1987) has recognized that it is best to have a decentralized, participatory approach to sustainable development. When decision making is decentralized, it increases flexibility and thus increases the range of possible solutions. The SP reinforces the PPP approach by making allowances for different standards and by not requiring complete harmonization. The Rio Declaration in 1992 followed the example set by the Brundtland Report by affirming the need for decisions to be made at a level which will allow for the full participation of all concerned citizens (Principle 10).

4.7.5　Intergenerational Equity Principle

The IEP is a central principle in the definition of sustainable development. Intergenerational equity requires, to quote the Brundtland Report, that 'the needs of the present generation are met without compromising the ability of future generations to meet their own needs'. This principle is the basis of the environmental accounting measures of sustainable income discussed in the previous chapter. More generally it is taken into consideration within the trilogy of economic, environmental and social objectives underlying sustainable development.

4.7.6　Implementation of Principles of Environmental Management

The five principles discussed above can be used to guide sectoral policies and budgeting processes. If implemented successfully they can facilitate a smoother transition to sustainable development within a sector. Establishing proper resource pricing policies and using these principles to guide policies can assist the market in providing appropriate signals to managers and users of environmental resources.

The principles have to be implemented by all institutions responsible for environmental management. Some institutional issues are discussed further in

Chapter 6 but we would like to make some remarks at this stage. First, there is a distinct advantage in having the implementing agency at 'arm's length' from the government. That requires, for example, that public sector activities are regulated in the same way irrespective of whether it is the state or the private sector that is responsible for them. This is particularly important in the energy and water sectors, where environmental regulation is often carried out by personnel who are too close to the managers of the activities. Second, and related to that, there is no presumption that the public sector is more able to deliver on the fulfilment of these principles than the private sector. Given the appropriate incentives, it may in fact be easier to have the private sector respond in an effective way than the public sector. More often a true partnership between all stakeholders involved will provide the best environmental remedies.

4.8 CONCLUSIONS

This chapter has discussed the issues that arise at the sectoral level in analysing natural resource-based projects and programmes. The basic tool of analysis is the pricing of resources resulting from the partial equilibrium, 'supply–demand' framework. Estimates of the demand and supply of the different resources is a key part of required analytical work necessary to guide environmental and sectoral policies.

The fundamental objective is to achieve full social cost pricing for the resources concerned. Market prices are not equal to the social prices because: (a) there are subsidies and taxes, (b) there are external costs and (c) there are user costs. In the absence of markets (b) and (c) these will not be reflected in the price. The use of the resource should be guided by the social price. In practice this may be difficult to achieve, but even if the price is not actively used, the government can try and regulate the resource so that its exploitation takes place *as if* the social price were in place. The fuller discussion of the appropriate instruments is provided in the next chapter, but one important mechanism available to policy makers is that of shadow pricing for investments. This is a method in which adjustments to the market prices are made when estimating the social benefits of a project or programme.

The chapter concluded with a review of some of the principles that should guide the sectoral policies and priorities. These include the polluter pays principle, the user pays principle (or resource pricing principle), the precautionary principle, the subsidiarity principle, and the intergenerational equity principle. Each has something to offer the policy maker, although none is a definitive guide to policy.

The case studies (Annexes 4A1–4) illustrate the practical issues that arise in sectoral policy making. In the first case study we revisit the reform of the Beef

Protocol examined in the previous chapter, using a partial equilibrium framework (Annex 4A1). The second one looks at the forestry sector (Annex 4A.2); the third at land use and sectoral policies (Annex 4A3); and the final case study examines the energy and industry sectors (Annex 4A4).

NOTES

1. For an overview of sectoral level analysis, see Bawm and Tolber (1985).
2. See discussion of the Coase theorem in Chapter 5, page 178.
3. For a detailed discussion of policy interventions in a 'second best' framework, see, for example, Friedman (1984). The concept is also discussed in Chapter 3.
4. Frequently a bond has to be placed with the authorities, to ensure that the remediation is carried out.
5. For a more detailed discussion on shadow pricing, see Chapter 8 and Ward and Deren (1991).

CITED BIBLIOGRAPHY

Bawm, W. and S. Tolber (1985), 'Sector analysis', in Ch. 5 *Investing in Development*, Oxford: Oxford University Press, pp. 69–80.
Friedman, I.S. (1984), *Microeconomic Policy Analysis*, New York: McGraw-Hill.
Gravelle, H. and R. Rees (1992), *Microeconomics*, London: Longman.
Harou P., H. Daly and R. Goodland (1994), Environmental sustainability and project appraisal', *Journal of Sustainable Development*, 2 (3): 9–13.
Markandya, A. (1994), *Financing Sustainable Development: Agenda 21*, Cambridge, MA: Harvard Institute for International Development.
Organization for Economic Cooperation and Development (OECD) (1995), *The Economic Appraisal of Environmental Projects and Policies: A Practical Guide*, Paris: OECD.
Panayotou, T. (1995), *The Use of Economic Instruments in Developing Countries*, Nairobi: UNEP.
Panayotou, T. (1996), 'Matrix of policy options and financial instruments', Paper prepared for the Third Expert Group Meeting on Financial Issues of Agenda 21, Manila, Philippines.
Pearse, Peter H. (1990), *Introduction to Forestry Economics*, Vancouver: University of British Colombia Press, 226 pp.
Ward, W. and B. Deren (1991), *The Economics of Project Analysis: A Practitioners' Guide*, Washington, DC: World Bank.
World Commission on Environment and Development (WCED) (Brundtland Commission) (1987), *Our Common Future*, Oxford: Oxford University Press.

ANNEX 4A1   CASE STUDY 1: ECONOMIC ANALYSIS OF THE BEEF PROTOCOL IN BOTSWANA

Introduction

This case study focuses on the key economic aspects of the preferential treatment that the European Union (EU) market gives to Botswana beef imports under the Lomé Convention. This is known as the Beef Protocol. In particular, it examines the impacts of changes in the Protocol, namely the discontinuation of the beef subsidy, on the cattle sector in Botswana. Changes in cattle stocks are of environmental importance due to their impact on rangeland degradation. A model of the cattle sector has been constructed, using data from 1966 to 1994, which quantifies the responses of the cattle suppliers and the consumers of beef and other cattle products, so that the impacts of a change in the subsidy can be analysed. Following a report of the results of the model, the case study goes on to discuss the results of other models, and to arrive at a consensus on the impacts of changes in beef prices on the cattle sector, on cattle holdings and the environment.

Cattle are an important part of the Botswana economy and society and have been so for a long time. In relative economic terms, however, the sector is declining in importance. Between 1966 and 1994, agriculture (which is dominated by livestock) as a whole has fallen from 42 per cent of GDP to 6 per cent. Nevertheless, it remains an important sector, providing income and livelihood to a wide range of income groups.

The number of cattle rose nearly threefold between 1967 and 1979, when they reached 3 million. Numbers were steady in the early 1980s but declined in 1983 and 1986 (as a result of drought); and then again in 1993, following the 1992 drought. Unofficial estimates of numbers for 1996 indicate that the stock was about 2.4 million cattle in that year. The Beef Protocol was initiated in 1975, by which time the stock had already increased from 1.1 to 2 million. It is difficult to see what impact the Protocol had on the stock, without carrying out an analysis, which requires a model of the supply and demand for cattle and for beef to be constructed. This case study looks at the development of such a model to answer some of the 'as if' questions that are being asked about the Protocol.

In Chapter 3, the economic analysis of the Beef Protocol was examined using a general equilibrium framework. Here a partial equilibrium framework is presented.

A Partial Equilibrium Model of the Beef Market and Cattle Numbers

This section examines the impacts of the discontinuation of the beef subsidy, on the cattle sector in Botswana, and on the households consuming beef and households owning and rearing cattle. A model of the cattle sector has been constructed in order to quantify the impacts. The underlying assumptions of the model are discussed below. The intention is to quantify the responses of the cattle suppliers and the consumers of beef and other cattle products, so that the impacts of such a change in the subsidy can be analysed. The main assumptions of the model that has been constructed are:

1. The product sold in the home and export markets is a single commodity, with differences in quality between the two markets that are constant over time. This allows us to treat the market as integrated, which simplifies the analysis considerably.[1]
2. The domestic demand for beef is driven by the 'real' price (the price adjusted for inflation), disposable per capita income and the level of the population. An econometric equation is estimated for this market and the results reported in the next section.
3. The international demand for beef is determined at a price that is given to Botswana producers. The BMC takes that price and pays domestic producers after deducting its operating, selling and other costs (including the payment of a 10 per cent levy for the EU market).
4. The supply of beef is a more complex issue. The holding of cattle is treated as an asset holding, in which the farmers adjust their holdings in order to have an optimal number of cattle. This optimal number is a function of the price of beef, the costs of producing beef and the returns on other assets, namely interest rates on bank deposits. Adjustments to the stock can be made by controlling births, off-take, and, to a lesser extent, mortality. Births are determined as a given percentage of the optimal stock and deaths are a function of the stock and external factors such as rainfall. The off-take is then the balance. Equations for each of the three (off-take, births and mortality) have been estimated and the results are reported below.
5. If the subsidy is removed, the price that the producer receives will fall by the amount of the subsidy. This will increase domestic demand at the same time as reducing the off-take. The adjustments will continue until demand and supply are in equilibrium again. Cattle numbers, however, will adjust at a rate depending on how close or far the farmers are from their optimal holding of cattle. This is a dynamic process, which has to be tracked to find out the final result on the stock.
6. The fall in the price will have a direct impact on household wealth and income for those households that have cattle. It will also impact on the disposal incomes of households consuming beef.

Main Results of the Modelling Exercise

The domestic demand for beef
The data suggest that the domestic demand for beef is sensitive to: the real price of beef, the per capita income level and the population of the country. After trying various forms of the estimating equation, the following 'elasticities'[2] were obtained:

Price elasticity:	–0.19
Per capita income elasticity:	+0.83
Population:	+0.68

These values were obtained from data for 1984 to 1994 and then used to project consumption in the earlier period (1966–83).[3]

The supply of beef
As described above, the supply of beef is estimated through equations for the off-take, the births and the deaths of cattle. The off-take was estimated as a function of the real price received by farmers (including the bonus paid by the BMC), the interest rates on deposits and the stock of cattle. As off-take responds to the price and interest rate with a lag, these variables were found to affect the off-take with a lag of one year. Longer and more complicated lags were tried but did not perform any better. The influence of the price and interest rates on the off-take is complex, and the sign of the coefficient linking these variables to price could be positive or negative. The stock variable is included with a lag of one year, to reflect the partial adjustment of the farmer to the desired stock. After some experimentation, the following elasticities were obtained:[4]

Price elasticity:	+0.64
Interest rate:	+0.31
Stock of cattle:	+0.79

It was expected that rainfall would influence the off-take rate but in spite of trying various forms of the rainfall variable, it was not found to work.

The births of cattle are estimated from limited data. It was found that the real price, and the interest rate were marginally significant in explaining the variations in births between 1980 and 1993. The estimated elasticities were:[5]

Price elasticity:	+0.23
Interest rate:	+0.28
Stock of cattle:	+0.67

The death estimates were made as a function of the previous years stock and a variable reflecting the average rainfall over the past three years. A decline in average rainfall induces an increase in the death rate. The estimated elasticities were:[6]

Stock of cattle: +1.15
Rainfall in Lobatse: −0.56

The Market Equilibrium and the Impact of the Lomé Agreement

The above estimates confirm the fact that the cattle market is sensitive to economic factors and that we can expect changes in the price if the beef subsidy is reduced or removed altogether. To see the possible impacts of changes in the Protocol we looked at the case where the subsidy was removed altogether. In 1994, the full price received by farmers for beef sold through the BMC was 4.8 pula/kg, or €1.4/kg. This includes payment of a bonus and is in 1995 prices. According to the BMC data, average revenue in 1994/95 from all its operations was 9.3pula/kg. At the same time, the analysis of expenses shows that chilled beef, which is the main exported product to the EU, has a cost of delivery of 3.9 pula/kg. This covers the export, transportation to EU, the EU tariff and costs of distribution within the EU. Of the total of 3.9 pula, the tariff accounts for 1.64 pula, or 41.53 per cent. If the tariff were raised to its full value, it would amount to 16.4 pula /kg. Add to that the other costs of delivery and we have a cost of 18.66 pula/kg. This exceeds the selling cost of chilled beef in the EU market (about 16 pula/kg), without paying anything to the farmers and allowing for administration costs in Botswana. Hence, with a full tariff, the BMC would not be able to sell in the EU market.

In such a case the market for beef would be reduced to domestic sales, plus what can be sold in third markets such as the Republic of South Africa (RSA). We assume, on the basis of existing sales that about 20 per cent of the present total exports would remain in such markets. This amounts to 6,040 tons a year. Furthermore, if the price varies in the future, overseas demand will be responsive to that price, to the extent of an elasticity of −0.5. To equilibrate the beef market we calculate that the price will have to fall from 4.8 pula/kg to 2.5 pula/kg, a fall of 48 per cent.[7] This is based on the assumption that the present stock is 2.4 million cattle. In 1993 the stock was 1.8 million cattle and unofficial figures suggest that a recovery of the amount indicated has occurred since then. The fall in price will raise domestic demand and reduce off-take, so that the new equilibrium involves total beef sales of 34 thousand tons, compared with about 53 thousand tons as the estimated total production with the Protocol.

With sales reduced to this level, the stock has to adjust over time as well, and Table 4A1.1 gives the expected changes in births, deaths and stock. It must be emphasized that these are projections based on: (a) an existing stock of 2.4 million cattle and (b) rainfall figures at the level of 490 mm/year.

Table 4A1.1   Projections of cattle numbers without subsidy

Year	Equilibrium price (pula/100kg)	Stock (000)	Births (000)	Deaths (000)	Sales (000)
1	249	2,400	458	316	175
2	270	2,366	464	315	175
3	298	2,340	475	311	178
4	319	2,327	492	307	182
5	351	2,328	503	305	186
6	365	2,340	521	305	192
7	405	2,365	535	307	195
8	405	2,398	560	310	203

Note: Sales are converted into cattle numbers assuming a carcass weight of 193 kg. The price with the subsidy is 4.5 pula/kg.

The projections reported above must be qualified. First, the equilibrium price is sensitive to exogenous shocks, and so the move from a current price of about 4.5 pula/kg, to one of 2.5 pula/kg, could involve large fluctuations in the price of beef. In fact, with the supply elasticity of 0.64 reported above, the system was very unstable. Hence the figures reported in Table 4A1.1 are based on a lower supply price elasticity of 0.33. This is taken from an earlier study by Ndzinge et al. (1984).[8]

The above projections show that domestic demand will soon rise to fill a good part of the gap created by the loss of foreign markets. Within eight years of the loss of the EU market, total supply has risen to 39,000 tons, which is 25 per cent below the total demand with the Lomé Convention. Furthermore the price has risen to 4.05 pula/100 kg, which is about 15 per cent lower than at present. This is an important aspect of the future for beef in Botswana, resulting mainly from the growth in domestic consumption. Domestic demand is expected to grow, as population grows (at 3.5 per cent) and because per capita incomes grow (at 3 per cent). Both these assumptions are built into the projections which are reported above.

The projections suggest that with a stock of about 2.4 million cattle, the removal of the subsidy will have virtually no impact on numbers. This is mainly because the stock level is not very sensitive to the movements in the beef market over the short term, and is more influenced by exogenous factors. Nevertheless, if the present stock was way out of line with what would be considered as optimal, there would be bigger changes in the stock over eight years. These are not predicted by the model.

The above analysis also suggests that if we are to have an impact on the stock of cattle, which is what has the negative effect on the environment, we must focus on increasing sales from a given stock (the off-take rate), and on increasing the productivity of cattle (the birth rate).

NOTES

1. To test this assumption we looked at the correlation between the full price received by farmers selling to the Botswana Meat Commission (BMC) and the domestic price of beef as reported in the price index statistics. Between 1986 and 1994 the coefficient of correlation between these two was 0.36. This indicates only partial association, but would still support the hypothesis that the two prices are linked together.
2. The elasticity gives the percentage change in consumption, given a 1 per cent increase in the variable whose impact is being measured (for example, price, income and so on). This applies for all the equations estimated.
3. All the above coefficients were statistically significant in the estimation equation. The explanatory power of the estimated equation was 95 per cent – that is, 95 per cent of the variation in the demand was explained by the above factors.
4. The explanatory power of the estimated equation was 63 per cent. Although all the above coefficients were statistically significant in the estimation equation, the price variable was sensitive to the specification of the equation. If a constant was added the coefficient became smaller and insignificant, and if other variables were added the coefficient fluctuated quite widely.
5. The explanatory power of the estimated equation was 57 per cent.
6. The explanatory power of the equation was 55 per cent. This equation is the poorest determined of the ones estimated, and the form needs further investigation.
7. The actual price received by sellers of livestock for domestic sales is not 4.8 pula/kg, which is the payment for sales to the BMC. The relation between the BMC sales price and domestic sales price is, however, assumed to remain constant. The drop is slightly sensitive to the export demand. If, for example that demand is only 4,530 tons, the equilibrium price is 2.3 kg.
8. Ndzinge, L., J.M. Marsh and Greer R. Clyde (1984), 'Herd inventory and slaughter supply response of Botswana beef cattle produce', *Journal of Agricultural Economics*, **35** (1), 97–107.

ANNEX 4A2   CASE STUDY 2: GAP ANALYSIS: FORESTRY SECTOR

Introduction

A sector analysis is based on an overall estimate of supply, demand and prices for that sector's goods and services. To keep prices of goods and services in line with the general price level, natural resource policies are designed to avoid creating a gap between supply and demand, keeping relative prices constant. If a product's prices rise in proportion to its increasing scarcity, substitutes must be produced. There are two ways to maintain prices at the general price level: keep demand levels in check and, if necessary, increase *supply in a sustainable way*. Policies can be set to influence supply and/or demand and we can simulate the impacts of policies through a supply/demand partial equilibrium model, as shown in the previous case study for livestock in Botswana. A simple gap analysis, as illustrated here, is often carried out in sector analysis work. In this annex, a gap analysis framework is presented for the forestry sector in Nigeria and also used later as a focus for a discussion of integrated land-use policies.

Gap Model

A 'gap model' (or 'gap analysis') typically attempts to quantify the gap between the potential demand for a product and the supply of a product over time, in a given sector and at a given product price. Usually, aggregate consumption and production are considered in gap analysis instead of demand and supply, because with aggregates there is no relationship with price. A gap between consumption and production is calculated for a given price level. If the future needs of a country for each of the major sector products is known (through cross-sectional analysis if necessary) the amount of resources required can be matched against the sustainable production of the resources.

Given a policy of price stability, especially for essential commodities, the size of the gap will lead to investments either on the consumption side (the preferred outcome for the environmentalist) or on the production side. Is it better to invest in a mass media campaign to encourage consumers to be more careful in their water use or should planners increase the capacity of a dam? Alternatively a policy change could be made to ensure that resource is properly priced so that it reflects extraction and management costs and the real value of the resource. A rapid gap analysis for natural resources in sector analyses improves understanding about environmental management issues such as deforestation. It can also guide a discussion on resources and environmental management policies and investments.

This representation of gap analysis has been kept simple and an example is provided below of an application for Nigeria. In practice, however, a full gap analysis can be very complex indeed for a resource such as forestry, which serves multiple uses. On the demand side, we should look at the demand for all these uses and on the supply side the amounts of different forest products supplied under different forest management policy regimes. To take an example, we expect the demand for recreational uses of certain kinds of forests to grow more rapidly than the demand for timber. At the same time the amounts of different kinds of forestry products that are supplied will depend on the policies in place that allow private and public owners of forest resources to charge for such services. As stated above we abstract from these issues for reasons of exposition.

Consumption forecasts

On the consumption side, projections are made by linking the use of different forest products through income–consumption curves (also known as Engel curves) which are used to derive income elasticities. Simple use ratios calculated for the base period are then extrapolated for the projection period. New technologies, substitution and changes in end-use characteristics (dwellings, cooking stoves and so on), influenced by movements in relative factor prices, all cause these use ratios to fluctuate over time. Therefore, future price assumptions are important but remain exogenous to the analysis. Projections for exports and imports are made on the basis of these future price assumptions.

Production forecasts

On the production side, the procedure is often determined by biological forces and is based on the forest area, the evolution of land use, the forest's physical stock and its sustainable growth. Harvest projections are made in round-wood volumes according to ownership categories and geographic regions. Future production estimates are consistent with the given base price and information on the forest area, inventory and growth which reflects current management practices. Some hypotheses can relate to the price responsiveness of private land harvests in addition to public land harvests.

Gap forecasts

The final step of the basic model involves comparisons of aggregate production and consumption estimates for each year of the projection period. Usually a gap is forecast between consumption and production for a given price level. A range of policies and programmes are then proposed to fill the gap. These models usually deal with aggregate consumption and production at the national level. The Food and Agriculture Organization has developed price demand elasticities for many countries that are applicable to major categories of forest products and that give demand projections for various price projections. Similarly, the level of timber supplied from private lands can also be adjusted according to assumptions on price responsiveness; (supply elasticities may be different for private lands). If independent elasticities have been estimated, 'supply–demand' gaps are recalculated for different future price-series scenarios, one of which should eliminate the gap.

In the gap model, the degree of sophistication in the forecast of consumption and production estimates can vary from a simple comparison of 'population–related consumption' or 'forest area–net annual increment' to a more complex analysis involving GDP and end-use elasticities. The ability to construct a model to varying degrees of sophistication is one of the key strengths of the method. It provides flexibility that can accommodate the different levels of data and analytical capabilities of the professionals involved. For that reason, the approach is frequently used for countries that do not have extensive statistics on the forestry sector and few trained professionals in the field. As forestry statistics and technical expertise build up in a country, a market equilibrium model could progressively replace this gap model.

Nigeria Example

A similar approach was used in a forestry sector work in Nigeria in the 1990s (Buongiorno et al. 1994). The gap analysis was complemented by a linear programming model which simulates the amount of investments in plantation and plant capacity required to meet consumption by 2010. The objective was to meet the needs of each Nigerian state at least cost. Although model simulations suggested that Nigeria should be able to meet long-term requirements in logs and fibres, at prices competitive with world prices, it was clear that this would require strong policies to halt deforestation and natural forest degradation. Consequently, special participatory forest management projects were proposed to save and manage the natural forests left. The urgency to undertake the investments and implement the participatory forest project was provided by the results of the gap analysis which took no more than two months to prepare.

Gap analysis raises important issues and facilitates more informed discussions about deforestation rates, pricing policies, land tenures, property taxes, incentives, institutional and other controls and so on. However, quality indicators also need to be discussed to supplement the gap analysis in order to more fully understand other aspects such as the biodiversity and health of forest ecosystems. In summary, a gap analysis can provide a useful framework for discussion and can lead to changes in both demand and supply policies and in public and private investment regimes.

Gap Analysis Exercise

The following values have been determined by planners seeking to undertake a gap analysis of lumber requirements in a small developing country:

Consumption

1. Assume constant relative prices of lumber.
2. GNP per capita is growing at 3 per cent per annum.
3. Population growth is 2 per cent per annum.
4. Income elasticity = 1.5.
5. Per capita consumption in 1998 is 2 M^3.
6. The population of the country in 1998 is 100,000.

Production of lumber

7. Total forest area = 80,000 hectares.
8. Mean annual increment (MAI) = 4 M^3 /ha/year.

Questions

1. What would be the gap between total consumption of lumber and production in 2008?
2. How can the policy maker react to the situation?

Solutions to Exercise

Question 1
To calculate consumption of lumber in 2008 the following four calculations must be made:

- Income elasticity = % change in quantity of lumber consumed / % change in GNP per capita per annum.
  Therefore, $1.5 = \%\Delta Q/3 \Rightarrow 1.5 * 3 = 4.5\%$ = percentage change in quantity of lumber demanded. Compound growth over 10 years means that by 2008, 55 per cent more lumber will be demanded per capita.
- Consumption per capita in 2008. $1.55 * 2 \text{ M}^3 = 3.1 \text{ M}^3$.
- By 2008 the population will have grown by 22,000, based on 2 per cent annual growth. Total population in 2008 = 122,000.
- Total demand in 2008. $122,000 * 3.1 \text{ M}^3 = 378,200 \text{ M}^3$.

The supply of lumber each year remains relatively static if it is based on off-takes of sustainable volumes of growing stock. The mean annual increment (MAI) over a full rotation is 4 M^3/ha per year. $\Rightarrow$ in 2008 total production and supply of lumber will be $80,000 \text{ ha} * 4 = 320,000 \text{ M}^3$. The GAP between consumption and production will be $378,200 - 320,000 = 58,200 \text{ M}^3$.

Question 2
The gap between production and consumption represents approximately 18 per cent of total lumber production in 2008. The government has a number of policy options which are briefly summarized below.

- Invest on the consumption side through media and educational campaigns to encourage users to reduce their overall consumption. Promote substitutes for lumber to be used by industry and large-scale users.
- Improve the pricing of lumber. It is possible that the resource price e.g. fuelwood price in developing countries is fixed by policy and is too low, or that all externalities have not been included. Extraction and management costs may be too low because of subsidies in other sectors, that is, fuel subsidies.
- Increase the production of lumber. This may involve national forestry programmes such as joint forest participatory management where village forest committees are encouraged to work with the state forestry departments in a programme of new plantations and protection to increase sustainable use of the forest and harvest outputs. This will only work if villagers are offered a range of incentives such as a share in the final harvest of lumber and non-timber forest products (NTFPs), employment

in the new plantations, supply of charcoal or efficient stoves and so on to reduce their own wood fuel demands. The villagers will then have a greater incentive to protect and maintain the forest growing stock which may increase the availability of timber for external use by industry and 'city' consumers.

Suggested Further Reading

Buongiorno, J., P. Harou, A. Omulabi and L. Ogundare, (1994), 'Timber demand and supply in Nigeria – models and forecasts to 2010', *Journal of World Resources Management*, (1), 101–27.

Harou, P. (1992), 'Minimal review of the forestry sector' in R. Haynes, P. Harou and J. Mikowski (eds), *Forestry Sector Analysis for Developing Countries*, Cintrafor special publication No. 10, Seattle, WA, pp. 3–15.

Kishor, N. and L. Constantino (1994), 'Sustainable forestry, can it compete?', *Finance and Development*, **31** (4), 36–9.

ANNEX 4A3   CASE STUDY 3: LAND USE AND SECTORAL POLICIES

A particular land use reflects the biophysical characteristics of the land as well as the socioeconomic and cultural context of sectors using the land at a given time. The suitability of land for forestry, or other uses, is not only based on its biophysical characteristics, economic and political factors play a significant role also. Macroeconomic and sector policies reviewed in sector analysis provide the framework, explaining the current and future prices of forest products and the prices of other sectors' products, such as agriculture and mining. These price changes will be reflected in the cash flows (therefore the land values) derived from the land. As new policies in each sector are implemented and relative prices change, land-use patterns will shift. The link between integrated land-use and forest policies is summarized in Figure 4A3.1.

Land-use management consists of directing the use of the land to its most efficient sustainable use. If marginal land is used for agriculture instead of forestry, one has to question the economic policies behind this unsustainable use of the land. If the overall policies cannot be changed, a preferred alternative is to use different instruments to redirect the use of the land to a more sustainable situation. To decide whether a public intervention is needed on private land, a dual financial–economic analysis can be undertaken.[1] If an individual suffers a financial loss by undertaking a socially desirable action on his/her land, for example by replanting after logging, an incentive may be justified if the economic (social) net benefit is positive.

A range of instruments exists to change land use (Harou 1990). Some of these instruments influence market behaviour, for example, improving land titling, while others affect the land management process through improved regulations, subsidies or provision of information. The instruments fall broadly into six basic categories: regulatory instruments, economic instruments, land acquisition, property rights, provision of infrastructure and information (see Box 4A3.1). No single instrument will be effective in achieving all land management objectives. The instrument used depends on the special characteristics of each problem and locality and the behaviour of the land owners.

NOTE

1. Further examples and methodologies for conducting financial and economic analysis of natural resources are set out in Part II of the handbook.

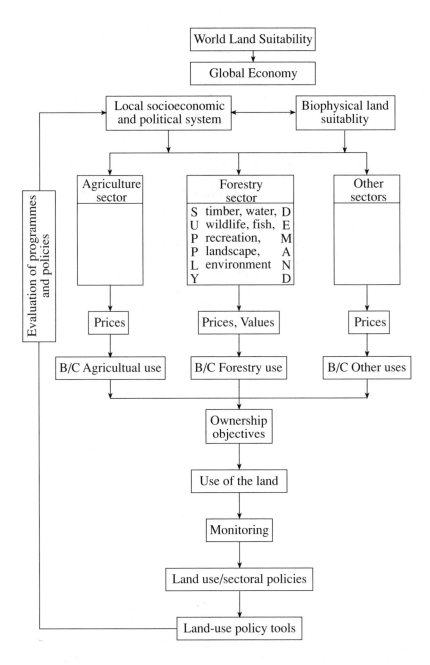

Figure 4A3.1   Sector and policy analyses linkage to land use

---

BOX 4A3.1   SIX INSTRUMENTS FOR LAND-USE MANAGEMENT

- *Regulatory Instruments* Includes zoning, subdivision regulations, transfer of development rights, and other types of land-use controls designed to protect sensitive land resources, public interests, and environmental and cultural values.
- *Economic instruments* Includes economic incentives such as preferential taxation schemes, transfer and development taxes, and subsidies, all of which can be used to encourage developers and landowners to develop (or keep in natural state) land in accordance with environmental objectives.
- *Land acquisition alternatives* Includes various types of land acquisition approaches, such as voluntary sales, expropriation, easements and land exchanges, which will enable urban land managers to meet conservation objectives.
- *Property rights* This approach involves the provision of secure land tenure to promote investment in land and infrastructure improvements.
- *Government provision of infrastructure* This approach involves the provision of appropriate infrastructure, such as roads, to guide development as well as to serve the special needs of land resources or hazard-prone areas.
- *Information and education* Methods for expanding knowledge of the issues, land conditions, and the environmental implications of various types of development on environmentally sensitive or hazard-prone lands. They can be used to support land-use decisions and to encourage landowners and public authorities to carry out voluntary conservation. They include land information systems, various types of assessments, and public information.

Suggested Further Reading

Harou, P.A (1990) 'Forestry taxes and subsidies for integrated land use', in M.C. Whitby and P.J. Dawson (eds), *Land Use for Agriculture, Forestry and Rural Development*, The Newcastle upon Tyne University Press, UK, pp. 85–94.

Harou, P.A. and H. Essmann (1990) 'Integrated land use and forest policies – a framework for research', in International Union of Forestry Research Organisations, *(IUFRO) Proceedings Division IV*, World Congress, Montreal, August, pp. 188–97.

ANNEX 4A4   CASE STUDY 4: ENERGY AND INDUSTRY SECTORS

Introduction

Energy planning and investments are carried out primarily by governments working (to various degrees), with private firms. The supply of commercial energy sources is dominated by large organizations such as national electric power companies and national and international oil companies. However, smaller private firms can participate fully in specific activities, for example, extracting oil, gas or coal; refining and marketing products to final consumers and generating power. In cases where private firms play one or more of these roles, the government, often as a parastatal organization, maintains a strong position through determining production agreements, pricing and profit sharing. The decisions made by governments and the private sector are, however, influenced by international and domestic market forces.

On the demand side, there are a number of decision-making units, that is, private and public firms, and many types of individual consumers. At the same time, the government retains a significant influence on the demand for energy through energy infrastructure provision and energy pricing. It can also influence energy demand via specific programmes to encourage energy conservation and to internalize the external costs of energy. Within the informal sector, which includes noncommercial fuels such as firewood, charcoal and dung, the government has less influence. It can instigate infrastructure and pricing policies for competing commercial fuels. Considering the pivotal role that the government plays within the energy sector and the integral nature of the sector *vis-à-vis* other sectors, there is an increasing need for policy makers to devise a framework for public action. The gap model discussed in Annex 4A1 can provide a useful framework, which can assist in the implementation of policies that utilize market mechanisms and develop options for decentralization.

Energy Pricing

An important prerequisite for an effective national energy policy is for government policy to be used to set up the appropriate enabling environment where energy can be priced correctly. This does not necessarily mean that the market-clearing price is the optimum price for the economy. Instead prices should also internalize environmental and user costs (as discussed earlier). To do this, regulations affecting both producers and consumers need to be established. Appropriate incentives, which favour benign environmental production processes and uses, should be set up (for example, incentives which encourage energy-saving capital investments). Product taxes can also be used to discourage consumption of polluting energy sources, for example, gasoline taxes.

Since the government influences pricing both as a regulator and producer of energy resources and fuel, it has a predominant role in establishing appropriate prices. New policies tend to incorporate more private actors with the objective of making the sector more responsive to market signals. In the absence of a perfectly competitive market and where externalities are prevalent, the supply/demand model needs to be adjusted. The supply curve is usually represented by the long-run marginal cost (LRMC). A longer-term perspective is required to address environmental problems because the benefits of emission reduction programmes and other similar programmes can take many years before they are realized. When considering the interventions required to address environmental problems, the LRMC is considered to be equal to short-term marginal cost (SRMC). Similarly, the LRMC is considered to be equal to the average total cost or long-term average cost. The literature on this point is voluminous and polemic. The cost curve can be readjusted to take into account market distortions. For this purpose, shadow prices should be used wherever applicable (Munasinghe 1985). The resulting price derived from the intersection of the corrected S and D curves would represent the *optimal efficiency price*. If all environmental externalities have been properly considered, the price will also be the *optimal social price*. Enforcement of regulations will be critical in ensuring that the social and environmental externalities are included within the price charged to consumers. Optimal social pricing means that society's investment in the energy sector fully reflects the values attributed to alternative uses, to the environment and to social equity.

An extra unit of supply should be priced according to its marginal cost. However, if a state monopoly is the agent responsible for producing the extra unit of supply, marginal cost pricing may not be the most efficient method. The private sector is now increasingly involved in energy production and supply expansion programmes. If effective regulations and institutions are set up which can ensure that the private sector internalizes environmental and social externalities, privatizing sections of the energy sector may prove to be a more efficient approach than through state monopolies.

Discriminatory pricing and distributional impacts

A key distinction to make in the design of energy pricing policies is the distinction between producer and consumer prices. Producer prices are the prices facing producers who buy energy to produce other goods (or other forms of energy, for example, electricity) while consumer prices are prices facing final consumers. Consumer prices can discriminate against large users and favour low-income consumers. To favour low-income consumers, progressive tariffs may be applied, which would allow an element of cross-subsidization from more wealthy households or the industrial sector to low-income households.

In order to understand fully the distributional consequences of energy pricing policies we need to look at the consumption of energy by income group in great detail. We also need to look at the distribution of the indirect benefits of these policies, through changes in environmental pollution and other public goods. This has been done in a number of World Bank studies, of which perhaps a state-of-the-art one is that of Eskeland and Kong (1998). They look at two regions of Indonesia (Jakarta and the 'Rest of Java') and develop a measure of the 'distributional characteristics' of a policy. This is an income-weighted measure of the increase in costs for different income groups resulting from measures that increase pollution control costs, or a similar measure of the increase in benefits resulting from the improved environment that results from the same measures. Environmental regulations in the areas of energy production and use, and transport are analysed in some detail. On the distributional effects of control costs the study shows that transport policies are more 'distribution friendly' than energy policies, mainly because transport environmental controls affect the rich relatively more than do energy environmental controls. Within transport, controls on private transport have a relatively smaller impact on the lower-income groups than do controls on public transport. Within energy, gas and electricity controls have the smallest impacts on the poor, and firewood, kerosene and coal have the biggest. All these differences become much smaller, however, when the indirect effects of the control measures are taken into account – that is, when the impacts of the measures on the production costs of other commodities are allowed for.

On the benefits side, the analysis is complicated by the fact that it is not known with any accuracy how the willingness to pay for the improvements changes with income. Eskeland and Kong take a range of values for the 'income elasticity of willingness to pay for environmental improvements' and estimate the distributional effects of the benefits.[1] These are roughly the same for the energy and transport regulations. With an income elasticity of demand for the benefits of one (a commonly assumed value) the resulting net distributional effects (taking both costs and benefits) are approximately neutral for energy and positive for transport. The lower the income elasticity of demand for the benefits, the greater are the distributional impacts of the benefits, and the greater the net benefits from both strategies.

Energy pricing in developing countries
Energy price reform is essential in developing countries. Electricity prices are barely one-third of supply costs and are often half the prices charged in industrial countries. These low prices are not a result of more efficient distribution systems, in fact, losses due to theft from illegal connections are as high as 30

per cent in many countries and there are likely to be more inefficiencies within the whole energy production, distribution and pricing system. The reasons for persistent underpricing are largely institutional. Utility managers have little influence in pricing or investment decisions, which are often politically motivated. The whole system of management lacks accountability and transparency. Subsidizing the price of electricity and energy causes both economic costs and negative environmental impacts. Demand is higher than it would be with proper pricing and there are few incentives for investing in new and cleaner technologies. Clearly, energy pricing should be considered within the context of broader energy demand management policies because the objectives of energy pricing are to lower demand and to change demand patterns. The next section identifies how a framework can assist governments in planning national energy programmes.

Integrated National Energy Planning

The oil crisis of the mid-1970s acted as a catalyst for governments by forcing them to consider their approach to energy sector planning. Different frameworks were proposed, one of which was integrated national energy planning (INEP) or integrated resource energy planning (IREP). The INEP/IREP proposes a gap model, supply and demand framework for the energy sector and its subsectors. (See Annex 4A1 for more information on GAP models.) This states that energy planning should be carried out and implemented in close coordination with a country strategy and its macroeconomic policies. The INEP conceptual framework is contained in Figure 4A4.1.

When formulating integrated energy strategies, governments review both supply- and demand-side options and set priorities, which attempt to improve the efficiency of energy production and consumption as well as protect the environment. The first step in the formation of a strategy is to target demand-side issues such as energy pricing and the promotion of competitive markets to improve the service and levels of information supplied to consumers. On the supply side, appropriate institutions and regulations are needed to minimize energy loss and make investments more efficient. Technology transfers and energy-efficient methods of transport can have a significant impact upon both supply and demand. INEP assists in setting priorities for planning supply and demand policies for the energy sector. An example of INEP in the US is set out in Box 4A4.1.

Demand-side management

Demand-side management (DSM) identifies and implements initiatives that improve the end use of energy supply by altering the characteristics of the demand for energy (for example, through education programmes). It involves a mix of

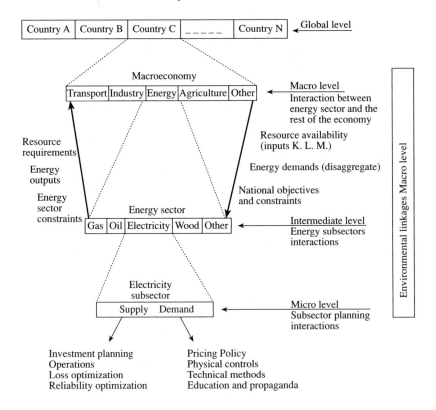

Source: Munasinghe and Meier (1993).

*Figure 4A4.1   Hierarchical conceptual framework for integrated national
(or resource) energy planning and environmental analysis*

pricing, load management, and conservation strategies designed to increase the
incentives for more efficient use of energy. The most important contribution
that DSM can make towards restructuring the demand for energy is by improving
the pricing regime so that all external and user costs are internalized.

DSM is the preferred approach when considering the environmental implications of energy sector interventions. There is considerable scope for demand
management to reduce negative externalities in the sector by internalizing
external and user costs through appropriate pricing. By reducing the demand
for energy through improving household or industrial conservation methods,
DSM can reduce the level of air pollutants, carbon dioxide emissions and CFCs
released into the atmosphere. An example of DSM in a developing country is
given in Box 4A4.2.

BOX 4A4.1   INTEGRATING DEMAND-SIDE MANAGEMENT WITH SUPPLY-SIDE PLANNING: THE US EXPERIENCE

Historically, US electric power utilities met the growth in demand by adding generating capacity. Loads were increased according to demand, with little effort to manage demand. The US approach to resource planning contrasted with practices in industrialized Asian and European countries, which had compatible growth rates. Constraints to increasing power supplies, in particular, limited access to fuel, led many industrial countries to increase loads according to demand and to suit whatever sources were available at that time.

During the early 1980s, pressure from regulatory commissions, and the increasing financial and environmental costs involved with building additional capacity, meant that the concept of demand-side management began to gain acceptance in the US. The evolution of demand management was part of a planning process called integrated energy resource planning (IERP) which is an example of integrated national energy planning (INEP). IERP is primarily a US process whereby utilities and their regulatory commissions work together to evaluate available demand- and supply-side options (including availability of power for purchase), and determine an optimal energy service strategy, taking into account economic and environmental factors. IERP means that all new energy sources which could be used to meet load growth are evaluated from a 'level playing field'. Conservation and other efficiency demand-side investments are integral components in the planning process. Demand- and supply-side investments are appraised using the same discount rate. The core concept of IERP is the 'equal' treatment, or integration, of energy-based and conservation-based energy services. Planners attempt to rank according to cost (beginning with the lowest-cost options), the different energy supply and end-use technologies, processes and programmes that could be used to provide energy services.

The concept is appealing. IERP has been used in the US to promote energy-efficiency investments as an alternative to capacity expansion. In the US, promotional activities are generally performed by the utility. IERP, as practised in the US, has developed in an environment where most end users purchase their electricity in a non-competitive market where strong regulatory regimes allocate costs and benefits across consumer groups. For example, if consumers are charged 8 cents per kWh but the peak cost to the utility is actually 10 cents, the utility, and presumably the country, can benefit by discouraging growth in demand during the peak period.

Regulatory commissions encourage the utility to negotiate with their customers by offering a range of methods and incentives to persuade them to reduce their overall consumption. The benefits and costs of consumption reductions are distributed in various ways between the utility, the customers, rate payers in general, and the taxpayer. Usually the risks and costs are borne by the ratepayers because regulators allow the utility to offset the costs of demand-reducing programmes against the general rates base. In many of these programmes, utilities use their preferential, and sometimes subsidized access to capital markets to finance new equipment and services for use by eligible customers. A variety of approaches are possible, but they all require the utility to identify investments, or practices for customers to adopt, which would reduce electricity consumption and thus avoid unnecessary capacity increases.

In the United States, implementation of IERP activities is forecast to reduce electricity demand by approximately 45,000 MW of generating capacity by 2010 and 90,000 MW by 2030. The net economic benefit would be approximately $35 billion for the period from 1990 to 2030.

Supply-side management
Energy supply planning can also play an important role by minimizing the impact of energy production and consumption on the local and global economy while utilizing the most efficient and advanced technology available. Sustainable, and politically viable energy supply schemes must consider a range of factors including: health (avoidance of respiratory diseases), safety (accident prevention), reliability, ecological impacts, non-renewability of resources, and employment. Once energy demands have been assessed and extrapolated for future requirements the normal approach is for economists to work with the design engineers and appraise the least cost option required to satisfy these demands. The least cost analysis should also take into account levels of efficiency and the environmental and social impacts of the options.

Integrated supply curves
A particularly useful technique for presenting and comparing the direct costs of supply and demand-side options is the use of integrated supply curves (ISCs)

BOX 4A4.2   RESIDENTIAL DEMAND-SIDE MANAGEMENT FOR THAILAND

A demand-side management (DSM) assessment was recently completed for the residential sector in Thailand. The investigation involved a comprehensive analysis of the major residential end uses of electricity: air conditioning, refrigeration, lighting, cooking, heating water, and other electric appliances. The study outlined 23 economically-viable DSM measures that would be achieved through improved use of existing technologies. If fully implemented, these improvements would reduce annual electricity use by up to 500 GWH and peak electrical demand by 160 MWE during the first year of the DSM programme.

The highest potential savings would be found through a programme to improve the energy efficiency of refrigerators. Improvements to the insulation and compressors of Thai refrigerators were predicted to reduce electrical use from 400 kWh to below 200 kWh per unit per year. Possible countrywide savings would be up to 170 GWh per year if more efficient refrigerators were introduced into the marketplace. Negotiations are under way with a large Thai refrigerator manufacturer to produce a high-efficiency prototype unit for testing and evaluation.

Estimates for savings were based on replacing less efficient equipment in existing housing when the equipment's natural life expired, and by installing cost-effective energy-efficiency measures in new houses. It was estimated that full implementation would take 10 years allowing time for new buildings to be constructed and inefficient equipment in existing buildings to be replaced. It was estimated that the strategy would result in cumulative savings of more than 6,000 GWh and peak reductions of more than 2,000 MW by 2005. This would represent a large proportion of total electrical consumption by the residential sector, which was 7,025 GWh and approximately 20 per cent of the peak utility load of 7,095 MW in 1989.

Source: World Bank (1993, p. 55).

(see Figure 4A4.2). The curves compare options for meeting energy needs by indicating the direct unit costs of electricity services. Ideally, all costs, including environmental and social, should be included for appropriate energy planning and pricing, however, usually only direct unit costs are shown. In the figure, the cumulative supply of electricity is shown on the horizontal axis and the incremental cost of supplying each additional service is indicated on the vertical axis. The ISC is not really a curve but a connected set of discrete costs. If necessary, the cost levels could be approximated by inserting a curve of best fit. Note that the lowest cost options in the figure do not involve generation. Rather they entail increased efficiency and DSM. Unfortunately the incentives to undertake these measures are often lacking, with the result that higher cost investment options are selected. Since these also have higher environmental costs, the problem is compounded.

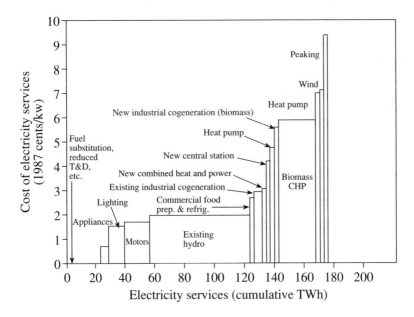

Note: T&D = transmission and distribution losses; CHP = combined heat and power; cents/kWh = centre per kilowatt-hours; TWh = terrawat-hours.

Source: Bodlund et al. (1989).

Figure 4A4.2   Example of an integrated supply curve for electricity

Theoretically, to improve efficiency and limit the extent of negative externalities an increase in energy supply should only be considered if all options for improving efficiency have been exhausted. The options available to improve efficiency should be compared using cost–benefit analysis. Other environmental and social criteria should be included in the analysis – tools such as environmental assessments, socioeconomic impact assessments, participatory approaches and surveys could be used to ensure that the environmental and social impacts of efficiency improvements are understood prior to implementation.

Improving the efficiency of private institutions to ensure that appropriate supply-side decisions are made may require a certain amount of restructuring and a more transparent regulatory mechanism between government and the institutions concerned. Supply-side reforms are discussed in Box 4A4.3.

BOX 4A4.3   SUPPLY-SIDE REFORMS

The World Bank's policy paper on electric power, 'The Bank's Role in the Electric Power Sector: Policies for Effective Institutional, Regulatory and Financial Reform' (1993) outlines a useful approach that is applicable to the energy sector. The guiding principles from the paper provide a clearer insight into current Bank policy:

- A requirement for all power sector loans is a clear indication that national and state policies are changing to incorporate a legal framework and regulatory process that meet certain Bank conditions. The conditions focus on economy-wide initiatives. For example, the Bank requires countries to set up transparent regulatory processes that are independent of the power suppliers and which do not allow the government to interfere in day-to-day power company operations (whether private or publicly owned). The regulatory framework should establish a sound basis for open discussion on power-sector economic, financial, environmental and service policies.
- In some of the least-developed countries, the Bank will assist in financing the importation of power services if this can be proved to improve efficiency. The Bank will pursue the increasing commercialization, corporatization and private sector participation in developing-country power sectors.
- The Bank will focus lending for electric power on countries with a clear commitment to improving sector performance in line with the above recommendations. To encourage private sector investment in the power sector, the Bank will use some of its financial resources to support programmes intended to facilitate the involvement of private investors.

Policy Instruments

For an energy policy to be fully effective the first requirement is to ensure that the correct macroeconomic policies are set in place, as discussed in Chapter 3. Trade liberalization can mean that newer, less-polluting technologies are imported and used instead of the original higher-polluting technologies. However, gains in efficiency are not guaranteed when new technologies are imported. The appropriate institutional and competitive market-incentive structures need to be set up to identify and manage the use of the new technologies, in combination with simple improved efficiency through 'housekeeping' and DSM.

Laws and regulations should be instituted which address environmental issues. The technology to decrease emissions of particulate matter during electric power production is relatively simple and inexpensive. However, appropriate emission standards need to be set to encourage the adoption of these appropriate technologies. Otherwise producers might still prefer to maintain high emissions and avoid additional expenditure on new technology. For regulations to be effective they should include some kind of financial penalties, which are greater than the cost of purchasing the new technologies. Other standards can be developed and enforced by capable institutions which could be either departments or sections within government, or independent institutions which are funded and/or regularized by government (see Chapter 6). For example, the use of coal as a fuel requires minimum standards for chimney sizes; vehicle standards can entail controls on specific items of equipment to reduce particulates, lead, SO_2 and CO_2 emissions in exhaust fumes; and building codes can lead to improved energy conservation within the home by enforcing double glazing and minimum levels of insulation and so on. Other technical measures including physical controls (lead shedding or rotating powercuts) and direct investment (extension of natural gas distribution networks) will also affect the environmental impact of energy production and consumption. Box 4A4.4 gives an example of how a developing country increased energy efficiency through deregulation and import restrictions.

Energy Conservation Efficiency Criteria

All policy instruments should ensure that energy conservation measures are efficient (see Chapter 5). An energy-conservation investment is economically efficient if the cost of reducing the demand for a unit of energy is no greater than the cost of supplying that amount of energy. The level of investment should be set at the equilibrium point where the cost of avoiding the need for a unit of energy (that is, the cost of reducing demand by one unit) is just equal to the cost of supplying that unit. Costs should include the costs to the environment.

BOX 4A4.4   DEREGULATION AND IMPORT RESTRICTIONS

Objectives within the Industrial Energy Efficiency and Moderniza-tion Project in India, initiated in 1990, included plans to develop and implement open-market policies and programmes that would improve incentives for efficient energy use; build stronger institu-tions in the public and private sectors to carry out energy conservation programmes; carry out demonstration projects in key subsectors; and conduct a programme for research and develop-ment needs.

The Indian government proposed to promote this plan by:

- deregulating the domestic economy to increase competition and provide stronger incentives for industry to use all factors of production, (including energy), more efficiently;
- adjusting the cost-plus pricing formulas which were estab-lished for most industries and allow enterprises to retain their financial savings derived from investments in energy con-servation;
- reducing tariffs on energy-saving devices to lower the capital cost of energy-efficiency investments;
- subsidizing plant-level energy audits and feasibility studies;
- subsidizing R&D programmes and expenditures by both public sector research institutes and the private sector;
- adopting fiscal incentives for energy-saving devices and systems, including 100 per cent depreciation allowance for income tax purposes, excise tax exemptions and customs duty exemptions for solar and wind energy generation equipment; and
- de-licensing equipment for the manufacture of mini-hydro and micro-hydro systems, electric vehicles, solar, wind and other renewable-source power-generating equipment.

Source: Gandhi (1996).

The equilibrium investment level, which internalizes environmental costs and accounts for energy conservation measures, will be lower than the technically achievable level of investment. Therefore, appropriate pricing and taxation should provide the correct signals if investment levels are not directly regulated or produced by the government.

Institutions

Institutional reforms remain the most effective supply-side reform available to policy makers (see Chapter 6). They are needed to make supply-side institutions more responsive to changes in demand and to government requirements. The creation of institutional frameworks to encourage efficient energy production and distribution must include initiatives on at least two levels: restructuring energy supply enterprises, and facilitating a transparent mechanism between government and energy-supply enterprises.

Energy sectors in many developing countries are structured so that a single company operates as a public monopoly. At earlier stages in the development of the sector, this allowed for economies of scale and more appropriate use of scarce technical skills. If the single company monopoly was financed and regulated according to private sector rules, this model might still work. However, in many countries, the public monopoly situation has resulted in the government combining the roles of operator, regulator and owner, leading to inefficiencies at all levels. Lack of transparency also prevents consumers and interest groups from monitoring the management and effectiveness of the energy supplier. A shift towards decentralization and market-based incentives, even with government ministries operating as regulators, is often more efficient. Essential features of a regulatory framework to encourage the use of market-based incentives and decentralization are: transparency and openness; clear articulation of reform objectives (including pricing); procedures limiting government interference and increasing managerial responsibilities in energy enterprises; and entry and exit conditions for investors and competitive enterprises.

New regulations should also address environmental issues. All energy enterprises, public, private, mixed or parastatal agencies, should abide by the same rules and regulations. The governments' role is to set these environmental laws and regulations, set up the appropriate institutions to enforce implementation and monitor the whole process

Privatization of energy supply enterprises or a broadening of their financial base – by switching some portion of their borrowing from government to financial intermediaries – might be recommended in countries where capital markets exist. With proper regulation and commercialization, the energy sector could help transform domestic savings into investments in long-term bonds and equity issues from energy companies. The precedent has already been set in developed countries where the privatization and broadening of financial markets led to the formation of capital markets. Privatization of plant management might also improve efficiency. In Sub-Saharan Africa, it is estimated that liberalizing procurement, eliminating government monopolies and instituting more transparent pricing in the energy sector could save the region up to $1.3 billion per year (World Bank 1993).

Exercise

The data in Table 4A4.1 are provided for generating an integrated supply curve for a country. They give the amount of electricity available for each source (in TWh), the private cost and the environmental cost per kWh for that source, and the social cost, which is the sum of the private and environmental costs.

Table 4A4.1   Data on sources and costs of electricity for a country

Source	TWh available	Total TWh	Private cost	Environmental cost	Social cost
				UScent/kWh	
Household insulation	1	1	–0.5	0	–0.5
Energy efficient home lighting	8	2		0	0
Reduced losses from transmission	2	4	1.0	0.1	1.6
Existing hydro	5	9		0.3	3.3
Existing coal	4	130	3.0	2.5	6.0
New gas	4	170		1.5	4.5
Combined heat & power (CHP)	1	185		2.0	6.0
Wind	5	190		0.2	5.2
Biomass	1	200		1.7	5.7
Diesel peaking	2	202		1.5	7.5

Answer the following questions

1. What do you understand by the negative cost for household insulation?
2. Sort the data by private cost, with the lowest cost option first and plot the integrated supply curve corresponding to that data.
3. Sort the data by social cost and plot the corresponding supply curve.
4. Assuming that 190 TWh are to be supplied, which sources would be privately cost effective and which would be socially cost-effective?
5. What measures would you need to introduce the socially optimal options in preference to the privately optimal ones?

Answers to the Exercise

Question 1

A negative cost implies that the cost of supplying electricity from this source is less than zero, *after taking account of other benefits*. For example, household insulation may provide reduced consumption of heating or air conditioning, less noise and cleaner air inside the house. Deducting these benefits from the cost of supply leaves us with a negative cost. Of course the difficult question is why such options have not already been undertaken if they are so beneficial? The answers are: (a) consumers may not be aware of the benefits (they lack the information); (b) there may be capital constraints which prevent them from exploiting the options; and (c) there are costs of making changes and implementing new programmes and these act as a barrier to the process.

Question 2

Sorting the data by private cost gives Table 4A4.2.

Table 4A4.2 Supply options sorted by private cost

Sorted by private cost

Source	TWh available	Total TWh	Private cost	Environmental cost	Social cost
				UScent/kWh	
Household insulation	12	12	−0.5	0	−0.5
Energy efficient home lighting	8	20	0	0	0
Reduced losses from transmission	20	40	1.5	0.1	1.6
Existing hydro	50	90	3.0	0.3	3.3
New gas	40	130	3.0	1.5	4.5
Existing coal	40	170	3.5	2.5	6.0
Combined heat & power (CHP)	15	185	4.0	2.0	6.0
Biomass	10	195	4.0	1.7	5.7
Wind	5	200	5.0	0.2	5.2
Diesel peaking	2	202	6.0	1.5	7.5

The integrated supply curve is shown in Figure 4A4.3.

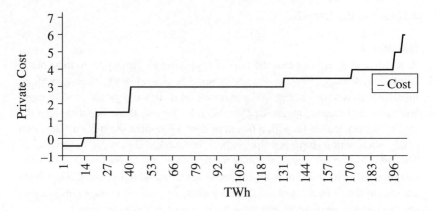

Figure 4A4.3   Private cost of electricity generation options

Question 3

Sorting the data by social cost gives Table 4A4.3.

Table 4A4.3   Supply options sorted by social cost

Source	TWh available	Total TWh	Private cost	Environmental cost	Social cost
			UScent/KWh		
Household insulation	12	12	−0.5	0	−0.5
Energy efficient home lighting	8	20	0	0	0
Reduced losses from transmission	20	40	1.5	0.1	1.6
Existing hydro	50	90	3.0	0.3	3.3
New gas	40	130	3.0	1.5	4.5
Wind	5	135	5.0	0.2	5.2
Biomass	10	145	4.0	1.7	5.7
Existing coal	40	185	3.5	2.5	6.0
Combined heat & power (CHP)	15	200	4.0	2.0	6.0
Diesel peaking	2	202	6.0	1.5	7.5

The integrated supply curve is shown in Figure 4A4.4.

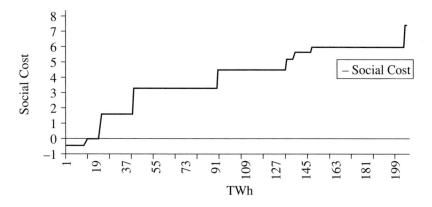

Figure 4A4.4   Social cost of electricity generation options

Question 4

If 190 TWh are to be supplied, the sources that are privately cost-effective are the following:

Household insulation
Energy efficient home lighting
Reduced losses from transmission
Existing hydro
New gas
Existing coal
Combined heat & power (CHP)
Biomass (only 50%).

If 190 TWh are to be supplied, the sources that are socially cost-effective are:

Household insulation
Energy efficient home lighting
Reduced losses from transmission
Existing hydro
New gas
Wind
Biomass
Existing coal
Combined heat & power (CHP) (Only 33%)

Thus the social supply curve includes wind whereas the private one does not. The social curve exploits all the biomass capacity and only 33 per cent of CHP, whereas the private one uses only 50 per cent of biomass capacity.

Question 5

The measures needed to achieve the social supply options could be the following:

(a) Impose a charge on each source equal to its marginal environmental cost. In that case the private sector will move to supply electricity in accordance with the social curve.

(b) Provide a subsidy to wind and to some of the biomass, paid for by a charge on the dirty fuels. The charge and subsidy could be worked out so that they induced the desired supply. The benefits of this method over (a) could be that the charges imposed on traditional fuels are lower than the environmental cost, thus imposing less of a fiscal burden.

(c) Put a restriction on supply from each source so that the social supply curve is satisfied. This is not practical when there are many producers and the market for electricity is decentralized. But with a single utility it can be done.

In addition to the above supply-side measures, DSM measures of household efficiency and reduced losses will be required. These may take the form of fiscal incentives to adopt insulation. The costs of the measures can be recovered from the benefits referred to in (a) above.

Note

1. They take a range of values from 0.1 to 2. A default value of one is often used and very crude income elasticity of the willingness to pay for health benefits of 0.35 estimate has been suggested by Krupnick et al. (1996), based on Mitchell and Carson (1986). But this *seriously* needs to be confirmed.

Cited Bibliography

Bodlund, B., E. Mills, T. Karlsson and T.B. Johansson (1989), 'The challenge of choices: technology options for the Swedish electricity sector', in T.B. Johansson, B. Bodlund and R.H. Williams (eds), *Electricity: Efficient End-use and New Generation Technologies and their Planning Implications*, Lund University Press, pp. 883–947.

Eskeland, G.S. and C. Kong (1998), 'Protecting the environment and the poor: a public goods framework applied to Indonesia', Policy Research Working Paper No. 1961, World Bank Development Research Group, Washington, DC.

Gandhi, V. (1996) *Macroeconomics and the Environment*, Washington, DC: International Monetary Fund.

Krupnick, A., K. Harrison, E. Nickell and M. Toman (1996), 'The value of health effects from ambient air quality improvements in Central and Eastern Europe', Environmental and Resource Economics,

Mitchell, R.C., and R.T. Carson 91986), Valuing Drinking Water Risk Reductions Using the Contingent Valuation Method: A Methodological Study of Risks from T.H.M. and Giardia. Report for the US Environmental Protection Agency, Washington DC.

Munasinghe, M. (1985), 'Energy pricing policy framework and exercise in developing countries', in C. Siddayao (ed.), *Criteria for Energy Pricing Policy*, London: Graham and Trotman, pp. 1–33.

Munasinghe, M. and P. Meier (1993), *Energy Policy Analysis and Modeling*, Cambridge: Cambridge University Press.

World Bank (1993), *Energy Efficiency and Conservation in the Developing World*, Washington, DC: World Bank.

5. Policies, instruments and the environment

OBJECTIVE

To present and evaluate different economic tools to internalize environmental externalities.

SUMMARY

Having set the proper macro and sectoral policies, the next task is to identify the externality problems and to design policies to address them. In the case of the environment, there is an important role for economic instruments in implementing such policies. This chapter provides the basis to design such instruments and gives examples of their application.

5.1 INTRODUCTION

The purpose of this chapter is to provide trainers, professionals and policy makers with tools, exercises and case studies they can refer to for illustrating economic tools to implement environmental policies. The chapter begins by presenting an analytical framework to which one can refer when discussing the advantages and disadvantages of the various policies and instruments typically used to internalize externalities. These instruments are reviewed in Section 5.4. Section 5.5 provides a brief review of experiences with these instruments, in particular with the implementation of economic instruments for pollution control. These experiences are reviewed with the intent of providing lessons for future use of economic instruments. The next chapter will review regulatory 'command and control' instruments.

5.2 ANALYTICAL TOOLS

The key concepts in integrating the environmental dimension in investment analysis are explained in Chapter 8 and have been alluded to earlier in Chapter 4. The analysis is based on the economic valuation of environmental impacts. To facilitate the comprehension of this chapter on economic instruments for environmental management, social costs and benefits are defined bearing in mind the externalities discussed in Chapter 4. These concepts will then be used to tailor the economic instruments for internalizing environmental externalities.

5.2.1 Externalities

Externalities arise because of market, policy or institutional failures, as explained in Chapter 4. Externalities exist when economic transactions between two or more parties result in an impact on a third party, who is not involved in the transaction. In other words, externalities exist when not *all* costs or benefits are taken into consideration by consumers and producers when conducting their consumption and production activities. A distinction is made between *positive* externalities and *negative* externalities. Positive externalities exist when the social benefits associated with a consumption or production activity are larger than the private benefits. This happens when an activity generates external benefits. Negative externalities exist when the social costs of a consumption or production activity are larger than the private costs. This happens when an activity is the source of external costs. Pollution is an obvious example of a negative externality.

5.2.2   Social Costs

In order to present the notion of social costs, a distinction has to be made between *private* and *external* costs. These concepts are defined here. Private costs are costs that are directly supported by the consumer in consumption or by the producer in production. Following from the above, external costs are costs that are borne by a consumer or producer other than the consumer or producer conducting the consumption or production activity. The social costs of an activity are the sum of its private and external costs.

As part of consumption activity, the consumer supports a large number of private costs: housing, transport, energy, time and so on. Market prices for goods and services are obviously close to private costs since these must be incurred in order to enjoy the consumption of the said good or service. Similarly, the enterprise must incur input costs (such as labour, capital, energy and so on) in order to produce output. A large number of these consumption and production activities are also the source of costs that are supported by other agents in the economy. For example, a consumer's decision to drive a car from point A to B (for which private costs are supported, for example, gasoline), is the source of costs for other individuals: noise, air pollution, contribution to traffic congestion and so on. These are costs *external* to the car user in the sense that they are not taken into account in the decision to drive or not to drive (or how many miles to drive). Similarly, a large number of enterprises discharge pollution while conducting their production activities. The damages created by this pollution are a cost that is external to the enterprise discharging the pollution – in that it does not support and therefore does not take into account this cost in its production (or location) decisions. The social costs include all private and external costs associated with any consumption and production activities.

5.2.3   Social Benefits

In order to define social benefits, a distinction has to be made between *private* and *external* benefits. Private benefits are those that are obtained directly by the consumer from consumption activities, or by the producer in production activities. External benefits are benefits obtained by a consumer or producer other than the consumer or producer conducting the consumption or production activities. The social benefit of an activity is the sum of its private and external benefits.

All consumption activities are undertaken because of the private benefits they generate: the consumer obtains satisfaction (or utility); the producer obtains profits. Some of these consumption or production activities also generate benefits to other individuals or enterprises. For example, a power plant that switches from mazut to natural gas as a source of fuel may do so solely to reduce its production costs. However, in doing so, it reduces the amount of air pollution it generates, which is a source of benefits (or reduced external costs) for those living in the vicinity of the plant. For example, these benefits may be a reduction in the health costs associated with air pollution. The social benefits include all private and external benefits associated with any consumption and production activities. Social benefits are not adjusted for their distributional impacts here. In some analyses of social environmental benefits, equity considerations may be included (Harou 1982).

5.2.4 Public Goods

Chapter 4 presented public goods as an important source of market failure. A public good is a good that has two important characteristics. First, if the good is made available to one person in the economy, then it becomes available to everyone else. In other words, if the good is made available to one person, it is not possible to exclude other persons from consuming the same quantity of the same good. *Exclusion* is not possible. Second, pure public goods are non-rival in consumption, as one person's use of the good does not diminish another person's enjoyment of it.

It is important to note that a public good is *not* defined by the nature of the supplier of the good (public authorities or private firm) but by the *technical* nature of the good. In other words, a public good can be produced by a private firm.

Typical examples of public goods are lighthouses and air quality. If a lighthouse is operational and through the light generated provides direction to a ship, it is not possible to exclude any other boat from using the same light for direction and the resource is non-rival. Similarly, air quality enjoyed by one person does not reduce in any way the quality and access for another person Equally, when the air becomes cleaner in a specific region, it becomes cleaner for everyone in that region.

The difficulty with a public environmental good is to get consumers to pay for the provision of such a good. Indeed, given that if the good is provided and it becomes available for everyone, there will be a tendency for a consumer not to reveal his/her true willingness to pay for this good. This phenomenon is usually referred to as a *free-riding* problem. As a result, there is a tendency for such a good to be undersupplied by private producers.

5.2.5 Open Access Resources

One source of market failure identified in Chapter 3 was that of a resource with undefined property rights. An open access resource, also called a common resource, is one that is available to everyone to use with uncontrolled access but is a rival good. Typical examples of open access include ocean fisheries. In many ways, the notion of open access resources is closely linked to the notion of external costs discussed above but the environmental goods are rival. For example, when a fisherman has to decide whether or not to take his boat to sea and fish, he takes into account his private costs and benefits to evaluate the profitability of his decision. However, the fisherman does not take into account the fact that if he goes fishing, there will be less fish available for other fishermen (current and future). There is therefore an external cost associated with the decision to fish. The same holds true for forestry. With open access resources, the problem is typically that *property rights* to the resource are either not defined, or if defined, not well enforced.

Using various examples below, a study of the impact of externalities, public goods and open access resources on the decisions of private consumers and producers is made. It will be shown that in the presence of externalities, private agents choose to consume or produce quantities of goods and services that are not *socially* optimal. It is on this basis that we are able to justify some form of intervention by public authorities, such as the design of an economic instrument to correct discrepancy between private and social costs and benefits.

5.3   OPTIMALITY OF PRIVATE DECISIONS

This section provides a number of examples and exercises with the purpose of studying optimality of consumption and production decisions in the presence of externalities. In each example, we show that private decisions lead to a level of consumption or production that is not socially optimal and propose economic instruments to redress the difference. These examples will ultimately lead to the notion of a *socially optimal level of pollution*.

5.3.1 Excessive Level of Production

For the benefit of the example, consider a pulp and paper plant that releases polluting emissions while producing its product. The firm has to decide how many tons of paper to produce. In a market economy, the firm will trade off the costs and benefits (revenues) associated with the production of each ton of paper. Standard microeconomics theory teaches us that the firm seeking to maximize profits will select a level of production such that marginal revenue equals marginal cost. These concepts are defined here. In a perfectly competitive industry (which is going to be assumed here), marginal revenue is simply the market price at which the firm sells each unit of its product. More formally, the marginal revenue is the contribution to total revenue associated with the production and selling of an additional unit of the good produced by the firm. In a discrete case marginal revenue is computed as follows:

$$\text{Marginal revenue } = \frac{\Delta \text{Total revenue}}{\Delta \text{Quantity produced}}$$

Marginal cost, as is customary, is assumed to be increasing with the additional level of output produced or:

$$\text{Marginal cost } = \frac{\Delta \text{Total cost}}{\Delta \text{Quantity produced}}$$

In Figure 5.1(a) at point P the optimal level of production is undertaken by the enterprise that seeks to maximize its profits. While the production of the paper is a source of costs supported by the firm, it is also the source of costs that it does not support: its activity generates a pollution source of environmental damages. Pulp and paper plants are indeed notorious for producing large quantities of water pollutants known as biological oxygen demand (BOD) and total suspended solids (TSS). There are therefore *external* environmental costs associated with the production of pulp and paper. In order to obtain the social cost of pulp and paper production, these external costs must be added to the marginal private costs. This is illustrated in Figure 5.1b. The distance between the marginal private cost and the marginal social cost may be here referred as the marginal external cost, that is the increase in external environmental cost associated with the production of an additional ton of paper. The same at an aggregate level is presented for a sector in the form of a supply curve in Figure 4.2 of the previous chapter.

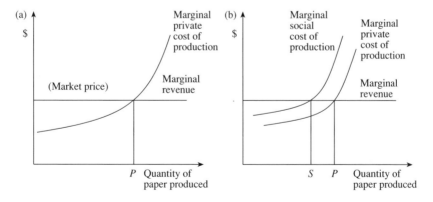

Figure 5.1   Production of paper: (a) optimal private choice; (b) optimal private choice versus optimal social choice

While the producer must trade off the marginal revenue to its own (private) marginal cost of production to determine the privately optimal quantity of paper to produce, the maximization of social welfare requires that the marginal revenue be equated to the marginal *social* cost of production. From society's point of view, *S* represents the optimal quantity of paper to be produced. One immediately notes the similarities of the supply curve drawn for a sector in the previous chapter (see Figure 4.2) and that *S* is smaller than *P*, thus indicating that the firm produces too much paper to be socially optimal.

5.3.2   Excessive Exploitation of Natural Resources

Forestry
Suppose there is a forest to which access is not controlled through community practices or clear property rights. The forest in this case is an open access resource, with villagers, households, enterprises, all having free access to the forested area. The wood is used for various purposes: construction, firewood, heating and so on. In Figure 5.2a, both the marginal private benefit and marginal private cost associated with the production (or cutting) of wood are represented. Note that a significant cost associated with wood production is typically the transport cost. For simplicity, we have once again assumed the marginal private benefit to be constant as for a competitive industry. The quantity *A* represents the number of hectares of forest that is privately optimal to cut under these circumstances.

In the decision of how many hectares of forest to cut, the decision maker (be it a single individual or a firm) ignores the fact that its decision imposes costs

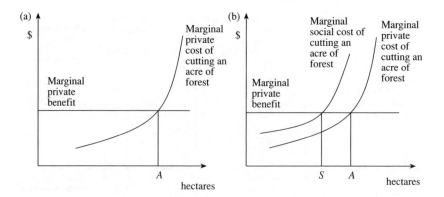

Figure 5.2   Forest exploitation: (a) optimal private choice; (b) optimal private choice versus optimal social choice

on other users of the forest. For example, for each acre of forest that the individual cuts, it means that other 'cutters' must go further away in the forest to obtain the wood, thus increasing transport cost. The decision maker may also ignore forest values other than the value of the logs obtained from the forest. For example, the forest may serve as a habitat for a large number of species, or it may prevent soil erosion and regulate water flows. In other words, there are external costs associated with cutting acres of forest: the marginal social cost is greater than the marginal private cost. In Figure 5.2b, S represents the socially optimal amount of hectares of forest to cut. As shown, decision makers that seek to maximize their own private net benefit (defined as benefit minus cost) will cut too many hectares of forest. The forest is overexploited.

Fisheries
The case of fisheries is conceptually similar to the forestry case presented above. Typically, fisheries are open access resources. In Figure 5.2b, *A* and *S* could stand for the privately and socially optimal amount of fish to be captured in tons, respectively. Our conclusion would be that the fisheries are overexploited. This appears to be the case indeed in many parts of the world. A particular characteristic of fisheries that exacerbates the overexploitation of resources is that fishing activities, throughout the world, are often subsidized, in various ways, by national governments. Our economic tools allow us to examine the impact of such subsidies. Subsidies reduce the private cost of fishing. This is represented in Figure 5.3a by a reduction (or a shift to the right) of the marginal private cost of fishing. *F* without subsidies is the quantity of fish that is privately optimal to capture. As can be seen, the immediate impact of subsidies is to *increase* the quantity of fish that is privately optimal to capture.

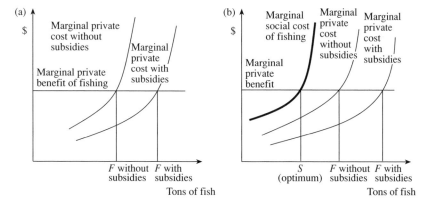

Figure 5.3   Fisheries exploitation: (a) optimal private choice with and without subsidies; (b) optimal private choice versus optimal social choice

As shown in Figure 5.3b, subsidies can only make an already bad situation even worse: subsidies exacerbate the difference between the private and social optimal amount of fish to capture. Such phenomena are also often observed in the energy and agricultural sectors. An immediate partial remedy to this situation is the removal of the subsidies which would reduce the fish catch to F without subsidies. However, the optimal social catch is S if external costs are included.

Underground drinking water

Suppose that a community obtains its drinking water for a groundwater well and that substitutes are available only at a very high cost. In Figure 5.4a, the marginal private benefit of consuming water is illustrated. Observe that this marginal benefit is declining as the amount of water consumption increases. This reflects the principle of diminishing marginal utility, which is often assumed in economics. Under this assumption, the first unit of a good gives more satisfaction (utility, or benefit) than the second unit, the second more than the third and so on. First assume that households have free access to the water and can consume any amount of water they desire at zero costs. In this situation, they will consume an amount of water W where the private marginal benefit of water consumption is zero.

Of course, this ignores the fact that there is a marginal social cost associated with the consumption of water. In particular, a cubic metre of water consumed by a household represents one less cubic metre of water to be consumed by another (current or future) household. Water is a rival good. In Figure 4.4b the marginal social cost of water consumption is shown and indicates that water is overconsumed.

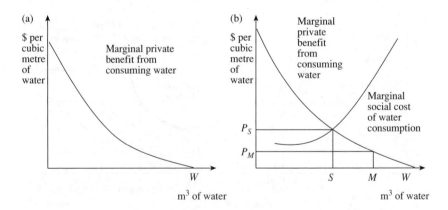

Figure 5.4   Consumption of water from groundwater well: (a) optimal private choice; (b) optimal private choice versus optimal social choice

It may be presumed that in such situations, public authorities would introduce a price for each unit of water being consumed (this price could be per cubic metre or per litre of water consumed and is shown as P_m in Figure 5.4b). The introduction of a price would obviously reduce the quantity of water (M) that is privately optimal to consume. However, in many circumstances, it has been observed that the price that consumers have to pay for water consumption fails to reflect the true social cost associated with water consumption. In other words, as illustrated in Figure 5.4b, the price set up by the authorities is below the price that would induce households to consume the socially optimal amount of water, S. The amount of water consumed with the price P_m is M, which is more than the optimal quantity S, which corresponds to the socially optimal price P_s. For numerous reasons, pricing water at its true social marginal value has been proven to be difficult for policy makers on equity grounds.

Water quality

Consider a number of individuals living around a polluted lake. Because of the degraded quality of the water in the lake, recreational activities (such as swimming, boating, fishing and so on) will be adversely affected, hence there is an insufficient provision of public goods in this case. Each individual could invest in cleaning up the lake so as to restore some of these recreational activities. In Figure 5.5a, the marginal cost of cleaning up the lake is depicted, in dollars per cubic metre of water cleaned. The larger the quantity of water cleaned up, the higher the marginal cost of cleaning up. The cleaner the lake becomes, the smaller the marginal private benefit associated with cleaning up an additional cubic metre of water. Any given individual will clean up the lake

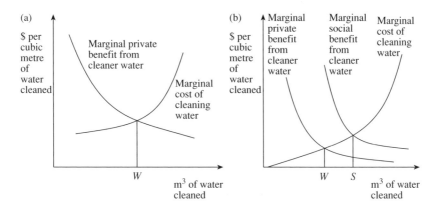

Figure 5.5   Improving environmental quality: (a) optimal private choice; (b) optimal private choice versus optimal social choice

until the marginal cost of cleaning up equals the marginal private benefit. The quantity *W* of water would thus be cleaned up.

However, if the lake becomes cleaner for one individual, it also becomes cleaner for everyone enjoying recreational activities from the lake: a cleaner lake is a public good. In other words, the marginal *social* benefit associated with cleaning up the lake is larger than the marginal *private* benefit. As shown in Figure 5.5b, *S* represents the *socially* optimal amount of water to clean up. Observe that *S* is larger than *W*. Private decisions lead to an *insufficient* amount of a public good, in this case clean water, being provided.

5.3.3   Efficient Level of Pollution

As for the production of any other goods and services, environmental protection or pollution control involves costs and benefits. Costs are measured in terms of the various inputs that must be devoted to pollution control. Benefits are measured in terms of the reduction in damages (health damages, ecological damages and so on) that is allowed by reducing the emissions of pollution. Costs and benefits must be traded off. To do so, the notions of marginal abatement cost and marginal damage need to be defined. The marginal abatement cost (MAC) is the cost of reducing pollution emissions by an additional unit. It is generally assumed that the MAC increases as abatement increases. In other words, the more one abates pollution, the more costly it becomes to reduce pollution by an additional unit. The marginal damage (MD) is the damage caused by an additional unit of pollution. It is generally assumed that the MD increases as pollution increases. It is also generally assumed that the environment has the capacity to absorb a limited amount of pollution without adversely affecting its quality. This represents the 'sink' function of the environment.

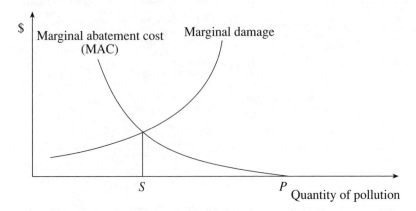

Figure 5.6   Optimal level of pollution

Facing no incentives to reduce its level of pollution, a polluter would produce the amount P of pollution, shown in Figure 5.6, where the marginal abatement cost is zero. However, the efficient, or socially optimal level of pollution is determined at the intersection of the marginal abatement cost and marginal damage functions: S is the optimal level of pollution. Left to themselves, polluters thus produce too much pollution. It is on this basis that interventions by the regulator may be justified. In the next section, the question of whether or not this intervention is indeed justified, and the various forms it may take is examined more precisely.

5.4   ENVIRONMENTAL INSTRUMENTS

The previous section provided a discussion of the basic concepts and ways in which they may be used for the optimal management of environmental pollution and natural resources. This section discusses the different economic instruments in greater detail.

Various instruments may be used by policy makers to induce consumers and producers to undertake a level of activity (be it pollution control, fishing, reforestation and so on) that coincides with the level that maximizes social welfare. These include the definition of property rights, the imposition of standards and the use of economic and financial instruments, among others. A large part of the literature in environmental economics is devoted to comparing the relative merits of these various instruments and how to tailor them to the specific policy case. In order to choose among these instruments, a number of criteria have to be considered, among them: cost-effectiveness, dynamic incentives directly related to pollution or overexploitation, implementation and flexibility. The application of these criteria is discussed in Section 5.4.4.

5.4.1 Property Rights

We have observed previously that consumers and producers make decisions on the basis of the private costs and benefits they are facing. However, social costs and benefits may differ from the private costs and benefits faced by consumers and producers. Private agents base their decision on private costs as opposed to social costs because they do not have to support in any way the external costs associated with their consumption and production activities. Similarly, they base their decision on private benefits as opposed to social benefits because they cannot extract a payment from the recipients of the external benefits.

The next question to ask is the following: why do consumers and producers not have to pay for the external costs their activities generate? Similarly, why can they not extract payment from those enjoying the external benefits? The answer to these questions often lies in the absence of clear property rights. Since many aspects of the environment, for example, a typical fishery or forest, do not belong to any private parties, there is no one to compensate for using these goods. The price of using the environment, a public good, or an open access resource is effectively nil. If these goods were to belong to private parties, a price would have to be paid for using these resources. The simple solution to externalities would therefore appear to be to *privatize property rights.*

However, a further crucial question is raised: to whom should private property rights be allocated? To those generating the external costs (such as the polluters), or to those whose welfare is adversely affected by the external costs (such as those whose health is damaged by the pollution)? Is it possible to allocate the property rights to ensure that the social optimum will be reached? In a classic article, Ronald Coase (1960) showed that in the absence of transaction costs, the social optimum will be reached (for example, the optimal level of pollution, the optimal amount of trees cut, of land protected, of reforestation, of environmental protection and so on) whether property rights are initially allocated to polluters or to those suffering from the pollution. This result has become known as the *Coase theorem.* This is illustrated here with the use of the example of a polluted lake given earlier.

Suppose that the lake is polluted because a plant is discharging pollution into it. The water of the lake is used for consumption and irrigation by a community living by the lake. Suppose that the benefit for the plant to discharge its pollution in the lake is $1,000. It would cost $1,000 for the plant to stop discharging in the lake by reducing its pollution or by discharging in some other location. Suppose that the benefit for the community of using the lake is $1,200. If the community had to stop using the water of the lake, it would have to pay $1,200 to obtain water from some other sources. Given these values, the social optimum in this case requires that the lake be used by the community for consumption and irrigation. It is in these uses that the lake provides the largest benefit. The Coase theorem tells us that if we allow negotiation between the plant owner and the community, the lake will be used for consumption and irrigation by the community, irrespective of who owns the property right over the lake.

First suppose that the property right is allocated to the polluter. Since it would cost $1,000 for the plant to stop using the lake to discharge its pollution, the plant would accept any compensation above $1,000 to stop discharging in the lake. On the other hand, it costs $1,200 for the community not to use the water of the lake. The community would be willing to pay up to $1,200 to be able to use the water from the lake and still be better off. Since the community is willing to pay more than what the plant would require to stop its discharges, there is room for negotiation. Negotiation will result in the community compensating the polluter to induce him/her to stop polluting the lake. The lake will be used for consumption and irrigation by the community. The optimum is reached even if the property right was allocated to the polluter.

Suppose instead that the lake belongs to the community. Since it would cost $1,200 for the community to stop using the lake, the community would accept a compensation greater than $1,200 to stop using the water of the lake. However, the plant would be willing to pay at most $1,000 to obtain the right to discharge in the lake. There is in this case no possibility for negotiation and the lake will be used for consumption and irrigation by the community.

The Coase theorem tells us that the optimum is reached whoever is allocated the property right. For this result to be obtained, however, important assumptions must be satisfied. First, it must be possible to precisely define the property right. Second, this property right must be enforceable and transferable. Indeed, the property right is of no meaning if abuse of the property right by a third party cannot be prevented. Third, parties to the transaction must be well defined. This may be particularly difficult when today's actions affect future generations; by definition, these cannot be part of current negotiation. Fourth, those owning the property rights must be able to capture *all* values associated with the environmental asset they own. In the forestry sector for example, this is generally a problem since the property right is typically defined solely over the wood value of the forest, and not over the entire environmental value of the forest. Finally, transaction costs must be small. When the number of polluters and pollutees is large, this condition will likely not be satisfied.

For all the above reasons, the conditions under which the allocation of private property rights may restore social efficiency restrict the applicability of property rights in practice. Hence it is necessary to look at other ways of achieving the optimal social solution.[1]

5.4.2 Command and Control Regulation

The traditional approach to environmental protection has often relied on command and control instruments. The regulator *commands* a desired behaviour, typically by imposing a limit on the amount of emissions that a polluter can produce. These limits are generally called *emissions standards*. The regulator then *controls* and enforces compliance with the chosen standard. Under this regime, the incentives for pollution control take the form of penalties or sanctions that the polluter is faced with if he/she does not comply with the command.

The laws, regulations and institutions required to implement command and control instruments are discussed in Chapter 6. In this section, the setting of environmental standards needed to implement this type of instrument is discussed from an economic perspective. A classification of regulatory instruments for different types of environmental issues with their limitations in comparison with economic instruments is also presented.

Standards are the predominant means for direct regulation of environmental quality throughout most of the developed world. They define environmental targets and establish the permissible amount or concentration of particular substances or discharges into air, water, land, or consumer products. Types of standards include: ambient environmental quality standards, effluent or emission standards, technology-based standards, performance standards, product standards and process standards (see Box 5.1). Standards also may include technological specifications for the performance or design of equipment or facilities and the standardization of sampling or analytical methods. In some cases, a

---

BOX 5.1   DEFINITIONS OF STANDARDS

Criterion   Scientific information (for example, concentration-effect or dose-effect data) used as a basis for setting environmental quality objectives. It assesses the risk to a given victim and the amount of damage caused by a known amount of pollution or dose of exposure.

Objective   A designated concentration of a pollutant in an environmental medium or a narrative statement (for example, adequate to support aquatic life, zero pollutant discharge). The objective is based on scientific criteria, local natural conditions, and socioeconomic and environmental factors.

Standard A legally defined regulatory instrument for limiting pollution. Several types of standards are commonly employed:

a. *Ambient environmental quality standard*   Establishes the highest allowable concentration of specified pollutants in the ambient air or water. For example, an ambient standard for a specific river may require that dissolved oxygen, averaged over a 24-hour period at a selected river mile point, must not fall below 4 parts per million on more than one day per year.
b. *Effluent or emission standard*   Establishes the legal ceiling on the total quantity or concentration of a pollutant discharged from a pollution source (for example, mg/litre, grams/24 hours, kg/ton). Effluent standards may include maximum effluent limitations for specified time periods (for example, maximum for

any one day, maximum averages of daily values for 30 consecutive days, or for one year) and monitoring requirements.

c. *Technology-based standard* A type of effluent standard that specifies a specific technology a firm must use to comply with environmental laws and regulations. For example, a utility may be required to use a scrubber to control sulphur oxide emissions.

d. *Performance standard* A type of effluent standard that defines a performance measure (for example, volume or concentration of a pollutant in a discharge, percentage pollutant removal to be achieved) and allows dischargers the flexibility to select the best means to meet this standard. For example, automobile companies may be required to develop a technology for new automobiles that limit tailpipe emissions to no more than 0.41 grams of hydrocarbons, 12.4 grams of carbon monoxide, and 1.0 grams of nitrogen oxides per mile.

e. *Product standard* Establishes a legal ceiling on the total quantity or concentration of pollutants that can be discharged into the environment per unit of product output (kg per 1,000 kg of product). Product standards also prohibit the addition of certain substances to products, for example, to eliminate lead discharges from the burning of gasoline, authorities prohibit the addition of lead to gasoline.

f. *Process standard* Limits the emission of pollutants associated with specific manufacturing processes (for example, the mandatory replacement of mercury cells by diaphragm cells to prevent mercury emissions from chlor-alkali manufacture).

regulator takes into account the transfer of pollutants from one medium to another as well as total environmental exposure to specific pollutants in determining ambient standards or discharge limits. Each of the various types of standards is used to provide a reference for evaluation or target for legislative action and control. Generally, standards are established by central governments. In some instances, central governments set out framework regulations to be carried out by local, state, or regional authorities. Subnational standards can be more stringent than those of the central government.

The granting or withholding of permits, licences, or other authorizations is another important tool for controlling pollution. The permits or licences are generally tied to an air or water quality standard and may be subject to the fulfilment of specific conditions such as compliance with a code of practice, selection of the location that minimizes environmental and economic impacts, installation of a treatment plant or pollution control equipment within a certain time period, or adoption of other environmentally protective measures. One major advantage of permits and licences is that they facilitate the enforcement of environmental programmes by including in one document all of a facility's pollution control obligations. Other advantages are that they may be withdrawn or suspended according to the needs of the national economy or other social interests and often require a fee that can be used to cover the costs of the pollution control programme. None the less, the use of permits and licences normally involves regular monitoring and facility reporting.

The command and control approach potentially gives the regulator maximum authority to control where and how resources will be spent to achieve environmental objectives. Under ideal conditions, the regulator would be able to identify precisely the marginal abatement cost and marginal damage functions characterizing each and every polluter, and would impose a ceiling on emissions of each polluter corresponding to the socially optimal level of pollution. In Figure 5.7, firm 1 would be facing a standard equal to S_1 and firm 2 equal to S_2. The regulator has to allocate the distribution of emission between firms in an optimal manner. The major advantage of this approach is that it provides the regulator a reasonable degree of predictability about how much pollution levels will be reduced.

In practice, however, there is great uncertainty and the regulator does not know firm-specific marginal abatement cost and marginal damage functions, whereas the firm itself knows them better. As a result, emissions standards in practice share the following principal characteristics: (i) standards are defined on the basis of the best available or economically achievable technology; (ii) standards are often defined and tailored to specific industries (for the same pollutant, standards are typically different across industries); (iii) standards are often different for old sources of pollution and new sources of pollution, generally being more stringent for new sources; (iv) standards are usually uniform and defined in terms of allowable emissions per unit of output.

Although command and control strategies have made substantial progress in reducing pollution, this approach has been criticized for not achieving various legislative mandates and deadlines and for being economically inefficient and difficult to enforce. These strategies are inefficient for the regulatory agency, which must have detailed information concerning production processes and the suitability of various pollution control devices. With diverse industries, it is extremely expensive and time-consuming to obtain the necessary information and expertise on each industry.

Other problems with this approach are the high costs for pollution control that leave little opportunity to take advantage of various forms of flexibility in meeting given ambient quality standards so as to be cost-effective. Although

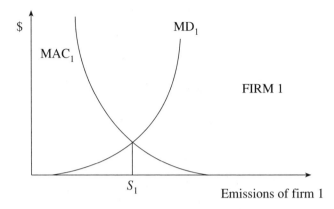

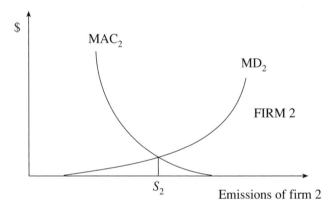

Figure 5.7 Optimal standards

standards may be applied differently depending on the age or type of facility, most polluters using the same production process are required to meet the same standards. Polluters who could reduce pollution at a lower cost are not given the opportunity. There is little flexibility for polluters who already have invested in some type of pollution control system. The command and control approach provides little incentive for innovation in pollution control technology once the standards are achieved. Moreover, this approach is insufficient or ineffective in addressing many of the more recent pollution control and waste management problems confronting environmental managers, such as non-point source pollution, for instance urban and agricultural run-off, solid waste disposal, and global environmental problems such as stratospheric ozone depletion and climate change. The advantages and disadvantages of the above regulatory instruments for different media are summarized in Box 5.2.

BOX 5.2 REGULATORY INSTRUMENTS

Regulatory Instruments	Existing applications					Advantages	Disadvantages
	Surface water pollution control	Ground water protection	Air pollution control	Solid waste management	Hazardous waste management		
Ambient environmental quality standards	X	X	X			Provide basis for evaluating effectiveness of existing controls	Require highly technical knowledge of pollutants' effects
Effluent and emission standards	X		X			Provide maximum government control	Involve high monitoring and enforcement costs
Technology-based effluent/emission standards	X	X	X			Provide maximum government control	Allow no flexibility in control technology
Performance-based effluent/emission standards	X	X	X			Promote cost savings Allow flexibility in control technology	Involve high monitoring and enforcement costs
Product/process standards	X	X	X			Eliminate or limit emission of pollutants prior to production	Require close substitutes for banned products

				Advantages	Disadvantages
Permits and licences	X	X	X	Require compliance with standards prior to facility operation Facilitate enforcement of effluent and emission standards Allow government to withdraw or suspend according to national needs	Involve high monitoring and enforcement costs
Land and Water use controls	X	X	X	Prevent inappropriate siting of polluting activities	Allow government to withdraw or suspend according to national needs Vulnerable to local political and economic pressures

5.4.3   Economic, Fiscal and Financial Instruments

Some regulatory measures also qualify as economic instruments. Box 5.3 provides a listing of the main economic instruments together with the related fiscal and financial instruments. Broadly speaking economic instruments are

---

BOX 5.3   ECONOMIC, FISCAL AND FINANCIAL INSTRUMENTS

Economic instruments

Charge systems	Pollution charges
	User charges
	Access fees
	Road tolls
	Administrative charges
Property	Ownership rights
	traditional management regimes
	land titles
	water rights
	mining rights
	Use rights
	licensing
	concession
Market creation	Tradable emissions permits
	Tradable catch quotas
	Tradable land permits
Liability system	Legal liability
	Natural resource damage liability
	Liability insurance
Bonds and deposit system	Environmental performance bond
	Land reclamation bond
	Deposit refund system

Fiscal instruments
Input taxes, Product taxes, Export taxes, Import tariffs, Tax differentiation, Royalties and resources taxes, Land-use taxes, Investment tax credits, Accelerated depreciation, Subsidies

Financial instruments
Financial subsidies, Soft loans, Grants, Location/relocation incentives, Subsidized interest, Revolving funds, Sectoral funds

ones that act *directly* on the pollution, whereas fiscal and financial instruments provide economic incentives through their effect on the prices paid for the inputs or received for the outputs to a production process. An analytical framework to discuss these environmental instruments was presented earlier and is now applied.

Pollution charges

The principle supporting the use of pollution charges, that is a charge (or price, or fee) per unit of pollution, is relatively simple. It was pointed out above that consumers and producers base their decisions on private costs and benefits as opposed to social costs and benefits. The private agents do not have to support the external costs associated with their activities. In the case of external benefits, they cannot extract payments from those enjoying these external benefits, since consumers and producers do not have to pay for the external costs they generate. The principle behind pollution charges and tradable emissions permits is simply to create a price equivalent to these external costs.

Let us first illustrate how pollution charges can be established. In Figure 5.8, upon facing a price P_1 for each unit of pollution that it discharges, the firm has a choice between reducing its pollution or paying the price P_1. A profit-maximizing enterprise will reduce its pollution up to the point where the price to be paid per unit of pollution is just equated to its marginal abatement cost. Facing a price P_1, the firm will reduce its emissions from Q_3 to Q_1. Facing a lower price (P_2), the firm will invest less in pollution abatement, and reduce its pollution only to Q_2.

The level of the charge, which equates the marginal abatement cost and the marginal damage functions is referred to as the *Pigovian tax* (after Alfred Pigou

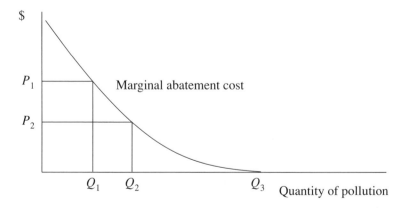

Figure 5.8   Impact of pollution charge on firm's pollution

who first worked on this issue). Under ideal conditions, the regulator would be able to identify precisely the marginal abatement cost and marginal damage functions characterizing each and every polluter, and would impose a Pigovian tax corresponding to the optimal level of pollution for each and every polluter. In Figure 5.9, firm 1 would be facing a price P_1 for every unit of pollution it produces, and firm 2 would face a price P_2.

   In practice however, firm specific marginal abatement cost and marginal damage functions are not known to the regulator. As a result, pollution charges tend to be uniform: a given pollutant will be charged the same price within given geographical areas across industrial sectors.

Tradable permits
Under this approach, markets can be created in which actors can buy 'rights' for producing pollution or where they can sell these 'rights' to other actors.

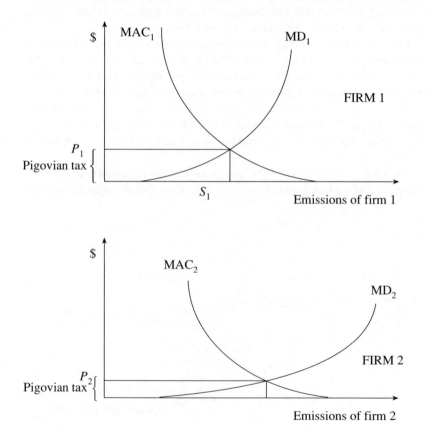

Figure 5.9   Differentiated Pigovian tax

Under a marketable or tradable permit system, the responsible authority determines a target level of environmental quality defined as an allowable level of emissions or an ambient environmental quality standard for a given region. This level of environmental quality is then translated into a total number of allowable emissions that can be discharged. Discharge rights are allocated to firms in the form of permits. Permits are then distributed to firms with each permit allowing the owner to discharge a specified amount of pollution. This permit to discharge may be transferred from one source to another. The demand for the permits is derived from the discharger's marginal costs of treatment. The discharger will reduce pollution or treat waste as long as the marginal cost of treatment is less than or equal to the cost of buying a permit. Hence, given a similar aggregate emissions target, the level of the (uniform) pollution charge necessary to achieve the target would be the same as the equilibrium price of a permit, assuming that the market for permits is perfectly competitive. An example is provided in Box 5.4 for three plants with different marginal abatement costs (MACs). The total abatement cost (TAC) of uniform reduction is 455 while the least cost way of getting the same reduction results is a cost of 420, which can be achieved with permit trading.

Assume that the regulator wishes to reach a given level of aggregate emissions by means of pollution charges. Lacking information on the MAC, it is not immediately clear what should be the level of the charge that will allow the pollution reduction objective to be reached. For two different firms with different MAC curves, as depicted in Figure 5.10, and for a given charge P, emissions are going to be Q_1, if the marginal abatement cost is MAC_1, and Q_2 if it is MAC_2. None of these may be the desired pollution standard. It has been suggested that the regulator may use an iterative approach by which it keeps adjusting the level of the charge until the target level of pollution is reached. A difficulty with this approach is that knowing the nature of the process into which the regulator is engaged, firms are going to adjust their emissions in a strategic manner. Of course, this difficulty does not exist with tradable permits since by definition the number of tradable permits determines exactly the level of aggregate emissions.

With permits, the problem is different. The regulator knows the reduction in emissions with certainty but does not know the costs of the reductions with certainty. Hence a target reduction could be easy to achieve, or may impose a heavy burden on industry. Another issue with permits is that of trading between pollutants whose emissions have very different environmental impacts. In a situation where environmental damages are not a function of the location of the polluter, this does not create problems. However, in many instances damages are a function of the location of the polluter. In such a situation, tradable permits may give rise to 'hot spots' of pollution.

BOX 5.4   COST-EFFECTIVENESS, PERMIT TRADING AND POLLUTION CHARGES

Suppose there are three plants characterized by the following MAC.

	MAC_1	MAC_2	MAC_3
6	0	0	0
5	15	40	20
4	30	75	40
3	50	110	75
2	75	150	120
1	100	200	170
0	150	260	230

At present 18 units of pollution are emitted. The objective is to reduce aggregate emissions to 9.

Solution 1 : A uniform reduction in pollution for each plant to 3
Then, TAC for each plant is the following: $TAC_1 = 95$
$TAC_2 = 225$ → TAC = 455
$TAC_3 = 135$

Solution 2: Allowing permits to be traded, hence minimizing total abatement cost

Unit 1:   1 : 15   Unit 6:   1 : 50
Unit 2:   3 : 20   Unit 7:   1 : 75
Unit 3:   1 : 30   Unit 5:   2 : 75
Unit 4:   2 : 40   Unit 9:   3 : 75
Unit 5:   3 : 40

Then, TAC for each plant is the following: $TAC_1 = 170$
$TAC_2 = 115$ → TAC = 420
$TAC_3 = 135$

If 9 permits are issued, 3 to each polluter, firm 1 will sell one permit to firm 2 at a price between 50 and 75 and the least cost solution is obtained. Note also that the marginal abatement cost for the last unit in the least cost case is the same in all 3 firms – that is, 75. This can also be the tax per unit that generates the least cost solution.

There are two basic approaches to implementing a marketable discharge permit system: government auction of permits or free distribution of permits to dischargers followed by trading among dischargers to establish a market price. Under the first approach, permits are sold for a single market-clearing price, which might be the lowest accepted bid, the highest rejected bid, or some value

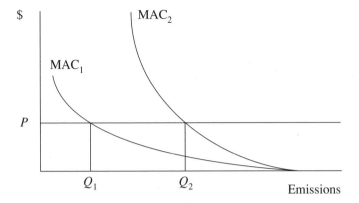

Figure 5.10   Marginal abatement cost curves

in between. Alternatively, the permits are allocated to the highest bidders. Under the second approach, permits might be distributed initially to duplicate the effect of uniform removal regulations or to allocate permits to communities on a basis such as population or to firms based on value added. Such an allocation is called 'grandfathering'. After the initial distribution, the method for exchange of the permits could be a centralized market or bilateral exchanges.

Other charge systems

User charges are direct payments for the costs of collective or public treatment of pollution. They are used most often in the collection and treatment of municipal solid waste and for the discharge of wastewater into sewers. With respect to water pollution control, for example, user charges are fees paid to water authorities to allow discharges of industrial wastes into public sewers. Through these charges, which are related to the quality and characteristics of the effluent, the public authority receiving the waste discharge is compensated for the effort involved in its disposal. At the same time, the scale of the charges should ensure that the plant has an economic incentive to improve the quality of the effluent. This approach, however, is not appropriate when disposing of certain toxic pollutants (for example, mercury) that should never be permitted to enter watercourses. Another application of user charges is in the area of vehicle-related taxes and charges.

Product charges are fees added to the price of products or product inputs that cause pollution in either the manufacturing or consumption phase or for which a special disposal system has been established. They function like effluent and emission charges in that they allow users to determine their own cost-effective means for reducing pollution. For example, all members of the

European Community (EC), except Denmark, have levied a product charge on lubricating oils as a result of a 1975 EC directive to adopt measures to recycle waste oil. The system involves a tax on lubricating oil and subsidies provided for recycling oil. In Germany, this programme was successful until the country encountered problems with illegal dumping. In France and Italy, where the systems have less of an incentive effect, oil collections have at least doubled since the beginning of the programmes. In Norway and Sweden, other product charges connected to environmental goals include charges on non-returnable containers, batteries, lubricating oil, fertilizers and pesticides.

The effectiveness of a charge on polluting products or product inputs will depend on the availability of substitutes. For example, where input costs are a small fraction of total costs, doubling or tripling the price through an input tax is unlikely to have a significant effect on consumption unless there are suitably priced substitutes. If less polluting substitutes are available, small increases in input prices may induce substitution and innovation over the longer term. Revenues from product charges can be used to treat pollution from the product directly, to provide for recycling of the used product, or for other budgetary purposes. Product charges also fail to provide an incentive for reducing emissions at the 'end of the pipe'. This issue is discussed further in Section 5.5.3. In general, however, we note charging inputs and outputs presumptively for emissions *is feasible* and has been carried out with beneficial environmental effects in many countries.

Administrative charges are fees paid to authorities for such services as chemical registration or the implementation and enforcement of environmental regulations. Usually they are a component of direct regulation and are intended primarily to finance the licensing and control activities of pollution authorities. In Norway, for example, these charges are levied to finance the registration and control activity for fish farming and agricultural pollution, control of emissions from industrial sources, and the licensing of chemical products. In some cases, administrative charges can have an incentive purpose as well. For example, a registration charge based on the relative hazards of pesticides or other chemicals may be imposed to encourage the use of less harmful products. In practice, administrative charges are similar to product charges in that the levels of such fees are usually low and do not provide significant incentives for changes in purchasing patterns. Revenues from administrative charges are usually added to the general budget rather than to the budget of the pollution authority involved.

Tax differentiation is used to promote consumption of products that are environmentally safe. This instrument involves a positive charge being levied on a polluting product and a negative charge, or subsidy, on a cleaner alternative. It is used primarily in the context of transport to discourage consumer purchases of polluting vehicles or fuels. Differential taxation of leaded and unleaded gasoline is a common practice throughout Europe. In the Netherlands, for example, unleaded gasoline is taxed at 0.1 ECU per 100 litres (about US$0.004 per gallon) and leaded gasoline at 1.74 ECU per 100 litres (about US$0.08 per gallon 1989). Other taxes are levied on diesel and other fuel oils. The fuel taxes are designed to have some incentive effects. Generally, the levels of the charge are calculated so as to keep the total financial effects budget neutral.

5.4.4   Choosing Among Instruments

Should we prefer uniform emissions standards, uniform prices, or tradable emissions permits to achieve the desired target? We have listed above a number of criteria that can be used to choose between instruments. We review these three instruments in view of these criteria.

*   *Cost-effectiveness*   It is easy to demonstrate that uniform pollution charges and tradable permits allow the desired objective to be reached at a lower cost than uniform emissions standards (see Box 5.2).
*   *Dynamic incentives*   certainly exist under economic instruments. Indeed, since the firm has to pay a price for every unit of pollution it produces, or alternatively must buy a permit for every unit of pollution it produces, the firm always has the incentive to reduce its emissions so as to reduce its total tax payments or to sell permits it no longer requires. Such incentives are much reduced under command and control since under this policy, the firm can pollute up to the standard free of charge. Once it complies with the standard, it has little incentive to do any better.
*   *Implementation issues*   None of the instruments possesses a distinctive advantage in terms of implementability. In all cases, firms must report their level of emissions (self-reporting), the regulator must verify the accuracy of these reports, it must monitor the firms, measure the firm's emissions, and enforce either the standards, misreporting by the firm, or compliance with the number of permits held by the firm.
*   *Flexibility*   While there is a tendency to group together economic instruments, tradable permits may benefit from an important advantage over pollution charges in terms of *flexibility*. Indeed, with pollution charges, the regulator must intervene to change the level of the charge in order to maintain aggregate emissions at their desired level when economic conditions are changing. For example, in times of increased economic activity, the pollution charge may have to be increased so as to keep aggregate emissions constant. With tradable permits, by definition aggregate emissions will remain constant; however, the price of a permit will reflect the intensity of the demand and adjust itself through market forces. There is in this case no need for the regulator to intervene. On the

other hand, for tradable permits to work efficiently, the market for permits must be relatively competitive (with a large number of firms trading the permits). This condition may not always be satisfied.

While pollution charges and tradable permits appear considerably superior, command and control has overwhelmingly been the preferred method of intervention. A large number of reasons may explain this phenomenon. Economic instruments have often been perceived as a 'licence to pollute' as opposed to a genuine instrument by which social optimality may be restored. The impact of economic instruments on the competitiveness of enterprises has also been a much-debated topic.

5.4.5   Disclosure Instruments

The above approaches have relied heavily on economic incentives for environmental regulation focusing exclusively on interactions between the regulator and the firm. However, recent research has suggested important roles for two additional 'players': the community and the market.

Recent evidence from Asia, Latin America and North America suggests that neighbouring *communities* can have a powerful influence on factories' environmental performance. Communities that are richer, better educated, and more organized find many ways of enforcing environmental norms. Where formal regulators are present, communities use the political process to influence the tightness of enforcement. Where formal regulators are absent or ineffective, 'informal regulation' is implemented through community groups or non-governmental organizations. The agents of informal regulation vary from country to country: local religious institutions, social organizations, community leaders, citizens' movements or politicians. However, these agents usually follow a quite similar process. Factories negotiate directly with local communities, responding to social norms and explicit or implicit threats of social, political or physical sanctions if they fail to reduce the damages caused by their emissions. In countries as diverse as China, Brazil, Indonesia and the United States, much of the variation in factories' environmental performance is explained by inter-community variation in income, education and bargaining power.

Factories operate in local, national and international *markets*, where many agents can affect revenues and costs. Environmental considerations now affect the decisions of many of these agents. In both industrial and developing countries, environmentalism in the middle and upper classes is a significant factor in consumer decisions. With the worldwide advent of environmental legislation, investors are also scrutinizing environmental performance. Among other factors, they have to weigh the potential for financial losses from regulatory penalties and liability settlements. In recent years, the importance of investor interest has been increased by the growth of new stock markets and the internationalization of investment. For similar reasons, international and local suppliers of financing, industrial equipment and engineering services are increasingly reluctant to do business with flagrant polluters.

Recent evidence from both the OECD and developing countries suggests that environmental reputation matters for firms whose expected costs or revenues are affected by judgements of environmental performance by customers, suppliers and stockholders. Many factors can affect firms' evaluation of their environmental reputation, including company size, export orientation and multinational ownership. For reputation-sensitive companies, public certification of good or bad performance may translate to large expected gains or losses over time corresponding to changes in market share. Investors are aware of this and consequently firms with a high level of pollution intensity or non-compliance may find their stock value affected. Several studies from the United States and Canada have suggested that gains from 'good environmental news' or losses from 'bad news' can be of the order of 1 to 2 per cent of the stock market value. Moreover there is also some evidence that such changes motivate firms to take action to reduce emissions (World Bank 2000).

Once we introduce a world of multiple agents and multiple incentives, as depicted in Box 5.5, we must also rethink the regulator's appropriate role in pollution management. No longer is this role confined to producing, monitoring and enforcing rules and standards. Instead, the regulator can gain leverage through non-traditional programmes, which harness the power of communities

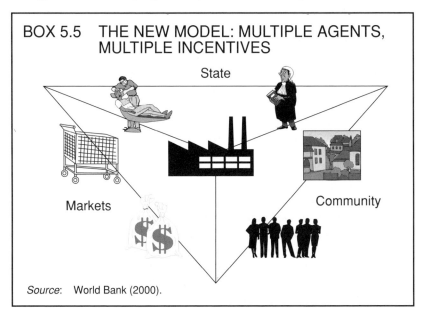

BOX 5.5   THE NEW MODEL: MULTIPLE AGENTS, MULTIPLE INCENTIVES

State

Markets

Community

Source: World Bank (2000).

and markets. Within the 'triangular' regulatory framework, for example, there is ample room for information-oriented approaches such as voluntary participation/compliance programmes and public disclosure of factories' environmental performance.

When markets and community are taken into account, together with the state, a different model of regulation emerges. Regulation, discussed in the following chapter, for developing countries may incorporate the following five key features:

- *Information intensity.* Effective pollution management by the state is impossible unless regulators have reliable data, integrated information systems and the capacity to set priorities which reflect comparative benefits and costs. Markets and communities need timely, accurate, public information to make appropriate assessments of factories' environmental performance. An effective regulatory agency will therefore allocate fewer resources at the margin to conventional enforcement and more to the generation and distribution of appropriate information products.
- *Orchestration, not dictation.* A pollution control agency is only one player in the environmental performance game. Agency activities, which influence polluters *indirectly*, through other agents, may be as important as direct enforcement. Potentially high-leverage programmes include community environmental education; public disclosure of factory performance ratings; voluntary, public agreements for pollution reduction by industry groups in environmentally degraded regions; and technical training programmes for environmental personnel in polluting factories.
- *Community control.* Should be accepted as a current reality, not as the goal of future programmes. A substantial role for local communities is appropriate from the perspective of environmental economics. Regardless of the state of formal regulation, local 'informal regulation' is stronger in areas with higher pollution loads, larger affected populations, higher incomes and education. Three implications can be drawn from the importance of community control. First, central regulatory agencies should impose uniform standards on heterogeneous communities under the guise of 'administrative efficiency' but rather allow local variation in regulation. Second, regulatory agencies can play a key role in facilitating negotiations between local communities and neighbouring factories by providing reliable information on emissions and local ambient quality, technical advice on abatement alternatives and the transfer of experience from other locations. Finally, regulators can use their authority to help communities which are excessively polluted because their lack of education, organization and bargaining power prevents them from negotiating effectively with local factories.

- *Structured learning.*   Environmental policy reform is a complex business which will inevitably be subject to many uncertainties. Because it is difficult to know exactly what will work in advance, reforms should emphasize structured learning. Rather than pre-committing to broad-based programmes, agencies should initiate a variety of pilot projects and build larger programmes as the lessons are absorbed.
- *Adaptive instruments.*   Newly industrializing economies can experience rapid changes in ambient quality across air and watersheds. Since regulation should primarily serve environmental quality objectives, it should be focused on adaptation to these rapid changes. Regulators should be empowered to counter environmental degradation by tightening existing regulations and yet should minimize disruption for investors. Meeting both objectives implies transparent adjustment rules, linked to publicly available data on ambient quality and emissions, and adjustment automatically triggered by deterioration of ambient quality below mandated levels and with sufficient lag for smooth adaptation by local economic agents.

An example of the use of disclosure instruments is the PROPER programme in Indonesia, which was implemented to improve compliance with water standards in 187 enterprises (World Bank 2000). It reduced the number of highly non-complying firms by 83 per cent within 18 months. At the same time, the number of firms meeting the standards or coming close to it increased.

5.5   INSTRUMENTS IN PRACTICE

So far this chapter has discussed different economic instruments for environmental regulation, somewhat in the abstract. This section looks at the actual experience with these instruments, largely in developing countries.

5.5.1   Environmental Charges and Taxes in Developing Countries

As mentioned above, the experience with environmental taxation in developing countries has been limited compared to that of the more industrialized nations. For simplicity, five main types of environmental taxes are identified: those on transport; natural resources; water; waste and industrial pollution.

Transport
Taxes and charges on fuels, road pricing and vehicle use have been applied in most developing countries. Petrol taxes are the most common, with most countries obtaining a large share of government revenues from duties on petrol. Some selected experiences of the application of economic instruments for the developing country context are presented in Table 5.1. Gupta and Mahler (1995)

Table 5.1 Experience with taxes and charges on transport in selected developing countries

Commodity	Type of tax and revenue	Location	Aim of tax	Reference	Environmental impact
Petrol	7 to 30% of total revenues	Various	Revenue	Gupta and Mahler (1995)	
Leaded petrol	Various	Various	Reduce fuel use prior to phaseout of lead	OECD(1999) for China	
Compressed natural gas vehicles	Tax exemption on CNG (compressed natural gas) cars	Argentina	Encourage use of less environmentally harmful transport	Seroa da Motta et al. (1999)	Widespread adoption of more environmentally benign vehicles.
Road pricing	Charge for peak hour use	Singapore	Attempt to reduce congestion	Watson and Holland (1978) cited in Panayotou (1998)	Reduced traffic by 73% in restricted zone in peak hours. Car pooling increased, 13% switched to public transport.
Road pricing	Auction system of rights to use certain roads. Simultaneous regulation of bus fleet.	Santiago, Chile	Reduce congestion and pollution	Hartje et al. (1994) cited in Panayotou (1998) and Seroa da Motta et al. (1999)	Overcapacity reduced by 30%. Reduced congestion, but some relocation to unregulated streets offsetting some gains

present a review of the differing rates of petrol taxes in different countries, including many developing nations. Although these taxes are largely applied for revenue purposes with no overall environmental objective, their imposition will reduce consumption, and thereby have some beneficial environmental effect.

Differential taxation on leaded and unleaded petrol has been introduced in many countries as a consequence of concerns over the health impacts of leaded petrol, including detrimental impacts on IQ in children. China, for example, has recently introduced a differential tax policy as part of a package of instruments to encourage the phase-out of leaded fuel (OECD 1999). This type of policy has proved effective in changing the share of unleaded to leaded fuel consumption in Europe, with many European countries now having successfully phased out the use of leaded petrol entirely (OECD 1999).

Road pricing has been used successfully in developing countries to reduce congestion, with examples of Singapore in the late 1970s and Santiago in the 1990s. This type of instrument may prove useful for large cities currently plagued by a high density of traffic and consequent high pollution densities, such as Bangkok in Thailand. However, differential pricing needs to be applied based on road use, as the experience in China has proved that lump-sum charges do not reduce environmental degradation though they are relatively simple to administer and are a good source of revenue. Geographical considerations such as the number of points of entry to the town are also important in determining whether such a programme can be a success.

Natural resources
Some taxes and charges have been raised on natural resources, such as minerals and forests in all countries. What we are interested in, however, is how the taxes can have an 'environmental' dimension. Examples of these are shown in Table 5.2. Wang et al. (1999) present a review of experience with these taxes to date in China, and suggestions for further integrating environmental concerns into this framework. The present structure does not consider the environmental impact *per se* of the commodities involved, for instance the tax on coal is only 0.3 yuan per ton in relation to the less environmentally damaging natural gas which is taxed at 2 yuan per thousand cubic metres.

In terms of forests, many countries have established harvesting taxes or stumpage fees. These, however, have broadly been aimed at raising revenue. Barbone and Zalduendo (2000) have reviewed experience with the imposition of fees for harvesting rights in Cameroon, Equatorial Guinea and Gabon. The environmental impact of these controls proved difficult to isolate, owing to the fact that these charges were implemented at the same time as other controls. Their importance to government revenue cannot be underestimated, particularly in Equatorial Guinea where revenues from harvesting fees amounted to 15.8 per cent of the government budget.

Table 5.2 Experience with natural resource taxes and charges in selected developing countries

Commodity	Type of tax and revenue	Location	Aim of tax	Reference	Environmental impact
Forest	Forestry tax charged for wood consumption when no reforestation activity. Tax set at low levels	Brazil, Colombia and Venezuela		Seroa da Motta et al. (1999)	Weakly enforced
Natural resource exploitation	Royalties: 4–6% of revenues from hydroelectric, mineral and oil production	Colombia	Preservation of natural resources. Earmarked for regulatory agencies	Seroa da Motta et al. (1999)	
Crude oil	8–30 yuan/ton	China	Incentive for sustainable management of resources	State Council (1993a) cited in OECD(1999)	
Oil royalties	Tax levy on oil passing through pipeline	Ecuador	Earmarked for use by Ecuadorian Institute for Eco-Development	Seroa da Motta et al. (1999)	
Various natural resources	Charges per unit of natural resource	China	Incentive for sustainable management of resources	State Council (1993a) cited in OECD (1999)	

Charges have also been raised on the extraction of oil in many countries, including China, Venezuela and Ecuador. Most of these charges have been established with the main aim of raising revenues, for example, the royalty tax in Venezuela (Seroa da Motta et al. 1999). However, some have aimed to encourage the sustainable use of natural resources. For instance, in China a major objective in levying the natural resource tax was to encourage the sustainable exploitation of natural resources through changing incentive patterns by forcing developers to pay for the right to exploit public resources (OECD 1999). Revenues from such charges and taxes may be earmarked for use in protecting the environment, as is the case in Ecuador, for example, where the revenues raised are earmarked for use in funding eco-development (Seroa da Motta et al. 1999).

Water charges

Water charges have been introduced in many countries. These have the dual objective of combating environmental degradation, including over-exploitation, and cost-recovery for infrastructure.

Seroa da Motta et al. (1999) report on the implementation of water charges in three countries: Mexico, Brazil and Colombia. A summary of the experience with these taxes is reported in Table 5.3. A lack of enforcement and other implementation problems have reduced the environmental impact of such charging systems.

Colombia has introduced a system of charges on organic emissions in its waterways (World Bank 2000). The scheme has been implemented in seven regions of the country, with each region being allowed to vary the rate until the target reduction has been achieved, at which point the charge is frozen in real terms. The scheme has resulted in significant reductions in emissions – in the Rio Negro, for example, BOD discharges fell by 52 per cent in the first six months of the plan and overall organic discharges in the areas covered have fallen by 18 per cent in the first year. This is seen as a real success story, with assessed charges being significant and collection rates high.

In the Philippines regulators at Laguna Lake, the second largest inland water body of South East Asia, have resorted to an environmental user fee to control industrial pollution (World Bank 2000). There is a fixed fee, plus a charge per unit of emissions with two rates, one for emissions below the permitted amount and one for emissions above. Rates have been set so that incentives are there for making reductions, at least for firms with low abatement costs. After two years of the programme, BOD discharges from the pilot plants to which it was applied have fallen by 88 per cent. The revenues from the scheme have helped the regulating authority improve its monitoring.

Table 5.3   *Water charges in selected developing countries*

Type of tax	Location	Aim of tax	Reference	Environmental impact
Water pollution charges for municipalities and industry exceeding organic matter and suspended solid standards. Revenue: $17.4 to $52.4m. since 1991	Mexico		Seroa da Motta et al. (1999)	Lack of enforcement has significantly reduced the potential impact of this measure. Revenues represent small percentage of potential
Water charges planned	Brazil	Reduction in level of degradation in rivers	Seroa da Motta et al. (1999)	Implementation difficulties expected
Charges on effluent discharge and water use. $160,000 collected from potential of $90m.	Colombia	Cost recovery to cover operation and maintenance costs of monitoring systems	Seroa da Motta et al. (1999)	Low enforcement
Charges on organic pollution discharge	Colombia – Antioquia district	Reduction in level of degradation in rivers	World Bank (2000)	Reported organic discharges fell by 18% in first year.

Waste charges

Charges on household waste, including sewage, have been levied in some developing countries in order to reduce the volumes of waste generated or to raise revenues. Table 5.4 reports some examples where such charges have been applied in Brazil, Bolivia and Venezuela. Landfill charges were found to face implementation barriers in Bolivia and Venezuela, with a lack of institutional capacity for the measurement of waste. In Brazil, sewage charges resulted in a reduction in the level of organic matter being disposed of.

Industrial pollution

Charges on pollution emanating from industrial sources have been raised in several developing countries, including China, Ecuador and Malaysia. A selection of these charges is presented in Table 5.5. China has introduced charges on a range of polluting activities, including industrial wastewater and air pollution. In Ecuador and Malaysia, charges have been raised on industrial wastewater. These have been proved to have an impact on the level of pollution in developing countries, though the rates charged need to be high enough to induce abatement by industry. China raises a particularly large amount of revenue from the pollution levy, amounting to 4.1 billion yuan, or approximately US$493 million, in 1996 (Wang et al. 1999). However, the charge in China relates to pollution above a certain pollution standard, hence is not as efficient from an economic viewpoint as a simple charge with no threshold. In Malaysia, charges on effluent from palm oil mills proved particularly successful, with a fall in pollution load of over 99 per cent from such facilities at the same time as the industry expanded production by three times (Panayotou 1998). It should be noted, however, that once the reduction had been achieved, the charge was abolished.

Summary

Pollution charges can serve as both an incentive to reduce emissions in a cost-effective way, as well as generating revenue for the regulator to invest in pollution reduction equipment. In terms of the incentive effects, these instruments are best used when the environmental goals can be defined in terms of relatively simple objectives with little spatial variation, such as a reduction in ambient concentrations of a pollutant nationally. If the goal is, for example, to limit ambient concentrations over a small area, or to have very different levels of concentrations in different areas, then the pollution charge is not the best instrument, or at best has to be supplemented by direct controls.

Pollution charges are also inappropriate where there are many small sources of the emissions, or where the sources are not stationary. Hence they are not appropriate for the regulation of vehicles, or run-off from the application of

Table 5.4 Selected waste charges

Commodity	Type of tax and revenue	Location	Reference	Environmental impact
Sewage disposal charges	Sewage tariff based on organic matter since 1983	Sao Paolo and Rio de Janiero, Brazil	Seroa da Motta et al. (1999)	Led to increased pollution control through improved housekeeping, raw material substitution and conservation
Landfill	Waste volume and tipping fees	Bolivia and Venezuela	Seroa da Motta et al. (1999)	Implementation difficulties restrict environmental benefit. Areas lack institutional capacity for waste monitoring. No mechanism to prevent illegal dumping

Table 5.5 Selected charges and taxes on industry in developing countries

Type of tax and revenue	Location	Aim of tax	Reference	Environmental impact
Levy charged on pollution exceeding pollution standard for metallurgy, chemicals, light industry, textiles, power and coal	China	Levies on industry to promote environmental management.	OECD (1999)	Notable environmental impact. But rates felt to be too low in comparison with costs of pollution control
$0.66 per kilo of discharge above a given level into rivers. Gradually increasing over time	Quito, Ecuador	Control industrial pollution and permit the use of water downstream for irrigation, cattle and human consumption (after primary treatment)	Huber(1997) quoted in Panayotou (1998)	
Variable licence fee with discharge on effluent from palm oil plants	Malaysia	Support pollution reduction	Panayotou (1998)	Pollution from crude palm oil mills reduced significantly. Growth in production of 300% concurrently. But standards imposed simultaneously, so hard to isolate impact of charge
Credit and tax incentives for environmental investments	Latin America and Caribbean	Encourage environmental investment	Seroa da Motta et al. (1999)	Subsidies for abatement investments have had a limited impact as environmental enforcement ineffective in increasing industry demands

fertilizers and pesticides. In such cases product charges (or presumptive taxes) are required.

Pollution charges can always be used as a revenue-raising device, but in this respect they are less effective than charges on inputs or outputs that generate the emissions in the first place (see below). The latter are easier to tax (there are fewer points of collection) and mechanisms for their taxation are already in place. In spite of this, it has to be said that in practice, pollution charges have been used more as a means of generating revenue than as an incentive to reduce emissions.

5.5.2　Environmental Subsidies

Subsidies to reduce emissions and to improve environmental performance are given in many countries, and indeed the rationale for the taxation of effluents is often that the revenues can be used to finance programmes of environmental remediation. Examples of such subsidies include: rebate for air and water effluent charges when investment is undertaken (France, Germany, all of Eastern Europe), accelerated tax depreciation of pollution abatement equipment, and rebates on import taxes for such equipment (several developing countries (CSD 1996a, 1996b).

Environmental subsidies can be effective in achieving reductions in pollution, but the reductions may be bought at an excessive cost.[2] If taxes are earmarked for environmental protection and the revenues recycled, the resulting level of protection may be too low or too high. Hence in industrialized countries, where tax regimes are sophisticated and budgetary provision for environmental protection is possible, earmarking for environmental protection is generally not desirable. In economies in transition and developing countries, on the other hand, such budgetary provision is very small or non-existent. Consequently the benefits of having access to some funds from this source for the environment probably outweigh the costs of an inefficient earmarking system, at least in the short run, and especially in the economies in transition in Eastern Europe where revenues from taxation of emissions are a critical source of funds for mitigation. The use of special tax treatment as a form of subsidy is more questionable. In general it does not provide the enterprises with incentives to choose the least cost options and they increase the polluters profits, which may lead to further pollution problems (Murty 1996).

A case where environmental subsidies have been applied is that of Ciudad Juàrez in Mexico, where the use of propane gas was subsidized for brick kilns (World Bank 2000). Other incentives were provided for brick makers to switch from scrap fuel burning (tyres, petrol) to the use of the cleaner propane fuel, including free technical assistance and equipment. From 1990 to 1992, over half of the brick makers in Ciudad Juàrez switched to propane. However, following the removal of subsidies as part of an economic reform programme, many returned to burning scrap to fuel the kilns.

In the light of the above discussion, the use of environmental subsidies outside of the recycling of tax revenues to support environmental investments is not an effective economic instrument. Even in the case of the former, strict guidelines are necessary to ensure that the investments that are supported are indeed cost-effective in terms of achieving the desired environmental goals.

5.5.3 Charges on Inputs or Outputs that Damage the Environment

Although ideally the pollution charge should be imposed on the emissions, in practice this is often impossible. Hence, as a second best, the charge can be levied on the input or output, frequently the energy source or chemical that is generating the pollution. Examples are taxes on petrol, including differentiated taxes where less damaging fuel is taxed at a lower rate,[3] taxes on diesel oil based on the sulphur content of the fuel, taxes on fertilizers and pesticides to take account of their environmental impacts, and taxes on ozone-depleting substances.

Taxing the source of the pollution rather than the pollution itself does not allow for (a) the possibility that mitigation measures can be undertaken at the 'end of the pipe' and (b) the fact that the impacts in terms of damages vary spatially, so that a general tax overtaxes use in a place where there is no environmental problem, and undertaxes it in places where the problem is very serious. The first issue can be addressed by giving rebates for payments when the polluter makes such an investment in end-of-pipe clean-up. Examples would be rebating a sulphur content tax for polluters who have flue gas desulphurization equipment. This is possible in a number of cases, but not always. The second problem of spatial variation is more difficult to address. To get round it we would have to have different rates of taxation depending on where the inputs were used and practically this is difficult to do, except at a rather crude level. The compromise in using input charges is acceptable in a number of situations, although the detailed analysis of the net benefits of moving to such a tax from a command and control situation are not available, certainly not in an *ex post* calculation.

The other big advantage of using taxes on polluting inputs and outputs is that they can be a major source of revenue, which can generate resources for environmental protection (see above), and even help shift the structure of taxation away from taxing 'goods' such as consumption and employment to taxing 'bads' such as pollution. The argument for using environmental taxes in this way has been elaborated and analysed in recent years and there is certainly a case for considering a shift to 'green taxation' as a number of countries are doing (Denmark, the Netherlands, Norway). There are, however, concerns that such a shift may not yield the 'double dividend' of improved economic performance as well as reduced environmental damage and these have to be taken into account.[4] A careful analysis of the impacts of the tax modifications has to be made before recommending its implementation. (For such an analysis, see Heady and Markandya 2000).

Eskeland and Devarajan (1996) examine the potential for fuel demand management in Chile and Indonesia. By examining the demand elasticities for different fuels, they concluded that firms could switch from dirty to clean fuels, thus if charges were raised on fuel as an input to production then pollution would decrease.

In conclusion, the case for using input/output charges as an economic instrument for environmental protection, and as part of the programme of action for a move to sustainable development, is strong but not without qualification. For many applications such as non-point sources, taxes on inputs are the only possibility for dealing with the issue. This will not solve the problem of 'hot spots' or local concentrations of the pollutant, for which direct controls of some kind will be required. Hence it is clear that the optimal mix of policy instruments is going to be one that combines economic instruments with direct controls. A second argument in favour of input/output charges is that they are easier to implement and to collect. Since emissions charges can be much more difficult to collect, and spatial variation may be impossible for them, the case for moving to input charges is even stronger. Finally, there may be a case for raising environmental charges as part of a broader tax reform. This has to be considered carefully in a detailed environmental– economic model before any conclusions can be made of what kinds of reforms are desirable.

5.5.4 Permit Trading Schemes

Permit trading in developing countries has been limited to date. However, the idea of allowing some trading in an attempt to achieve environmental goals is catching on. One form that has had some application is that of transferable development rights (TDRs) (Panayotou 1994). The idea is that if a conservation area is declared, the owner of the land or buildings does not completely lose the right to develop the property. Rather s/he can exercise that right elsewhere, in a place where further development is restricted and the right has some value. Usually the terms allow an increase in development beyond existing legal limits by about 10–15 per cent. Such rights have been used in urban areas in the United States and for coastal development in Puerto Rico. TDRs are somewhat different from marketable permits in that they consist of giving groups who would lose out from the development, a compensation that is acceptable and that does not involve raising a large amount of resources through taxation. Marketable permits exploit trade between different agents all of whom have to meet a given environmental objective.

More generally permit trading schemes can be seen as having considerable potential, in industrialized as well as developing countries. They can play a role in the control of air emissions, during the transition to a phase out of a damaging chemical, and protection for biodiversity. Practical experience shows, however, that they almost always have to be implemented in conjunction with direct controls, and, like emissions taxes, they are not suitable for dealing with local pollution problems, where the number of traders may be very few. Related to this, if the restrictions on trades is too great, there will be less chance of success. The choice between tradable permits and emissions taxes will depend partly on cultural factors (how acceptable taxes are) as well as on technical considerations about the costs of making errors in fixing the tax rates or the number of permits.

For developing countries, the use of permit trading has been limited to date, though some developing countries are examining the implementation of carbon trading. For air pollution, Almaty (Kazakhstan), Santiago (Chile) and Mexico City are considering the implementation of permit systems. Implementation of these systems were delayed in Santiago and Mexico City due to a lack of regulation (Blackman and Harrington 1998).

Permit trading has been shown to be successful in reducing national and international air emissions, the phase-out of lead and CFCs, and trading in development rights over conservation and urban land. Permit trading is particularly useful in the phasing out of environmentally damaging substances, as it allows those who reduce faster to sell permits for the use of the substance in question. This provides incentives for increasing the speed of phase-out and ease the burden on industries which take longer to phase out the use of the substance. Gradual phase-in and limited regulation of the process are important ingredients to the success of permit trading.

5.5.5 Subsidizing of Recycling Schemes

Under recycling schemes are included deposit-refund programmes, as well as subsidies to recycling. They could be considered under taxes and subsidies, respectively, but they are separated because they raise special issues. Many countries have such schemes. In the OECD, deposit refund schemes operate in Austria, Belgium, Canada, Denmark, Finland, France, Germany, the Netherlands, Norway, Sweden, Turkey and the United States (OECD 1993). Within developing countries, deposit refund schemes have been introduced in Bangladesh, Indonesia, Korea and Singapore, among others.

For both the deposit refund schemes and the recycling there is evidence that they have reduced waste (OECD 1993). Deposit refund schemes are largely justified in economic and environmental terms but some recycling subsidies, which are quite popular with governments and the public, and which can be very effective, may be oversold, with too much being devoted in resources to collect waste that can be safely and cheaply disposed of. This is one area where the economic instruments could be too successful. If recycling results in a reduction of one ton of waste per annum at a cost of $100, and the marginal social cost of one ton disposed is $50, then there is too much recycling; it would be better to dispose of the last ton of waste and save $50.

The marginal social costs of the different options that are available – deposit refund schemes, waste landfill, waste incineration and manufacturer recycling schemes – should therefore be equalized. In order to know whether this is the case, the correct marginal costs of each of the options have to be ascertained. Such a calculation has not been carried out, although some estimate must have been made of the relative costs of landfill versus incineration. Certainly a *full social cost* comparison has not been carried out before deciding on the selection and relative use of the different instruments related to recycling. At the same time the rationale for subsidizing recycling has not been fully analysed. As a second-best policy it may be justified to subsidize one form of waste reduction when other forms are underpriced. The analogy is with subsidizing public transport when private transport is priced below its social cost. But it is generally better to price private transport at its social cost, as it is to price waste disposal properly. The economics of what the subsidy should be and how it should be phased out as waste-disposal prices increase has not been studied in a policy context.

5.5.6   Conclusions on the Introduction of Different Economic Instruments

In this section the actual experience with the main economic instruments used for environmental regulation have been reviewed. The purpose of the review was to see where they can be most effectively employed, and where their use is less desirable. In promoting the different instruments it is important to bear in mind what the strengths and weaknesses of the economic instruments are and how cases where they have been successfully applied evolved.

From this review it appears that *emissions charges and taxes* have a role to play when the goal is a national reduction in emissions, and when the sources of the emission can be easily monitored. They are not the best instrument when the spatial dimension is important, when the sources are 'non-point' and when the goal is to raise revenue. In this context it is important to note that for historic reasons, the use of such charges in economies in transition in Eastern Europe is justified. Reforms would be desirable but will take time to implement and temporarily the present structure serves a useful purpose. *Environmental subsidies* can be effective in reducing pollution but the costs in economic terms are high. If the subsidies come from earmarking of environmental taxes, this is not a desirable system to introduce, and not as effective as non-earmarked programmes, for OECD countries. In Eastern Europe, earmarking is still desirable because it is virtually the only source of local funds for environmental protection. Programmes of accelerated depreciation and tax write-offs are not as efficient as other economic instruments that could achieve similar goals.

The use of *charges on inputs and outputs* that are environmentally damaging can work as a very effective environmental instrument. Costs of compliance are generally lower than for emissions charges and rebates can be offered to deal with end-of-pipe clean-up. They would probably be the easiest to integrate into the general system of taxation, although care should be taken in proposing tax increases on the grounds that they will substitute for other economic taxes. As with all economic instruments, they will need to be imposed in conjunction with some direct controls, to deal with local, and specific problems.

Permit trading schemes are an important part of the arsenal of tools at the disposal of a regulator. They have somewhat wider application than pollution charges, and can be introduced in stages, making them more acceptable to the affected parties. Applications where successes have been noted are national and international air emissions reductions, phase-out of lead and CFCs, and trading in development rights over conservation and urban land. Gradual phase-in and limited regulation to the process are important ingredients to their success.

Recycling schemes can and have been successful in reducing waste. There is definitely a role for such schemes. There is a slight concern that the levels of subsidies given may be too high, in which case the reductions will be achieved at an excessive cost, compared to a more balanced use of instruments for the regulation of waste.

5.6   LESSONS AND CONCLUSIONS TO THE CHAPTER

A number of useful lessons can be drawn from the implementation of economic instruments in these various countries. We list below what we think to be the most important lessons.

1.   *Experience to Date*

- A growing number of developed and developing countries are adopting a *mix* of instruments that combine command and control and economic instruments.
- Pollution charges mainly have a financial (revenue-raising) role rather than an incentive effect.
- The fee structure is sometimes extremely complex, with hundreds of rates, which vary across many pollutants, many polluters and many regions. This is especially the case in the Eastern European transition economies.

A complex structure often opens the door for polluters to challenge the pollution charge scheme.
- High inflation has reduced the impact of pollution charges. Reviewing the charge to account for inflation is difficult, and often politically difficult.
- Despite opposition by industries, there is no indication that the introduction of economic instruments has had a detrimental effect on competitiveness and trade.

2.   *Policy reforms required*

- Cost-effectiveness is a very important argument in favour of economic instruments. But, it is not a very effective argument in the political/public arena. Indeed:
  - (a) for the uninitiated, cost-effectiveness is a very vague concept. It needs to be explained and made precise in the context in which it is to be applied;
  - (b) the gains obtained from using economic instruments (reduction in aggregate abatement costs) are likely to be large only at high levels of aggregate abatement; and
  - (c) except for a very limited number of cases (for example, SO_2 trading emissions in the United States), cost-effectiveness has not been the most important reason why economic instruments have been introduced, even in developed countries.
- From a purely theoretical point of view, revenues should *not* be earmarked for specific environmental investments. A dollar of 'environmental revenues' should be used wherever it can yield the greatest social benefit (for example, education, hospitals, reducing other taxes and so on). However, revenues have typically been earmarked for environmental investments: financing of abatement activities by those paying the tax, financing of public abatement activities (for example, wastewater treatment plant), increasing the capacity of the environmental agency to protect the environment and so on.
- Where the fee structure is highly complex, reforms are needed to reduce administrative costs and make the pollution charge scheme transparent and simple. It should not be open to manipulation. In this context we should note that:
  - (a) including a large number of pollutants is comprehensive but costly to monitor;
  - (b) including a large number of (regional) coefficients may approximate damages, but it is costly to implement. Moreover, there is a high likelihood that the value of the coefficients will be set arbitrarily; and
  - (c) it may be best in the first phase to use estimated emissions factors for small sources and actual monitoring of emissions for large sources.

- To avoid the problems of inflation automatic indexing of the charge (using for example the consumer price index) should be built into the pollution charge programme. Removing revisions away from the political arena is generally a good idea.
- Reliable, comprehensive, easy-to-use environmental management systems (EMSs) are often lacking in enterprises impacted by pollution charges and so on. This is important since it reduces the potential impact of the pollution charge scheme, and prevents the achievement of the overall purpose of the scheme, namely reducing industrial discharges and improving environmental quality. The EMS should be able to answer in a very simple way implementation questions as well as management/ policy decision questions such as:
  (a) How do changes in industrial discharges affect ambient quality?
  (b) Which plants have not self-reported their emissions?
  (c) What kinds of plants are complying with the regulations?
  (d) What kind of plants should we inspect more often than others?
  (e) Is ambient quality improving as a result of the introduction of the pollution charge scheme?
  (f) What is the impact of enforcement actions on emissions?
- Putting in place a reliable and credible environmental management system is absolutely crucial. It gives information to the environmental agency about the behaviour of polluters; it gives polluters a greater incentive to control their emissions since the environmental agency knows 'what's going on'; and it gives the general public some faith in the capacity of the agency to protect environmental quality. The costs of such a system should not be attributed to the introduction of economic instruments. A similar system is required for the proper implementation of a command and control approach.
- To increase acceptability of the pollution charge scheme by the industrial sector the following measures need to be introduced:
  (a) consultation with the industrial sector;
  (b) increasing the charge according to a clear and transparent procedure instead of starting with a very high charge; and
  (c) clear use of the funding.

3. *Calibrating economic instruments*

To establish in a very practical way whether an economic instrument is necessary and to efficiently calibrate the subsidies or taxes, a dual financial-economic analysis as explained later (see 8.5) is helpful. If the financial analysis is negative but the net economic return is positive, a transfer calibrated to make the financial analysis break even would be appropriate and efficient from Society's view. Harou (1985 and 1987) used the dual analysis approach to calibrate forestry incentives in North America and Europe.

5.7   PROBLEM SET

Exercise 1

Suppose there are two firms characterized by the following marginal abatement cost (MAC) functions:

$$MAC_1 = 200 - P_1; \; MAC_2 = 300 - P_2/2.$$

(a) Represent these two functions graphically and determine the total quantity of emissions these two plants produce in the absence of any public intervention.

Suppose the regulator wishes to reduce total emissions to 350 units ($P_1 + P_2 = 350$). In order to do so, suppose the regulator imposes a uniform limit of 175 units of emissions for each plant.

(b) What is the value of MAC_1 and MAC_2 at that level of emissions?
(c) Calculate the total cost of pollution control for these two firms.

Exercise 2

In Exercise 1 above, suppose instead that the regulator wants to achieve its objective of 350 units by using solely a uniform tax per unit of emissions.

(a) Calculate the level of the tax that will allow the regulator to achieve this objective.
(b) At that level, what are the levels of emissions of firm 1 and firm 2?

5.8 SOLUTION TO PROBLEM SET

Exercise 1

The graph of the MAC is shown in Figure 5.11.

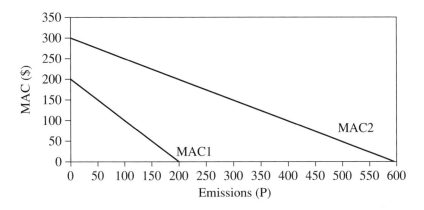

Figure 5.11 Solution: Marginal abatement cost

(a) Without regulation, firm 1 and firm 2 will emit pollution until MAC_1 and MAC_2 is zero.
$MAC_1 = 0$ when $P_1 = 200$; $MAC_2 = 0$ when $P_2 = 600$; total level of emissions is 800.

(b) With $P_1 = 175$, then $MAC_1 = 25$; with $P_2 = 175$, then $MAC_2 = 212.50$.

(c) Total cost of pollution of firm 1 = [(200 -175) · 25] / 2 =312.50.
Total cost of pollution of firm 2 = [(600 – 175) · 212.50] / 2 = 45,156.25.

Exercise 2

Denote by T the tax rate. We know that firm 1 will reduce its emissions up to the point where $T = MAC_4$. We also know that firm 2 will reduce its emissions up to the point where $T = MAC_2$. Since the tax rate is the same, we will therefore have $MAC_1 = MAC_2$:

$$200 - P_1 = 300 - P_2/2$$

from which we get:

$$P_1 = P_2/2 - 100.$$

We also know that we must have $P_1 + P_2 = 350$. This can be rewritten as $P_1 = 350 - P_2$. Hence, we can write:

$$P_2/2 - 100 = 350 - P_2$$

We therefore find that $P_2 = 300$. Consequently, we must have $P_1 = 50$. We also find that $T = 150$.

NOTES

1. We discuss the reform of property rights as an instrument for environmental management because it can play an important role in specific cases. Of course the whole issue of such rights is much more complex and the environmental dimension is only a small part. Property rights are also social constructs and any reforms undertaken have to be evaluated in this wider context.
2. Raising general taxes to pay the subsidies had a significant welfare cost. In developing countries this cost is even higher than in developed countries.
3. Arguably this is an example of an environmental subsidy, where the 'clean' fuel pays a lower rate of tax.
4. The idea is that a pollution charge is beneficial, not only because it addresses the environmental problem, but also because it provides revenue to the government from a (paradoxically) 'clean' source; clean in the sense that there is no loss of welfare associated with its collection. One should be careful, however, in using the double dividend argument, as careful analysis shows that the presence of a double dividend is dependent on many complex factors. (See Goulder (1994) for a further discussion of this topic.)

CITED BIBLIOGRAPHY

Barbone, L. and L. Zalduendo (2000), 'Forest taxes, government revenues and the sustainable exploitation of tropical forests', World Bank Africa Region Working Paper Series No. 5, Washington, DC: World Bank.

Blackman, A. and W. Harrington (1998), 'Using alternative regulatory instruments to control fixed point air pollution in developing countries: lessons from international experience', Resources for the Future Discussion Paper 98–21, Washington, DC: Resources for the Future.

Coase, R. (1960), 'The problem of social cost', *Journal of Law and Economics*, **3**, 1–44.

Commission for Sustainable Development (CSD) (1996a), 'Financial resources and mechanisms', E/CN.17/1995/8, Economic and Social Council, United Nations, New York.

Commission for Sustainable Development (CSD) (1996b), 'Financial resources and mechanisms: addendum', E/CN.17/1996/4/Add.l, Economic and Social Council, United Nations, New York.

Eskeland, G. and S. Devarajan (1996), *Taxing Bads by Taxing Goods: Pollution Control with Presumptive Charges*, Washington, DC: World Bank.

Goulder, L.P. (1994), 'Environmental taxation and the double dividend: a reader's guide', Paper presented to the 50th Congress of the International Institute of Public Finance, Harvard University, Cambridge, MA.

Gupta, S. and W. Mahler (1995), 'Taxation of petroleum products: theory and empirical evidence', *Energy Economics*, **17** (2), 101–16.

Hahn, R.W. (1990), *Meeting the Growing Demand for Environmental Protection: A Practical Guide to the Economists Toolchest*, Washington, DC: American Enterprise Institute.

Harou, P.A. (1982), 'Including equity in the evaluation of outdoor recreation benefits', *Canadian Journal of Forest Research*, **12**, 337–42.

Harou, P.A. (1985), 'Comparison of methodologies to evaluate subsidy programs to non-industrial private forests', *Silva Fennica*, **19** (4), 365–75.

Harou, P.A. (1987), 'The EC context for private forestry incentive valuation', *Silva Fennica*, **20** (4), 366–72.

Heady, C.J. and A. Markandya (2000), 'Study on the relationship between environmental/energy taxation and employment creation. Special Report', Brussels: European Commission DG, Environment.

Jeanrenaud, C. and M.-A. Stritt (1994), 'Market-based instruments: a way to reduce the cost of air pollution control: some empirical results for Switzerland', IRER Working Paper No. 9301, Neuchâtel University, Switzerland.

Klarer, J. (ed.) (1994), 'Use of economic instruments in environmental policy in Central and Eastern Europe: Case Studies of Bulgaria, the Czech Republic, Hungary, Poland, Romania, the Slovak Republic and Slovenia', Regional Environmental Centre, Budapest, Hungary.

LaPlante, B. (1998), 'Policies, instruments and the environment', mimeo, Washington, DC: World Bank.

Markandya A. (1998), 'The cost of environmental regulation in Asia: command and control versus market-based instruments', *Asian Development Review*, **16** (1), pp. 1–30.

Markandya, A. and Z. Lehoczki (1994), 'Environmental taxation: a review of OECD countries and prospects for economies in transition', REC Paper Series No. 1, Regional Environmental Centre, Budapest, Hungary.

Murty, M.N. (1999), 'Role of government in environmental management', in M.N. Murty, A.J. James and S. Misra (1999), *Economics of Water Pollution: The Indian Experience*, Oxford: Oxford University Press.

OECD (1993), 'Environmental taxes in OECD countries: a survey', OECD Monographs No. 71, Paris: OECD.

OECD (1995), *Environmental Taxes in OECD Countries*, Paris: OECD.

OECD (1999), *Environmental Taxes: Recent Developments in China and OECD Countries*, Paris: OECD.

Panayotou, T. (1994), 'Conservation of biodiversity and economic development: the concept of transferable development rights', *Environmental and Resource Economics*, **4**, 95–110.

Panayotou, T. (1998), *Instruments of Change: Motivating and Financing Sustainable Development*, London: Earthscan.

Ray, A. (1984), *Cost Benefit Analysis: Issues and Methodologies*, Baltimore, MD: Johns Hopkins University Press.

Rico, R. (1995), 'The US allowance trading system for sulfur dioxide: an update of market experience', *Environmental and Resource Economics*, **5**, 115–29.

Seroa da Motta, R., R. Huber and H.J. Ruitenbeek (1999), 'Market based instruments for environmental policymaking in Latin America and the Caribbean: lessons from eleven countries', *Environment and Development Economics*, **4** (part 2) 177–202.

Wang, J., C. Ge, J. Yang, A. Song, S. Wang and Q. Liu (1999), 'Taxation and the environment in China: practice and perspectives' in OECD (1999) pp. 61-105.

World Bank (2000), *Greening Industry: New Roles for Communities, Markets and Governments*, New York: Oxford University Press.

6.   Laws, regulations and institutions

OBJECTIVE

To provide the proper legislative and institutional context for implementing economic and non-economic instruments for environmental management.

SUMMARY

Laws and regulations should be conceived and implemented through a participatory and evolutionary process aimed at the implementation of clear policy goals. Such goals will be more attainable if they have been established participatively through an environmental strategy backed by an environmental plan. Laws and regulations may be more readily implemented by institutions that have the support of political will, appropriate funding and a mechanism by which the institution can coordinate its activities with other relevant institutions.

6.1 INTRODUCTION

The objective of sustainable development requires a coordinated approach to environmental law making which should be based on a comprehensive statement of policy. This policy should be backed by a vision (Chapter 2), appropriate macroeconomics and sectoral policies (Chapters 3 and 4) implemented through economic (Chapter 5) and other instruments, including laws and regulations which are the focus of this chapter. This policy should also be spelled out in an environmental strategy (Chapter 7) or more appropriately, a sustainable economic development plan. While policies have focused more on the national level, with global externalities, such as climate change, international laws are appearing as a result of evolutionary thinking about two new themes – environmental protection and sustainable development (Boyle and Freestone 1999).

In the most fundamental sense the law defines who can do what. It does this mainly though not exclusively, but importantly for environmental matters, through a system of property rights. Then the law stipulates how these property rights are to be enforced. Hence, it provides the basis of any system of environmental management. This was recognized in Chapters 8 and 39 of Agenda 21 (see Chapter 2 of this book), which deals with the significance of laws, regulations and institutions. Laws are seen as a key tool for environmental planning and management and generally include statutory and court decisions ('case law'). They are often supplemented by administrative regulations in order to ensure more detailed, correct and consistent interpretation of the requirements laid down in national legislation.

6.2 LEGAL SYSTEM FOR ENVIRONMENTAL PROTECTION

A framework of environmental management should include the following three elements:

1. an environmental policy applicable to all government levels – national, provincial and local;
2. legislation and regulations at all levels and for all sectors which bind government agencies, the private sector and the community at large; and
3. an integrated and coordinated administration at all levels of government working in cooperation with the private sector and civil society.

The broad environmental policy applicable to all government levels was discussed in earlier chapters at the national and sectoral levels. In this chapter we address the legal, regulatory and institutional aspects of environmental management which allows the implementation of the environmental instruments discussed in the preceding chapter.

Once environmental priorities are established, the most efficient instruments should be used to address the priorities. Environmental laws are always part of the mix of tools to ensure sound management of natural resources and to prevent and control pollution. A legal system of environmental protection includes international treaties, constitutional environmental rights and sometimes an overall framework of sectoral laws and regulations, as well as appropriate institutional arrangements. These different components will be discussed briefly in this chapter.

6.3   INTERNATIONAL LEGAL INSTRUMENTS

Multilateral and bilateral treaties dealing with environmental protection cover a vast area of subject matter such as marine environment, protection of the atmosphere, trade in hazardous waste and substances, conservation of nature and living resources and conservation of marine living resources. Some apply globally and others only to a particular region. Implementation mechanisms of these treaties increasingly reflect and promote the integration of environment and development issues to ensure more effective implementation. A list of major international treaties is provided in Annex 6A1. Specifically, the financial mechanisms (trust funds) and technology transfer provisions in these treaties are designed to ensure compliance while not curtailing development. In addition, the relationship between trade and environment has become an important new consideration in discussions related to the General Agreement on Tariffs and Trade (GATT)/World Trade Organization (WTO).

While treaties are binding on the signatories, other international instruments are non-binding or voluntary, and they are referred to as 'soft law'. Incentives to follow soft law instruments are multiple, despite the non-binding character of these. Compliance with broadly accepted principles reflected in non-binding international environmental legal instruments is a means of demonstrating credibility and trustworthiness in the international community.

6.4   ENVIRONMENTAL LAWS

6.4.1   Constitutions

At the first level in the legal framework of any country is the constitution. No doubt, constitutional provisions help highlight national priorities and thereby influence future legislative policies and executive actions. Since 1972, a new constitutional trend has begun to appear, whereby the basic principles of environmental protection are being incorporated into political constitutions of countries throughout South America, Asia and Africa.

6.4.2 National Framework Legislation

In addition to environmental provisions in constitutions, national framework environmental legislation was developed in the decade following the 1972 United Nations Conference on the Human Environment (Stockholm Conference). In some jurisdictions, it covers various aspects of the environment, while in others it merely establishes the enabling act and the central environmental agency, defining the latter's responsibilities, or provides a procedure whereby environmental considerations can be fed into decision-making routines, commonly constituting an environmental impact assessment system. For example, Indonesia developed Act No. 40 concerning Basic Provisions for the Management of the Living Environment in 1982. In addition to laying out principles and objectives, the act makes participation in the management of the environment a right as well as an obligation of every person. The act serves as the basis for the evaluation and adjustment of all valid legislation containing provisions related to aspects of the living environment, that is, legislation regarding irrigation, mining and energy, settlements, land use and so forth. In this fashion, all these laws are included within one system of Indonesian environmental law. Zambia also adopted a holistic approach to environmental problems through the Natural Resources Conservation Act (NRCA) (1970). Another example of framework legislation is the document prepared by a group of independent experts within the framework of the cooperation programme between the Council of Europe and the Central and Eastern European countries to design a model for the revision of the existing legislation or the adoption of new legislation. The document is divided into several parts, which include: General Provisions; Organizational System of Environmental Protection; Distribution of Responsibilities Among Different Tiers of Government; Right to Information and Public Participation in the Protection of the Environment; and Devices and Enforcement.

6.4.3 Environmental Assessment (EA) Laws

EA can be an important environmental instrument to mainstream the environment in the decision-making process. Often, administrative guidelines on EA procedures also exist. Nevertheless, these guidelines may lack the status of law. Strategic EA is a new instrument attempting to mitigate potential adverse environmental consequences from new policies and programmes. It seeks to avoid the project pitfalls of cumulative impacts. New laws on strategic impact assessment in Europe, Canada and the United States have been promulgated with this goal in mind.

There are a number of different options in the development of EA rules. Whereas some countries have adopted specific EA laws, others use framework environmental laws to cover EA-relevant issues in the wider context of general environmental legislation. Specific laws typically comprise detailed EA provisions, whereas framework laws usually contain only the basic principles of EA. The latter are therefore frequently supplemented by regulations or guidelines in order to ensure correct and consistent interpretation of the requirements laid down in national legislation. For instance, South African regulations under Section 26 of the Environmental Conservation Act 1989, a framework environmental law, provide explicit and clear guidance to engage in EA. In Syria, EA Decree (1995) requires EA according to Articles 1 and 13 of the Environmental Protection Act. The annexes of this decree include a list of activities for which EA or permit conditions is/are compulsory, as well as a classification of sensitive areas.

6.4.4   Sectoral Legislation

In some countries, there may be an environmental framework law dealing with overall policy and coordination. This law may be coupled with sectoral legislation, which regulates specific sectors or industries. In the absence of a consolidated environmental code, an understanding of a country's body of environmental legislation requires a review of the statutes (including statutory amendments) and subsidiary legislation. A check-list is provided in Box 6.1 to aid in the collection and assessment of a country's legislation related to environmental and natural resources management. Each item is further developed in Annex 6A2.

Generally, strong sectoral institutions and laws still represent the bulk of the existing environmental regulatory framework in developing countries. These sectors and related laws may be classified into three groups: (i) laws on natural resources; (ii) laws on the management of the man-made environment, such as land-use laws; and (iii) laws on the protection of human health.

Sectoral legislation initially geared towards use of national resources, for instance forest law, is now more oriented towards sustainable management. However, deforestation, and the loss of biodiversity and marine resources have not been halted by the existence of these sectoral laws.

In regard to legislation on the management of man-made environments, land-use planning and zoning law is increasingly a topic of concern in developing countries. Examples of this legislation include the 1981 Brazilian Act on Environmental Protection Areas and Botswana's 1977 Town and Country Planning

---

BOX 6.1   SECTORAL LEGISLATION: CHECK-LIST

1. Obligations under International Law
2. Constitutional Provisions
   General right of citizens to a clean environment
   General right to information about the environment
3. Comprehensive Environmental Law
4. Land-Use Related Laws
   (a) General land-use planning and development control
   (b) Land tenure
   (c) Agriculture
   (d) Coastal zone conservation
5. Resource-specific Laws
   (a) Soil conservation
   (b) Forestry
   (c) Water resource management
   (d) Fisheries/marine
   (e) Wildlife and wildlife habitat (parks, reserves)
6. Pollution Control
   (a) General law
   (b) Health code
   (c) Pesticides
   (d) Hazardous waste
   (e) Air pollution
   (f) Noise
7. Institutional Framework

Note: Each item is developed in Annex 6A2. The list is not exhaustive.

Act. Departing from an emphasis on negative terms such as 'prohibitions' or 'restrictions', new legislation in this area emphasizes positive planning to encourage and promote economic land uses that are considered compatible with environmental objectives. The protection of cultural heritage is also an important element in land-use plans.

In laws targeting the protection of human health, industrial pollution is generally managed through a combination of regulatory controls, standards and economic incentives. Frequently, the quality of a country's anti-pollution legislation is one of the best indicators of a country's seriousness in responding to environmental changes. Malaysia's 1974 Environmental Quality Act (EQA) authorizes the regulation of most forms of pollution. This is effected through the licensing of polluting activities as well as certain prescribed premises. Such activities range from pollution of inland waters, land, air, coastal waters and noise pollution.

Before turning to regulations and institutions, it is important to note that the responsibility for the enactment of laws does not only reside in a country's parliament or similar body or bodies. Executive officers also have the power to adopt by-laws and regulations. More recently, some countries are making efforts to issue truly 'environmental' legislation as evidenced by the fact that drafting of legislation is increasingly entrusted to environmental agencies. In Chile, for example, the preparation of environment-related bills was carried out by the Environmental Legislation Commission under the Ministry of the Interior. Furthermore, the drafting of environmental laws is not solely confined to government agencies. In Costa Rica, preparation of an environmental bill was undertaken by the School of Law of the State University. In Ecuador, the Natura Foundation, a non-governmental organization (NGO), was promoting the preparation of a bill on its area of interest.

6.4.5   Environmental Regulations

Legislative bodies, in conjunction with executive leaders of government, enact laws designed to remedy certain societal problems. While such legislation spells out the goals and intent of the law, legislative bodies often leave it up to agencies to write and enforce detailed regulations and guidelines. Regulation drafted by agencies, however, should be seen as a component of the larger policy formation and implementation process. As such, regulations should be viewed as means for achieving policy goals, determined by the legislature, in conjunction with other mechanisms. However, the promulgation of regulations is meaningless and can be misinterpreted if not considered along with an assessment of their implementation.

Environmental statutes generally empower an administrative agency to develop and promulgate regulations. Executive agencies can sometimes promulgate regulations through an executive order. The laws are implemented through regulations and other vehicles for implementing environmental requirements.

Laws provide the vision, scope and authority for environmental protection and restoration. In some countries, laws also encompass the types of general requirements described by other countries in regulations. Regulations establish, in greater detail than can be specified by law, general requirements that must be met by the regulated community, for example, how harmful substances should be tested, registered, handled, monitored, emitted, discharged and/or disposed of. These requirements generally apply at a national, state or regional level depending on the scope specified in the law. Some regulations are directly enforced. Others provide the criteria and procedures for developing facility-specific requirements via permits and licences that provide the basis for enforcement. Some countries do not include the step of developing regulations but rely solely on facility-specific permits or licences to implement their laws.

Permits usually control activities related to construction or operation of facilities that generate pollutants. The requirements in permits are often based on specific criteria established in laws, regulations, and/or guidance.

- General permits specify exactly what a class of facilities (for example, gasoline stations) is required to do. General permits and licences are used when it is impractical and/or unnecessary to issue a specific permit for each facility (for example, when there are numerous small facilities that have very similar operations).
- Facility-specific permits specify exactly what a particular facility is required to do. Permits often take into account the particular conditions at the specific facility.

Licences are similar to permits. Licences are permits to manufacture, test, sell and/or distribute a product, such as a pesticide, that may pose an environmental or public health risk if improperly used. Licences may be general or facility specific.

Often government regulators must interpret requirements, even those that have been carefully drafted, because not all applications can be anticipated. Written guidance and policies for interpreting and implementing requirements help ensure consistency and fairness when the requirements are applied in practice. Guidance and policies are also useful in situations where regulation is achieved solely by facility-specific permits or licences (either because the regulatory system does not include more general requirements or because it is impractical to issue general requirements, for example, due to wide variability in regulated community characteristics). In this case, guidance and policies for creating requirements will help ensure consistency and fairness. These instruments were discussed in Chapter 5.

Other legal instruments for environmental management include environmental taxes, eco-labelling practices, information disclosure requirements and emission trading. These instruments are not mutually exclusive. Combination of all the above may be used to attain effective improvement of the environment. It is worth noting that those instruments are created by law or other legal instruments.

To be effective, regulations have to be prepared with the participation of civil society, the private sector, NGOs, and government institutions and political bodies concerned and affected by their implementation. Regulations should also be backed by a functioning judicial system and implementing institutions. The first step to ensure compliance is to build capacity in the governmental institution and judiciary. If the institutional and court systems are already well established, the first step may be implemented through greater cooperation among interested parties and transparency in regulatory drafting work. Different means exist to ensure full participation in the development of these regulations (Box 6.2).

BOX 6.2   WAYS TO INVOLVE THE REGULATED COMMUNITY IN DEVELOPING GENERAL REQUIREMENTS

Informal consultations

Policy makers can informally consult with key representatives of the regulated community and NGOs before developing general requirements. These consultations can be helpful in sorting out future problems early, and in eliminating resistance.

Private/business guidelines

The Dutch National Environmental Policy Plan of 1989 encourages the creation of innovative economic and environmental instruments under Dutch civil and environmental law. One of these is the covenant, a public–private contract that makes government and business partners in environmental protection, rather than adversaries.

The Japanese system sometimes uses the method of administrative guidance – negotiations between the regulator and regulated entities prior to establishing regulations. Pollution control agreements are often developed in this way among enterprise, local government and citizen groups. These agreements contain an obligation by the private sector to undertake mutually acceptable pollution control measures to achieve quantitative emission targets. In persuading business to cooperate, local governments often use incentives such as low-interest loans and tax reductions in exchange for timely compliance with government requirements and guidelines. One of the main advantages of this administrative tool has been the immediate action following the agreement as opposed to lengthy legislation and implementation.

Formal comment

The US legal system requires that the federal government publish draft regulations and solicit comments from the regulated group and the public. Widely distributed, low-cost government periodicals provide advance notice that new regulations are being developed and announce when they will be available. Any organization or individual can easily obtain and review the proposed regulations when issued.

Written comments from the public are usually accepted for a limited period of time, 30 to 90 days in the US, after the proposed regulation has been issued. The environmental agency prepares and publishes detailed responses to the comments. Many of the comments directly concern the difficulty or unanticipated effects of compliance. These comments provide regulators with an opportunity to rethink their approach. The formal responses to comments reassure commentators that their comments were considered.

Field testing

In field testing, specific members of the regulated community volunteer to test general requirements to determine, for example, whether the requirements are clear and understandable, and/or the ease and cost of compliance. Policy makers can then make changes to the general requirements before they are finally implemented. Although field testing can lengthen the total time it takes to develop a general requirement, it can expose weaknesses that might otherwise render it unenforceable. As of 1991, field testing is being pilot-tested for use in the US.

Not all proposed requirements can realistically be field tested. For example, with those requiring substantial investment in new equipment it may be impractical to field test because of the cost and time required for planning, permitting, construction, and start-up of new equipment. Field testing may be more appropriate for requirements that concern operation and maintenance of existing equipment; record-keeping and reporting by regulated sources; new methods of testing compliance; and/or the ability of existing equipment to meet new standards. Field testing of these types of requirements generally should not delay the process of developing the requirements or pose too great a financial burden on the prospective regulatory community. Where field testing is used, one needs to determine the funding of the enforcement programme and the choice of the test facility itself.

Regulations should be realized through strategic planning. The environmental strategy and national environmental action plan, considered in Chapter 7, should establish the reasons and priority for the proposed regulation. The previous chapter presented the choice between command and control or market incentives in the implementation of environmental policies. The search for market-based regulations, while appropriate in many cases, has sometimes resulted from a misinterpretation of the relative success of regulations, which may simply not have been properly developed, that is, without involving key actors. In some cases, the use of market mechanisms is reasonable. In other situations, grant programmes may be appropriate, and in yet other cases, the use of typical regulatory standard setting and enforcement (direct command and control regulation) may be necessary.

The point of strategic regulatory planning is to focus attention on the behaviour of regulated parties, to identify the positive and negative incentives

---

BOX 6.3   A SEVEN-STEP MODEL FOR STRATEGIC REGULATORY PLANNING

I.	Problem recognition	What is at issue?
II.	Identification of parties	Who is involved?
III.	Historical analysis	How have different levels of government and the parties involved responded to this issue in the past? Why?
IV.	Situational analysis	
	A. Mission/objectives	What outcomes are desired?
	B. Party analysis	What are the motivations, goals, positions, and resources of each party to either comply with, ignore, or fight the desired behavioural changes?
V.	Strategic regulation formulation	Determination of the conditions in the regulated community, regulating agency, and the outside arena that affect the cost and level of coerciveness of alternative regulatory devices. The most appropriate devices are then chosen to influence target group behaviour and achieve compliance.
VI.	*Ex-ante* review	Addresses the fit and feasibility of the regulatory plan before implementation.
VII.	*Ex-post* review/revision	Following implementation, how successful has the regulatory plan been at modifying behaviour? Is further modification needed?

Source: Cohen and Kamioniecki (1991).

the government can offer, or to stimulate others to increase compliance. Attention is shifted from bureaucratic and legislative processes to the behaviour of the regulated community. Such an approach, outlined in Box 6.3, differs markedly from traditional approaches to the regulatory planning process. All too often, policy makers skip directly to the 'strategic regulation formulation' step, bypassing entirely the preliminary steps that are necessary to create a dynamic rather than static formulation process. Perhaps this tendency is due to impatience on the part of officials to solve the problem at hand. Operating within a very short time frame or believing the issue to be extremely serious can nurture this feeling. In many cases, however, a lack of thoroughness is the culprit. The result generally is the adoption of regulatory devices that are neither cost-effective nor in agreement with legislative intentions. Policy makers overseeing the most successful regulatory programmes are likely to have gone through the preliminary stages in the model. While some may believe that following the seven steps listed in Box 6.3 makes the regulatory process painstakingly slow, they are vital to a tactical approach to regulatory planning.

6.4.6   Enforcement and Compliance

Legislation is really not the critical factor in environmental improvements. The major problems result from the difficulty of establishing control and enforcement mechanisms to apply the legal provisions. Most countries rely on fines and sanctions for achieving compliance. There are not many countries with explicit plans in their legislation to rely on cooperative agreements, self-monitoring, or voluntary economic incentives. This was alluded to in Chapter 5 under disclosure instruments (Box 5.5).

6.5   ENVIRONMENTAL INSTITUTIONS

In many cases, there is no lack of laws, but rather a lack of political will to apply or implement environmental laws and regulations. This translates into poor management organizations. To implement environmental laws and regulations requires political clout, skilled personnel and appropriate budgets. In addition, all institutions concerned with environmental regulations should be well coordinated. Overlapping responsibilities among ministries at different levels of government may send contradictory signals to polluters and lead to conflicting objectives among the various agencies charged with pollution control. To avoid this situation, a small but high-level supervisory environmental agency is usually preferred to a new ministry of the environment.

Factors that contribute to institutional ineffectiveness include: lobbying by powerful interest groups; short-term planning horizons; and lack of accountability by public institutions. Other problems that particularly affect environmental institutions are: mismatches between assumed responsibilities and the available resources; lack of qualified personnel; penalties for non-compliance with regulations that are not strict enough; inadequate communication; and a weak judiciary.

When deciding which instruments are appropriate for achieving particular environmental objectives and when deciding the comparative cost-effectiveness of these instruments, it is very important to take into account the administrative capacity of the proposed implementing agencies. These agencies will have to undertake complex measures that are frequently associated with carrying out environmental strategies, such as charging and collecting taxes and fees, monitoring fuel and gas emissions, or determining environmental impacts. Such actions also often require careful coordination between different government agencies.

Without a clear legislative framework and effective institutions, well-conceived policies and actions to address priority environmental problems cannot be translated into effective practice. Most national environmental strategies emphasize three key areas for improving institutional performance: (i) assigning clear institutional responsibilities; (ii) establishing consistent and transparent legislation; and (iii) ensuring effective implementation capacity. Clarifying institutional responsibilities is important because environmental problems cut across sectoral boundaries and involve many different agencies. In establishing institutional responsibilities, the following actions are important: minimizing opportunities for conflict; clearly defining the status and functions of relevant agencies; and ensuring effective coordination among government agencies and other actors.

In establishing consistent and transparent legislation, minimum air and water quality standards should be established at the national level because competition between localities in attracting industrial development may lead subnational jurisdictions to adopt lower environmental standards. In contrast, decisions regarding the provision of local environmental services, such as solid waste collection, should be left primarily to local governments. However, decentralization of environmental management responsibilities must be accompanied by adequate transfers of financial resources or revenue-raising powers in order to permit the proper delivery of these services.

While individual agencies should carry out their own specific environmental management responsibilities, some type of organizational mechanism is generally needed to ensure effective coordination. This requires empowering an agency with enough political status to coordinate policies and provide technical and political support to state, local and sectoral agencies. It is also desirable for effective environmental management that autonomous agencies of various legal status have good coordination.

To increase interministerial coordination, the Environmental Action Programme for Central and Eastern European Countries recommends:

1. creating a deputy minister or equivalent senior position for environmental policy and regulations to focus on economic policy issues, strategy development, and policy implementation;
2. designing task-oriented teams to connect existing departments and to provide links between ministries;
3. setting up cabinet-level committees to bring together the ministries of environment (MoE) with economic and sectoral ministries;
4. establishing temporary task forces of high-level officials to prepare the work for these committees and to provide career and other professional incentives to encourage participation;
5. designating staff from the MoE to participate in strategy development in sectoral ministries and invite staff from those ministries to working groups in the MoE on relevant issues; and
6. creating the capacity within the MoE to evaluate policies and set long-term targets for key environmental indicators.

Specifically with regard to Bulgaria, the environmental strategy paper recommends establishing a Supreme Ecological Council of Experts to ensure interministerial coordination in addressing pollution control. As an advisor to the MoE, the Council's functions include reviewing applications for project support and reviewing work on research and development of pollution abatement activities (World Bank 1998).

Establishing consistent legislation via a transparent procedure will facilitate implementation. Regulations and standards that support such laws should be spelled out clearly. Environmental laws should be consistent with other relevant laws and economic or other incentives. Agents responsible for causing environmental degradation often respond more readily to economic incentives than to restrictive regulations. To be effective, environmental laws should not conflict with these incentives. In some cases, ensuring a lack of conflict between laws and incentives will require alterations in the latter. Fiscal incentives applying to cattle ranchers in the Brazilian Amazon in the early 1980s, for example, encouraged the conversion of primary tropical forests, despite laws requiring that 50 per cent of the total area in all agricultural and ranching establishments be left in its natural forested state. Only after these incentives were eliminated did deforestation decline.

Another way to improve institutional performance is to build implementation capacity for environmental policies through the application of laws and regulations. Many national and local institutions lack the necessary resources, incentives and trained staff to carry out environmental management functions properly. In some cases, weak institutional performance reflects a lack of political commitment to environmental goals. To address these concerns, political will should exist, funding and expertise should be available, a system of incentives and penalties must be put in place, the private sector should be involved and the judiciary should be effective.

Political decisions are usually the responsibility of those at the centre of the government. One way to ensure political will is to empower people and to facilitate their participation in the governmental decision-making process through environmental education, awareness-raising programmes and the involvement of people on the periphery in the conduct of legislative and administrative responsibilities. The adoption of transparent procedures, development of accountable institutions, promulgation of legislation to effect devolution, and administrative reorganization are essential to ensure effective implementation of environmental laws and regulations.

Matching management responsibilities with funding and available expertise is necessary. Environmental management responsibilities should be assigned only to those agencies that have the necessary funding and technical expertise to execute them. Financial resources may be obtained from the national budget, from revenues specifically raised for environmental purposes (such as those related to environmental services) and from external sources. The conversion of debt for environmental management presents another possible source of revenue for certain countries (see Chapter 3).

Whether in the private or the public sector, people need incentives to comply with environmental laws. For private polluters, the threat of fines and jail terms can be a powerful incentive limiting environmental damage. Such sanctions also need to be applied to government agencies or state-owned companies when they cause pollution or do not live up to their environmental responsibilities.

Apart from formal economic sanctions, sometimes a policy of good and bad publicity can be quite effective. In China, for example, environmental protection agencies conduct annual inspections of environmental quality in each urban district. The National Environmental Protection Agency is responsible for inspecting 37 major cities; other cities are examined by provincial environmental protection boards (EPBs). The results of the examinations are compared, and the ten best and ten worst cities are published in the newspaper. The mayors of the top ten cities each receive an award; the mayors of the ten worst cities are criticized in newspapers. Progress is monitored by the EPBs. The local EPB is under the control of the mayor but the mayor must report to the provincial EPB.

To alleviate the burden on institutions responsible for environmental management, there is a need to expand opportunities for private sector involvement. The private sector (community groups, local and international NGOs, private firms, research institutes) can play a key role in developing and implementing an environmental strategy. Community groups are in a unique position to identify the most important local problems and propose ways of addressing them. NGOs can play an important role in monitoring the performance of government agencies, carrying out traditional public sector tasks (when this is more cost-effective) and disseminating information. These points have already been emphasized in Chapter 5.

Finally, to build capacity for implementing environmental management, it is important to ensure that an effective judiciary is in place. Although rarely acknowledged in national environmental plans, weak enforcement systems motivate polluters and other offenders to delay investment in environmental improvements. Therefore, a strong and efficient judiciary can help ensure timely and effective enforcement of environmental laws and regulations.

6.6 CONCLUSIONS

Although we have separately discussed laws, regulations and institutions, the interconnection between the three is evident. Each is mutually supportive of the others and all require a clear mandate through a proper environmental strategy and clear policies. A transparent and open process at each level of the law–regulation implementation process helps enterprises and other economic actors adapt to changing regulatory conditions. Companies and other stake-holders are more likely to comply with policy instruments when they understand how and why they were chosen, or when they were part of the decision-making process.

In the promulgation of laws, the design of regulations and incentives and the application of laws and regulations, it is important to maintain flexibility to respond to specific circumstances and unexpected events. During times of environmental crisis standards can be strengthened (for example, factories could be closed during a smog alert) while during times of economic crisis standards can be made less stringent.

To adjust policies and instruments to accommodate new circumstances, a system of monitoring and evaluation needs to be established. A key question is how to measure progress in reaching environmental objectives and meet standards. At the macro level, a recent trend has been the development of performance indicators, which can provide essential information on progress in priority areas. At the local level, the affected citizens and NGOs have often initiated the monitoring of pollution or of other actions negatively impacting their environment and lives. Institutions should assist in this regard and take actions when necessary.

Performance indicators compare how actual measures of environmental quality, such as levels of suspended particulate in ambient air, relate to the targets or objectives established in standards set by policy makers. For example, the concentration of suspended particulate can be compared to the levels recommended by World Health Organization guidelines. The Dutch performance indicator for eutrophication shows an improvement from 332 in 1987 to 287 in 1991; deposition of acidic compounds (sulphur dioxide, oxides of nitrogen, ammonia) fell from 242 to 171 during the same period. In aggregating performance indicators to derive a composite measure of national environmental quality, the Dutch give equal weight to each component; other countries use a weighted system to aggregate indicators. For example, using the Dutch method, overall environmental pressure fell from 219 to 195 between 1987 and 1991 (reaching all goals would put the indicator at 100). This average annual decline of nearly 3 per cent is impressive against a backdrop of real GNP growth averaging 3.8 per cent a year, but less than the declines of nearly 7 per cent per year required to reach the country's national goal for the year 2000.

In conclusion, laws, regulations and institutions play a supportive role in the market. The key to efficient markets is low transaction costs. Transaction costs are the costs involved in measuring what is being exchanged and in enforcing agreements. Goods and services or the performance of agents have multiple valuable attributes. The ability to measure those attributes at low cost is a necessary condition for capturing the gains from trade that were the keys to Adam Smith's *Wealth of Nations*. But a sufficient condition requires, in addition, that the contracts embodying the exchange process be enforced at low cost. Those conditions are not easily met when dealing with environmental goods and services. Internalization of environmental externalities through laws, regulations and economic incentives requires well-tuned institutions as well as effective organizations. Different countries will structure their legal, regulatory and judicial systems differently as a result. There is not a single recipe for success.

In practice, this concept may translate into 'regulatory negotiation', negotiated rule making, or laws that set the stage for implementation with optional or voluntary agreements. In the case of negotiated rule making, negotiators try to reach a consensus through a process of evaluating their own priorities and making trade-offs to achieve an acceptable outcome on the issues of greatest importance to them. If a consensus is achieved, the rules will be easier to implement.

Voluntary agreements are part of an emerging body of regulations. Under the pressure of a growing number of regulations, companies engaged in manufacturing activities, particularly industrial activities, are assuming responsibilities for performing more complex tasks which play a decisive part in the environmental protection field: identification and assessment of risks and harm to the environment coupled with control, limitation or possible reduction of these. Companies are stimulated to enhance their public image and strengthen their legal security by following a policy of information to the public.

CITED BIBLIOGRAPHY

Agenda 21: Programme of Action for Sustainable Development (1992), Chapters 8 (8.13–25) and 39 (39.1–9), New York: United Nations.

Boyle, A. and D. Freestone (1999), *International Law and Sustainable Development*, Oxford: Oxford University Press.

Brack, D. (1996), *International Trade and the Montreal Protocol*, Royal Institute of International Affairs, London: Earthscan.

CBD (2001), Convention on Biological Diversity website – http://www.biodiv.org.

Cohen, S. and S. Kamioniecki (1991), *Environmental Regulation through Strategic Planning*, Boulder, CO: Westview Press.

Grubb, M. with C. Vrolijk and D. Brack (1999), *The Kyoto Protocol: A Guide and Assessment*, Royal Institute of International Affairs, London.

Jha, V., A. Markandya and R. Vossenaar (1999), *Reconciling Trade and the Environment*, Cheltenham: Edward Elgar.

Krueger, J. (1999), *International Trade and the Basel Convention*, Royal Institute of International Affairs, London: Earthscan.

Markandya, A. and I. Milborrow (1998), 'Trade and industrial impacts of a multilateral agreement to phase out ozone-depleting substances – a case study of the Montreal Protocol', *European Economy*, No. 1, 1998, pp. 39–90.

FURTHER READING

Ewing, K. and R. Tarasofsky (1998), 'The "trade and environment" agenda: survey of major issues and proposals', Environmental Policy and Law Paper No. 33. Available from IUCN website: http://www.iucn.org/themes/law.

Firestone, D. and F. Reed (1993), *Environmental Law for Non-Lawyers*, 2nd edn, Vermont: SoRo Press.

International Law Institute (1994), 'Environmental policy and regulation', Seminar, 23 May to 3 June, in cooperation with Georgetown University, 2 Vols, Washington, DC.

Mercuro, N., F. López, and K. Preston (1994), *Ecology, Law and Economics: The Simple Analytics of Natural Resource and Environmental Economics*, New York: University Press of America.

World Bank (1998), Environment Action Programme for Central and Eastern Europe: setting priorities, World Bank, Washington, OECD: Paris.

ANNEX 6A1   LIST OF MULTILATERAL TREATIES AND OTHER AGREEMENTS IN THE FIELD OF THE ENVIRONMENT

A.   General Environmental Concerns

1. *Declaration of the United Nations Conference on the Human Environment* (Stockholm, 16 June 1972)

   - Objectives: To lay down common principles to inspire and guide the people of the world in the preservation and enhancement of the human environment.
   - Non-mandatory; global. After adoption by the Conference, recorded in UNGA Resolution 2994 (XXVII) of 15 December 1972.
   - Related instrument: (a) *World Charter for Nature* (UNGA Resolution 37/7 of 28 October 1982).

2. *Convention on Environmental Impact Assessment in a Transboundary Context* (Espoo, 25 February 1991)

   - Objectives: To prevent, reduce and control significant adverse transboundary environmental impact from proposed activities, by the establishment of an environmental impact assessment procedure that permits public participation.
   - Not yet in force; regional. Membership restricted to ECE (Economic Commission for Europe) member states, the EC, and states having consultative status with ECE.
   - Appendices: I. List of activities; II. Content of the environmental impact assessment documentation; III. General criteria to assist in the determination of the environmental significance of activities not listed in appendix I; IV. Inquiry procedure: V. Post-project analysis; VI. Elements for bilateral and multilateral cooperation; VII. Arbitration.

B.   Nature Conservation and Terrestrial Living Resources

1. *African Convention on the Conservation of Nature and Natural Resources* (Algiers, 15 September 1968)

   - Objectives: To encourage individual and joint action by African states for the conservation, utilization and development of soil, water, flora and fauna for the present and future welfare of mankind.

- In force 16 June 1969; regional. Membership restricted to African States; 30 parties, all developing countries.
- Annex: List of protected species.

2. *Convention Concerning the Protection of the World Cultural and Natural Heritage* (Paris, 23 November 1972)

- Objectives: To establish an effective system of collective protection of the cultural and natural heritage of outstanding universal value, organized on a permanent basis and in accordance with modern scientific methods.
- Including 95 developing countries.
- Related instrument: World Heritage List.

3. *Convention on International Trade in Endangered Species of Wild Fauna and Flora* (Washington, 3 March 1973) as amended

- Objectives: To protect certain endangered species from overexploitation by means of a system of import/export permits.
- In force 1 July 1975; global. Membership open; 113 parties, including 85 developing countries.
- Related instruments: Amendment Protocols (a) Bonn, 27 June 1979, in force 13 April 1987; (b) Gaborone, 30 April 1983.

4. *Convention on the Conservation of Migratory Species of Wild Animals* (Bonn, 23 June 1979)

- Objectives: To protect those species of wild animals that migrate across or outside national boundaries.
- In force 1 November 1983; global. Membership open; 39 parties, including 20 developing countries.
- Related instrument: (a) *Agreement on the Conservation of Seals in the Wadden Sea* (Bonn, 17 November 1988, in force 10 October 1991); (b) Agreement on Bats in Europe (Geneva, 25 November 1991).

5. *International Tropical Timber Agreement* (Geneva, 18 November 1983)

- Objectives: To provide an effective framework for cooperation and consultation between countries producing and consuming tropical timber, to promote the expansion and diversification of international trade in tropical timber and the improvement of structural conditions in the tropical timber market, to promote and support research and development with a view to improving forest management and wood utilization, and to encourage the development of national policies aimed at sustainable utilization and conservation of tropical forests and their genetic resources, and at maintaining the ecological balance in the regions concerned.

• In force April 1985; global. Membership open to any state which produces or consumes tropical timber; 48 parties, including 25 developing countries.

C. Atmosphere and Outer Space

1. *Convention on Long-range Transboundary Air Pollution* (Geneva, 13 November 1979) and related protocols

   • Objectives: To protect man and his environment against air pollution and to endeavor to limit and, as far as possible, gradually reduce and prevent air pollution, including long-range transboundary air pollution.
   • In force 16 March 1983; regional. Membership restricted to ECE member states, the EC and states having consultative status with ECE; 33 Parties, including 4 developing countries.
   • Related instruments: (a) *Protocol on Long-term Financing of the Cooperative Programme for Monitoring and Evaluation of the Long-range Transmission of Air Pollutants in Europe* (Geneva, 28 September 1984, in force 28 January 1988); (b) *Protocol on the Reduction of Sulphur Emissions or their Transboundary Fluxes by at least 30 Percent* (Helsinki, 8 July 1985, in force 2 September 1987); (c) *Protocol Concerning the Control of Emissions of Nitrogen Oxides or their Transboundary Fluxes* (Geneva, 18 November 1991, not yet in force).

2. *Vienna Convention for the Protection of the Ozone Layer* (Vienna, 22 March 1985) and Montreal Protocol, 1987, as amended

   • Objectives: To protect human health and the environment against adverse effects resulting from modifications of the ozone layer.
   • In force 22 September 1988; global. Membership open; 81 parties, including 49 developing countries.
   • Related instruments: (a) *Montreal Protocol on Substances That Deplete the Ozone Layer* and amendments (Montreal, 16 September 1987, in force 1 January 1989); (b) *Amendment to the Montreal Protocol on Substances That Deplete the Ozone Layer* (London, 29 June 1990, in force 10 August 1992).

D. Global Marine Environment

1. *Convention on the Prevention of Marine Pollution by Dumping of Wastes and Other Matter* (London, 29 December 1972) as amended

   - Objectives: To control pollution of the sea by dumping, and to encourage regional agreements supplementary to the Convention.
   - In force 30 September 1975; global. Membership open; 67 parties, including 38 developing countries.

2. *International Convention for the Prevention of Pollution from Ships* (London, 2 November 1973) as amended

   - Objectives: To preserve the marine environment by achieving the complete elimination of international pollution by oil and other harmful substances and the minimization of accidental discharges of such substances.
   - In force 2 October 1983; global. Membership open; 70 parties, including 41 developing countries.
   - Related instruments (a) *Protocol of 1978 Relating to the International Convention for the Prevention of Pollution from Ships* (London, 17 February 1978, in force 2 October 1983).

3. *United Nations Convention on the Law of the Sea* (Montego Bay, 10 December 1982)

   - Objectives: To set up a comprehensive new legal regime for the sea and oceans, including protection and preservation of the marine environment.
   - Now in force as of 1994; global. Membership open.

4. *UNEP Montreal Guidelines for the Protection of the Marine Environment against Pollution from Land-based Sources* (Montreal, 19 April 1985)

   - Objectives: To assist governments in the process of developing appropriate bilateral, regional and multilateral agreements and national legislation for the protection of the marine environment against pollution from land-based sources.
   - Non-mandatory; global. After adoption by a UNEP Working Group of Experts, endorsed by UNEP Governing Council Decision 13/18 (II) of 24 May 1985.

ANNEX 6A2   DISCUSSION NOTES TO CHECK-LIST

1. *Obligations under International Law*

   Increasing concern over transboundary environmental pollution has led to the creation of several international environmental treaties. These have focussed in particular on the issues of climate change (the Kyoto Protocol, see Grubb et al. (1999)), ozone depletion (the Montreal Protocol, see Brack (1996), Markandya and Milborrow (1998)), endangered species (Convention on International Trade in Endangered Species (CITES), see Jha et al. (1999)), biodiversity (Convention on Biological Diversity (CBD), see CBD (2001)) and the transport of hazardous wastes (the Basel Convention, see Krueger (1999)). These treaties commit signatories to measures and to actions, in some cases with quantified targets, in others with less precise qualitative measures. The enforcement mechanisms for them also vary. Some use trade sanctions against violators, others rely on moral suasion and political pressure to ensure compliance. What is important, however, is that all such treaties have to be taken into account in the formation of environmental regulation if the country is a signatory.

2. *Constitutional Provisions*

   In recent years, many countries have included environmental provisions in their constitutions. These may be related to substantive rights to a healthy environment; or to procedural matters, for example, in a federal system, as to which level of government has jurisdiction over various issues (for example, forests, land, water, wildlife); or to access to information about the environment. Thus, the first basic question is whether environmental provisions exist in the Constitution of the country concerned.

3. *Comprehensive Environmental Law*

   The second basic question is whether the country has a comprehensive environmental and natural resources law. If that is the case, such a law will normally have 'environment' or 'natural resources' subject matter in the title, and will probably cover several sectors (for example, all pollution control matters, or natural resource management of forests, soils, parks and so on).

4. *Land-use Related Laws*

   a. General land-use planning and development control: Land-use and development control laws are among the most basic and important legal groupings for environmental protection and natural resources management in developing countries. Land-use planning and development control laws (sometimes still called 'Town and Country Planning' laws) include basic concepts of physical planning, national planning, zoning and development permitting.

b. Land tenure: Laws related to land tenure (ownership or use rights), may be found in distinct codes of their own or under headings ranging from land registry, land titling, land lease and tenancy, and land sales (especially agricultural land sales). These laws may have long-range environmental implications especially with rural land use and the security of claims where investment in conservation is concerned.

c. Agriculture: Many of the issues relating to the environment may be dealt with in general agricultural legislation. The most important issues that might be covered are soil conservation, agricultural land use and leasing conditions, and pesticides (see also discussion below under soils and pesticides). Other areas of interest include plant and animal protection.

d. Coastal zone conservation: In recent years, coastal states have been paying more attention to overall coastal management from the perspective of development control. Special coastal conservation laws may exist in some countries, which set out the principles and requirements for development and conservation of coastal resources. Topics covered by specific coastal legislation may include set-back zones for development, special zoning for different uses, conservation and pollution control measures.

5. *Resource-specific Laws*

a. Soil conservation: A few countries, such as China, have legislation directed specifically at soil erosion control. Most countries, however, deal with this issue through agricultural, forest, water, or other resource-sector laws. If the country has serious soil erosion problems, it may be necessary to investigate laws and subsidiary legislation in such related sectors.

b. Forestry: This is normally a recognized area of law in many jurisdictions. In almost all the Commonwealth countries and the former French colonies, forestry legislation was promulgated by the colonial power. It is therefore advisable to inquire about general forest legislation, and also more specific regulations dealing with the processing of forest products or trade thereof which may have a bearing on the forestry sector. In considering such an inquiry, recent amendments should also be taken into account. The Food and Agriculture Organization (FAO) has for many years been assisting countries in the updating of such laws.

c. Water resource management: This area generally relates to watershed management, that is, the management and protection of water sources, watercourses and lakes. Unless there is a comprehensive water code covering water management and water pollution control, legislation for this sector may be scattered among other laws dealing with forests, river basin authorities, agriculture, health or land-use planning, which may need special attention if the country has water-related problems. This sector may also have numerous pieces of subsidiary legislation related to specific water uses or regional problems.

d. Fisheries/marine: Legislation in this area may cover fishing rights, the types of fishing craft and equipment to be used as well as marine pollution, and conservation of breeding areas, or endangered or fragile sites. Specific regulations may exist dealing with the handling, processing and distribution of fish. Commonly, this legislation will be separate from wildlife legislation, although there is some cross-referencing in the context of protected species and marine parks. Where coastal fisheries projects are concerned, inquiries should also be made to determine whether the country concerned has declared a 200-mile exclusive economic zone because this may have legal and institutional implications for management and control of fishing.

e. Wildlife and wildlife habitat (parks, reserves): Historically, legislation in this area was commonly part of the forestry law except where the country had vast resources in which case there may be special legislation for wildlife conservation (commonly focused on fauna, not flora) and for parks and reserves. In the past couple of decades, particularly with help from the FAO, the World Conservation Union (IUCN), and more recently, the secretariat for the international Convention on International Trade in Endangered Species (CITES), many countries have undertaken legal reform in this sector and have updated wildlife laws and regulations. Therefore, both forestry and wildlife sectors should be researched. Wildlife legislation may also be combined or split into different laws covering domestic possession and trade, and international trade.

6. *Pollution Control*
   a. General law: A few countries have consolidated several pollution-related laws into one environmental law, for example, Malaysia's Environmental Quality Act. However, it is more common for a country to have a spectrum of laws and regulations dealing with different pieces of the pollution problem, for example, the factories act, mining code, fisheries or coastal law, water law, traffic code, or health code.
   b. Health code: The health code in many countries is the principal instrument for regulating pollution affecting human health. Many of these laws are relatively old and rely on the theory of nuisance for establish-

ing and controlling pollution. Where this is the case, the laws are general, without specific standards, and frequently inefficient in dealing with modern pollution problems; however, there may be detailed subsidiary legislation which may better define the use of enforcement notices or measures for minimizing pollution. In this case, subsidiary legislation is perhaps the key and needs special inquiry as to its effectiveness.

c. Pesticides: With the assistance of an FAO legal project in the early 1970s, several countries have enacted specific pesticide control legislation covering all aspects of the use of agricultural chemicals, their registration, labelling, storage, transport, packaging, sale and disposal. The model FAO statute from which most countries developed their national law, relies heavily on regulations for listing pesticides and controlling use. In view of difficulties in procurement, an inquiry should be made into the means of regulating (both in terms of laws, rules and administrative notices) importation, manufacture, sale, use and storage of fertilizers and pesticides.

d. Hazardous waste: A general law regarding waste management provides regulations and methods for waste treatment and indicates the responsible party for waste treatment. Hazardous waste is either defined in general waste management law, or it is dealt with in separate legislation. In addition, countries that are signatories to the Convention on the Control of Transboundary Movements of Hazardous Wastes and their Disposal (the Basel Convention) should have domestic legislation to implement the Convention.

e. Air pollution: Countries with major air pollution problems, especially in urban areas, are likely to have some form of legislation to control activities that are major contributors to air pollution. Provisions may also exist in traffic, health or industrial codes.

f. Noise: Some countries have noise pollution control laws, particularly for cities, and controls are based on the need to protect public health and welfare. These may be found in the health code.

7. *Institutional Framework*

The institutional framework associated with the administration and enforcement of all the laws in the sectors indicated above should be identified and studied. The first line of inquiry is whether there is a central environmental body, which, as noted above, a few countries have created or are considering creating. The functions of such bodies may range from purely advisory or coordinating roles that may have some review authority for projects affecting certain sectors, to regulatory or enforcement agencies with responsibility to oversee all environmental performance. There was much enthusiasm shortly after the 1972 Stockholm Conference for the creation of environmental agencies. Today, many different institutional arrangements exist for environmental regulation and the various specialized responsibilities will probably be disbursed throughout the public administration system even if there is a distinct ministry of the environment. Therefore, information should be obtained on the institutional responsibilities and capabilities of any centralized environmental body as well as any specialized units within the key sector ministries charged with implementing the sector laws, for example, agriculture, public works, public health, planning, finance, local government and related departments. In addition, particularly in federal governmental systems, a check should be made of local or regional agencies responsible for the monitoring and enforcement of environmental legislation and licensing and other permitting procedures required in the country concerned.

7. National environmental strategies

OBJECTIVE

To present national environmental strategy (NES) experiences and the tools used in their development, and to show how these strategies can be helpful in setting environmental priorities and corresponding policies.

SUMMARY

Following a review of past experiences with NESs made at the World Bank,[1] three key elements for a successful environmental strategy are highlighted: identifying priority problems, defining priority actions and ensuring effective implementation. For the latter, it is paramount that technical and economic analysis be tempered by active participation and commitment of key stakeholders. Effective environmental management requires strategy objectives to be realistic and integral to broader political, economic and social concerns.

7.1   INTRODUCTION

The drawing up of a national environmental strategy (NES) is an exercise undertaken to systematically analyse environmental impacts of macroeconomic and sectoral policies, programmes and projects in a given country. To the extent that the environmental dimension has been well integrated, or mainstreamed, in regular economic analyses, and acted upon, NESs or other types of environmental strategies would be redundant. During a transition to a sustainable development path, however, an environmental strategy can force ecological and social considerations into the policy-making process and the budget allocation. A NES helps provide the priorities for setting a sustainable environmental plan of actions for a country. This chapter covers the steps needed in order to set environmental priorities within the existing policy-making process.

A NES should recognize the global context of environmental issues. International treaties and conventions placed on a country provide the starting point for developing a more detailed national strategy. While developing countries should focus their limited resources on environmental problems that pose the most severe threats to national development, in many cases successfully tackling domestic problems will also contribute to solving global ones.

There is no one approach to devising a NES but, to set environmental priorities correctly, three elements are crucial: prioritizing problems, proposing actions and following their implementation (see Box 7.1). Tackling each element requires a balance between proper economic analysis and involvement of key stakeholders. A brief review of past NESs, however, shows that the setting of priorities was often missing in the strategies – resulting in an unrealistically long list of 'important' environmental actions to be undertaken.

7.2   PAST EXPERIENCE

Since the mid-1980s international donors and non-governmental organizations (NGOs) have been helping countries prepare national environmental strategies and action plans. Building on earlier experiences with national tropical forestry action plans, national conservation strategies, and similar documents, these plans tend to be based on environmental profiles and sectoral and economic analyses done by the countries themselves or with the assistance of international and bilateral organizations. In 1990 the International Development Association (IDA), a World Bank affiliate that provides interest-free loans to the world's poorest countries, urged IDA borrowers to complete national environmental action plans (NEAPs). By the end of 1994 most IDA borrowers and some other countries had prepared NEAPs or similar documents. Some of these plans were partly implemented. Different approaches to national strategies are summarized in Box 7.2 (IIED 1994).

Box 7.1   FORMULATING PRIORITIES FOR AN ENVIRONMENTAL STRATEGY

Key element	*Description*
1. Identifying priority problems	Consists of analysing the extent and severity of environmental concerns and identifying those considered to be most critical based on specified criteria.
2. Defining priority actions – diagnosing causes	Probably the most important component of a strategy, this comprises three major steps: identifying the causes of problems, setting goals, and identifying alternative policy instruments to address the causes of problems based on the expected benefits and costs of each, and other, relevant criteria and considerations.
3. Ensuring effective implementation	Involves integrating the proposed actions with the government's macroeconomic and sectoral policies; participation by key stakeholders in the planning and implementation phases; finding incentives that ensure clear assignment of institutional responsibilities, consistent and transparent legislation, and adequate implementation capacity; mobilizing resources to finance strategy implementation; and making provisions for monitoring, evaluation, and revision of priorities during implementation.

A limited review of past experiences from 30 NESs and similar exercises was presented in World Bank (1995a). This examined six components in the preparation of a NES: screening problems; prioritizing problems; identifying the causes of the problems for the diagnosis of the environmental situation; choosing policies and instruments; identifying legal and institutional reforms for tackling the problems; and ranking environmental actions.

The review of the screening of problems showed that the major environmental problems are seen as: urban (in 82 per cent of the NES across regions);

land degradation and erosion (73 per cent); industrial pollution (64 per cent); water resources and deforestation (61 per cent each); sanitation (42 per cent); biodiversity and wildlife (39 per cent); and cultural heritage (18 per cent).

The review of prioritization practices showed that 50 per cent of the NESs reviewed had clearly defined criteria for setting problem priorities while 10 per cent did not identify any criteria. The criteria used were: monetary damage estimates (36 per cent); human health (27 per cent); irreversibility (24 per cent); ecological effects (18 per cent); and equity (3 per cent). Damages valuation is the most important criteria but is not used enough because of a lack of local expertise and the absence of reliable data. Techniques for valuation that may be appropriate in drawing up NESs from the individual project level are described in detail in Part II of this book.

The principal causes of the problems identified above are cited in the review as: population (70 per cent); poorly defined property rights (48 per cent); economy-wide policies and political instability (30 per cent); poverty (24 per cent); and economic growth (15 per cent). Government policies identified as having negatively affected the environment are: inadequate institutional coverage (86 per cent); inappropriate pricing (51 per cent); development plans (23 per cent); fiscal policies (14 per cent); and the absence or inadequacy of land-use plans (12 per cent). Many NESs did not identify underlying causes – the reason most commonly given being that they are intersectoral and so not easy to trace.

On the basis of this diagnosis, appropriate policies or legal and institutional reforms can be identified. The categories of policies classified in the review include: awareness building (88 per cent); regulatory instruments (85 per cent); market-based instruments (58 per cent); property rights (27 per cent); and direct investments (24 per cent). However, most NESs are not specific about their choice of instruments. They rarely discuss their costs or implications, or spell out the criteria for their choice or ranking.

A review of environmental instruments is provided in Chapters 4 and 5. Once policies have been set and appropriate instruments proposed to reduce or prevent environmental damage, it is necessary to rank them. The criteria used for ranking actions in the NES are reviewed as: ecological effects including irreversibilities (33 per cent); cost-effectiveness and benefit–cost analysis (30 per cent): financial and institutional capacity (30 per cent); equity (21 per cent); compatibility with other programmes (18 per cent); and win-win situations (18 per cent).

The review of the implementation aspects of the actions proposed indicates that NESs often tend to rely on legislative reform to improve environmental management emphasizing 'command and control' instruments over the economic instruments. However, regulatory instruments require strong institutions that in practice are often missing. Institutional problems highlighted in

BOX 7.2   DIFFERENT APPROACHES TO NATIONAL STRATEGIES

Governments have adopted a number of strategic approaches to national environmental management. Some focus narrowly on environmental issues and others are broader and deal with the integration of environmental, development and social concerns. These approaches fall into several categories:

Comprehensive National Strategies

- *National environmental action plans (NEAPs)*   Supported by the World Bank and other donors, NEAPs describe countries' major environmental concerns, identify the principal causes of environmental problems, and formulate policies and actions to deal with them. NEAPs are intended to contribute to the continuing process by which governments develop comprehensive environmental policies, including programmes to implement them. This process forms an integral part of overall national development decision making.
- *National sustainable development strategies (NSDSs)* Called for by Agenda 21, NSDS is a generic name for a participatory and cyclical process to achieve economic, ecological, and social objectives in a balanced and integrated manner. The process encompasses the definition of policies and action plans, their implementation, monitoring and regular review. NSDSs may take many forms and incorporate or build on the approaches briefly described above.
- *National conservation strategies (NCSs)*   Promoted by the World Conservation Union (IUCN), NCSs are intended to provide a comprehensive cross-sectoral analysis of conservation and resource management issues to help integrate environmental concerns into the development process. They identify a country's most urgent environmental problems, stimulate the national debate, and raise public consciousness; they assist decision makers in setting priorities and allocating human and financial resources; and they build institutional capacity to manage complex environmental issues.

Sectoral and Thematic Strategies

- *National tropical forestry action plans*   Sponsored by the United Nations Food and Agricultural Organization (FAO) and promoted under the Tropical Forestry Action Programme, national TFAP exercises involved a multisectoral review of forest-related issues and formulation of strategic plans that define national targets and actions regarding afforestation and forest management, forest conservation and restoration, and integration with other sectors.
- *National plans to combat desertification*   Sponsored by the Permanent Committee for Drought Control in the Sahel, these plans analyse the socioeconomic and ecological situation, review current activities, and discuss policies and actions to combat drought for a number of Sahelian countries. In addition, national plans are now also being developed in response to the UN Framework Convention on Climate Change and Convention on Biological Diversity adopted at the United Nations Conference on Environment and Development (UNCED) held in June 1992.

Documents Contributing to the Strategic Process

- *Country environmental profiles and state of the environment reports*   These are prepared by governments, bilateral aid donors and NGOs. Generally they present information on conditions and trends, identify and analyse causes, linkages, and constraints, and indicate emerging issues of relevance to national environmental management.
- *UNCED national reports (1991–92)*   These documents were prepared by national governments, often in consultation with the private sector and local, regional and international NGOs, prior to UNCED. Each report addressed development trends, environmental impacts, and responses to environment and development issues through policies, legislation, institutions, programmes, projects, and international cooperation. Some UNCED reports also considered issues of equity and social justice. Others are intended as the basis for future NSDSs.

the review are: poor monitoring and enforcement (79 per cent); inadequate skills and personnel, competition and lack of coordination (58 per cent); inadequate legislative framework, gaps and duplication (39 per cent); and lack of political and public awareness (27 per cent).

The recommendations made to redress these inadequacies are: new legislation and standards (73 per cent); training and capacity building (70 per cent); working group/coordinating body (55 per cent); new agency/environmental unit (39 per cent); and decentralization (27 per cent). Shortcomings in institutional analysis included: the lack of cost analysis of the proposed reform; insufficient attention given to the capacity of courts; and the inadequate consideration of incentives to improve institutional performance.

The above summary of the review of some NES experiences mentioned here offers a broad range of environmental problems and solutions that are seen to be important in different countries. However, this range is not solely due to the conditions specific to individual countries. Country experiences also differ as a result of a lack of developed method on which to base the NES. The three key elements of a good environmental strategy contained in Box 7.1 are discussed further in the following sections.

7.3   IDENTIFYING AND PRIORITIZING PROBLEMS

Experience from past NESs and similar development strategies has shown that an essential first step for effective environmental management is identifying priority problems. Because resources are scarce, the range of problems to be addressed needs to be restricted. Consensus on the most critical environmental problems confronting a country should be sought among the groups of people involved in causing the environmental degradation and those directly affected by the degradation itself as well as experts in various environmental fields, NGOs and relevant government agencies. In arriving at this list of priorities an important part is played by a careful estimation of the additional costs and benefits attached to each environmental concern. Indeed, much of this book is devoted to assisting the policy analyst in providing this information.

Where attempts are made to undertake rigorous economic analyses by quantifying the damages of environmental problems and the costs of tackling them, however, the process of using them would gain from being reviewed by local stakeholders. Only affected individuals know the effects of different environmental problems on their welfare, and only through direct involvement can their preferences be articulated. However, the ranking of priority problems will often have to balance economic, social, political and environmental objectives. It is not an easy task because of lack of information, lack of organization in the participatory process that leads to paralysis or a blurring of the priorities, and the presence of vested interests.

For the participatory process to work therefore, priority problems need to be identified on the basis of further transparent (comprehensible) criteria. These include:

- *Ecological impacts.* Ecological impacts are especially important when dealing with natural resource management. Typical examples are the number of animal species or hectares of forest or arable land lost each year. To determine which activity causes the most serious damage, these data should be complemented by data on productivity losses.
- *Number of people affected.* This variable is one of the main indicators of the social impact of environmental problems. For instance, the relative importance of air and water pollution can be compared by estimating the size of the population at risk: for example, 40 per cent of the population is exposed to elevated sulphur dioxide and particulate concentration levels, while 35 per cent of the population lacks access to potable water. Additional information about the toxicity of air and water pollution permits a rough priority ranking of air pollution over water pollution.
- *Effects on health.* Health impacts are usually the most useful criteria for setting priorities among urban environmental problems. One reason is that when pollution is severe enough to affect human health, there are usually related impacts on productivity, ecosystems and aesthetic values. Moreover, health impacts impose economic losses due to increased illness (morbidity) and premature death (mortality). These are tangible costs influencing the general well-being of the affected population and tend to be higher than the costs associated with decreased productivity and losses of aesthetic value.
- *Effects on the poor.* Equity is seldom used as a criterion because it is difficult to measure the impact of a problem over a group of people. However, a NES can give distributional equity a numerical ranking based on an assessment of the income level of the group affected by the environmental problem. Where no income data are available, proxies can be used.
- *Effects on economic productivity and growth.* The most critical environmental problems can be identified, in theory, by comparing the social costs that they generate. These costs can help identify priority problems both within a sector and in relation to problems in other sectors. Although this method is a reasonable way to set priorities, it is seldom applied because the links between environmental problems and outcomes are not easy to establish. Even when a connection can be made, it may be difficult to value the impacts in monetary terms though recent advances in economic valuation presented in Part II of this book are reducing some

of these difficulties. The Sierra Leone NES, recognizing the importance of this type of analysis but lacking monetary estimates for many values, produced a non-monetary cost–benefit analysis. In Box 7.3. costs and benefits are ranked by various experts on a three-point scale, thus avoiding extensive data requirements.

- *Risk and uncertainty.*   A number of important environmental problems are characterized by long-term effects (for example, the impact of toxic waste disposal on air or water) or great uncertainty (for example, the 'value' of biodiversity, or the ability of polluted ecosystems to purify themselves). Since traditional economic analysis does not handle these dimensions well, it is necessary to use other, multidisciplinary approaches to identify priority concerns. The precautionary principle, or the safe minimum standard, that suggests no action if there is the likelihood of significant environmental damage, is one approach to deal with these factors, although it may imply much higher control costs.

BOX 7.3   NON-MONETARY COST–BENEFIT ANALYSIS FOR PRIORITIZING ENVIRONMENTAL PROBLEMS: SIERRA LEONE

Each environmental problem is rated by experts on a three-point scale as high, moderate, or low for each of the three factors: environmental significance, potential intervention benefits, and potential intervention costs. An overall priority is then computed for each problem by multiplying the environmental significance by the difference (benefits – costs).

Problem	Environmental significance	Intervention benefits	Intervention costs	Overall priority
Water contaminants	High	High	Moderate	High
Water availability	High	High	Low	High
Living conditions				
Urban	High	High	Moderate	High
Rural	Moderate	Moderate	Moderate	Low
Land degradation	High	High	Moderate	High
Deforestation	Moderate	High	Low	High
Forest degradation	Moderate	Moderate	Low	Moderate
Biodiversity loss	Low	High	Low	Moderate
Mangrove loss	Low	High	Low	Moderate
Pollution from mining	Low	Low	Low	Low
Land degradation from mining	High	High	Moderate	High

7.4 DEFINING PRIORITIES FOR ACTION: DIAGNOSING CAUSES

Identifying the causes of environmental problems is a prerequisite for designing the right solutions. Most environmental problems stem from a combination of two broad sets of factors, depicted in Figure 7.1: 'pressure' factors such as population growth, human and economic activity and poverty on one hand, and 'enabling' factors, such as market, government and institutional failures which allow the 'pressure' to cause environmental damage. Diagnosing these causes and targeting policies and investments towards them is key to successful action. However, the review of NESs presented earlier found only a minority of plans that had followed such an approach. An example of a plan with this approach has proposed phasing out price subsidies to fossil fuels that cause excessive fuel consumption and thus excessive emissions of air pollutants.

Pressure factors include rapid population growth, human and economic activity, and poverty. When not adequately managed any one of these may cause extensive environmental damage. In most countries, however, these factors are not regarded as environmental problems *per se* and are addressed in broader national development plans rather than in environmental strategies.

Population growth affects environmental conditions in both rural and urban areas. Population growth in rural areas tends to: force people into exploiting

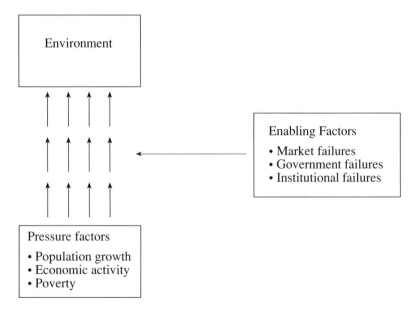

Figure 7.1   Causes of environmental problems

more fragile natural ecosystems; increase the demand for arable land and fuelwood, often resulting in deforestation; and shorten fallow periods, thereby reducing land productivity. Similarly, the inability to make provisions for rapid urban population growth often results in inadequate urban waste management, air and water pollution, a shortage of supplies of clean water, land degradation and congestion.

Human and economic activity depends directly or indirectly on the use of natural resources. Even in the presence of rapid technological change, the expansion of economic activity coupled with population growth threatens both the environment's capacity to assimilate change at the national as well as the global scale, and its stock of non-renewable resources.

In terms of poverty, the poor are usually the first to suffer the consequences of environmental degradation, and poverty on its own can have a significant negative impact on the environment. When other alternatives break down, poor people are often forced to use land and water in ways that threaten the productivity of these vital resources in the future. For example, in many low-income countries people living at subsistence levels have encroached on forests, wetlands, mangrove zones and coral reefs causing large-scale deforestation, erosion and loss of terrestrial and marine biodiversity. Likewise, in many developing nations the urban poor lack the financial resources to compete for housing in safe locations or for land where basic services are established. As a result, they are frequently forced to establish illegal settlements on hazard-prone or environmentally sensitive land poorly suited to residential uses.

Enabling factors exacerbate environmental problems because pressure factors are not properly managed. Most national environmental strategies and plans identify three general types of 'enabling' factors that strongly contribute to the severity of environmental problems: market failures, government failures and institutional failures which were described in Chapter 4.

Many market failures can be traced to the lack of markets or prices attached to the use of natural resources. Individuals may dispose of waste products in a way that is harmful to the atmosphere or to water systems because they may have no reason not to believe that these resources are limitless (and hence 'free') or that a third party will be negatively affected. Unless governments intervene to adjust prices or through the introduction of environmental instruments, producers may have no incentive to stop polluting the atmosphere or to treat harmful effluents, with the consequence of negative impacts on the population's health.

Government failures may also exacerbate environmental problems. Macroeconomic reforms can lead to environmental degradation in certain circumstances when such reforms coincide with specific policy and/or market failures. For instance, when environmental resources are not correctly priced, serious distortions in resource use and allocation can result. Indeed, in previously centrally planned economies systematic underpricing of energy and other inputs has contributed to severe pollution problems.

Property rights failures provide frequent examples of government or institutional failures. A lack of definition over property rights can lead to numerous natural resource management problems. Non-private ownership of resources in the absence of proper common management regimes, for example, has often led to open access, giving rise to the overexploitation or degradation of tropical rainforests, mangroves, rivers and fisheries. Among the environmental plans prepared by African countries to date, the majority indicate that unclear rights over the use of natural resources have led to poor management of these resources. Private and communal forms of land ownership are preferable to open access. However, such forms of land ownership may also result in unsustainable management practices if the potential adverse effects on neighbouring farms or the rupture of traditional sociocultural arrangements are not taken sufficiently into account.

Inadequate public awareness and commitment may also heighten environmental problems and is another frequent government or institutional failure. Factors that perpetuate environmental degradation also include: a lack of information, inadequate public awareness about environmental problems and about what causes them, and insufficient political will to address the problems.

Institutional failures related to environmental issues are frequent. Most national environmental strategies and action plans identify institutional weaknesses as a vital factor in contributing to the perpetuation of environmental degradation. Unclear definition of institutional responsibilities and/or weak implementation capacity can undermine well-intentioned efforts to improve environmental management. In many countries, overlapping responsibilities among agencies at different levels of government may send contradictory signals to polluters and lead to conflicting objectives among the various agencies charged with pollution control. Factors that contribute to institutional ineffectiveness include: lobbying by powerful interest groups; short-term planning horizons; and a lack of accountability by public institutions. Other problems that often particularly affect environmental institutions are: a mismatch between assumed responsibilities and the available resources; a lack of qualified personnel; penalties for non-compliance with regulations that are not strict or high enough; inadequate communication; and a weak judiciary.

7.5 DEFINING PRIORITIES FOR ACTION: FINDING SOLUTIONS

As with the selection of priority environmental problems, choosing the most urgent actions to solve them is, in the end, a political matter. However, policy makers need to base their decisions on a sound analysis of both the problems that exist and their possible solutions, given the existing political constraints. They need to be informed about the costs and benefits of alternative actions. The technicalities of benefit–cost analysis are covered later in this book. The usefulness of the analysis is discussed here to set environmental policy priorities.

Once priority environmental problems and their causes have been identified, it is necessary to set realistic objectives and choose the most appropriate policy instruments for intervention. The two parts of the process are interlocked. Before deciding what objectives are most realistic, policy makers need to be familiar with the available instruments for curbing pollution and natural resource degradation, and must gauge the administrative and financial feasibility of alternative ways of attaining desired results in terms of environmental quality and control. Establishing practical environmental goals and targets is also a consensus-building process which requires consultation with relevant stakeholders.

Environmental policy instruments including regulations, economic tools, property rights and other mechanisms such as information, education and direct government investments have been described earlier. These policy instruments may require different incentives, different types of information, and different degrees of institutional capacity in order to be well implemented. To select them, it is important to make maximum use of cost–benefit (Box 7.4) or cost-effectiveness analysis in order to achieve the greatest gain relative to given objectives and available resources. Other criteria to consider in choosing instruments include transparency, through participation with the key stakeholders for instance, flexibility to adjust taxes and fees as conditions change, and their administrative and financial feasibility. Transparency requires an open process of adopting and implementing environmental standards and helps enterprises and other economic actors adapt to changing regulatory conditions. Firms and other stakeholders are more likely to comply with policy instruments when they understand how and why they were chosen and when the stakeholders are part of the decision making process.

Once priorities have been assessed as to the most appropriate instruments and other investments to tackle the most serious environmental problem in the different sectors of the economy, the costs of implementing these actions have to be quantified and proposed in the annual national budget. To the extent that this exercise is backed by an economic analysis, and adequate participation by the key stakeholders, the environmental portion of the national budget should be defended easily as the least cost path on the road to sustainable development.

7.6   PLAN IMPLEMENTATION

Once the strategy has been prepared and transformed into an environmental plan that is backed by a reasonable budget allocation, everything is yet to be

BOX 7.4   THE COSTS AND BENEFITS OF AIR
POLLUTION ABATEMENT IN
SANTIAGO, CHILE

Several air pollution control options for the Santiago metropolitan region were compared using cost–benefit analysis: emission standards for light-duty gasoline vehicles, emission standards for trucks, compressed natural gas for buses, and conversion of wood-burning industrial sources to distillate fuel oil. The following steps were taken to assess the benefits of each option: a dispersion model was used to estimate the improvements in ambient air concentrations from emission reductions; population-based weights were used to estimate exposure above acceptable ambient standards; dose–response functions were used to estimate the health effects of the control strategy, and a simple valuation (lost productivity – see Chapter 10) was used to estimate health benefits in terms of lost workdays; finally, the average daily wage was used to approximate a monetary measure for the health benefits.

Because the costs of each intervention are known, it is possible to compare the (partial) benefits to the known costs. As shown in the table below, a number of the interventions had very high benefit/cost ratios: for example, fixed source measures would cost $9 million per year to implement and would yield expected benefits of over $26 million per year. The study also allowed comparison across various air pollutants to help set priorities among air pollution control investments.

Because the estimated benefits are on the low side (only including health and not other benefits such as damage to infrastructure or aesthetics), the study indicates that the proposed control strategy is attractive on the basis of health benefits alone, and would be even more attractive if other benefits were included.

Costs and benefits of intervention strategies in Santiago

Source	Benefits	Costs	Ratio of benefits to costs
Fixed sources	26.7	9.0	3.0
Gasoline vehicles	32.8	35.0	0.9
Buses	36.6	18.0	2.0
Trucks	7.7	5.0	1.5
Control strategy	103.4	67.0	1.5

Source: Eskeland, G.S. (1994).

done. Rigorous analysis and priority setting will not by itself guarantee effective implementation. Experience in both industrial and developing countries demonstrates that environmental improvement occurs when there is public pressure for change and governments have the necessary commitment and capacity to respond. To ensure successful implementation, it is important for the strategic process to integrate environmental concerns with broader development objectives, involve participation by key stakeholders, ensure well-functioning institutions, mobilize the necessary financial resources, and include provisions for adequate monitoring and evaluation.

Integrating environmental objectives with broader development objectives is critical at the macro and sectoral levels, as highlighted earlier in this book. The search for sustainable development requires that environmental objectives be integrated with broader development goals and that they conform to the social and cultural values of the country. Treating the environment as a separate 'sector', divorced from the overall economy is mistaken and often counterproductive.

For macroeconomic policies, greater knowledge is needed to fully understand their effects on the environment. These have been discussed in some detail in Chapter 3 and existing evidence suggests that: (i) economic instability is generally not good for the environment, because it often leads to accelerated consumption and the rapid depletion of natural resources, and stabilization is necessary but not sufficient for the attainment of environmental objectives; and (ii) the effects of macroeconomic policies on the environment are generally ambiguous and difficult to predict – though in some cases quite straightforward and significant. Instruments other than macroeconomic and sectoral ones, moreover, are normally more appropriate for achieving particular environmental objectives.

Involving key stakeholders is central to a successful national environmental strategy. It should therefore not be developed by government alone. Numerous examples attest to the fact that strategies are more likely to be successful if key stakeholders participate in their preparation. A participatory approach will be more realistic, and will have embedded within it a broader base of knowledge, understanding and commitment from the groups involved.

NESs are generally most effective when their preparation involves the ministries responsible for economic as well as environmental decisions. In Nicaragua, involvement of the Ministry of Economy as the coordinating agency in the planning process, with technical support from the other ministries, raised the political status of the resulting document, which was ultimately signed by the President as the country's official strategy for the environment.

Some groups, especially the very poor, women, indigenous peoples or others not fully mobilized, may not have the organizational or financial ability to participate effectively. These are often the exact stakeholders whose interests are critical to the successful and sustainable implementation of critical aspects of environmental strategies. Special efforts need to be made to balance the disequilibrium of power, prestige, wealth or knowledge that exists when powerful and more established stakeholders are supposed to collaborate in the implementation of a strategy with weaker, less-organized groups.

Most strategies identify well-functioning institutions as one of the most important prerequisites for effectively implementing a national environmental agenda. Without a clear legislative framework and capable institutions, well-conceived policies and other actions to address priority environmental problems cannot be translated into practice. This general lesson is demonstrated across countries. To enhance institutional performance it is important to promulgate transparent and flexible regulations to implement the laws. Although the existing legal framework may provide for comprehensive protection, most countries still need to establish supporting standards and regulations. As demonstrated in numerous NESs, it will be necessary to revise existing standards and regulations where they are excessively stringent, unclear or obsolete. It is also important for institutional effectiveness to ensure the consistency of environmental laws with the laws and incentives of other sectors. Because agents causing environmental degradation tend to respond better to economic incentives than to restrictive regulations, environmental laws should avoid conflicting with the incentives in other sectors. As mentioned earlier (section 6.5), the fiscal incentives provided by the regional development agency in the Brazilian Amazon to attract investments in cattle ranching in the early 1980s encouraged the conversion of virgin forests despite laws requiring the preservation of 50 per cent of the original forest.

Most national, state and local institutions in developing countries lack the necessary financial resources, incentives, and trained staff to carry out their environmental management functions effectively. To a large extent, weak institutional performance reflects a lack of political will. To address these concerns, environmental strategies for several countries (for example, Poland, Indonesia) highlight the need to: increase political awareness by empowering people at the periphery and to facilitate their participation through awareness programmes and devolution of legislative and administrative responsibilities; match management responsibilities with funding and available expertise; create a system of incentives and penalties by the threat of fines and jail terms for the private sector, but also for government agencies, who are themselves polluters; and expand opportunities for private sector involvement as local community groups, local and international NGOs, private firms and research institutes can play a key role in planning and implementing an environmental strategy, since they are in a unique position to identify the most important local problems and propose ways of addressing them and sometimes to implement or monitor the performance of government agencies.

Mobilizing financial resources is important in supporting a NES. However, implementing an environmental strategy is not always expensive. Environmental improvements may often be achieved at little or no financial cost – that is, they are 'win–win' opportunities – simply by removing existing policy distortions, for example removing subsidies that encourage excessive use of natural resources (fossil fuels, irrigation water, trees for logging); and clarifying land rights to promote better land management. These 'win–win' opportunities should be pursued as a first priority.

Even so, in many cases environmental improvements require new investment. Financial support for the national environmental strategy can be mobilized through internal and external sources. Many countries have established national environmental funds to channel revenues from pollution charges, taxes and other sources for environmental improvement purposes. Domestic funding for the implementation of NESs is therefore helped by involving central planning and finance ministries, and national development banks in their preparation. External sources of financing such as the Global Environment Facility can be made available for tackling global externalities such as the loss of biodiversity and climate change.

Effective implementation requires monitoring actions and their consequences in order to understand what works, and what does not. Moreover, new priorities may emerge in response to new information or changing environmental and institutional conditions. Changes in government structures and institutional capacity may also alter the effectiveness of the policies selected. In all of these cases it is important to learn from experience. The use of performance indicators is one way to meet the need for information on the pace and direction of environmental change. This information can then be used to adjust policies as appropriate. Some performance indicators are based on regularly collected statistical data for resources such as forests and fish stocks. In other cases, such as urban air pollution, special monitoring systems may need to be established and maintained. Many countries have only begun to set up environmental information systems and fewer still have developed performance indicators that draw upon this database.

7.7   CONCLUSIONS

Environmental strategy making is an ongoing process, not a one-off event. Effective policy making will require environmental strategies to be updated on a regular basis. Much has been learned to date with respect to national environmental management and these findings are now being applied to the next generation of environmental strategies. Two lessons, in particular, stand out for future application: the need for rigorous analysis in establishing priority actions, and the importance of public participation. Box 7.5 presents some key lessons on the political economy of establishing environmental priorities and strategies.

BOX 7.5   KEY LESSONS FOR POLICY MAKERS

Set priorities   Strategies cannot be effectively implemented without defining the priority actions. Priority setting requires clearly defined criteria and agreement among key stakeholders. In choosing priority actions, each stakeholder group must be committed to its role in implementing the strategy and understand what will be gained and lost in meeting environmental objectives.

Balance analysis and participation   Analysis and participation are both critical for effective priority setting. The overriding challenge is achieving the right balance between the findings of economic and technical analyses on one hand, and stakeholder concerns and preferences on the other.

Involve the right actors   A plan is more likely to be effectively implemented when those responsible for economic as well as environmental decision making participate in its preparation. An environmental document has more political influence when ministries involved with the environment work closely with those responsible for overall national resource allocation. Well-trained and experienced staff are also needed to manage the strategic process and ensure its continuity.

Clarify the objectives   Misconceptions about the purpose of an environmental strategy on the part of the public and donors can lead to disappointment and ultimate abandonment of the strategy. The public needs to be aware that strategies are not funding instruments and investments will not necessarily follow. Likewise donors cannot expect their investments to solve problems unless the necessary policy reforms and intersectoral coordination are undertaken. To ensure that expectations are realistic, a strategy's objectives and scope need to be well defined at the time of its initiation.

Ensure quick victories   Local populations need evidence of positive change to build and sustain their commitment to environmental management. The implementation of pilot programmes or demonstration projects can show the importance of environmental strategies in improving the quality of life.

Insist on donor coordination   Although the many external donors involved in environmental programmes frequently resist coordination, successful implementation of environmental strategies and action plans will depend on coordinating the investments of the external actors involved in environmental management to reduce duplication and inconsistencies. One possible mechanism to increase collaboration and coordination is to form a coordinating group composed of international agencies, major donors, recipient countries and NGOs, to exchange information, promote consistency of projects with environmental strategies, and coordinate investments.

Monitor the results   Inadequate information places considerable constraints on effective environmental management. In the earliest stages of environmental strategy making, particular attention needs to be given to expanding and updating the information base. In addition, the resulting strategy or plan needs to include arrangements for monitoring, evaluating, and updating them to incorporate lessons learned from experiences and ensure appropriate adjustments to ongoing programmes and investments.

The future of national environmental strategies certainly lies in incorporating environmental concerns into the broader process of decision making for sustainable development. This will require increased attention to monitoring implementation, revising existing national environmental policies, and improving coordination within and among countries, donors and other international organizations. Particularly important challenges are the need to develop environmental strategies at both the subnational and international levels, as well as to incorporate global concerns into national environmental priority-setting.

NOTE

1. This chapter draws heavily on World Bank (1995a).

CITED BIBLIOGRAPHY

Eskeland, G.S. (1994), 'A presumptive Pigovian Tax: complementing regulation to mimic an emission fee', *World Bank Review*, **8** (3), 373–94.

International Institute for Environment and Development (IIED) (1994), 'National sustainable development strategies: experience and dilemmas', *Environmental Planning Issues*, No. 6 October.

World Bank (1995a), *National Environmental Strategies – Learning from Experiences*, Washington, DC: World Bank.

World Bank (1995b), *Taking Stock of National Environmental Strategies*, World Bank Environmental Management Series, Washington, DC: World Bank.

ANNEX 7A1   QUESTIONS FOR DISCUSSION

Question 1
(a) Does an NES exist for the country you are considering?
(b) If one does exist, when was it most recently updated?

Question 2
(a) What do you consider the major environmental problems in your country?
(b) How could you practically prioritise these problems further – given your data constraints?

Question 3
Identify the main 'pressure' and 'enabling' factors that are causing environmental degradation.

Question 4
(a) Which environmental policy instruments are currently used in the country considered?
(b) Are there any additional instruments that you think should be used in the light of your study of the likely causes of the existing environmental problems and after reading about environmental instruments (Chapters 5 and 6)?

Question 5
(a) What are the key stakeholders that need to be consulted when drawing up the NES in your country?
(b) Do these groups participate at present in policy development?
(c) From the political economy view, what factors should be emphasized for your NES?

8. Economy-wide policies and the valuation of environmental impacts

OBJECTIVE

To link economy-wide policies and the environment (Part I) with the valuation of environmental impacts of projects, programmes and policies (Part II).

SUMMARY

Correction for possible negative environmental consequences of otherwise appropriate economy-wide policies can be made through the use of instruments or programmes seen here as the aggregation of many small projects. At the project level the environmental assessment (EA) needs to be integrated into the economic analysis. The likely negative environmental impacts of projects have to be identified early in the project cycle. The differences in the analysis for projects with environmental impacts are (a) extending the physical input–output schedule in time and space using the EA; (b) shadow pricing not only for policy failures but also for market and institutional failures; (c) comparing costs and benefits using net present value (NPV) type criteria, a real social discount rate, and a with–without analysis format; and (d) considering various objectives in a participatory decision-making process.

8.1 INTRODUCTION

This chapter links Part I of the book, which looks at economy-wide policies from the macro and sectoral levels, with Part II, which deals with environmental valuation at the project and programme levels. Much of the analysis at the macro and sectoral levels involves defining priorities and selecting policy instruments to achieve stated objectives. In doing so, some measure of the costs and the benefits is required to enable the comparison of instruments. Valuation is also needed to quantify external costs for pricing policies, to estimate environmental damages resulting from macroeconomic reforms, and to estimate depletion of resources for environmental accounting, among others. So far, the valuation methods have not been discussed. The next part of the book is devoted exclusively to that.

To clarify the link between the two parts of the book, let us return to the framework contained in Chapter 1 explaining the sequence of the chapters. With a vision of global sustainability (Chapter 2), we have looked at economy-wide policies (Chapters 3 and 4) and the environment and proposed environmental instruments to mitigate some of the environmental impacts of these policies (Chapters 5 and 6). The prioritization of environmental impacts and remedies was considered through consideration of the design of national environmental strategies (NESs) (Chapter 7). We now need to examine the valuation methods used in benefit–cost analysis, particularly the shadow pricing of environmental goods and services.

Classical project analysis estimates shadow prices to correct for policy failures. For environmental shadow pricing one needs to further correct for market and institutional factors (see Chapter 4, Figure 4.2). Didactically it is useful to note here that if the environmental impacts of macroeconomic and sectoral policies had been addressed properly through the use of environmental instruments (taxes, subsidies and regulations, among others), there would be no need to shadow price. The market prices in the economy would give the right signals to allocate resources to maximize social welfare sustainably. However, this hypothetical case never exists, so there is a need to use valuation techniques correctly to elicit the shadow price of environmental goods and services. The institutional frameworks that can be used to integrate the environmental impacts into the decision-making process were discussed in Section 6.5.

In the remaining part of the book, we shall often explain the valuation concept at the level of a project or investment, but the same method can be applied at the programme or policy level. It is useful to conceive policy instruments as programmes consisting of a great number of small projects: many farmers planting subsidized seedlings, for instance, or the addition of catalytic converters to a fleet of taxis. In this way the link between the valuation methods at project or policy level are easier to visualize.

The difference in the analysis of projects or investments with environmental impacts is that they need to incorporate the information provided by both the environmental and social assessments in the economic cash flows of the investment. Soil nutrient leaching caused by erosion resulting from a project, for instance, will have to be valued and entered into cash flow analysis. Four steps in the analysis of projects with environmental impacts are described in this chapter. The following chapters will describe in more detail the valuation methods and offer some examples.

8.2   THE PROJECT CYCLE AND ENVIRONMENTAL ASSESSMENT

Baum (1982) distinguishes five main steps in the project cycle: identification, preparation, appraisal, implementation with monitoring and evaluation. The environmental aspects should be considered early on and all along the project cycle (see Figure 8.1).

Recently, a new project cycle has been proposed to give more flexibility in the appraisal of projects. It consists of a four-stage process: listening, piloting, demonstrating and mainstreaming (Piccioto and Weaving 1994). The cycle starts with small activities which try innovative ideas proposed by the beneficiaries themselves, building on successes along the new circle of learning. Once the project is shown to be sustainable, a full-scale investment is envisaged.

8.3   APPRAISAL OF A PROJECT WITH ENVIRONMENTAL IMPACTS

The differences between the analysis of projects when environmental impacts (EIs) are included and when they are not are summarized in Table 8.1. Inclusion may involve the following steps:

- extending the physical input–output (I/O) table in time and space using an environmental assessment;
- extending the economic analysis by shadow pricing inputs and outputs to account not only for policy failures but also for market and institutional failures;
- comparing benefit/cost (B/C) with NPV criteria (annuity or periodic) using a real long-term discount rate and a long or indefinite time span; and
- comparing projects with different objectives through real participation.

The with–without analysis principle is particularly useful in assessing the environmental impacts of projects. The worth of a project has to take into con-

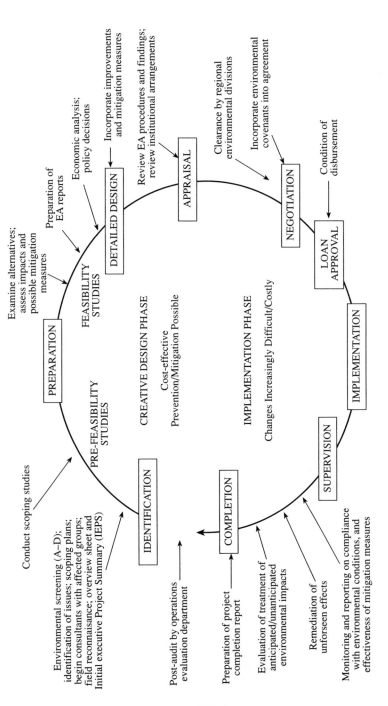

Figure 8.1 Environmental assessment and the project cycle

273

Table 8.1 Appraisal of projects with environmental impacts

Steps in project analysis	EIs not included	EIs included
1. I/O of the project	Direct production	Production function plus an EA (expand the physical analysis in space and time)
2. Valuation	Market prices or shadow prices correcting mostly for policy failures	Shadow prices rectifying for policy but also market and institutional failures
3. B/C	Use NPV, IRR*, B/C criteria together with risk analysis	Mostly NPV kind of criteria, but also cost-effectiveness, often with an unlimited time span, together with uncertainty analysis
4. Decision making	Mostly efficiency objective	Efficiency plus social and environmental objectives balanced through public participation

Note: * Internal Rate of Return.

274

sideration the opportunity cost of the resources used. The economic benefit of a project is the difference in present value between the with and without project alternatives. The with–without project situation should not be confused with a before–after situation.

What the analyst needs is an estimate of what *would* have happened in the period over which the project has impacts, had there been no project. For instance, the decrease in soil productivity for agriculture should be considered when appraising forestry projects in an area where marginal agriculture and grazing are taking place and for which yield will decrease over time (see Figure 8.2). The policy framework, laws and regulations, for instance, can also change over the life span of the project. Environmental assessments, like the economic analysis, are also based on the with–without principle: the ecosystems with or without the project have to be compared to assess the environmental impacts.

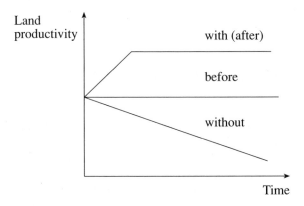

Figure 8.2   Land productivity: with and without analysis

The consideration of interdependence and separability of project components is important in analysing projects with environmental impacts. Different components of projects may damage the environment. The EA may recommend some mitigation measures and some alternative project designs. The mitigation alternatives need to be compared economically and a separate appraisal made for each alternative. The separation of physical inputs and outputs by component is thus important in appraising projects with environmental impacts.

8.4   STEP 1: EA AND THE WITH–WITHOUT ANALYSIS

Simply put, an EA describes the impacts on the environment with a project and compares them to the impacts on the same environment as the impacts would have occurred without the project. The same approach is taken by the economic analysis. To do this systematically, different attempts to categorize the elements comprising the environment, also called attributes, have been made. Changes in the environmental attributes provide indicators of changes in the environment. The EA describes and quantifies, then aggregates the effects of project activities on these attributes.

The EA measures attributes with and without the project, or an activity within the project, at a given point in time. Figure 8.2 illustrates the measure of productivity with and without a project over time. The measure of attributes may also change over time without the activity (avoid a 'before' analysis, as was said for the economic analysis). The impacts have to be measured in terms of the 'net' changes in the attribute at a given point in time. The main steps in an EA are thus: (i) describe the baseline; (ii) identify the potential impacts (screening, scoping); (iii) measure the impacts; (iv) aggregate impacts on the environment; and (v) propose mitigation measures to minimize the environmental impacts which need to be monitored during the project.

8.5   STEP 2: FINANCIAL AND ECONOMIC APPRAISAL

Once in possession of the technical and EA studies, the financial appraisal analyses an investment from an individual point of view, while economic analysis takes a societal point of view (see Table 8.2). Financial and economic values are similar if there are no policy failures and no environmental or social impacts of using resources in producing goods and services. If policies such as minimum prices or price ceilings, quotas or subsidies for production, imports or exports, monopoly or 'monopsony' (single buyer), oligopoly or 'oligopsony' (few buyers), speculation on market prices among others, are not rectified by macroeconomic or sector adjustments, prices have to be approximated for what they really would be if the right policies were in place. Shadow prices may be higher or lower than market prices. Subsidies for natural resources lower prices and so increase demand. Most of the time, this would create negative environmental impacts. Shadow pricing for policy failures may eliminate many investments that could have negative effects on the environment. These issues have been discussed previously in Chapter 4.

Shadow-pricing investments has been mentioned earlier and will not be covered in detail here. The economic value represents consumers' willingness to pay (WTP). In theory, a perfectly competitive market provides the right values of goods and services in that market, given existing policies affecting WTP. In the case of input values or costs, the term 'opportunity' cost is often used – it is the value forgone by not being able to use the input in its next best alternative and it is measured in terms of consumers' WTP for the goods and/or

Table 8.2   *Financial and economic analysis*

	Financial analysis	Economic analysis
Point of view	Net returns to equity capital or to private group or individual	Net returns to society
Purpose of analysis	Indication of incentive to adopt or implement	Determine if government investment is justified on economic efficiency basis
Treatment of prices	Market or administered (may assume that markets are perfect or that administered prices have compensated for imperfections)	May require 'shadow prices' (e.g., monopoly in markets, external effects, unemployed/underemployed factors, overvalued currency)
Taxes	Cost of production	Part of total societal benefits
Subsidies	Source of revenue	Part of total societal cost
Loans	Increase capital resources available	A transfer payment; transfers a claim to resource flow
Interest or loan repayment	A financial cost; decreases capital resources available	A transfer payment
Discount rate	Marginal cost of money; market borrowing rate	Opportunity cost of capital; social time preference rate
Income distribution	Not normally considered in financial analysis although data on income flows is available	Is not considered in economic efficiency analysis. Can be done as separate analysis or as weighted efficiency analysis

services forgone. So, for both inputs and outputs, WTP is the basis for valuation in economic analysis.

In practical terms, the actual market prices, sometimes local, often international, are taken as a good approximation of economic values. The need to calculate shadow prices at the project level will depend on how much economic policies are distorted and the importance of the value of an input or output in the project – that is, its impact on profitability. Often, shadow prices may have been pre-calculated at the national or sectoral level for important inputs or outputs. The importance of the project in the overall economy – that is, its impact on supply – is also a factor that will indicate the need to shadow price a particular investment proposed to foster economic development.

Economic cash flows ignore transfer payments such as taxes, subsidies and interest paid within the society from which point of view the analysis is made. The reasoning behind it is that transfers do not use resources *per se* but are merely transfer payments from one group or individual to another within a society. In environmental economics, many costs and benefits are evaluated at the global level. In this case, even interest on a loan paid outside a country is considered as a transfer. The correction of price for transfer payments may have important impacts on resources used and the environment. A subsidy on land clearing speeds up deforestation, but on kerosene it can slow down fuelwood harvesting.

8.6 STEP 3: SHADOW PRICING FOR MARKET FAILURES

Since most environmental goods and services are characterized by externalities, further shadow pricing is sometimes necessary. If markets are perfect and externalities internalized through effective institutional arrangements, prices of environmental goods and services would be found in the economy, which reflect their real value. However, prices should be corrected often for policy failures, as reviewed in the preceding section. When no market prices exist or prices need to be corrected for externalities, one can use direct proxies for valuing environmental impacts which are usually cost based, or indirect proxies, for example by revealing embedded environmental values from property assets, such as land prices. When no proxy is available, we are forced to survey WTP directly such as in the contingent valuation method. Valuation techniques can be organized along the lines of Figure 8.3. Most valuation techniques are enumerated in Box 8.1, however, many other groupings can be imagined (OECD, EDI, ODI 1995). These techniques are discussed further in the following chapters.

The valuation methods mentioned here generate prices that are not corrected for institutional failures or intergenerational externalities. The user costs associated with them and with non-renewable resources will often be added to the price found with these techniques (Harou et al. 1994). It includes the present value of the future capital required to produce substitute goods and services when the ones enjoyed now will be exhausted. This assumes perfect substitutability between the two natural resources or environmental goods.

8.7 STEP 4: DISCOUNT RATE AND COMPARISON OF COSTS AND BENEFITS

To compare the benefits and costs of an investment over time, especially long-term environmental investments, the discount rate is crucial. The appropriate discount rate to use for an economic analysis, especially where the project has environmental impacts, is a controversial topic.

The discount rate should not be different for a project with environmental impacts. The crux of the analysis consists in quantifying the appropriate I/O

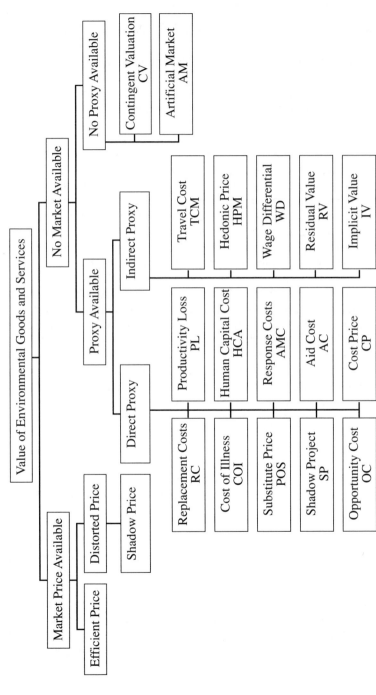

Figure 8.3   A possible taxonomy of valuation techniques

279

BOX 8.1   EXAMPLES OF VALUATION TECHNIQUES

Direct proxies to estimate environmental impacts do not pretend to reflect WTP but to estimate a lower, or sometimes upper, bound of that value. Direct proxies involve costs or price information which approximate values of environmental externalities. The advantages of using costs or existing prices as proxies for WTP is that they are easily observable. Cost-based approaches should be used with caution because these costs do not necessarily equal the benefits of environmental improvements or the damages from degradation. The actual costs incurred as a result of environmental degradation can estimate the minimum benefits of avoiding environmental impacts. So, the loss of agriculture productivity (productivity loss), the cost of medical expenditure (cost of illness), the cost of an ill person or premature death (human capital cost), the cost of averting or mitigating negative environmental impacts (response cost), the cost of replacing environmental goods or services (replacement costs), the cost of an aid project such as grants, debt-for-nature swaps, subsidized loans or donations (aid costs), the reconstruction of an environmental good (shadow project), the cost per unit of output (cost price) or the price of a close substitute are all ways of approximating the value of environmental goods and services using directly observable costs or prices. All these costs could be called opportunity costs. Note that some authors define an 'opportunity cost approach' in the valuation literature specifically for the value of lost opportunities due to environmental protection, that is, the cost of environmental protection. Different costs of the same impact can value different functions of an environmental good or service. The cost of illness, human capital and productivity loss are often complementary in that each reflects a specific aspect of a healthy life. If all three approaches are used to value the different facets of human health impact, one has to be cautious not to double count these different values.

Indirect proxies cannot be found readily for estimating WTP but have to be derived from observed markets, or behaviour in markets, related to the environmental commodity. By examining the prices people pay, or the benefits they apparently derive from environmental services or goods, in these closely related markets, peoples' environmental preferences can be uncovered. The value of these environmental impacts is embedded in the value of an asset (hedonic price) or a job (wage differential) or the time and cost incurred in visiting and enjoying a national park (travel cost method). Residual and implicit values are inferred from final product market prices or environmental values that make a project break even. While the indirect proxy methods involve more calculation they will not necessarily provide a better estimate of willingness to pay for environmental goods and services than the direct proxies. However, they have the advantages of relying on observed behaviour and existing market prices directly related to the environmental attribute being valued.

The contingent valuation method (CVM) consists of asking people directly, via a questionnaire or experimental techniques, what they would be willing to pay for a benefit or what they would be willing to receive as compensation for a deterioration of their environment. The questionnaire simulates a hypothetical (contingent) market of a particular environmental good in which individuals (demand) are asked to state their WTP for a change (improvement or deterioration) in the provision (supply) of the good in question. The questionnaire has to provide the institutional context in which the good would be provided and on the payment vehicle. CVM may apply equally to changes in public goods such as air quality, landscape or the existence values of wildlife but also to goods and services sold to individuals, like water supply and sanitation. It may apply to both use and non-use (existence) values which was not the case for the 'proxy' techniques. The accuracy and reliability of consumer preferences obtained using the CVM have been criticized on grounds of biases inherent in the technique: free-rider, starting-point, information, vehicle and hypothetical bias. The disparity between WTP and WTA can also be important.

While *transfers* of values are usually made with non-market values, it can also be useful to transfer existing prices to environmental goods or services where such a market does not exist. Likewise, costs and benefits can be transferred. In the literature, some define benefit transfer (BT) to mean specifically the transfer of non-market values such as air and water quality, and recreation. The location where the data are generated (study site) could be from a totally different place or country from the area to where the benefits are transferred (policy site). Sometimes only the methodology is transferred; in other cases the data and values are transferred. This method is useful when time and budget are limited, the study site and issues are similar, and the original valuation procedures were sound.

schedule that should be provided by an environmental assessment and in valuing properly these inputs and outputs over the long-term. The value of environmental goods as they become scarcer should appreciate accordingly. The relative price increase of environmental goods and services over time will have to be properly reflected in the cash flow table.

The discount rate used for the economic analysis of projects with environmental impacts is therefore the same as without these impacts, but both are different from the rate used in the financial analysis in which only the opportunity cost of capital is considered. The choice of the discount rate and calculations using the discount rate are now discussed.

8.7.1   Use of the Discount Rate in Project Appraisal

The practice of *discounting* arises because individuals attach less weight to a benefit or cost in the future than they do to a benefit or cost now. Impatience, or 'time preference', is one reason why the present is given more weight than the future. The second reason is that, since capital is productive, a dollar's worth of resources now will generate more than a dollar's worth of goods and services in the future. Hence an entrepreneur is willing to pay more than one dollar in the future to acquire one dollar's worth of these resources now. This argument for discounting is referred to as the 'marginal productivity of capital' argument; the use of the word marginal indicates that it is the productivity of additional units of capital that is relevant.

If a form of damage, valued at X today, but which will occur in T years time is to be discounted at a rate of r per cent, the value of X is reduced to $X/(1 + r)^T$. Clearly the higher is r and the greater is T, the lower will be the value of the discounted damages.

In the appraisal of projects the selection of the discount rate is of critical importance. For a proper economic analysis the relevant rate is the social discount rate, while for a financial analysis the market rate applicable to the sector being analysed is appropriate.

8.7.2   Real and Nominal Discount Rates

Note that all the values in the economic cash flow tables should be in real terms. For financial analysis both real and nominal values may be of interest.

The difference between a real and nominal discount rate is important for long-term environmental impacts to be valued and discounted (Harou 1983). It is recommended that the real rate be used. The appropriate relationship between nominal and real rates of discount is a multiplicative one:

$$(1 + n) = (1 + f)(1 + r)$$

where n is the nominal (inflated discount rate), r is the real discount rate and f is the average annual percentage rate of inflation.

If a nominal rate of discount is used without valuing environmental benefits including an inflation factor, it will bias the analysis against projects with positive environmental impacts. Forecasting inflation is often impossible so that working with real values and discount rates is highly recommended on practical grounds for appraising projects with long-term environmental impacts. Only real price increases in environmental goods and services have to be estimated.

The comparison of costs and benefits is often made over a long period of time if long-term environmental impacts of a project are important. The cash flow table should start in year zero, so that initial outlays of funds, often important in the first year of environmental projects, are appropriately reckoned in the net present worth (NPW) equation. Since the approach is to estimate benefits and costs with and without the projects having the impacts (mutually exclusive project alternatives), an NPW type of criteria is used with an infinite, periodic, annual, or simply long enough period to be considered infinite when discounted. For instance, if a limited time span is used to compare mitigation alternatives, an equal time frame has to be chosen for both the with and without situations if the comparison is to be meaningful.

8.7.3   The Social Discount Rate

Excluding questions of risk, the three main contenders for the choice of the social discount rate are (i) the *individual rate of time preference*, based on the rate of individual trade-off between present and future benefits and costs; (ii) the *opportunity cost of capital*, based on the marginal productivity of capital; and (iii) the *social rate of time preference*, based on ethical considerations about the rate at which present and future costs should be traded off.

The individual rate of time preference would be equal to the opportunity cost of capital if there were efficient markets and no taxes. In practice the range of individual time preference rates is large and does not coincide with the rates for the opportunity cost of capital. The individual rate of time preference in developing countries would range widely, from as low as 6 to as high as 100 per cent and above (depending on whether the individual is borrowing or lending). The (risk-free) opportunity cost of capital rate in developing countries is about 10–15+ per cent.

The social rate of time preference, on the other hand, is different to both of the above. Broadly speaking, economists and philosophers would regard it as ethically unjustifiable to discount future benefits and costs at more than 1–3 per cent.

Thus there are two approaches to discounting: an *ethical* approach based on what rates of discount *should* be applied; and a *descriptive* approach based on what rates of discount people (savers as well as investors) *actually* apply in their day-to-day decisions. The former leads to relatively low rates of discount (about 2–3 per cent in real terms) and the latter to relatively higher rates (at least 4 per cent and, in some cases, very much higher rates). As a consequence of the different rates resulting from these techniques, if the prescriptive approach is applied more projects with long-term benefits are accepted. This favours the environment, by and large. On the other hand a lower rate can result in more projects in total, some of which may have damaging environmental consequences. Hence we cannot say a priori what the implications of a lower rate of discount are.

As noted above, a low social rate would result in more projects being selected on the B/C criteria. This might imply that there were not enough resources to fund all of them. In that case a further rule would be needed to select projects. One possibility is to use a shadow price of capital of more than one to allocate scarce funds.

8.7.4   The Market Rate of Discount

Financial analysis would normally apply discount rates that reflected market opportunities for the sector (the opportunity cost of capital). As noted above, these range from 10 to 15 per cent and higher. Of course it is important to note that at such high rates projects with benefits spread over a long term, or where benefits do not start until several years from now, are unlikely to be selected.

Although the above analysis suggests that a low rate of discount be applied to economic analysis, this is not the practice in all multilateral institutions. The World Bank, for example, requires a rate closer to the opportunity cost of capital for the economic as well as the financial analysis. This varies from country to country but is usually around the 10 per cent level.

8.7.5   Discounting Projects With Very Long-term Impacts: The Case of Climate Change

The above analysis, while satisfactory for most projects with impacts over periods as long as 50 years, is not suitable for situations where the effects are likely to take place over much longer periods. A case in point is climate change, where the consequences of actions today will be felt for over 100 years. Here the long-term nature of the problem is the key issue. Any 'realistic' discount rate – that is, one that applies in capital markets in developing countries – would render the damages, which occur over long periods of time, very small. With a horizon of about 200 years, a discount rate of 4 per cent implies that damages of one dollar at the end of the period are valued at 0.04 cents today. At 8 per cent the same damages are worth 0.0002 cents today. Hence at discount rates in this range the damages associated with climate change become very small and even disappear (Cline 1993).

The choice of discount rate has been shown to be a key parameter in the determination of the social costs of CO_2 emissions, and hence the benefits of mitigation policies. Fankhauser (1995) illustrates the sensitivity of the social costs per ton of carbon emitted to changes in the level of the discount rate. Setting the discount rate at 3 per cent, Fankhauser estimated the expected shadow value of 1990 CO_2 emissions at \$5.50/tC and for 2030 emissions the value was \$8.30/tC. Taking a discount rate of 0, however, yielded an expected value of \$48.8/tC in 1990 and \$62.9/tC in 2030. This high sensitivity is as a result of the long time horizon over which the damages of climate change occur.

In view of the above, many economists feel that climate change impacts have to be discounted at a lower rate, perhaps close to the social rate referred to above. This is formally justified by empirical and theoretical arguments that point to a rate that declines with time. An important paper in this area is Cropper et al. (1994). From surveys of individual trade-offs over time, they estimate a nominal rate of time preference of about 16.8 per cent, based on a sophisticated questionnaire approach to valuing present versus future risks. Most importantly, however, the Cropper et al. paper points to a *declining* rate of discount – that is, to a rate that is not constant over time but gets smaller as the time horizon lengthens. So whereas the 16.8 per cent rate applies to a five-year time horizon, a rate of only 3.4 per cent applies to a 100-year horizon. In another innovative survey, Weitzman (1998) found that the discount rate suggested by professional economists falls progressively, from 4 to 0 per cent as the perspective shifts from the immediate (up to 5 years hence) to the far distant future (beyond 300 years). Weitzman suggests that the appropriate discount rate for long-lived projects is less than 2 per cent, based upon this analysis.

8.7.6   Recommended Approach to Discounting

The approach recommended here for its practicability is to calculate a discount rate embodying both the opportunity cost of capital and the social time preference, that is, the weights society places on consumption at different points in the future (Harou 1985). The economic NPW of a project is

$$NPW = \sum_{t=0}^{\infty} \frac{B_t - C_t}{(1+r)^t} - \alpha K_0 \tag{8.1}$$

where B_t and C_t are the social benefits and costs in year t, r is the rate of social time preference (also called social discount rate, SDR), K_0 is the capital invested in terms of year zero, and α is the opportunity cost per dollar of public investment usually in terms of private investment forgone.

The term α in the above formula is sometimes called the shadow price of investment. It replaces the nominal price of funds of one rupee per rupee or dollar per dollar. If $\alpha = 2$, the investment must show a present value of $2 per dollar invested instead of $1 per dollar invested. It depends on the percentage of funds diverted from the private sector, if any, and on the opportunity cost of capital from the private sector. In its simplest form α could be derived as

$$\alpha = \frac{\rho}{r} \tag{8.2}$$

if we assume that reinvestments in perpetuity in the private sector are included in the private sector opportunity cost of capital ρ. To the extent that capital markets are not perfect and that externalities exist, ρ and r are different. The social rate of time preference is usually lower than the opportunity cost of private capital and so $\alpha > 1$.

8.8   STEP 5: DECISION-MAKING WITH PARTICIPATION

The EA should involve people from the outset. Public participation plays a key role in assessing environmental impacts, comparing alternatives, designing appropriate mitigation measures, and building local ownership and participation into the development. If real consultation has occurred, most social externalities are incorporated into the project analysis at that point. However, participation is also important in the final step of the decision process when comparing final investment alternatives, given budget constraints when different objectives and criteria are considered simultaneously. The more participative the project appraisal had been, the faster and easier will be the last step in the appraisal of projects with environmental impacts. Different participatory tools exist to organize the inputs of stakeholders (World Bank 1996).

8.9   CONCLUSION

Environmental impacts have to be considered early on in the project cycle. If biophysical impacts exist, they have to be described or quantified through an EA comparing environmental impacts with and without the project and by project components. Environmental impacts have to be identified on a wider space and time scale than projects without impacts. Cash flow tables with and without the project have to be estimated in real terms and discounted with a rate reflecting both the opportunity cost of capital and the rate of social time preference. Valuations for correcting policy failures are done through classical shadow pricing mimicking perfect policies and market. Prices still have to be corrected for externalities and institutional failures. Appropriate environmental shadow prices should correct not only for policy but also, to the extent possible, for externalities, and institutional failures. Underlying the entire process of appraisal of projects with environmental impacts is the biophysical I/O schedule that should be produced by a relevant EA. By appraising projects and programmes following this approach, Harou, Daly and Goodland (1994) suggested that environmental sustainability policies could be implemented incrementally.

CITED BIBLIOGRAPHY

Baum, W. (1982), *The Project Cycle*, Washington, DC: World Bank.

Cline, W.M. (1993), 'Give greenhouse abatement a fair chance', *Finance and Development*, **30** (1), March, 3–5.

Cropper, M., S.K. Ayedale and P.R. Portney (1994), 'Preferences for life saving programs: how the public discounts time and age', *Journal of Risk and Uncertainty*, **8**, 243–65.

Fankhauser, S. (1995), *Valuing Climate Change: The Economics of the Greenhouse*, London: Earthscan.

Harou, P. (1983), 'On the real rate of discount', *Forest Science*, **29** (2), 249–52.

Harou, P. (1985), 'On a social discount rate', *Canadian Journal of Forest Research*, **15** (5), 927–34.

Harou, P., H. Daly and R. Goodland (1994), 'Environmental sustainability through project appraisals', *International Journal of Sustainable Development*, **2** (3), 13–21.

Intergovernmental Panel on Climatic Change (IPCC) (1996), *Climate Change 1995: Economic and Social Dimensions of Climate Change*, edited by J. Bruce, H. Lee and E. Haites, Cambridge: Cambridge University Press.

Organization for Economic Cooperation and Development, Economic Development Institute and Overseas Development Institute (OECD, EDI, ODI) (1995) *The Economic Appraisal of Environmental Projects and Policies: A Practical Guide*, Paris: OECD.

Picciotto, R. and R. Weaving (1994), 'A new project cycle for the World Bank?', *Finance and Development*, **31** (4), December, pp. 42–44.

Weitzman, M. (1998), 'Gamma discounting for global Warming', Discussion Paper, Harvard University, Cambridge, MA.

World Bank (1996), *The World Bank Participation Sourcebook*, Washington DC: World Bank.

PART II

Environmental Valuation Methods for Policies
and Projects

9. Economic principles and overview of valuation methods

OBJECTIVE

This chapter introduces the main valuation methods and the basic economic concepts underlying them.

SUMMARY

The chapter introduces the basic concept of the total economic value (TEV) of an environmental change, reviewing its main components. To express in monetary terms the TEV of an environmental change, the individual willingness to pay (WTP) or willingness to accept compensation (WTA) need to be estimated. A classification of valuation methods is presented.

9.1   INTRODUCTION

The previous chapter has shown the importance of extending the methods of project appraisal to include environmental impacts. These impacts need to be valued as, due to the various market, policy and institutional failures discussed earlier, often environmental goods and services have no market price or have the wrong price.

A major difficulty in the analysis of projects with environmental impacts is to identify the complete range of costs/benefits and then to place a monetary value on those that are not marketed. The environmental assessment (EA) helps to identify the full range of environmental inputs and outputs that need to be considered. The valuation methods described in this chapter help to provide values where no price exists for these environmental inputs and outputs.

This chapter provides the underlying theoretical principles for the measurement of the economic value of environmental goods and services and an overview of the available techniques.

9.2   TOTAL ECONOMIC VALUE OF AN
ENVIRONMENTAL ASSET

Before proceeding with the analysis of the techniques available for expressing in money terms the value of environmental assets, the nature of such a value must be explored. The economic value of environmental goods has a composite nature. Two broad categories of values are defined in the literature: *use values* and *non-use values.*

Use values are defined as those benefits that derive from the actual use of the environment. For example, people can derive a benefit from burning firewood, using herbs for medicinal purposes, walking in a forest, watching birds or admiring the landscape. In turn, use values are divided, depending on the author, into *primary values* or *marketed goods and services* or *consumptive values*, and *secondary values* or *non-marketed goods and services* or *non-consumptive values* (Pearce and Turner 1990; Sharma 1992; Bateman 1993). Some authors have also suggested an additional category of use values to include those values that are not readily perceived when individuals are asked to evaluate the value of a natural resource. For example, an individual may not be aware of the value of trees on greenhouse effects and the importance of the latter.

In addition to the above use values, economists have also introduced the concept of *option values*, that is, the additional value placed on a natural resource by those people who want to have the option of using the goods and services in the future. This concept is based on two basic arguments: uncertainty and irreversibility related to environmental issues. It is assumed here that if an individual is uncertain whether the asset will be available in the future, s/he will be willing to pay a sum in excess of his/her expected consumer surplus to ensure that the environmental asset will be available in the future. The option value, therefore, can influence decision making regarding the most efficient allocation of natural assets (that is, conservation versus development).[1]

Non-use values are also described as 'existence values'. The argument behind existence value is that people care about the environment not only because they, or their heirs, can get some sort of benefit, or can avoid some sort of loss, by using or preserving environmental assets. People wish to maintain or improve environmental assets out of sympathy for animals and nature or from moral conviction. There is therefore an intrinsic value, 'a value that resides 'in' something and that is unrelated to human beings altogether'.[2] Sometimes a bequest value is also added to non-use values (Bateman 1993), although this is controversial. This value involves altruism such as, for example, the desire to preserve environmental assets for the enjoyment of other people of both the present and future generations. Some authors distinguish, however, between pure existence value and bequest value, which is also sometimes considered as an option value.

Table 9.1 provides an example of the taxonomy described above with reference to the forest resources.[3]

Table 9.1   Forest assets and their service flows

		Use values		Non-use values	
Non-perceived	Primary	Secondary	Option	Bequest	Existence
Climate mitigation Air quality Soil quality Water flow	Timber Fruits, nuts, latex, gum arabic, litter, etc. Fuelwood Forage and fodder Developed recreation	Wildlife Scenery Non-developed recreation Biodiversity Community integrity	Biodiversity Recreation Community integrity Scenery Wildlife	Biodiversity Scenery Recreation	Biodiversity Wildlife Scenery

Following Table 9.1, the total economic value is obtained as follows:[4]:

$$TEV = UV + NUV, \qquad (9.1)$$

where

TEV = total economic value
UV = use values
NUV = non-use values.

$$UV = NPV + PG + SG + OV,\qquad(9.2)$$

where

NPV = non-perceived values
PG   = primary goods/services
SG   = secondary goods/services
OV   = option value.

and

$$NUV = EV + BV\qquad(9.3)$$

where

EV   = existence value
BV   = bequest value.

Even if, in practice, it is not easy to untangle these different components, and frequently this is not required, it is worth bearing in mind the above concepts when estimating the value of environmental goods and services.

In many circumstances it is of crucial importance to assess the total value of environmental assets, or that of some components of it, in monetary terms. It will often be the case that the benefits of a proposed development will be much greater than the primary use value of a resource but much less than the TEV of the resource. In order to have a convincing argument that the development should not proceed, or that a different development scheme is preferable, it is important to assign monetary values to as many categories of economic value as possible, while avoiding double counting of some of the environmental benefits. If the analyst manages to measure with a monetary yardstick environmental goods or bads, it will be possible to include these monetary values within the framework of benefit–cost analysis (BCA) of projects, in policy analysis, as well as in the construction of green national accounts. In such a way project/policy makers will be provided with more powerful information for decision making. The primary purpose of this handbook is to provide some of the tools to quantify these values.

9.3   BASIC CONCEPTS OF VALUATION METHODS

9.3.1   The Willingness to Pay/Accept as a Measure of the Economic Value

The monetary valuation of an environmental good is usually based on the monetary value that individuals place on it.

The maximum amount of money an individual is willing to pay for obtaining a benefit or avoiding a loss in most situations reflects the intensity of his/her preferences for such a benefit or loss.[5] These preferences in turn are based on the values s/he attaches to goods. The maximum willingness to pay (WTP) can be considered an expression of the individual's values. Analogously, the minimum willingness to accept (WTA) is an amount of money considered as compensation for forgoing a benefit or for incurring a loss and this reflects the value of such a benefit or loss.

When an individual buys an asset paying the market price, the price paid directly reveals a lower bound of his/her maximum WTP. It indeed reveals that his/her WTP to pay for such an asset is at least equal to the price paid. For example, if we observe an individual paying 10 monetary units (MU) for a kilogram of sugar, this means that he/she is willing to pay at least 10 MU for each kilogram of sugar of that quality, otherwise s/he would not buy it at that price. His/her maximum WTP must be equal to or greater than 10 MU.

Similarly, when an individual sells an asset receiving the market price, the amount of money received directly reveals an upper bound for his/her minimum WTA for forgoing the use of such an asset. For example, if we observe an individual selling a kilogram of sugar at 10 MU, it means that his/her minimum WTA as compensation for giving up one kilogram of sugar is not greater than 10 MU. This is illustrated in Figure 9.1.

When there is no market for an asset, obviously there is no market price that reveals the lower bound of the individual's maximum WTP and the upper bound of the minimum WTA. In this case there is no useful yardstick for the value that individuals attach to such an asset. To evaluate people's WTP or WTA, that is, to obtain a monetary measure of the value individuals attach to a non-marketed asset, it is necessary to use alternative means. These alternative means are the techniques presented in the following chapters. Before dealing with these, however, some general concepts regarding WTP / WTA need to be introduced.

Both maximum WTP and minimum WTA of individuals for a change in the level of an environmental asset can be measured looking at the variations of the individual's monetary expenditure required to keep him/her indifferent in terms of satisfaction (welfare), when the change occurs.[6] Maximum WTP and minimum WTA can then be taken to be monetary indicators of the individual's welfare changes.

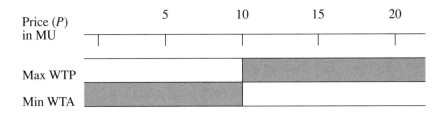

Note: For example, a kilogram of sugar is traded at $P = 10$ MU. It means that the lower bound to max WTP to get a kilo of sugar is 10 MU. Besides, 10 MU is the upper bound to min WTA to give up a kilo of sugar. Max WTP and min WTA are somewhere above 10 MU and below 10 MU respectively.

Figure 9.1   Price as lower bound to max WTP and upper bound to min WTA

Changes in the level of provision of an environmental asset can affect the welfare of individuals in different ways, according to basic economic features of the asset. An environmental asset may be priced, such that individuals have to pay some amount of money to secure its use (for example, piped water). However, many environmental assets are public or semi-public goods, which, while affecting the welfare of each individual, are not under the control of each individual (for example, the quality of the air). According to these specific features of the asset, an individual therefore may be willing to pay or accept as compensation, to obtain or avoid the following types of changes in the asset: (a) decreases in price; (b) increases in price; (c) improvement in the quantity/quality available; and (d) degradation of the quantity/quality available. In these different contexts the individual's maximum WTP and minimum WTA are measured using the economic concepts of compensating variation (CV), equivalent variation (EV), compensating surplus (CSU) and equivalent surplus (ESU). A summary of the various cases analysed is provided in Figure 9.2, and the concepts are elaborated in the next section.

The concepts of CV and EV, and CSU and ESU, are discussed in the following section. The concept of consumer surplus (CS), a device for estimating valuation measures in practice, is examined in Section 9.3.3.

9.3.2   Measures of Welfare: Compensating and Equivalent Variations

One of the major issues in welfare economics is how to derive the measures of a change in welfare as described above. Two main approaches are practicable:

1. One can analyse the actual consumer behaviour, the consumer's reactions in adjusting the bundle of goods consumed in response to changes in the

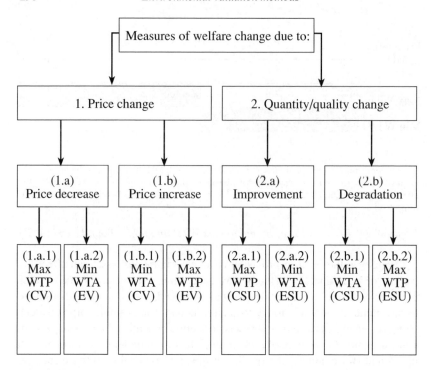

Legend
CV = Compensating variation
EV = Equivalent variation
CSU = Compensating surplus
ESU = Equivalent surplus

Figure 9.2   Measures of max WTP and min WTA for price and quantity changes

     set of prices faced or in the change in quantity consumed of an environmental good/service. In such cases the analyst looks at the so-called 'revealed preferences', that is, s/he recovers from the actual behaviour the consumer's preferences and uses this information to work out money measures of the consumer's welfare changes.

2. Asking the consumers directly their willingness to pay or willingness to accept for a proposed price change or for the envisaged quantity change. This approach utilizes the family of techniques sometimes called 'stated preferences techniques', that is, based on what the consumer states when directly asked to express his/her value judgement.

This is why it is important to have a closer look at the reactions of the consumer to changes in prices or quantities consumed of environmental goods or services.[7]

Consider a typical 'two good' case, where X_e is the quantity of environmental good/service, X_a is a composite bundle of all the other consumer's goods and m is income. Let us start by considering a price decrease of the environmental good/service e. Suppose it were possible to operate an income compensation that leads the consumer to be indifferent to a decrease in the price P_e, taking from him/her enough income to leave him/her on the current welfare level U_0 (see Figure 9.3a). The CV for the price decrease is the amount of money that has to be deducted from the income of the consumer to keep him/her at the same utility level as without the price decrease. The CV corresponds to the maximum WTP of a rational individual to obtain such price decrease. In this way, the 'income effect' of the price reduction is removed. Due to the substitution effect, however, the consumer will increase the optimal demand of X_e to X_{e1}, because now the good e is relatively cheaper. In Figure 9.3b, we can therefore draw the 'income compensated' demand curve for the good X_e, given the utility level U_0, or the demand as a function of price P_e, and utility U_0 – that is the so-called 'Hicksian demand curve', $h_e(P_e, U_0)$. Drawing the compensated demand curve $h_e(P_e, U_0)$ allows us to geometrically represent the CV for the price decrease as the area (a) in Figure 9.3b, that is, the area $P_{e0} AB P_{e1}$ under the compensated demand curve $h_e(P_e, U_0)$ between the line of the prices. The proof of the correspondence between the CV and the area under the compensated demand curve is complex and cannot be reported here.[8]

If we were not constraining the individual to the utility level U_0 by taking away some income and compensating for the price reduction, with the income m_o, the individual facing the price decrease would have had the possibility of increasing the demand for e up to X_{e2}, enjoying the utility level U_1. This enables us to draw the so-called 'Marshallian demand curve' $X_e(P_e, m_o)$ reported in Figure 9.3b.

Aware of the fact that enjoying both the price decrease and the current level of income the consumer could enjoy the utility level U_1, s/he can work out his/her consumption of X_e, which allows him/her to stay at the utility level U_1 *facing* the current price P_0 (see Figure 9.3a). S/he would consume the quantity X_{e3}, but s/he would require some additional income to afford the increase in consumption from X_{e0} (current level of consumption) to X_{e3}. The EV for a price decrease is the additional income to be given to the consumer to bring him/her to the same level of utility U_1, s/he would attain with the current income if the price decrease from P_{e0} to P_{e1} occurred. It corresponds to the rational consumer's minimum Willingness To Accept as compensation (min WTA) for giving up the price decrease. We can therefore draw a demand curve of the individual, $h_e(P_e, U_1)$ which is 'income compensated' on the level of utility U_1 (see Figure 9.3b). The EV for the price decrease is represented by the area $P_{e0} CDP_{e1}$ that is, the surface (a+b+c) under the Hicksian demand curve $h_e(P_e, U_1)$ between the lines of the two prices.[9] Note that for a price decrease, assuming that X_e is a normal good, that is, its demand increases as the income of the individual

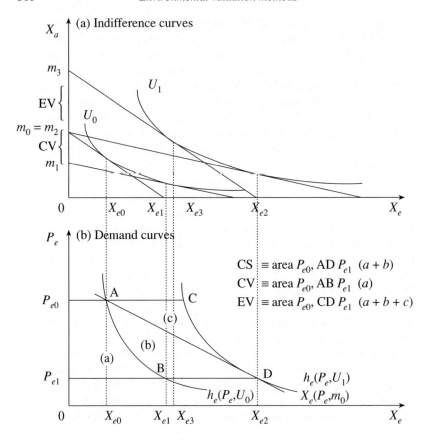

Figure 9.3   Price decrease: CV, EV and CS

increases, EV exceeds CV, that is, the minimum WTA a compensation to give up the price decrease exceeds the maximum WTP to obtain it.

The case of a price increase is illustrated in Figure 9.4. Note that in the case of a price increase the correspondences between CV and maximum WTP, EV and minimum WTA are reversed with respect to the case of a price decrease.

In the case of a price increase the CV is defined as the amount of money that is required by the consumer to keep him/her to the same utility level as without the price increase; it measures the minimum WTA of a self-interested individual to consent to the price increase. The EV is defined as the amount of money to be taken away from the consumer to bring him/her to the same level of utility s/he would attain with the current expenditure if the price increase occurred; it measures the maximum WTP of the individual to avoid the price increase. In Figure 9.4b both the Hicksian curve and the Marshallian curve are shown. Note

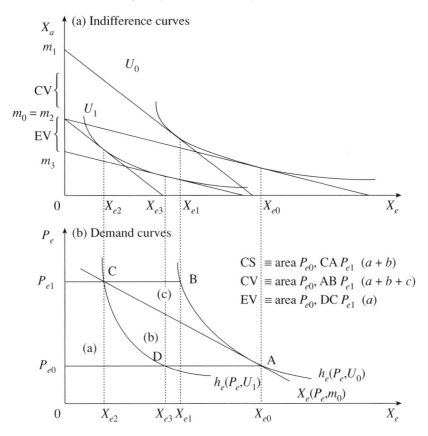

Figure 9.4   Price increase: CV, EV and CS

that for a price increase of a normal good generally it holds that: EV < CV. Only if the income elasticity for good e is zero does it hold that: EV = CV.

9.3.3   Divergence between CV and EV and the Consumer Surplus

The divergence between CV and EV is theoretically grounded. Indeed:

> The divergence between CV and EV is inescapable without severe restrictions on consumer's preferences. If the income effect of a price change is not zero, then the answer to the question how much income can we take from the consumer to cancel out the welfare gain resulting from the fall in price from P_0 to P_1 is bound to differ from the answer to the question: how much income must we give to the consumer to make him just as well of with price P_0 as he would be with price P_1? (Gravelle and Rees 1992, pp. 120–21)

The divergence between CV and EV poses the problem of the most suitable measure to be used. In the case of a unique price decrease, the main consideration is about the property rights implied by each of the two measures. The CV measures the WTP to obtain the price decrease using the initial level of utility as a reference point, implicitly assuming that the individual has no claim on the price change. The EV measures the WTA to forgo the price decrease, considering the utility level the individual would reach with the price decrease as a reference point, implicitly assuming that the individual has a right to the price decrease and needs to be compensated if it is not attained.

In the case of multiple price changes there is an additional issue to be considered. As Freeman (1979, p. 920) states: 'The CV is independent of the order of evaluation. The EV will be independent of the order of evaluation only in the special case ... that is, where income elasticities of the goods are unitary. Unless this unlikely condition is met, there is no unique EV in the case of multiple price changes'. In such cases the CV is therefore the best measure.

A third issue to be considered arises when the measures of welfare change have to be used for the ranking of two alternative policies. In this case EV is shown to be superior to CV. Starting with the same initial indifference curve U_0, consider two alternative policies, say A and B, both of which contain multiple price changes, which lead the consumer to the same final indifference curve U_1. For both policies the measure of the welfare change should be the same. The EV is the same whatever price change is considered, as long as the initial and final indifference curves are the same for the two policies, due to the fact that EV is based on the initial set of prices. On the other hand, CV is different for the two policies, the final set of prices being different, even if both sets of prices allow the consumer to reach the same utility level U_1.[10]

As we have noted, CV and EV measures of welfare take different given utility levels as benchmarks – the current utility level U_0 and the utility level U_1 attainable if the price change occurred, respectively. Unfortunately this feature of both CV and EV makes them not directly derivable from the observed behaviour of the consumer, who acts in a context where his/her income, rather than his/her utility, is fixed when prices change. Fortunately, both measures can be approximated by a simpler measure, which can be estimated from observed data, namely the 'Marshall consumer surplus'.

The concept of consumer surplus, as first described by Dupuit (1844) is the difference between the willingness to pay for purchasing a given commodity and the price actually paid by the consumer to have it. If one varied the price of the good X_e in Figures 9.3 or 9.4 keeping the income ATA fixed level M, say $M = m$, and traced out the changes in its demand, one would obtain a relationship such as is drawn in Figure 9.5. This is called the 'Marshallian' demand curve $X_e(P_e, M)$, where M is the income available to the consumer for consumption. It differs from the compensated demand curve in that price changes are not compensated by changes in money income to keep utility constant. For this reason it is also called the *uncompensated demand curve*. Note that when M is fixed at m_0 the demand curve can be drawn as in Figures 9.3b or 9.4 b. Hence the Marshall demand curve can be derived from the same analysis as was used for CV and EV.

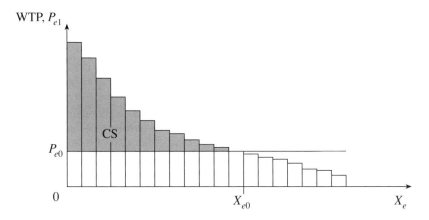

Figure 9.5   Dupuit or Marshall consumer surplus

From its definition, it is clear that for a fall in price from P_{e1} to P_{e0} the Marshall/Dupuit surplus is represented as the shaded area in Figure 9.5. It is also equal to the area under the uncompensated demand curve $X_e(P_e, M)$ between the price lines P_{e0} and P_{e1}, that is, the area (a+b) in Figure 9.3b.

Due to its features of being observable and lying between the theoretically grounded measures of welfare change CV and EV, the CS has been and is currently used in much empirical work as a proxy of these measures.

For a price decrease of a normal good generally it can be shown that: CV < CS < EV. For a price increase of a normal good generally it holds that: EV < CS < CV. Only if the income elasticity for good e is zero does it hold that: EV = CS = CV. Indeed a close inspection of Figures 9.3b and Figure 9.4b will show that this is indeed the case.

On the importance of the difference between these measures and on the use of CS as an approximation of CV and EV a considerable amount of work has been done.[11] Willig (1976, 1979) indicated that in most practical situations the difference between CS and the two measures (CV and EV) does not exceed 5 per cent, depending on the income elasticity of the good and the share of the consumer surplus (related in turn also to the quantity demanded) of the good in question in the total consumer expenditure. The empirical evidence, however, is somewhat different and Willig's bounds have been criticized for this reason and for the fact that to determine the bounds in empirical work the analyst would require the same information required to exactly calculate EV or CV. On these grounds, Hanemann (1980), Hausman (1981) and Vartia (1983), worked out methods for the 'exact' calculation of welfare measure starting with information on the observed consumer behaviour. These approaches overcome a further limit of CS as a measure of welfare change: the fact that when multiple price changes occur, the CS is shown to be 'path dependent'. In other words, its measure varies according to the sequence of price/quantity adjustments assumed to lead to the new consumer equilibrium.

Despite these remarkable efforts to extend and improve welfare change measurements, the CS is currently used in many empirical works based on revealed preferences techniques, at least as a rough and ready approximation of the 'exact' measures of welfare change. In most practical situations additional analytical efforts to go beyond the CS are not possible due to lack of time, money and data. Besides, often they would not add very much in terms of understanding of the economic phenomena under investigation. That is why the use of CS is so widespread in the estimation of monetary measures of welfare change.

9.3.4 Measures of Welfare for Free/Uncontrolled Goods/Services

When considering environmental goods/services outside the control of the consumer, sometimes referred to in literature as 'quantity constrained goods/services', it is apparent that any change in their level affects the utility of the individual.[12] Such effect will lead the self-interested consumer to make the following commitments/requests for payment:

1. In the case of an environmental improvement, to be willing to pay something to bring about the environmental improvement, or to require compensation if the expected (claimed) environmental improvement does not occur.
2. In case of environmental degradation, to require compensation for the environmental damage or to be willing to pay something to prevent such damage.

In both cases there are measures of the WTP/WTA of the consumer for the environmental change. They can be analysed as follows. Let us draw an indifference curve reflecting the same level of welfare for different combinations of a generic good (say, money available for purchasing whatever good or service) (see Figure 9.6). If an environmental improvement, from E_0 to E_1 occurs, other things equal, the consumer will enjoy an increase in utility from U_0 to U_1. Indeed, to keep the utility of the individual constant at U_0, all increases in E, say from E_0 to E_1, need to be compensated by reductions in money available for consumption X.

The compensating surplus for an environmental improvement is the amount of money that needs to be deducted from the income of the consumer to keep him/her at the same utility level as without the environmental improvement.

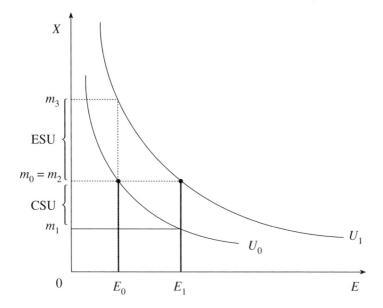

Note: The segments in bold are the budget sets and the points in bold are budget constraints for different levels of environmental good. The good X is money allocated to consumption.

Figure 9.6   Environmental improvement: CSU and ESU

Note that the compensating surplus is defined with respect to the level of utility U_0, that is, the utility the individual attains without the environmental improvement. It is shown as CSU in Figure 9.6.

If we were not constraining the individual to the utility level U_0, by taking away some income to compensate for the environmental improvement, the individual would have had the opportunity to increase his/her utility to the level U_1. Aware of the fact that, enjoying both the environmental improvement and the current level of income, the individual could reach the utility level U_1, s/he can determine the additional income needed to reach the utility level U_1 without the environmental improvement (see Figure 9.6). The equivalent surplus (ESU in Figure 9.6) for an environmental improvement is the additional income to be given to the consumer to bring him/her to the same level of utility U_1 that s/he would attain with the current income if the environmental improvement from E_0 to E_1 occurred. It corresponds to the self-interested consumer's minimum willingness to accept as compensation (min WTA) to give up the environmental improvement. Notice that the Equivalent Surplus is defined over the level of utility U_1, that is, the level of utility that could be reached with the current income if the environmental improvement occurred.

The case of environmental degradation is illustrated in Figure 9.7. Note that in the case of environmental degradation the relationships between CSU and maximum WTP, ESU and minimum WTA are reversed compared to the case of an environmental improvement. In the case of environmental damage the CSU is defined as the amount of money to be given to the consumer to keep him/her at the same utility level prior to the environmental damage; it measures the minimum WTA of a rational individual to consent to the environmental damage. The ESU is defined as the amount of money to be taken away from the consumer to bring him/her to the same level of utility s/he would attain with the current income if the environmental damage occurred – it measures the maximum WTP of the individual to avoid the environmental damage.

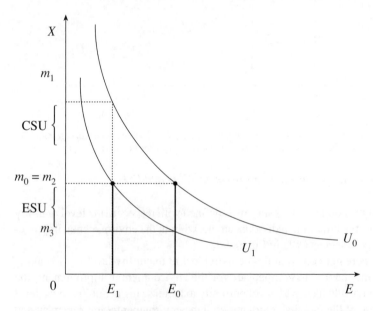

Note: The segments in bold are the budget sets and the points in bold are budget constraints for different levels of environmental good. The good X is money allocated to consumption.

Figure 9.7   Environmental damage: CSU and ESU

Table 9.2 summarizes the definitions of CV, EV, CSU and ESU. The reader is referred to Annex 9A1 for more analytical details.

Practical applications of the above-mentioned concepts are examined in depth in Chapters 11 and 12. In particular, the consumer surplus concept is widely used in the travel cost method and hedonic price method in Chapter 11 and the willingness to pay concept is directly applied in the contingent valuation methods presented in Chapter 12.

Table 9.2 CV and EV for price changes, CSU and ESU for environmental changes

	CV; CSU	EV; ESU
Price decreases/environmental improvements	*Max WTP to obtain the price decrease/environmental improvement*: amount of money to take away from an individual to keep him/her at the same level of welfare s/he is at without the price decrease/environmental improvement	*Min WTA to forgo the price decrease/environmental improvement*: amount of money to give an individual to bring him/her to the same level of welfare as if the price decrease/environmental improvement occurred
Price increases, environmental damage	*Min WTA to consent to the price increase/ environmental damage*: amount of money to give an individual to keep him/her at the same level of welfare s/he is at without the price increase/environmental damage	*Max WTP to prevent the price increase/environmental damage*: amount of money to take away from an individual to bring him/her to the same level of welfare as if the price increase/environmental damage occurred

9.4   OVERVIEW OF VALUATION METHODS

In using WTP to value environmental goods it is rarely the case that market data are available. Many such goods are public goods in nature as discussed in Chapter 5. In such cases the value of an increase/decrease in supply is equal to the sum of the marginal WTP/WTA. This is not easy to obtain. Discussed below are some techniques for eliciting such values.

The following sections offer an overview of the most popular and accepted valuation techniques in the absence of complete markets, providing a brief description of each technique and pointing out the advantages and the limitations as well as the areas for which their application is most suitable.

A number of techniques for placing a value on non-marketed goods and services are available. These techniques have been classified in several ways. Mitchell and Carson (1989) offer a classification based on:

1. whether the data comes from observation of people acting in the market (revealed preferences) or from people's responses to hypothetical questions on their willingness to pay for a change of the environmental services (stated preferences); and
2. whether the methods yield monetary values directly or indirectly.

Munasinghe (1993) distinguishes three possible approaches: (i) conventional market approaches; (ii) implicit market approaches; and (iii) constructed market approaches.

OECD (1995) classifies the valuation methods according to their appropriateness in the measurement of the various types of impacts. Four categories of impact are identified for different sectors, namely: (i) productivity; (ii) health; (iii) amenity; and (iv) existence values. This classification is particularly useful in identifying the most appropriate technique to place a monetary value on the environmental impact according to the sector generating the impact (Table 9.3).

For illustrative purposes, however, this book will refer to the classification provided earlier in Figure 8.3, reproduced here as Figure 9.8, which is a summary of the classifications described above.

9.4.1   Revealed Preference Direct Proxy Methods

From Figure 9.8 we consider first the methods to be used when no market price is available for the environmental impact but where proxies are available. The methods developed here do not claim to measure WTP exactly but to estimate a lower, or sometimes upper bound of that value. Direct proxies involve cost or price information which approximate values of environmental externalities.

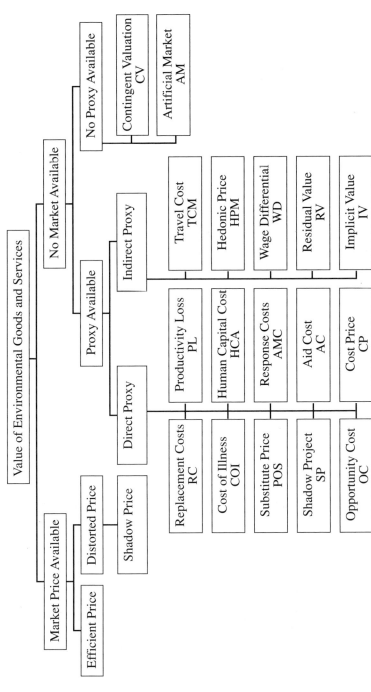

Figure 9.8   A possible taxonomy of valuation techniques

Table 9.3 Environmental impacts, welfare issues, and relevant valuation methods

Environmental impacts	Welfare-related Issues			
	Productivity	Health	Amenity	Existence
Green (natural resources)				
Soil erosion and fertility	X			
Land degradation	X		X	X
Desertification	X			
Salinization	X			
Deforestation	X		X	X
Loss of habitats (inc. wetlands)	X		X	X
Wildlife	X			X
Depletion of finite resources	X			
Brown (pollution)				
Air pollution	X	X	X	
Waste disposal	X	X	X	
Hazardous waste	X	X	X	
Congestion, noise	X	X	X	
Blue (water related)				
Groundwater depletion, contamination	X	X	X	
Surface water pollution	X	X		
Marine environment	X		X	X
Overfishing	X			X

	Productivity change method (PCM), Response costs (AMC), Shadow project (SP), Replacement costs (RC), Substitute price (POS)	Human capital approach (HCA) or Cost of illness (COI), Response costs (AMC)	Contingent valuation (CV), Travel cost (TC), Hedonic pricing (HP)
Red (social aspects)			
Resettlement	X		X
Community disruption	X	X	
Indigenous threat			X
Global			
Global warming, ozone layer	X	X	X
Biodiversity, species loss	X	X	X
Possible valuation methods	⇒	⇒	⇒

Source: OECD (1995).

Two main characteristics of these methods are:

1. They are usually based on the estimation of costs incurred as a result of a change in the provision of the environmental good or service (also sometimes named 'cost based').
2. They value the environmental change by observing the physical relationships (that is, the dose–response relationship) existing between the environmental change and a receptor (for example, erosion/agricultural production, pollution/health, water quality/fish catches and so forth).

The most widely used techniques among those listed in Table 9.3 are: productivity change method (PCM), opportunity cost approach (OCA), defensive expenditure (DE), cost of illness (COI), human capital approach (HCA), shadow project (SP), substitute cost (SC) and cost-effectiveness approach (CEA).

In the *productivity change method* the environment is considered an input into the production function of a marketed good. Changes in an environmental attribute lead to changes in the output of the marketed, good other things equal. The value of the change in the environmental attribute is therefore estimated as the change in the market value of production. Caution should be taken, however, in the use of the proper output price. Let us assume, for example, a soil protection project where it is expected that the reduction of soil erosion will allow for an increase of the crop production. Two possible scenarios can be considered here:

1. The prices of agricultural crops may decrease because of increases in crop supplies. In this case, the change in the environmental attribute will have an effect on the market equilibrium price and, as a consequence, on the consumers' welfare and producers' benefits. A proper measure of the real benefits/losses determined by the soil protection project, should take account of both the consumers' and producers' welfare effects.
2. The second possibility is one where the changes in crop production determined by the reduction of soil erosion do not affect the market equilibrium prices. In this case only the producers' welfare will be affected and the environmental benefit of the project can be measured as the additional benefit in terms of crop production generated by the reduction of soil erosion in the with-project scenario as compared to the without-project scenario. The second scenario is the one usually assumed in actual studies.

The *opportunity cost approach* estimates the value of unpriced goods and services by measuring the forgone benefits of using the same resource for other alternative objectives. For example, conserving a natural area rather than using it for agricultural development will be measured using the forgone income from selling agricultural products instead of estimating the income generated with preservation. In brief, this approach measures what has to be given up for the preservation of the natural area.

This OCA measures the cost of preservation and can be used when a decision must be taken on whether to choose a proposed development project with positive net benefits without preservation or the preservation alternative. In this case, if the preservation alternative is chosen, it is implicitly assumed that the benefits of the preservation alternative are at least equal to the benefits forgone. When using this method, careful consideration should be made regarding option and existence values as well as the irreversible impacts of the development project. The OCA is a very useful technique when benefits of certain uses such as preservation, protection of habitats, cultural or historical sites, cannot be directly estimated.

The *defensive expenditure* method is based on the assumption that individuals and communities spend money on mitigating or eliminating damages caused by adverse environmental impacts. This is the case, for example, of double-glazed windows for reducing traffic noise, extra filtration for purifying polluted water, air conditioning for avoiding polluted air and so forth. These expenses can be considered as minimum estimates of the benefits of mitigation, since it is assumed that the benefits derived from avoiding damages are higher than or at least equal to the costs incurred for avoiding them. The advantage of this technique is that it is easier to estimate the expenses incurred than to estimate the environmental damage.

The *cost of illness and human capital approaches* are used to estimate the monetary value of an environmental change through its impact on illness or life. Dixon et al. (1994) report on a study carried out in Mexico in 1991 aimed at assessing the costs of increase in morbidity and mortality[13] due to air pollution on the basis of treatment costs, loss of wages and loss of life (sometimes also called loss of earnings approach). The COI approach is more comprehensive than the HCA as the former includes expenses and lost wages and puts a monetary value on suffering and the possibility of reducing the risk of mortality. The HCA, while technically simpler to undertake, only measures the lost output of the worker due to illness or death.

The *shadow project* method refers to the costs of providing an equal alternative good or service elsewhere. The possible alternatives are: asset reconstruction (that is, providing an alternative habitat site for a threatened wildlife habitat); asset transplantation (that is, moving the existing habitat to a new site); or asset restoration (that is, enhancing an existing degraded habitat). The cost of the chosen option is added to the basic cost of the proposed development project in order to estimate the full cost. The development project will be accepted if the benefits are at least equal to the development project costs plus the SP costs.

The *substitute cost* method or alternative cost approach refers to the cost of available substitutes for the particular non-priced service or good. The non-priced good can be either a consumer good (for example, parks) or an input factor (for example, non-priced forage substituting for sorghum in livestock). In both cases, if the two substitutes provide an identical service, the value of the non-priced good is the saved cost of using the substitute.

The validity of this approach depends upon three main conditions being maintained: (i) that the substitute can provide exactly the same function of the good or service substituted for; (ii) that the substitute is actually the least-cost alternative; and (iii) that evidence indicates an actual demand for the substitute. It should be noted, however, that often natural resources and the environment also provide other services in addition to the one that substitutes for the marketed good or service. In this case the SC should be considered as a lower bound of the value of the environmental asset.

The *cost effectiveness approach* (CEA) is a technique generally used for selecting among competing options to achieve a pre-established decision. The rationale of the technique is to compare the relative costs of the alternatives available with the effects and to choose the least-cost option. With this approach, benefits are not valued in money terms. So, for example, if the decision makers have decided to fix water pollution standards to a certain level, the analysts will try to find out the least-cost option to achieve the goal. Similarly, if a limited amount of money has been made available by the decision makers to install pollution monitoring systems in one town, and several options exist to achieve the goal, the preference will go to the alternative that allows the installation of the highest number of monitoring systems.

Cost-based approaches should be used with caution because costs do not necessarily equal the benefits of environmental improvements or the damages from degradation. Cost-based measures are readily observed and generally can provide a useful lower-bound estimate of environmental benefits or damages. When costs are not actually incurred, such as for the shadow project technique, there is a risk of under or overestimation of the value of the environmental asset. Furthermore, different costs of the same impact can also be valued using different functions of the environmental good or service. The cost of illness, human capital and productivity loss are often complementary in that each reflects a specific aspect of a healthy life. If all three approaches are used to value the different facets of human health impact, one has to be cautious not to double count these different values.

9.4.2   Revealed Preference Indirect Proxy Methods

These methods are based on the assumption that the non-marketed environmental good or service affects the preferences expressed by consumers about other marketed goods or services. The purpose of these techniques is to identify the relationship between the environmental change and the affected prices of marketed goods or services. This is done through the application of some of the techniques illustrated in Chapter 11. The main techniques that fall into this category are the travel cost method, the hedonic price method and the wage differential method.

The travel cost method (TCM) is based on the expenditures incurred by households or individuals to reach a site as a means of measuring willingness to pay for the recreational activity. The sum of the cost of travelling (including the opportunity cost of time to travel and visit the site) and any entrance fee gives a proxy for market prices in demand estimation. By observing these costs and the number of trips that take place at a range of prices, it is possible to derive a demand curve for the particular environmental good or resource. The area under the demand curve (that is, the consumer surplus) measures the WTP of consumers for that environmental good or resource.

There is general agreement in considering the TCM as one of the most effective approaches in valuing recreation services (Bockstael et al. 1991; Smith 1989; Ward and Loomis 1986). Nevertheless, as Smith (1993) points out, this model has been used so far to define 'the demand for and value of services provided by specific types of recreation sites and not estimating the value people place on changes in the sites' quality features'. Furthermore, the decision between the zonal and the individual TCM approaches (as described in Chapter 10) is likely to have a significant impact on the results obtained. Similar to the other techniques addressed above, the TCM only measures the 'use value' of recreation sites. Other potential problems encountered with this method are the following: (i) difficulty in the determination of the opportunity cost of on-site and travel time; (ii) the issue of the treatment of substitute sites; and (iii) the problem of the choice of the appropriate functional form and its impact upon consumer surplus estimates. A detailed presentation of this method is provided in Chapter 10.

The hedonic pricing method (HPM) estimates the differential premium on property value derived from proximity to some environmental attribute. In order to obtain a measure of how the environmental attribute affects the value of houses or other properties, all other variables of the house (number of rooms, central heating, garage space and so on) are standardized. Moreover, any unit of housing is completely described by geographical, neighbourhood and environmental attributes.

Let us assume, for example, that we want to assess the landscape improvement value of a forest. The HPM will first estimate the marginal WTP of individuals/households who decide to buy or rent a house with the same attributes but differing quality of landscape. Then it will specify the demand function for this attribute and will estimate individual/household consumer surplus. The last step will be to aggregate all the individual consumer surpluses in order to obtain the total value of the landscape improvement. A detailed presentation of the technique is provided in Chapter 10.

Although it has been widely used, this method has several limits in its application. The most important of these is perhaps the high quality of data required on variables that are seldom recorded in the official statistics even in developed countries. Brookshire et al. (1982) identified no less than 18 variables necessary for the analysis of the housing market, most of which must be estimated. Another disadvantage is the huge amount of data required. To use this method the housing market must also be competitive. Finally, as for the TCM, the HPM does not capture non-use values.

The wage differential method (WDM) assumes that the wage rate paid for a job reflects a set of attributes, including safety. It follows that other things being equal, employees will seek higher wages to compensate for higher risks. The price for safety (also called hedonic wage) is the difference between what the wage would be for a job with the same attributes but no risk and the wage of a job including risk.

Strong assumptions that are needed for this technique to work are that: (i) the labour market functions freely; (ii) labour is mobile; (iii) it is possible to isolate the exclusive impact of risk on wages; (iv) there is perfect comparability between different types of risks; and (v) there is a good quality of information on risks. This method is a special case of the hedonic method, and is not considered further in this book.

9.4.3   Stated Preference Contingent Valuation Methods

Among the various direct or stated preferences techniques, the CVM is by far the most widely applied. Basically it consists of asking people (usually via a questionnaire or by experimental techniques)[14] what they are willing to pay for a benefit or what they are willing to receive as compensation for the damage caused. In fact, the questionnaire simulates a hypothetical (contingent) market of a particular good (for example, landscape quality) in which individuals (who demand the good) are asked to reveal their willingness to pay for a change (better/lower quality) in the provision (the supply) of the good in question. The questionnaire also provides information on the institutional context in which the good would be provided and on the payment vehicle.

The major advantage of this approach when compared with the others is that it may, in theory, be applicable to value all goods and services and it is the only possible technique for the evaluation of non-use values. Another attraction of this method lies in the fact that in simpler cases it does not require the huge amount of data (often not available or unreliable) necessary for the other techniques. Data can be treated at different levels of complexity according to the time and financial resources available and the specific format of the question used to capture the individual's value judgement.

Several criticisms have, however, been raised as to the accuracy and reliability of consumer preferences resulting from CVM. The major criticism concerns the biases inherent in the techniques[15] (mainly strategic bias or the free-rider problem, starting-point bias, information bias, vehicle bias and hypothetical bias). Another source of scepticism about this method is the disparity emerging in empirical studies of CVM between willingness to pay and willingness to accept (Mitchell and Carson 1989; Knetsch 1990; Pearce and Turner 1990). This issue is addressed in more detail in Chapter 12.

Although many of these problems are not yet totally resolved, steps have been taken in the last decades, particularly in the design of questionnaires and in the interpretation of results, which have considerably improved the findings (Brookshire and Coursey 1987). As pointed out in the review by Smith (1993), the comparison between findings obtained with CVM and other methods are substantially consistent.

The following chapters offer a detailed analysis of the most popular direct and indirect techniques. For each technique analysed, examples are proposed which are partly drawn from simulations conducted by the authors during training courses and partly from actual studies carried out by the authors in several parts of the world. A stepwise approach is used to facilitate the understanding of the methodology as well as the major problems faced when applying these methods. Each example consists of four sections: (i) methodology of the technique; (ii) problem set; (iii) solution set; and (iv) discussion. Boxes have also been added to provide the users with valuable information on how to compute the main statistical indicators, mathematical formulae and economic values. Finally, some exercises are also proposed which will allow the reader to become familiar with the practical use of the techniques.

NOTES

1. It is not guaranteed that the option value attached to a resource's use on the future will be positive. It depends on how factors relating to supply and demand for the resource interact in the future. Theoretical analysis indicates, however, that the option value is likely to be positive in many interesting cases.
2. Pearce and Turner (1990, p. 135).

3. For other proposed classifications, see Munasinghe (1993); Pearce and Warford (1993); Freeman (1993).
4. In some ways the use of the term total economic value is unfortunate because it uses the word 'total' in a different way from that commonly used in economics. What is being sought here is the full value of an environmental asset or service. This may be for a *change* in the amount of the asset or for the whole asset. It does *not* imply that the valuation is for the asset in its totality.
5. It is common sense to say that if we are willing to pay more for the asset A than for the asset B, then we prefer A to B.
6. In Annex 9A1, the concept of the expenditure function and its relationships with the measure of max WTP to min WTA are illustrated in some more detail.
7. For more comprehensive treatment of this topic, see, for example, Freeman (1993, pp. 72–80) and Annex 9A1.
8. This differs from the 'normal' demand curve, in which demand is represented as a function of prices and money income.
9. The argument is the same as in the previous case.
10. On the superiority of EV with respect to CV for the ranking of policies, see, for example, Johansson (1987).
11. The reader is referred to Freeman (1993 pp. 61–6) for a survey of the works of Willig (1976, 1979), Hanemann (1980), Hausman (1981) and Vartia (1983).
12. In this section only the free of charge public goods are considered. For a review of the welfare measures for quantity changes of taxed public goods, see Freeman (1993, pp. 72–85).
13. Monetary estimations of the value of life have raised some ethical as well as theoretical criticisms (Markandya and Pearce 1989). A more appropriate and accepted definition of this technique is that it seeks to place a value on *changes in the statistical probability of illness or death*.
14. People are asked to respond to stimuli in laboratory conditions.
15. For a detailed discussion on biases in CVM, see Mitchell and Carson (1989).

CITED BIBLIOGRAPHY

Bateman, I.J. (1993), 'Evaluation of environment: a survey of revealed preference technique', CSERGE/GEC Working Paper 93–06, University of East Anglia, Norwich.

Bockstael, N.E., K.E. McConnell and I.E. Strand Jr. (1991), 'Methods for valuing classes of benefits: Recreation', in J. Braden and C. Kolstad (eds), *Measuring the Demand for Environmental Commodities*, Amsterdam: North Holland, pp. 227–70.

Brookshire, D. and D. Coursey (1987), 'Measuring the value of a public good: an empirical comparison of elicitation procedure', *American Economic Review*, **77** (4), September, 554–66.

Brookshire, D.S., R.C. D'Arge, W.D. Schultze and M.A. Thayer (1982), 'Valuing public goods: a comparison of survey and hedonic approaches', *American Economic Review*, **72**, 165–77

Dixon, J., L.F. Scura, R.A. Carpenter and P.B. Sherman (1994), *Economic Analysis of Environmental Impacts*, London: Earthscan.

Dupuit, J. (1844), 'On the measurement of the utility of public works', Annales des Ponts et des Chaussées, second series, vol. 8; reprinted in D. Munby (ed.), *Transport: Selected Readings*, Harmondsworth: Penguin Books Ltd, 1968.

Freeman, A.M., III (1979), 'Approaches to measuring public goods demands', *American Journal of Agricultural Economics*, **61**, 915–20.

Freeman, A.M., III (1993), *The Measurement of Environmental and Resource Values: Theory and Methods*, Washington, DC: Resources for the Future.

Gravelle, H. and R. Rees (1992), *Microeconomics*, London: Longman.

Hanemann, M. (1980), 'Measuring the worth of natural resource facilities: comment', *Land Economics*, **56** (4), 482–90.

Hausman, J.A. (1981), 'Exact consumer surplus and dead weight loss', *American Economic Review*, **71** (4), 662–76.

Johansson, P.O. (1987), *The Economic Theory and Measurement of Environmental Benefits*, Cambridge: Cambridge University Press.

Knetsch, J.L. (1990), 'Environmental policy implications of disparities between willingness to pay and compensation demanded measures of values', *Journal of Environmental Economics and Management*, **18**, 227–37'.

Markandya, A. and D.W. Pearce (1989), *Environmental Policy Benefits: Monetary Valuation*, Paris: OECD.

Mitchell, R.C. and R.T. Carson (1989), *Using Surveys to Value Public Goods: The Contingent Valuation Method*, Washington, DC: Resources for the Future.

Munasinghe, M. (1993), 'Environmental economics and sustainable development', World Bank Environment Paper No. 3, Washington, DC: World Bank.

Pearce, D.W. and R.K. Turner (1990), *Economics of Natural Resources and Environment*, New York: Harvester Wheatsheaf.

Pearce, D.W. and J.J. Warford (1993), *World Without End: Economics, Environment, and Sustainable Development*, Oxford: Oxford University Press.

Sharma, N.P. (1992), *Managing the World's Forests*, Dubuque, IA: Kendall/Hunt.

Smith, V.K. (1989), 'Taking stock of progress with travel cost recreation demand methods: theory and implementation', *Marine Resource Economics*, **6**, 279–310.

Smith, V.K. (1993), 'Nonmarket valuation of environmental resources: an interpretative appraisal', *Land Economics*, **69** (1), February, 1–26.

Vartia, Y.O. (1983), 'Efficient methods of measuring welfare change and compensated income in terms of ordinary demand functions', *Econometrica*, **51** (1), 79–88.

Ward, W.A. and J.B. Loomis (1986), 'The travel cost demand model as an environmental policy assessment tool: a review of the literature', *Western Journal of Agricultural Economics*, **11** (2), 164–78.

Willig, R.D. (1976), 'Consumers' surplus without apology', *American Economic Review*, **66**, (4), 589–97.

Willig, R.D. (1979), 'Consumers' surplus without apology: reply', *American Economic Review*, **69** (3), 471–4.

ANNEX 9.A1   ECONOMICS UNDERLYING VALUATION METHODS

As mentioned in the text, the expenditure function is a very useful conceptual tool in defining the individual's maximum WTP and the minimum compensation required (minimum WTA) both for a price change of a priced environmental asset and for a quantity change of non-priced environmental goods or services. Indeed both maximum WTP and minimum WTA can be measured looking at the variations of expenditure required to keep the consumer indifferent in terms of utility (satisfaction, welfare) when the change occurs. Maximum WTP and minimum WTA can then be assumed as money measures of the individual's welfare changes. Some of the most important welfare measures used to derive maximum WTP and minimum WTA for the afore-mentioned two cases are discussed. These measures are worked out considering: (a) price decreases; (b) price increases; (c) quantity decreases; and (d) quantity increases.

Measures of the WTP/WTA: Changes in the Consumer's Expenditure

Individuals consume goods and services, to obtain satisfaction. According to conventional consumer theory, one way to model the consumer's behaviour is to describe a situation where, given a vector of prices at time 0, say P_0, (where $P_0 = p_1, ... p_n$), after specifying the functional form of the utility and fixing a given level of utility (satisfaction) U_0 to be reached, the individual chooses his/her consumption bundle X (where $X = x_1, ..., x_n$), such that, while allowing to exactly obtain the level of utility U_0, s/he minimizes the expenditure: $m = x_1 p_1 + ... + x_n p_n$. Changes in the vector of prices P lead to changes in the level of the minimum expenditure needed to attain U_0, and adjustments of the bundle X chosen by the consumer. The same holds for shifts of the level of utility U to be attained. The minimum expenditure is therefore a function of the utility level and prices:

$$m = m[P, U(X)].   \tag{9A1.1}$$

The minimum expenditure as a function of the utility level and of the prices is usually called the 'expenditure function'.

Environmental goods and services enter this framework in two different ways according to their economic features:

1. Environmental goods and services implicitly or explicitly priced, which enter the bundle the consumer adjusts in order to minimize the expenditure.

This category can be viewed as a component of the vector X, say X_e, with prices P_e, besides the other goods X_a with prices P_a. The expenditure function becomes:

$$m = m[P_e, P_a, U(X_e, X_a)] \qquad (9A1.2)$$

2. Non excludable environmental goods and services E, that, while affecting the utility of the consumer, are not under his/her control, that is, whose level of consumption (fruition) is exogenous. They are assumed free of charge, that is, they enter the utility function without requiring a direct allocation of money to them.[1] Examples of this kind of good are air and natural scenery. When including this set of goods and services, the expenditure function becomes:

$$m = m[P_e, P_a, U(E, X_e, X_a)]. \qquad (9A1.3)$$

The expenditure function is a very useful conceptual tool in defining the individual's maximum WTP and the minimum compensation required (minimum WTA) both for price change of a priced environmental asset and for a quantity change of a non-priced environmental good or service.

WTP/WTA for a Change in Prices of Priced Environmental Goods

Consider first the case of a priced environmental good. Suppose a case, where the individual consumes a priced environmental good e (say, water) and another marketed good a. In the period 0 they are consumed in quantity X_{e0} and X_{a0} and the prices paid are, respectively, P_{e0} and P_{a0}. P_{a0} can be assumed $= 1$, that is, set as a numeraire.[2] The consumer also benefits from a non-excludable non-priced environmental good (say air) which is fixed at the level E_0. The expenditure function is therefore as follows:

$$m = m[P_e, P_a, U(E_0, X_e, X_a)]. \qquad (9A1.4)$$

Changes of the price of water P_e will affect the consumer's minimum expenditure required to attain a given level of utility. This will lead the self-interested consumer:

1.a. In the case of a price decrease:
    (1.a.1)   to be willing to pay an amount to bring about the price decrease, or:
    (1.a.2)   to require compensation if the expected (claimed) decrease does not occur.

1.b. In case of a price increase:

   (1.b.1)   to require a compensation for the price increase; or

   (1.b.2)   to be willing to pay something to prevent the increase.

According to the level of utility we take as benchmark of the analysis, we can have two measures of the changes in expenditure: the compensating variation (CV) and the equivalent variation (EV).

1.a.   WTP/WTA for a price decrease

In the case of a price decrease, the following definitions of CV and EV hold:

1.a.1. The CV of the expenditure is the amount of money to be taken away from the consumer to keep him/her at the same utility level as without the price decrease. CV measures the self-interested consumer's maximum WTP to obtain the price decrease.

1.a.2. The EV of the expenditure is the amount of money to be given to the consumer to bring him/her to the same level of utility s/he would attain with the current expenditure if the price decrease occurred. EV measures the rational consumer's minimum WTA to forgo the price decrease.

These measures are analysed in detail hereafter, referring to Figure 9.3 in the text.

1.a.1. Maximum WTP to obtain a price decrease (measured by CV)   If a price decrease, from P_{e0} to P_{e1} occurs, other things being equal, the consumer will enjoy a reduction in its expenditure to attain the same level of utility U_0. The new expenditure will be:

$$m_1 = m[P_{e1}, P_{a0}, U_0(E_0, X_{e1}, X_{a1})]. \qquad (9A1.5)$$

the difference $(m_0 - m_1)$, that is, the savings in expenditure s/he would obtain to keep the utility level U_0 if the price decrease occurs. The compensating variation is the difference $(m_0 - m_1)$, representing the maximum WTP of a rational individual for obtaining the price decrease:

$$\begin{aligned}
\max \text{WTP} \equiv \text{CV} = (m_0 - m_1) &= m[P_{e0}, P_{a0}, U_0(E_0, X_{e0}, X_{a0})] \\
&\quad - m[P_{e1}, P_{a0}, U_0(E_0, X_{e1}, X_{a1})] \qquad (9A1.6)
\end{aligned}$$

Note that the CV for a price decrease of an ordinary good is positive.[3] Also note that the CV is defined over the level of utility U_0, that is, the current utility level before the change.

1.a.2.   Minimum required compensation (minimum WTA) to forgo the price decrease (measured by EV).   A price decrease, say from P_{e0} to P_{e1}, *ceteris paribus*, allows, the consumer an increase of utility, say from U_0 to U_1. The expenditure function in such a case would be:

$$m_2 = m[P_{e1}, P_{a0}, U_1(E_0, X_{e2}, X_{a2})] \text{ with } m_2 = m_0^4 \qquad (9A1.7)$$

'*Ceteris paribus*' implies that all other things are equal, in this case it refers to the prices of the other goods and the consumer's expenditure.

If the level of utility U_1 has to be reached facing the price P_{e0}, the expenditure needs to be increased from m_0, to the level m_3:

$$m_3 = m[P_{e0}, P_{a0}, U_1(E_0, X_{e3}, X_{a3})]. \qquad (9A1.8)$$

Suppose we ask the individual now how much s/he would be willing to accept, as a minimum payment, to forgo the price decrease. Assuming the individual behaves in a rational (economic) way, s/he would be willing to accept at minimum the difference $(m_3 - m_2)$, that is, the increase in expenditure s/he would incur to reach the utility level U_1 if the price decrease does not occur.

The equivalent variation of the expenditure (EV) is the difference $(m_3 - m_2)$, measuring the minimum compensation (min WTA) required by a self-interested consumer, to forgo the price decrease.

$$\text{min WTA} \equiv \text{EV} = (m_3 - m_2) = m[P_{e0}, P_{a0}, U_1(E_0, X_{e3}, X_{a3})]$$
$$- m[P_{e1}, P_{a0}, U_1(E_0, X_{e2}, X_{a2})]. \qquad (9A1.9)$$

Note that the equivalent variation is defined over the level of utility U_1 that can be reached with the price decrease, maintaining the current expenditure.

1.b.   WTP/WTA for a price increase
In the case of a price increase the CV and the EV are defined as follows :

1.b.1   The CV of the expenditure is the amount of money to be given to the consumer when a price increases, to keep him/her at the same utility level as without the price increase. CV measures the rational consumer's minimum WTA to agree to the price increase.

1.b.2.   The EV of the expenditure is the amount of money to be taken away from the consumer to bring him/her to the same level of utility s/he would attain with the current expenditure if the price increase occurred. EV measures the rational consumer's maximum WTP to avoid the price increase.

1.b.1. Minimum required compensation (min WTA) for a price increase (measured by CV). If the price P_e increases from P_{e0} to P_{e1}, other things equal, the consumer will experience a fall in the attainable level of utility, leading him/her at U_1. To attain the same level of utility U_0 as before, s/he will have to increase his/her expenditure at least up to m_1 (Figure 9.4). The new expenditure will be:

$$m_1 = m[P_{e1}, P_{a0}, U_0(E_0, X_{e1}, X_{a1})] \qquad (9A1.10)$$

The CV of the expenditure for such a price increase is the difference $(m_0 - m_1)$. This measures the minimum compensation required (min WTA) by a rational consumer for consenting to the price increase.

$$\min \text{WTA} \equiv \text{CV} = (m_0 - m_1) = m[P_{e0}, P_{a0}, U_0(E_0, X_{e0}, X_{a0})]$$
$$- m(P_{e1}, P_{a0}, U_0(E_0, X_{e1}, X_{a1})] \qquad (9A1.11)$$

Note that the CV is again defined with respect to the level of utility U_0. Defined as above, the CV for a price increase is a negative value. Also note that the CV for a price increase corresponds to minus EV for a price decrease, that is, it is the same amount with the opposite sign.

1.b.2. Maximum WTP to avoid the price increase (measured by the EV). If the price P_e increased from P_{e0} to P_{e1}, other things equal, the consumer would experience a fall in the attainable level of utility, leading him/her at U_1 (Figure 9.4). In such a case the expenditure would be:

$$m_2 = m[P_{e1}, P_{a0}, U_1(E_0, X_{e2}, X_{a2})], \text{ with } m_2 = m_0^5 \qquad (9A1.12)$$

To avoid the price increase s/he will be prepared to forgo at maximum the sum of money without which, given P_{e0}, s/he would reach the lower level of utility U_1. The expenditure in that situation would be:

$$m_3 = m[P_{e0}, P_{a0}, U_1(E_0, X_{e3}, X_{a3})]. \qquad (9A1.13)$$

The difference between the expenditure m_3 that allows him/her to stay at U_1 with P_{e0} and the expenditure $m_2 = m_0$ that allows him to stay at U_1 with P_{e1} is the equivalent variation of the expenditure for the price increase:

$$\max \text{WTP} \equiv \text{EV} = (m_3 - m_2) = m[P_{e0}, P_{a0}, U_1(E_0, X_{e3}, X_{a3})]$$
$$- m(P_{e1}, P_{a0}, U_1(E_0, X_{e2}, X_{a2})] \qquad (9A1.14)$$

The EV for a price increase is negative. Note that the EV for a price increase from P_{e0} to P_{e1} corresponds to minus CV for a price decrease from P_{e1} to P_{e0}.

Change in the Quantity/Quality of a Free Uncontrolled Environmental Asset

When considering the second class of goods, that is, environmental goods/services outside the control of the consumer, sometimes referred to in the literature as 'quantity constrained goods/services', it is apparent that any change in their level of fruition E affects the utility of the individual.[6] Such an effect will lead the rational consumer :

2.a. In the case of an environmental improvement:
    (2.a.1)   to be willing to pay an amount to favour the environmental improvement, or:
    (2.a.2)   to require compensation if the expected (claimed) environmental improvement does not occur.
2.b. In the case of environmental damage:
    (2.b.1)   to require compensation for consenting to the environmental damage;
    (2.b.2)   willing to pay something to prevent such damage.

2.a.   WTP/WTA for an environmental improvement

2.a.1. Maximum WTP for an environmental improvement (measured by CSU).
If an environmental improvement from E_0 to E_1 occurs, other things equal, the consumer will enjoy a reduction in its expenditure to attain the same level of utility U_0 (see Figure 9.6). The new expenditure will be:

$$m_1 = m[P_{e0}, P_{a0}, U_0(E_1, X_{e1}, X_{a1})]. \qquad (9A1.15)$$

Indeed, to keep constant the utility of the individual, all increases in E, say from E_0 to E_1, this needs to be compensated by reductions of income available for consumption X.[7]

Suppose now that the individual is asked how much s/he would be willing to pay at maximum to get the environmental improvement. Assuming the individual behaves in a rational (economic) way, s/he would be willing to pay at maximum the difference $(m_0 - m_1)$, that is, the savings in expenditure s/he would obtain to keep the utility level U_0 if the environmental improvement occurs. The difference $(m_0 - m_1)$, representing the WTP of a rational individual, to get an environmental improvement, is the compensating surplus (CSU) of the consumer's expenditure for the environmental improvement.

$$\max \text{WTP} \equiv \text{CSU} = (m_0 - m_1) = m[P_{e0}, P_{a0}, U_0(E_0, X_{a0}, X_{e0})]$$
$$- m[P_{e0}, P_{a0}, U_0(E_1, X_{a1}, X_{e1})] \tag{9A1.16}$$

Note that the compensating surplus is defined with respect to the level of utility U_0, that is, the utility the individual attains without the environmental improvement.

2.a.2. Minimum required compensation to forgo the envisaged (claimed) improvement (measured by ESU). An environmental improvement, say from E_0 to E_1, leads, *ceteris paribus*, to an increase of utility, say from U_0 to U_1 (see Figure 9.6). The *ceteris paribus* assumption here refers to the prices of other goods and related expenditure.

The expenditure function in such a case would be:

$$m_2 = m[P_{e0}, P_{a0}, U_1(E_1, X_{e2}, X_{a2})], \text{ with } m_2 = m_0. \tag{9A1.17}$$

If the level of utility U_1 has to be reached increasing the consumption of other goods, rather than with the environmental improvement, the expenditure on other goods need to be increased to the level m_3:

$$m_3 = m[P_{e0}, P_{a0}, U_1(E_0, X_{e3}, X_{a3})]. \tag{9A1.18}$$

Suppose the individual is now asked how much s/he would be willing to accept, as a minimum, to forgo the environmental benefit. Assuming the individual behaves in a rational (economic) way, s/he would be willing to accept at minimum the difference $(m_3 - m_2)$, that is, the increase in expenditure s/he would incur to reach the utility level U_1 if the environmental improvement does not occur.

The difference $(m_3 - m_2)$, representing the minimum compensation required (min WTA) of a rational individual, to forgo an environmental improvement, is the equivalent surplus (ESU) of the consumer's expenditure for the environmental improvement. It is defined as the amount of money to give an individual to allow him/her to reach the utility level s/he would reach if the environmental improvement occurred.

$$\min \text{WTA} \equiv \text{ESU} = (m_3 - m_2) = m[P_{e0}, P_{a0}, U_1(E_0, X_{e3}, X_{a3})]$$
$$- m[P_{e0}, P_{a0}, U_1(E_1, X_{e2}, X_{a2})]. \tag{9A1.19}$$

Note that the equivalent surplus is defined over the level of utility U_1, that is, the level of utility that could be reached with the current expenditure if the environmental improvement occurred.

2.b. WTP/WTA for environmental damage

2.b.1. Minimum required compensation (minimum WTA) to consent to the damage (measured by CSU). If environmental damage occurs, leading to a fall in the quantity of the environmental good or service from E_0 to E_1 (see Figure 9.7), the consumer will experience a fall in the utility level attainable with the current expenditure from U_0 to U_1. To attain the level of utility U_0 there needs to be an increase in the consumption of the other goods and services X. This leads to an increase of the minimum expenditure necessary to attain the utility level U_0:

$$m_1 = m[P_{e0}, P_{a0}, U_0(E_1, X_{e1}, X_{a1})] \qquad (9A1.20)$$

Suppose now that the individual is asked how much s/he would be willing to accept, at minimum, to consent to the environmental damage. Assuming the individual behaves in a rational (economic) way, s/he would be willing to accept as a minimum the difference $(m_0 - m_1)$, that is, the increase in expenditure s/he would have to afford to keep the utility level U_0 if the environmental damage occurred. The compensating surplus (CSU) of the consumer's expenditure for the environmental damage is the difference $(m_0 - m_1)$. It measures the minimum compensation (min WTA) required by a rational consumer to consent to an environmental damage.

$$\min \text{WTA} \equiv \text{CSU} = (m_0 - m_1) = m[P_{e0}, P_{a0}, U_0(E_0, X_{e0}, X_{a0})]$$
$$- m[P_{e0}, P_{a0}, U_0(E_1, X_{e1}, X_{a1})]. \qquad (9A1.21)$$

Note that the compensating surplus is again defined with respect to the level of utility attainable with the current expenditure m_0 without the environmental damage.

2.b.2. Maximum WTP to avoid the environmental damage (measured by ESU). Environmental damage, leading to a decrease in the fruition of environmental goods or services, say from E_0 to E_1, (see Figure 9.7) leads, *ceteris paribus*, to a decrease of utility, say from U_0 to U_1.

In such a case the expenditure function is defined as:

$$m_2 = m[P_{e0}, P_{a0}, U_1(E_1, X_{e2}, X_{a2})], \text{ with } m_2 = m_0. \qquad (9A1.22)$$

If the lower level of utility U, has to be reached decreasing the consumption of the other goods/services X, rather than affording the environmental damage, the resulting minimum expenditure m_3 is given by:

$$m_3 = m[P_{e0}, P_{a0}, U_1(E_0, X_{e3}, X_{a3})]. \qquad (9A1.23)$$

Table 9A1.1 CV and EV for price changes; CSU and ESU for environmental changes

	CV; CSU	EV; ESU
Price decreases/ environmental improvements	*Max WTP to obtain the price decrease/environmental improvement*: amount of money to be taken away from an individual to keep him/her at the same level of welfare s/he is at without the price decrease/environmental improvement Price decrease: $\max \text{WTP} \equiv \text{CV} = (m_0 - m_1) = m[P_{e0}, P_{a0}, U_0(E_0, X_{e0}, X_{a0})] - m[P_{e1}, P_{a0}, U_0(E_0, X_{e1}, X_{a1})]$ (9A1.6) Environmental improvement: $\max \text{WTP} \equiv \text{CSU} = (m_0 - m_1) = m[P_{e0}, P_{a0}, U_0(E_0, X_{a0}, X_{e0})] - m[P_{e0}, P_{a0}, U_0(E_1, X_{a1}, X_{e1})]$ (9A1.16) $m_0 > m_1 \Rightarrow \text{CV, CSU} > 0$	*Min WTA to forgo the price decrease/ environmental improvement*: amount of money to be given to an individual to bring him/her at the same level of welfare as if the price decrease/environmental improvement occurred Price decrease: $\min \text{WTA} \equiv \text{EV} = (m_3 - m_2) = m[P_{e0}, P_{a0}, U_1(E_0, X_{e3}, X_{a3})] - m[P_{e1}, P_{a0}, U_1(E_0, X_{e2}, X_{a2})]$ (9A1.9) Environmental improvement: $\min \text{WTA} \equiv \text{ESU} = (m_3 - m_2) = m[P_{e0}, P_{a0}, U_1(E_0, X_{e3}, X_{a3})] - m[P_{e0}, P_{a0}, U_1(E_1, X_{e2}, X_{a2})]$ (9A1.19) $(m_3 > m_2) \Rightarrow \text{EV, ESU} > 0$
Price increases/ environmental damage	*Min WTA to consent the price increase/environmental damage*: amount of money to be given to an individual to keep him/her at the same level of welfare s/he is at without the price increase/environmental damage Price increase: $\min \text{WTA} \equiv \text{CSU} = (m_0 - m_1) = m[P_{e0}, P_{a0}, U_0(E_0, X_{e0}, X_{a0})] - m[P_{e1}, P_{a0}, U_0(E_0, X_{e1}, X_{a1})]$ (9A1.11) Environmental damage: $\min \text{WTA} \equiv \text{CSU} = (m_0 - m_1) = m[P_{e0}, P_{a0}, U_0(E_0, X_{e0}, X_{a0})] - m[P_{e0}, P_{a0}, U_0(E_1, X_{e1}, X_{a1})]$ (9A1.22) $m_0 < m_1 \Rightarrow \text{CV, CSU} < 0$	*Max WTP to prevent the price increase/environmental damage*: amount of money to be taken away from an individual to bring him/her to the same level of welfare as if the price increase/environmental damage occurred Price increase: $\max \text{WTP} \equiv \text{EV} = (m_3 - m_2) = m[P_{e0}, P_{a0}, U_1(E_0, X_{e3}, X_{a3})] - m[P_{e1}, P_{a0}, U_1(E_0, X_{e2}, X_{a2})]$ (9A1.14) Environmental damage: $\max \text{WTP} \equiv \text{ESU} = (m_3 - m_2) = m[P_{e0}, P_{a0}, U_1(E_0, X_{e3}, X_{a3})] - m[P_{e0}, P_{a0}, U_1(E_1, X_{e2}, X_{a2})]$ (9A1.24) $(m_3 < m_2) \Rightarrow \text{EV, ESU} < 0$

Suppose now the individual is asked how much s/he would be willing to pay, at maximum, to prevent the environmental damage. Assuming the individual behaves in a rational (economic) way, s/he would be willing to pay at maximum the difference $(m_3 - m_2)$, that is, the reduction in expenditure necessary to reach the utility level U_1, if the environmental damage does not occur.

The difference $(m_3 - m_2)$, is the equivalent surplus (ESU) of the consumer's expenditure for an environmental damage. It measures the maximum willingness to pay (Max WTP) of a rational individual, to prevent the environmental damage:

$$\text{max WTP} \equiv \text{ESU} = (m_3 - m_2) = m[P_{e0}, P_{a0}, U_1(E_0, X_{e3}, X_{a3})]$$
$$- m[P_{e0}, P_{a0}, U_1(E_1, X_{e2}, X_{a2})] \tag{9A1.24}$$

Note that the ESU is again defined over the level of utility U_1, that is, the utility that would be reached with the current expenditure if the environmental damage occurred.

Table 9A1.1 summarizes the concepts of maximum WTP and minimum compensation required (WTA), related to price decreases and environmental improvements or to price increases and environmental damages.

Notes

1. Of course, there may be an indirect allocation of money for these environmental goods if, for example, the consumer drives somewhere or moves house to take advantage of them. When such options for increasing the consumption of the environmental goods are not permitted, the consumer's choice is referred to in the literature as 'choice under quantity constraints' (Johansson 1987). For a good review of the discussion about priced and free of charge quantity constrained commodities, see Freeman (1993, pp. 73–85) and the original references listed.
2. This assumption implies that the expenditure is expressed in units of good a. Indeed good a can be considered as money for the purchase of all the other consumer goods.
3. For a price decrease, the CV is conventionally considered positive even if actually it is a reduction in the expenditure, that is, a negative variation of the expenditure.
4. The expenditure is kept constant by assumption: $m[P_{e1}, P_{a0}, U_1(E_0, X_{e2}, X_{a1})] - m[P_{e0}, P_{a0}, U_0(E_0, X_{e0}, X_{a0})]$. This means that the expenditure required to attain the utility level U_1 with the new set of prices P_{e1} is assumed to be equal to the expenditure required to attain the utility level U_0 with the old set of prices P_{e0}.
5. The expenditure is again kept constant by assumption. See note 4.
6. In this section only the free of charge public goods are considered. For a review of the welfare measures for quantity changes of taxed public goods, see Freeman (1993, pp. 72–85).
7. The vector X is the vector of all the priced goods and services, including the environmental ones, under the control of the consumer.

10. Revealed preference: direct proxy methods

OBJECTIVE

This chapter aims at illustrating the application of the productivity change and substitute cost methods.

SUMMARY

After presenting the reference analytical framework, examples of the productivity change method and the substitute cost method are presented to estimate the economic value of a non-marketed environmental good or service by measuring their influence on the output of a marketed good. Step-by-step exercises with questions and full analytical solutions using the productivity change method and the substitute cost method follow. A discussion of the exercises ends the chapter.

10. Revealed preference: direct proxy methods

OBJECTIVE

SUMMARY

10.1 INTRODUCTION

The techniques belonging to the revealed preference category assume that some kind of direct or indirect relationships exists between the marketed good or service and the non-marketed environmental good and service. Depending on the type of relationship, different techniques can be used to infer the economic value of the non-priced environmental good or service.

This chapter will focus on the indirect relationship between the environmental good and the marketed good, where the environmental good is an input in the production of a marketed good and the value is inferred by looking at the changes in the value of the production or costs of the marketed good due to a change in the quality or quantity of the environmental good. Many possible examples exist of such a relationship. Air pollution, for example, can affect agricultural and forestry production levels as well as production costs. Water pollution affects agricultural, forestry and fisheries outputs and production. Water pollution may also influence the cost of domestic water supply. Natural fertility and erosion can be considered a factor input in the production function of agricultural commodities.

The frameworks within which these relationships are analysed are called the production function approach (PFA) and the cost production function (CPF) (Freeman 1993). These methods consider the environmental attribute as an input. They relate the output of particular marketed goods or services (that is, agricultural production, timber, fish catches) to the inputs necessary to produce them (labour, capital, land), including the environmental goods or services (soil stability, water quality and so forth).

The production function will be of the type:

$$Q = f(X_m, X_e),$$

where X_e is the non-marketed environmental attribute and X_m is a vector of the other marketed inputs.

The cost-minimizing function for producing the marketed good is:

$$C = f(X_m, X_e, Q),$$

where C is the cost.[1]

A change in the provision of the environmental attribute (for example, improvement of the quality of water or reduction of erosion) will generally influence both the output level (Q) and the production costs (C). Profits can be directly derived considering the difference between the value of the production and the inputs costs:

$$\text{Profits} = P.f(X_m, X_e) - WX_m,$$

where P is the price of the output and W is the vector of the prices of the marketed inputs. Note that the environmental input contributes to the production of the output but it is not paid for. The implicit value of the environmental input is then the change in the profits which results from a change in that input. If X_e, say, increases to X_{e1}, then the profits increase by:

$$\Delta \text{ profits} = P \left[f(X_m, X_{e1}) - f(X_m, X_e) \right].$$

This can be taken as the implicit value of the change in the level of the environmental input. For important changes in the environmental inputs it is also likely that the level in the marketed inputs will adjust, respectively, upward for complementary inputs and downward for substitute inputs. Still the change in profits would represent the value in the change of the environmental input.

These changes may affect market prices, which will affect the consumers' and/or producers' surpluses. The value of X can therefore be inferred by observing the changes in the market data for the above-mentioned products.

Let us assume, for example, that the change in the environmental good or service reduces the production costs of a large number of producers. Let us also assume that prices of the other inputs remain constant. The impacts of this are illustrated in Figure 10.1. The supply curves of the producers will shift downward (from S_1 to S_2) causing a fall in the prices (from P_1 to P_2) and an increase in the output Q (from Q_1 to Q_2). Benefits will accrue to the consumers and can be measured by looking at the changes in the consumer surplus. The consumers' surplus increases by the area P_1P_2EC. Producers may obtain net benefits or losses, depending on the elasticities of demand and supply. In this case, the producers' surplus changes from area P_1CB to area P_2EA. Part of the change in consumers' surplus, therefore, notably the area P_1P_2CE, is offset by part of the change in producers' surplus. The total net benefits of the reduction of prices is thus the area $ABCE$.

In many cases, the environmental changes being contemplated will only affect a small proportion of producers. This may be the case, for example, when the environmental changes are concentrated in a single region, whose producers account for only a part of total production, or in cases where trade with other regions or countries is easy. In such cases, the demand curve can be depicted as a horizontal line, as shown in Figure 10.2. Under these conditions, the downward shift in the supply function in the project will be unlikely to influence the market equilibrium and the benefit generated by the change in the environmental good will totally accrue to the producers. Benefits generated by the environmental improvement can be measured by observing only the changes of producers' surplus. This situation is illustrated in Figure 10.2, where the producer surplus change corresponds to the area $ABCE$.

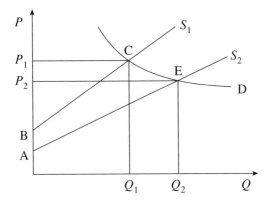

Figure 10.1   Equilibrium price change due to changes in environmental inputs and related welfare measures

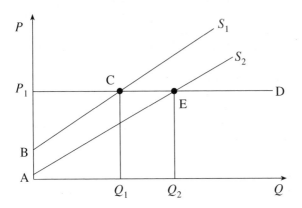

Figure 10.2   Change in environmental inputs and related welfare measure

The use of this approach can be very complex in that it implies the knowledge of the effects of changes in the environmental good or service on the cost of production, the supply of outputs, the demand for Q, and factor supplies. Moreover, the models will change depending on whether the case analysed is a single-product firm or a multi-product one; whether the changes induced by the environmental attribute are marginal or non-marginal; and whether there is a situation of joint-production technologies.

It is also important to note here that the measures of changes in welfare are the private changes, captured by the farmers or consumers. If the shift in the supply curve is achieved, for example, through increased open access to land that was previously commonly managed, then there will be external costs associated with that shift. These have not been taken into account here, but are clearly something that needs to be checked when the method is actually applied. Where such external costs are substantial, their measurement would be based on the changes in output/loss of amenity to other users of the resource.

It is beyond the scope of this chapter to address all the possible situations in detail.[2] The following sections are rather aimed at providing the reader with a practical guide in the use of the techniques generally applied for estimating the value of the influence of an environmental attribute on a marketable good. The valuation techniques presented are the productivity change method and the substitute cost method.

10.2   PRODUCTIVITY CHANGE METHOD (PCM)

In the PCM, as defined earlier, the environment is considered as an input in the production function of a marketed good. Changes in an environmental attribute lead to changes in the output of the marketed good, *ceteris paribus*. The value of the change in the environmental attribute is therefore estimated as the change in the value of production.

This method has been widely applied in real projects. Studies which have applied this technique include: Anderson (1987) in his study on afforestation in Nigeria showed that shelterbelts increased agricultural yields 10 to 30 per cent. Hodgson and Dixon (1988) used this approach to estimate the value of the impacts of logging on fisheries and tourism in the coastal area. It was estimated that a logging ban yielded larger revenues in so far as increased revenues of tourism and fisheries more than compensated logging revenue losses. In a study by Lal (1990) this method was used to evaluate the alternatives of conservation and conversion of mangroves in Fiji. The author estimated that the value of forestry production within the mangroves was less than 10 per cent of the off-site fishery benefits due to the mangroves. Barbier et al. (1991) studied the trade-offs between conserving or converting tropical wetlands. Böjo (1991) applied this technique in the analysis of a land improvement project in Lesotho. Heck et al. (1983) used the production function approach to measure the benefits to agriculture of reducing ozone air pollution.

In the following exercise a simplified model is assumed where the environmental improvement will allow producers to expand the output, and production costs are constant (prices and quantities of inputs and factors do not change). Furthermore, producers face a perfectly elastic demand curve. This assumption implies that the price of the output will remain unchanged and the benefits generated by the environmental improvement will only accrue to producers.

10.2.1 Methodology

The basic assumption of this method is that a dose–response relationship exists between the non-marketed environmental attribute (that is, forage) and the production of the marketed good (that is, milk and meat). The environmental benefit (value) of the project is the additional benefit in terms of additional milk and meat production generated by the increase in the availability of forage in the 'with-project' situation as compared to the 'without-project' situation.

As pointed out earlier, the proposed exercise assumes that benefits of increased availability of forage only accrue to producers and that the change in the provision of the environmental attribute will not affect the output prices, the quantity and prices of the other factor inputs, or external costs. These assumptions are illustrated in Figure 10.3. Notice that the demand curve is infinitely elastic at the equilibrium, that is, the producers in the zone of the project are small with respect to the market of both for milk and meat (price takers). The producers incur negligible costs of production and the supply of milk and meat is only constrained by the availability of forage. These assumptions hold in the context of the specific project analysed, if, for example, the opportunity cost of labour (the major production factor) is close to zero.

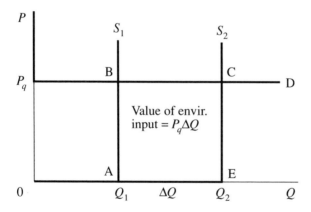

Figure 10.3 Demand and supply framework of the productivity change exercise

The PCM follows a path with some steps common to most applications. These are:

1. Determine the technical relationship between the marketed output Q and the environmental input X: $Q = f(X_m, X_e)$.

2. Estimate the change in the marketed output due to the unit change of the non-marketed input: (marginal product of X): $\partial Q / \partial X^e$.
3. Collect the market unit price of the marketed output: P_q.
4. Calculate the value of the input P_e as the unit price of output P_q times the change in the production of Q $(\partial Q / \partial X_e)$: $P_e = (\partial Q / \partial X_e) * P_q$.
5. Calculate the value of change in the non-marketed input X_e as the physical change of the non-marketed input times its price: $V_e = \Delta X_e * P_e$. (If it is not possible to measure in physical units the change of the environmental good, the value of change of the output is directly taken as a measure of the value of the environmental change: $V_e = \Delta Q * P_q$ (net of the change in the cost of the marketed inputs, if any).)

Note that the estimated value of the environmental asset is the area ABCE in Figure 10.3. A graphical illustration of the procedure is provided in Figure 10.4.

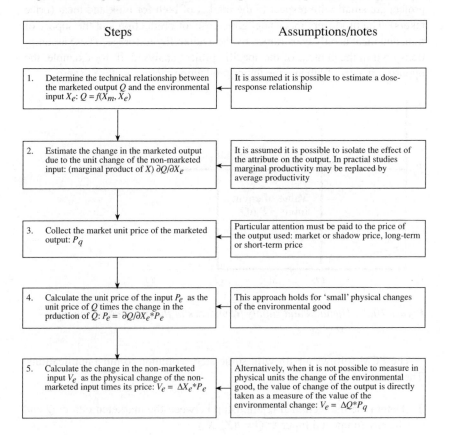

Figure 10.4   Procedure for the productivity change method

10.3 SUBSTITUTE COST METHOD (SCM)

The SCM can be used to estimate both the value of a non-traded consumption good and the value of an intermediate non-traded good. In either case, the money saved using the environmental good instead of a priced input is a possible measure of the benefits of an environmental good or service.

In this section only the case of non-traded intermediate goods will be illustrated, although the methodology for non-traded consumption goods is similar. It is assumed here that the environmental attribute is a substitute for other inputs in the production process. In this case a change in X_n (the environmental good or service) will cause a reduction in the cost of other inputs. For a fixed production level, if the marginal rate of technical substitution (MRTS) is known and is constant, the valuation of a unit of the environmental good is straightforward: it is the unit price of the substitute (the priced input) times the MRTS.[3] If the MRTS is not constant, allowance has to be made for the rate at which the marginal productivity of each factor changes, using techniques such as those illustrated in Annexe 10A1.

In essence, the SCM is just a special case of the production function approach with output held constant in presence of an environmental change.

We can imagine a producer of meat who can use both forage (the environmental input) and sorghum (the priced input) to feed his/her livestock. To get a given quantity K of meat in one period s/he can use all the bundles of the two inputs on the isoquant,[4] as illustrated in Figure 10.5a. S/he can therefore substitute sorghum for forage, and vice versa, without altering the quantity of meat produced. So, the value of the forage can be measured by looking at the saved cost of sorghum.

In the exercise at the end of this chapter we shall look at a particular case in which the forage (the environmental input) fully substitutes for the sorghum in the production process. It follows that the value of the forage is represented by the shaded area in Figure 10.5b that is, the market price of sorghum times the quantity of sorghum saved.

This method has been used extensively in developing countries, an example is provided by Misomali (1987). In a study on fuelwood plantations in Malawi, the author priced fuelwood on the basis of the saved kerosene imports. Newcomb (1984) looked at fuelwood as a substitute for dung for domestic heating. Dung was thus made available as a fertilizer and costs for chemical fertilizers imports (imports plus internal marketing costs) were saved. Therefore, the resulting shadow price for fuelwood was the saved cost of imports of chemical fertilizers. Examples of applications of SCM for estimating the value of non-traded consumption goods are provided in Ward et al. (1991).

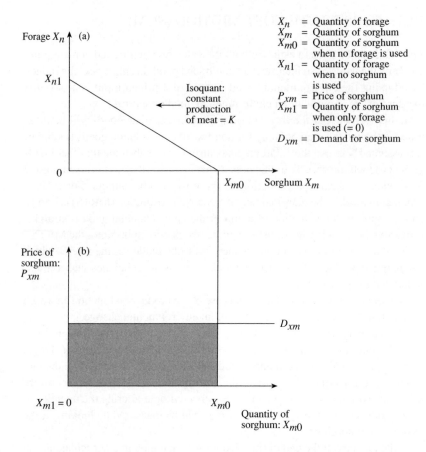

Forage X_n (a)

X_{n1}

Isoquant:
constant
production
of meat $= K$

0

X_{m0} Sorghum X_m

Price of   (b)
sorghum:
P_{xm}

D_{xm}

$X_{m1} = 0$ X_{m0}

Quantity of
sorghum: X_{m0}

X_n = Quantity of forage
X_m = Quantity of sorghum
X_{m0} = Quantity of sorghum
when no forage is used
X_{n1} = Quantity of forage
when no sorghum
is used
P_{xm} = Price of sorghum
X_{m1} = Quantity of sorghum
when only forage
is used ($= 0$)
D_{xm} = Demand for sorghum

Figure 10.5   Value of the environmental input using the substitute cost method

10.3.1 Methodology

The procedure may vary according to the specific context of the valuation exercise but the main steps are those listed below:

1. Choose the closest market substitute X_m to the non-marketed good X_n on the following grounds:

   • Consumer preferences (if the output is a final consumption good).
   • Technical relationships and observed habits of producers (if the good is an intermediate good).

2. Calculate the price of the traded good in the project area, P_{xm}, either by adding transport costs and margins to dealers to the border price (in the case of an import substitute) or subtracting from the local market price the same component (in the case of a locally tradable substitute).
3. Identify the differences between the two goods in terms of their substitutability, considering both their technical features and other characteristics, such as location and availability.
4. Estimate the rate of substitution R_s of the non-marketed good with the marketed one (that is, the value of the non-traded good in terms of the traded good) taking into account the technical features of inputs (for example, the digestible energy content of fodder) or consumer preferences (in the case of final products, for example, fresh milk) identified in the previous step. If the R_s is not constant, the calculation will be more complex.
5. Multiply the price of the marketed good in the project area times the substitution rate to get the benefit of the increase in the environmental input:
$P_{xn} = P_{xm} * R_s$.

An illustration of the procedure is contained in Figure 10.6.

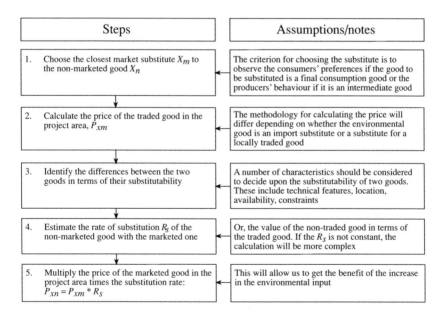

Steps	Assumptions/notes
1. Choose the closest market substitute X_m to the non-marketed good X_n	The criterion for choosing the substitute is to observe the consumers' preferences if the good to be substituted is a final consumption good or the producers' behaviour if it is an intermediate good
2. Calculate the price of the traded good in the project area, P_{xm}	The methodology for calculating the price will differ depending on whether the environmental good is an import substitute or a substitute for a locally traded good
3. Identify the differences between the two goods in terms of their substitutability	A number of characteristics should be considered to decide upon the substitutability of two goods. These include technical features, location, availability, constraints
4. Estimate the rate of substitution R_s of the non-marketed good with the marketed one	Or, the value of the non-traded good in terms of the traded good. If the R_s is not constant, the calculation will be more complex
5. Multiply the price of the marketed good in the project area times the substitution rate: $P_{xn} = P_{xm} * R_s$	This will allow us to get the benefit of the increase in the environmental input

Figure 10.6   Procedure for substitute cost method

NOTES

1. The production function and cost function approaches can be considered two possible alternatives to achieve the same measure of the welfare change (Freeman, 1993; Bowes and Krutilla 1989). The choice of one or the other will generally depend on the availability of data for the estimation of the production function or the cost function.
2. For a comprehensive and in-depth treatment of these topics the reader is referred to the specialized literature: Freeman (1993); Hufshmidt et al. (1983); Baumol et al. (1982); Just et al. (1982); Just and Hueth (1979).
3. The MRTS of the environmental good with the priced good is the quantity of the marketed good required to substitute one unit of the environmental good, keeping the level of output fixed.
4. An isoquant is the locus of all technically efficient bundles of inputs that allow the production of the same quantity of outputs. In Figure 10.5 the isoquant is drawn so that there is a constant rate of substitution whatever the levels of inputs used.

CITED BIBLIOGRAPHY

Anderson, D. (1987), *The Economics of Afforestation: A Case Study in Africa*, Baltimore, MD: Johns Hopkins University Press.

Barbier, E.B., W.M. Adams and K. Kimmange (1991), 'Economic valuation of wetland benefits: the Hadejia-Jama' are floodplain, Nigeria', London Environmental Economics Centre (LEEC) Discussion Paper No. DP91–02.

Baumol, W.J., J.C. Panzer and R.D. Willig (1982), *Contestable Markets and the Theory of Market Structure*, New York: Harcourt, Brace, Jovanovich.

Böjo, J. (1991), 'The economics of land degradation: theory and application to Lesotho', Dissertation for Doctorate in Economics, Stockholm School of Economics.

Bowes, M.D. and J.V. Krutilla (1989), *Multiple-use Management: The Economics of Public Forestlands*, Washington, DC: Resources for the Future.

Freeman, A.M., III (1993), *The Measurement of Environmental and Resource Values: Theory and Methods*, Washington, DC: Resources for the Future.

Heck, W.W., M.A. Richard, W.W. Cure, A.S. Heagel, H.E. Heggestad, R.J. Kohut, L.W. Kress, J.O. Rawlings and O.C. Taylor (1983), 'A reassessment of crop loss from ozone', *Environmental Science and Technology*, 17, 572A–581A.

Hodgson, G. and J.A. Dixon (1988), 'Logging versus fisheries and tourism in Palawan: an environmental and economic analysis', Environmental and Policy Institute Occasional Paper No. 7, Honolulu: East–West Center.

Hufschmidt, M.M., D.E. James, A.D. Meister and B.T. Bower (1983), *Environment Natural Systems and Development: An Economic Evaluation Guide*, Vols I and II, Baltimore, MD: Johns Hopkins University Press.

Just, R.E. and D.L. Hueth (1979), 'Multimarket welfare measurement', *American Economic Review*, 69 (6), 947–54.

Just, R.E, D.L. Hueth and A. Schmitz (1982), *Applied Welfare Economics and Public Policy*, Englewood Cliffs, NJ: Prentice-Hall.

Lal, P.N. (1990), 'Conservation or conversion of mangroves in Fiji', Environment and Policy Institute, Occasional Paper No. 11, Honolulu: East–West Center.

Misomali, E.D. (1987), 'Economic cost–benefit analysis in relation to fuelwood plantations in Malawi', BSc Dissertation, Department of Forestry and Wood Sciences, Bangor.

Newcomb, K. (1984), 'An economic justification for rural afforestation: the case of Ethiopia', Energy Department Paper No. 16, Washington, DC: World Bank.

Pétry, F. (1995), *Sustainability Issues in Agriculture and Rural Development Policies*, Rome: Food and Agriculture Organization.

Ward, H.W., B.J. Deren and E.H. D'Silva (1991), *The Economics of Project Analysis. A Practitioner's Guide*, Washington, DC: Economic Development Institute of the World Bank.

ANNEX 10A1   CASE STUDY 1: A NUMERICAL EXAMPLE OF PCM

Background

The following exercise draws on the Sylvo-Pastoral Management and Reforestation Project of the Mani forest area (Djibouti Republic) reported in Pétry (1995).

The Mani forest is an area of about 26,000 hectares (ha) which lies to the south east of the Gulf of Rahjou, extending south-east from the Mani forest towards Lake Lossa. The project area includes:

1. An area of about 2,000 ha with the highest elevation at 1,800 m that includes the Mani Forest. It lies within the 300 mm isohyet[1] and receives the highest rainfall in the country.
2. An area of about 4,000 ha which is severely desertified, composed of plateaux and hills with altitudes between 900 and 1,400 m. It lies between the 300 and 250 mm isohyets.
3. An extremely rugged area of 20,000 ha called Karam, with altitudes between 500 and 1,200 m. It lies between the 250 and 200 mm isohyets. Seventy-five per cent of the rainfall is concentrated in the hot season.

The forest plays a central role in the ecological system as well as in the economic activities of the pastoralists living in the area. In years of severe drought, the Mani forest is considered the last resort for all cattle. The multifunctional role of the forest also includes its use as a source of fuelwood and minor forest products, as well as its micro-climatic functions and its key role in determining the region's hydrology.

Due to overexploitation the forest is suffering irreversible degeneration and would disappear within ten years without intervention. Moreover, this, together with rangeland degradation will threaten the livelihood base of subsistence pastoralists. It is therefore of foremost importance to introduce more sustainable resource management practices.

To relieve the pressure on the Mani forest and assist its regeneration, the project aims at a more balanced utilization of both overexploited and under-exploited sylvo-pastoral resources. In the meantime it aims at diversification in the range of income-generating opportunities for the subsistence pastoralists in order to reduce pressure on the forest resources.

The project, as outlined in Pétry (1995), has six components:

1. *Sylvo-pastoral management.* The progressive introduction of a system of deferred grazing over 24,000 ha of land; the creation of 750 ha of permanent pasture; the establishment of 400 ha of forage plantation and livestock support activities.
2. *Forest conservation and regeneration.* With the aim of conserving and regenerating the Mani forest, the project promotes the natural and assisted regeneration of *juniper procera* at various sites within the forest, the planting of 86 ha of community woodlots and the construction of windbreaks near livestock water points.
3. *Water development.* The project, with the beneficiary's participation, would construct 39 drinking water storage tanks and 25 livestock water points.
4. *Soil and water conservation.* Soil and water conservation measures over an area of 900 ha would enhance the productivity of pasture resources.
5. *Income diversification.* This would be promoted through charcoal production using excess dead wood, wood carving, aviculture and apiculture.
6. *Institutional support.* The project would enable the creation of a project management unit, the provision of a core of local and expatriate staff, training and monitoring and evaluation support.

Problem Set

For the project to be appraised, all the costs and benefits of the project must be priced. The following example demonstrates how the analyst proceeded to place a monetary value on a non-marketed good provided by the forest, that is, the forage.[2]

The value of the milk and meat obtainable with one unit of forage is chosen as a measure of its value. The problem is how to calculate the value of the change in production due to the increased availability of forage. To find the answer, some further assumptions and data are required.

Table 10A1.1 shows the livestock by species existing in the project's area before the project's implementation.

Table 10A1.1   Existing livestock by species in project area

Species	Number
Camels	472
Cattle	1,324
Sheep	1,244
Goats	3,331
Donkeys	218

The feed requirement of a camel is 2.3 metric tons of forage dry matter per year. Table 10A1.2 shows the sorghum feed requirements of every species of animal in terms of the sorghum feed requirement of one camel. These values are called 'tropical livestock standard units' (TSUs).

Table 10A1.2   Tropical livestock standard units

Species	TSUs
Camels	1.00
Cattle	0.73
Sheep	0.12
Goats	0.12
Donkeys	0.40

Table 10A1.3 shows the annual per unit production of milk obtained from lactating females and the production of meat obtained from all animals.

Table 10A1.3   Annual production parameters

Species	Milk (litres/year/animal)	Meat (kg/year)
Camels	600	14.0
Cattle	400	16.0
Sheep	30	4.7
Goats	40	6.6
Donkeys	0	0.0

Table 10A1.4 gives the number of lactating females by livestock species in the project area.

Table 10A1.4   Number of lactating females by species

Species	Lactating females
Camels	54
Cattle	245
Sheep	87
Goats	473
Donkeys	0

Table 10A1.5 gives the average observed price of milk and meat.

Table 10A1.5   Price of milk and meat

Commodity	Price
Milk	150B$/litre
Meat	600 B$/Kg

Solution Set

When an input of a production process is not marketed, its value can be elicited from the value of the production obtainable with the use of the input by considering the contribution of the input to the product. In this case the non-marketed forage contributes substantially to the production of milk and meat. The value of one kilogram of forage dry matter can therefore be assumed equal to the value of the production of milk and meat at present obtainable in the project's area with one kilogram of forage dry matter. The following figures are calculated:

- the total value of milk and meat obtainable in one year from the existing livestock;
- the theoretical annual consumption of forage dry matter by the existing livestock;
- the value of one kilogram of forage dry matter by the ratio of total value of milk and meat by quantity of forage dry matter consumed.

Calculation of the value of milk and meat annually obtainable in the area
This value is obtained by multiplying the total annual production of milk and meat by their average market prices. The annual total quantity of meat is obtained by multiplying the annual production of every animal by the number of animals present in the project area by species, then summing across the different species, as shown in Table 10A1.6.

Table 10A1.6   Total meat produced

Species	Number of animals in project area	Meat per animal (kg/year)	Total meat by species (kg/year)
Camels	472	14.0	6,608.0
Cattle	1,324	16.0	21,184.0
Sheep	1,244	4.7	5,846.8
Goats	3,331	6.6	21,984.6
Donkeys	218	0.0	0
Total meat (kg/year)			55,623.4

Analogously, the total annual quantity of milk is obtained by considering the number of lactating females by species and the relative milk production per unit, then summing across the species, as shown in Table 10A1.7.

Table 10A1.7   Total milk produced

Species	Lactating females	Milk (litres/year)	Milk by species (Litres/year)
Camels	54	600	32,400
Cattle	245	400	98,000
Sheep	87	30	2,610
Goats	473	40	18,920
Donkeys	0	0	0
Total milk (litres/year)			151,930

The total value of the annual production is obtained by multiplying the annual quantities by the relative prices, as shown in Table 10A1.8.

Table 10A1.8   Total value of production

Commodity	Price	Annual quantity	Annual value (B$/year)
Milk	150 B$/litre	151,930 (litres/yr)	22,789,500
Meat	600 B$/kg	55,623.4 (kg/yr)	33,374,040
Total annual value (B$/year)			56,163,540

Calculation of the annual forage dry matter requirements
The total forage dry matter requirement of the existing livestock in the project area is calculated by following these steps:

- The different animals are expressed in TSUs according to their feed requirements and added up across species.
- The total TSUs are multiplied by the annual forage dry matter requirement of the standard animal (the camel), to get the total annual forage dry matter requirements of the existing livestock in the project area.

The estimates of TSUs are given in Table 10A1.9.
The annual standard animal requirement of forage dry matter is 2,300 kg/year. The existing livestock's requirement per year is therefore:

TSU	$2,074.72 \times$
Kg/year	2,300 =
Kg/year	4,771,856

Table 10A1.9   Total tropical livestock standard units by species

Species	TSUs	Animals in project area	Total TSUs by species
Camels	1.00	472	472.00
Cattle	0.73	1,324	966.52
Sheep	0.12	1,244	149.28
Goats	0.12	3,331	399.72
Donkeys	0.40	218	87.20
Total TSUs in the area			2,074.72

Calculation of the value of one kilogram of forage dry matter
The value of one kilogram of forage dry matter is obtained as the ratio of the total value of annual production to the total forage dry matter requirements.

B$/year	56,163,540 ÷
Kg/year	4,771,856 =
B$/kg	11.77

The value of the forage dry matter, according the change in production approach is therefore 11.77B$/kg.

Discussion

To support the above analysis from the economic point of view, a number of assumptions have been made.

First, it is assumed that the average product equals the marginal product of forage. This means that the incremental quantity of forage produced leads to a proportional increase in the quantity of milk and meat. Following on from this, the assumption is made that the incremental production of forage leads to an increase of meat and milk sellable at a constant price, that is, the prices of milk and meat do not fall due to the increase of the supply.

Furthermore, all the value of the output (the selling price) is allocated to the production input 'forage'. This is correct only if we assume that production costs are negligible. For example, if the major production factor is labour we assume that its opportunity cost is close to zero, that is, no other output is forgone when additional labour is employed in milk and meat production. By the same token, we should assume that the value of leisure time forgone is zero. This assumption might not be realistic in other projects. In such cases, the remuneration of all other production factors and input costs that allow the production of milk and meat should be deducted from the selling price, as in Figure 10A1.1.

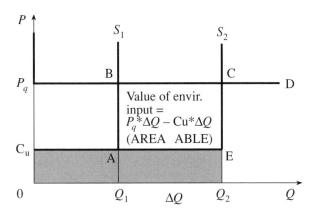

Figure 10A1.1   Demand and supply framework of the productivity change exercise: case with constant unit production costs

It should be noted also that once the benefits of the increased availability of forage have been estimated, the costs of producing the forage should also be estimated and accounted for in the framework of the cost–benefit analysis. The net benefits obtained will provide the decision maker with an indicator of the viability of the project.

Notes

1. An isohyet is a line connecting points with equal rainfall levels.
2. It is assumed here of course that the expansion of grazing does not lead to 'overgrazing'. If that is the case, the project is badly designed and should be reconsidered. An assessment of any costs associated with such overgrazing could be made to show policy makers of the implications of their project design.

ANNEX 10A2 CASE STUDY 2: A NUMERICAL EXAMPLE OF SCM

Background

The project context of this exercise is the same as that described for the productivity change method exercise. This exercise focuses on the derivation of the value of a non-marketed asset, namely forage, looking at the value of a marketed asset (sorghum) that can be a substitute for it. The substitution can be on preference grounds when referring to final consumption goods, or on technical grounds when considering inputs, as in the present case.

Problem Set

In the particular socioeconomic context of the project, forage is an important output.[1] Thanks to sylvo-pastoral management activities, the project would increase the annual forage production by 113 per cent, from 4,264 tons in a base year to 9,115 tons at full development.[2] Since no market for forage exists, its shadow price, that is, the value to the economy of one unit of forage, must be estimated in order to appraise the benefits of the project.

The value of forage is estimated by looking at the value of sorghum, which can be its substitute for animal feeding. The sorghum is imported from abroad. The price of sorghum (sorghum dry matter) for the final user is composed of FOB (free on board) price, freight, insurance and transport costs on site, as shown in Table 10A2.1.

Table 10A2.1   Imported air-dried sorghum costs

Description	Values
FOB price US$/ton	96
Freight US$/ton	100
Insurance US$/ton	5
Local transport B$/ton	5,337
Exchange rate B$/US$	156.65

The air-dried sorghum contains 90 per cent of dry matter and 10 per cent of moisture.[3]

The digestible energy, that is, the quantity of energy that animals obtain from the feed is shown in Table 10A2.2, expressed in mega-calories per kilogram (Mcal/kg) of dry matter of feed.

Table 10A2.2   Digestible energy of different feeds

Description	Values
Sorghum dry matter	3.88 Mcal/kg
Forage dry matter	2.40 Mcal/kg

Questions

1. Using the information provided, estimate the price of the forage in the project area using the substitute cost method assuming sorghum is a substitute.
2. Briefly discuss the advantages and the disadvantages of the technique, high-lighting the assumptions that require a note of caution.[4]

Solution Set

We are interested in evaluating the price of a kilogram of forage dry matter in the project area. Since no market for forage exists, the prices prevailing for a surrogate can, after appropriate adaptations, be used to assess the value of forage. The procedure described in Section 10.3.1, the substitute cost method, will be followed systematically in order to yield an estimate of the price of forage dry matter.

Step 1   Determination of the appropriate substitute
First, the determination is made that the suitable substitute for forage is sorghum. To elicit the value of forage from the value of sorghum we have to consider:

- the price of a kilogram of sorghum dry matter in the project area; and
- the quantity of digestible energy present in a kilogram of forage dry matter relative to the quantity of digestible energy contained in a kilogram of sorghum dry matter.

In order to understand why we have to look at the digestible energy present in feed it is worth recalling that the value of a feed is roughly determined by its feeding capacity, which in turn is closely related to the quantity of digestible energy present in it.

Step 2   Calculation of the price of sorghum dry matter in the project area
The sorghum is an imported commodity. It is usually transported after being dried. The price of the air-dried sorghum in the project area is therefore determined by the CIF (cost, insurance and freight) price plus the transportation cost from the border to the project area.
    The CIF price in US dollars of one ton of the air-dried sorghum is obtained by adding the cost of freight and insurance to the FOB price:

FOB price of air-dried sorghum US$/ton	96	+
Freight US$/ton	100	+
Insurance US$/ton	5	=
CIF price of air-dried sorghum (US$/ton)	*201*	

The CIF price in US$ of a ton of air-dried sorghum is converted into local currency (B$) using an appropriate exchange rate:

CIF price of air-dried sorghum (US$/ton)	201	×
Exchange rate (B$/US$)	156.65	=
CIF price of air-dried sorghum (B$/ton)	*31,486*	

The transport cost from the border to the project area is added to the CIF cost in local currency to obtain the cost of a ton of air-dried sorghum in the project area:

CIF price of air-dried sorghum (B$/ton)	31,486	+
Local transportation (B$/ton)	5,337	=
Local price of air-dried sorghum (B$/ton)	*36,823*	

The cost per ton is converted into a cost per kilo:

Local price of air-dried sorghum (B$/ton)	36,823	÷
Conversion factor (kg/ton)	1,000	=
Local price of air-dried sorghum (B$/kg)	*36.823*	

In calculating the local price of the sorghum dry matter we have to consider that one kilogram of air-dried sorghum contains 0.9 kg of sorghum dry matter:

Local price of air-dried sorghum (B$/kg)	36.823	÷
Dry material content of air-dried sorghum (kg/kg)	0.9	=
Local price of sorghum dry matter (B$/kg)	*40.914*	

The cost of one kilogram of sorghum dry matter in the project area is therefore B$40.91.

Step 3   Identification of the differences between forage and sorghum
The main difference between these two kinds of fodder is their digestible energy content. It is worth noting that little imported sorghum is used in the project area, despite the technical substitutability of forage with sorghum.

Step 4   Calculation of the substitution rate of forage with sorghum
The substitution rate of forage with sorghum shows how many kilograms of sorghum dry matter are required to yield the same digestible energy as a kilogram of forage dry matter. The substitution rate is obtained as the ratio between the digestible energy of forage and the digestible energy of sorghum:[5]

Forage dry matter (Mcal/kg)	2.40	÷
Sorghum dry matter (Mcal/kg)	3.88	=
Conversion of forage into sorghum	*0.6186*	

Step 5 Calculation of the value of forage based on digestible energy content

To elicit the value of a kilogram of forage dry matter from the value of a kilogram of sorghum dry matter, it is necessary to multiply the value of one kilogram of sorghum by the substitution rate of forage with sorghum:

Price of sorghum dry matter(B$/kg)	40.914	×
Conversion factor of forage in sorghum	0.6186	=
Value of forage dry matter (B$/Kg)	*25.308*	

The forage dry matter contains 62 per cent of the digestible energy of sorghum dry matter, therefore, under these assumptions, the value of forage dry matter is 62 per cent of the value of sorghum dry matter.

Alternatively, we can calculate the cost of one unit of digestible energy (one megacalorie) obtainable from a kilogram of sorghum dry matter:

Price of sorghum dry matter(B$/kg)	40.914	÷
Sorghum digest. energy (Mcal/kg)	3.88	=
Price of a Mcal of digestible energy (B$/Mcal)	*10.545*	

This calculation highlights the value of a megacalorie in the project area, when it is obtained from sorghum dry matter. Assuming that the value of a megacalorie produced from sorghum dry matter is equivalent to that of the forage dry matter, to obtain the value of a kilogram of a forage dry matter we can multiply the value of the sorghum megacalorie by the megacalories obtainable from a kilogram of forage dry matter.

Price of a Mcal (B$/Mcal)	10.545	×
Forage digest. energy (Mcal/kg)	2.400	=
Price of forage dry matter (B$/kg)	*25.308*	

As can be seen, the same result as above is obtained.

Discussion

Whenever the sorghum is actually consumed and the project allows for the substitution of sorghum with forage, this value can also be interpreted as the savings on the sorghum bill we have per kilogram of forage locally produced.

Whenever forage is technically substitutable with sorghum, but sorghum is not actually used in the project area, the analyst must be careful in using the value of the forage equivalent as the opportunity cost of forage.

If there is a fair degree of competition in input markets and farmers are assumed to be well informed, it is likely that sorghum is not used (imported) because its marginal cost exceeds the value of its marginal product. For instance, transport costs can generate a natural protection against imports of sorghum. Assuming that the price of forage is equal to the price of the substitute in this case leads to an overestimate of the value of forage, which is better estimated by considering the value of its marginal product (see the productivity change exercise).

It is possible that some sorghum dry matter is temporarily used for assuring livestock survival whenever forage shortages occur. In this case, however, the sorghum bill must be considered as an investment, based on long-run economic rationale, rather than an operating cost. In this case, its value is not a good proxy for the forage, although it is currently used as an operating input.

The productivity change and the substitute cost methods give substantially different results. The value of one kilogram of forage dry matter evaluated by the SCM is more than twice the value obtained with the change in production approach.

According to economic theory, in a perfect competitive economy the equilibrium value of each input should be equal to the value of its marginal product. In our example, the value of a kilogram of forage dry matter should be equal to the value of milk and meat obtainable by increasing the use of the input by one kilogram. At the margin therefore, the PCM, given a competitive economy, leads to a theoretically better result. On the other hand, in a perfectly competitive economy the price of two almost perfectly substitutable inputs such as forage dry matter and sorghum equivalent dry matter should not differ substantially. If this is the case, the demand for the cheaper input should increase, leading to a price increase and, conversely, the demand for the more expensive input should decrease, leading to a price decrease. However, if the price of one of the inputs is exogenous, this will not be the case.

For better understanding of the meaning and the reliability of our estimates it is worth focusing on the causes that lead to such a different value. Some explanations, not mutually exclusive on theoretical grounds and likely to occur simultaneously in practice, can be put forward:

- *Technical versus observed substitutability.* The more expensive input – the sorghum – is technically substitutable for forage but it is not actually substituted due to its high price. If farmers were compelled to use the sorghum for feeding the livestock then they would go out of the market, due to the relatively low price of milk and meat. Therefore no well-informed and rational farmer would use an input costing B\$25.30 to obtain a production value of B\$11.70. Given the price of milk and meat, and assuming that the sorghum is not actually used, the surrogate market technique can give misleading results, that is, an overestimate of the value of a digestible megacalorie in the project area that leads to an overestimate of the forage dry matter's value.
- *Existence of further outputs.* There could be other outputs, other than milk and meat, that increase the value of forage calculated with the PCM, for example, the wool, the hides, the animals' traction or the animals' transport capability. This last could apply to donkeys, which produce neither milk nor meat. Lacking these kinds of outputs, we should assume either that donkeys have an 'existence value' or that farmers behave in an irrational way in allowing them to consume feed without an appreciable output.
- *Short-run and long-run prices.* The prices of milk and meat could be short run in nature. They could be at a low level due to a temporary excess supply in that region. In this case the PCM leads to an underestimate of the forage value in the long run. On the other hand, if the price of sorghum considered is higher than the long-run price, the SCM leads to an overestimate of the forage value in the long run.

Notes

1. The value of fodder production is considered a proxy of the total value of the pasture land. However, other benefits of protecting the Mani forest are in the form of 'non-use benefits'. The forest indeed:

   - serves as a recreational resource for residents of Bouassa Town and international tourists;
   - represents a centre of biodiversity of international significance; and
   - provides other service functions that are difficult to identify, qualify and value, along with its productive function explicitly considered in the economic analysis.

2. Project benefits would derive not only from planting and rangeland management but also from the prevention of degeneration of the Mani forest and of the pasture.
   Note that in this exercise, 'ton' means metric ton.
3. This is due to a partial drying effect of air, the atmospheric humidity and other causes.
4. A spreadsheet is available for driving the trainee and easing calculations.
5. Once the substitution rate has been estimated then, with a given quantity of forage, we can obtain the equivalent quantity of sorghum, in terms of digestible energy, by multiplying the quantity of forage by the conversion factor, that is, the substitution rate.

ANNEX 10A3   TECHNICAL SUBSTITUTABILITY OF INPUTS AND FACTORS

Non-marketed inputs or factors used in production processes may be substitutable with other marketed inputs or factors. When the production function is known or estimable, it is possible to define in an analytical way the substitution rates between factors or inputs. The marginal rate of technical substitution of factor i for factor j ($MRTS_{ij}$) expresses how much the quantity of factor j must change when the factor i changes by one unit, in order to keep output constant. This is the variation in input j that exactly compensates for a unit variation in factor i. Analytically, for all continuous and differentiable production functions, the MRTS of factor i with factor j can be calculated by setting the total differential of the production function to be zero, keeping all other factors constant:

$$Y = f(x_k), \quad k = 1...l \Rightarrow dY = \frac{\partial Y}{\partial x_i} + \frac{\partial Y}{\partial x_j},$$

where $\partial Y/\partial x_i$ and $\partial Y/\partial x_j$ are the marginal productivities of factors i and j respectively.

Therefore,

$$dY = MP_i dx_i + MP_j dx_j . dY = MP_i dx_i + MP_j dx_j = 0 \Rightarrow \frac{dx_j}{dx_i} = -\frac{MP_i}{MP_j} = MRTS_{ij}.$$

This means that the variation of factor j due to a unit variation of factor i (when the output is fixed), is the ratio of the marginal productivities of factors i and j. The MRTS of i with j is negative (if i decreases then j must increase to keep output constant) and in absolute terms is directly proportional to the coefficient of factor i. That is, the larger the relative weight of factor i in the production, the greater the quantity of factor j required to replace one unit of factor i. Moreover, it is inversely proportional in absolute value to the quantity of factor i used. When X_i is relatively low, a large quantity of X_j is required to compensate for one unit of X_i and when X_i is relatively high, a smaller quantity of X_j is required to compensate a unit of X_i. In the case of the Cobb–Douglas production function, the $MRTS_{ij}$ is given by:

$$Y = A \prod_{n=1}^{u} X_n^{\alpha_n} \quad n = 1...i...j...u$$

$$\delta Y_{ij} = A \prod_{\substack{n=1 \\ n \neq j \neq i}}^{u} \overline{X}_n^{\alpha_n} \left[\alpha_j X_j^{(\alpha_j - 1)} X_i^{\alpha_i} \right] dX_j + A \prod_{\substack{n=1 \\ n \neq j \neq i}}^{u} \overline{X}_n^{\alpha_n} \left[\alpha_i X_i^{(\alpha_i - 1)} X_j^{\alpha_j} \right] dX_i$$

$$dY = 0 \Rightarrow \left[\alpha_j X_j^{(\alpha_j - 1)} X_i^{\alpha_i} \right] dX_j + \left[\alpha_i X_i^{(\alpha_i - 1)} X_j^{\alpha_j} \right] dX_i = 0$$

$$MRTS_{ij} = \frac{dX_j}{dX_i} = -\frac{\alpha_i X_i^{(\alpha_i - 1)} X_j^{\alpha_j}}{\alpha_j X_j^{(\alpha_j - 1)} X_i^{\alpha_i}} = -\frac{\alpha_i X_j}{\alpha_j X_i}.$$

11. Revealed preference: indirect proxy methods

OBJECTIVE

The purpose of this chapter is to: (i) analyse the theoretical concepts of two main techniques which fall within the category of revealed preference indirect proxy methods, namely the travel cost method (TCM) and the hedonic price method (HPM); (ii) provide a detailed presentation of the methodology for their application; (iii) illustrate the methodology and present an exercise which will enable the reader to become familiar with the application of the techniques; and (iv) discuss possible interpretations and policy implications of the results.

SUMMARY

As was noted in the previous chapters, the indirect proxy methods attempt to estimate the value of an environmental resource by observing the effects of a change in the quality/quantity of the environmental service on the quantity or price of the good consumed by individuals. Two variants of the TCM model, notably the zonal and the individual TCM, are analysed and illustrated by step-by-step exercises. The major assumptions made in the application of these methods will also be highlighted. The hedonic price method is also presented. After a review of the basic theoretical concepts underlying the method, a step-by-step exercise is proposed.

11.1   TRAVEL COST METHOD

The TCM uses a survey technique based on interviews where visitors of recreational sites are invited to provide information on the trip (the cost, length, purpose of trip and other sites visited) and on other socioeconomic features (their income, age and sex). This method can be used to measure the use value of a recreation area or historic site, as well as to estimate increases in this use value if the site were to be improved. One application of this methodology is to see whether a recreation site has a greater total use value than a proposed agricultural, urban or industrial development. The use of this technique is particularly appropriate when the site is publicly owned and the government is contemplating improving the site or changing its use, and where there are not likely to be significant option values or non-use values attributed to the site.

The fundamental insight that drives this model is that if a consumer wants to use the recreational services of a site s/he has to visit it. The travel cost to reach the site is considered as the implicit or the surrogate price of the visit, and changes in the travel cost will cause a variation in the quantity of visits. Observation of these variations across individuals will permit the estimation of demand functions and of the value of the site.

Two main variants of the travel cost method exist: the zonal travel cost model (ZTCM) and the individual travel cost model (ITCM). The ZTCM divides the entire area from which visitors originate into a set of visitor zones and then defines the dependent variable as the visitor rate (that is, the number of visits made from a particular zone in a period divided by the population of that zone). The ITCM defines the dependent variable as the number of site visits made by each visitor over a specified period. The following sections provide a summary of these methods.

11.1.1   Zonal Travel Cost Method (ZTCM)

In mathematical terms the trip demand curve for a given recreational site from the zone j will be defined as:

$$V_j/P_i = f(C_{ij}, X_i)$$

where: V_j is the total number of trips by individuals from zone j to the recreational site per unit of time; P_i is population of zone j; and C_j is the travel cost from zone j to the recreational site;[1] and X_j represents the socioeconomic characteristics of zone j. These socioeconomic characteristics include, among others, factors such as income levels, spending on other goods, the existence of substitute sites, entrance fees and quality indices of n substitute sites.[2] The visitor rate V_j/P_i is generally calculated as visits per unit of population, usually assumed in thousand persons, in zone j.

Assuming that the above relationship is a linear one, in each zone the average consumer surplus (ACS) per person for all visits to the site in a period of time is calculated by integrating the equation of the type:

$$V/P = a + bTC$$

between the price (cost) of visits actually made from each zone and the price at which the visitor rate would fall to 0, that is, the choke price (CP), intercept of the demand curve with the TC axis. Assuming we have defined three zones, as in Figure 11.1, the ACS of zone 1 will be:

$$ACS_1 = \int_{TC_1}^{CP} (a + bTC)dTC$$

The annual total consumer surplus for the whole recreation experience can be estimated in each zone by multiplying the annual average ACS per population unit times the population units of the zone. Cumulating the annual zonal consumer surplus across all zones gives the estimate of total consumer surplus per year for the whole recreational experience of visiting the site.

11.1.2 Individual Travel Cost Method (ITCM)

The demand curve in this model relates individual annual visits to the costs of those visits. That is:

$$V_i = f(TC_i, X_i)$$

where: V_i is the number of visits made in a period time, say a year, by individual i to the site; TC_i is the visit cost faced by individual i to visit the site; and X_i is all other factors determining individual i's visits (income, time, and other socioeconomic characteristics).

This demand function can be extended to allow for the specification of a number of explanatory variables. These include the individual's estimate of the proportion of the enjoyment of the overall trip imputed to the specific site under investigation; the individual's view of the availability of substitute sites; the size of the individual's household; and whether the individual is a member of an environmental organization, as well as other socioeconomic data.[3]

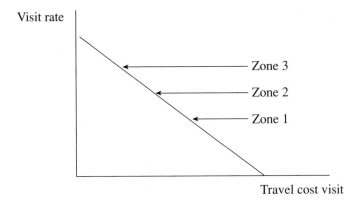

Figure 11.1   Zonal travel cost

Integrating the demand curve between the actual travel cost TC_i and the choke price gives an estimate of the individual annual consumer surplus (ICS) for individual i:

$$ICS_1 = \int_{TC_1}^{CP} f(TC, X)dTC.$$

The total annual consumer surplus for the site is obtained by multiplying the individual annual consumer surplus (ICS) by the number of individuals visiting the site annually. The modelling of individual socioeconomic features enables the estimation of consumer surpluses of different socioeconomic groups of visitors. Alternatively, the average ICS per visit can be calculated and can then be multiplied by the total annual number of visits to the site to get the total annual consumer surplus of the site.

In the basic model described above, several assumptions are made which deserve careful attention when the method is applied:

- The basic method assumes the case of a pure visitor, that is, that the trip to the site is for the sole purpose of visiting the site. This case is only one possible scenario. Other possibilities are that the visit to the site forms only part of the recreation experience or that the visit coincides with other activities (for example, a visit to relatives). The travel cost and time should in these cases be allocated among the different purposes.
- It is also assumed that driving to the recreational site produces neither utility nor disutility. In fact it may be the case that the trip itself produces

some benefits to the driver. In this case the travel cost would be overestimated.

- The opportunity cost of the time spent on-site and for travelling is generally assumed to be the wage rate. No general consensus exists on this point.[4]
- The basic model assumes that there is only one site to visit. In the real world visitors often choose among substitute sites. In this case, the number of visits that consumers make to the site surveyed will depend not only on its implicit price but also on the implicit prices of any substitute. If these are not accounted for, the parameters will be biased upwardly.

In order to obtain a reliable estimation of the welfare change due to recreational services, all the above issues should be considered in the design of the questionnaire as well as in the travel cost function itself.

11.1.3   Methodology

There are five main steps in carrying out a TCM study. Figure 11.2 provides an illustration of how these steps are organized.

1. *Identification of the environmental good/service to be valued.*   This activity is based on information provided by preliminary studies, which will define precisely the good/service to be valued. This method is usually applied in the valuation of recreational sites, services/attributes of the site (that is, walking, fishing and so forth), or for a change in the quality/quantity of the environmental attribute. In the exercises developed below, this method is used for the valuation of sites.
2. *Preparation of the questionnaire/scenario.*   Particular care should be devoted to the identification of the variables required for the valuation. After an introduction where the purpose of the survey is explained, the questionnaire should carefully analyse the main features of the visit[5] and the socioeconomic characteristics of the visitors.[6] If the questionnaire is also used for a CVM survey, it should also include: (i) a scenario that simulates the hypothetical market of the environmental good/service; (ii) the payment vehicle; and (iii) the elicitation form (see Chapter 12 for more details on CVM).

   The number of variables will depend on which travel cost model is used (either ZTCM or ITCM) and on the particular situation. The design of the questionnaire should not be too lengthy, which could cause annoyance to the interviewees.

   Finally the questions should be formulated as clearly and concisely as possible and should not lead to misinterpretation on the part of either the enumerators or the interviewees.

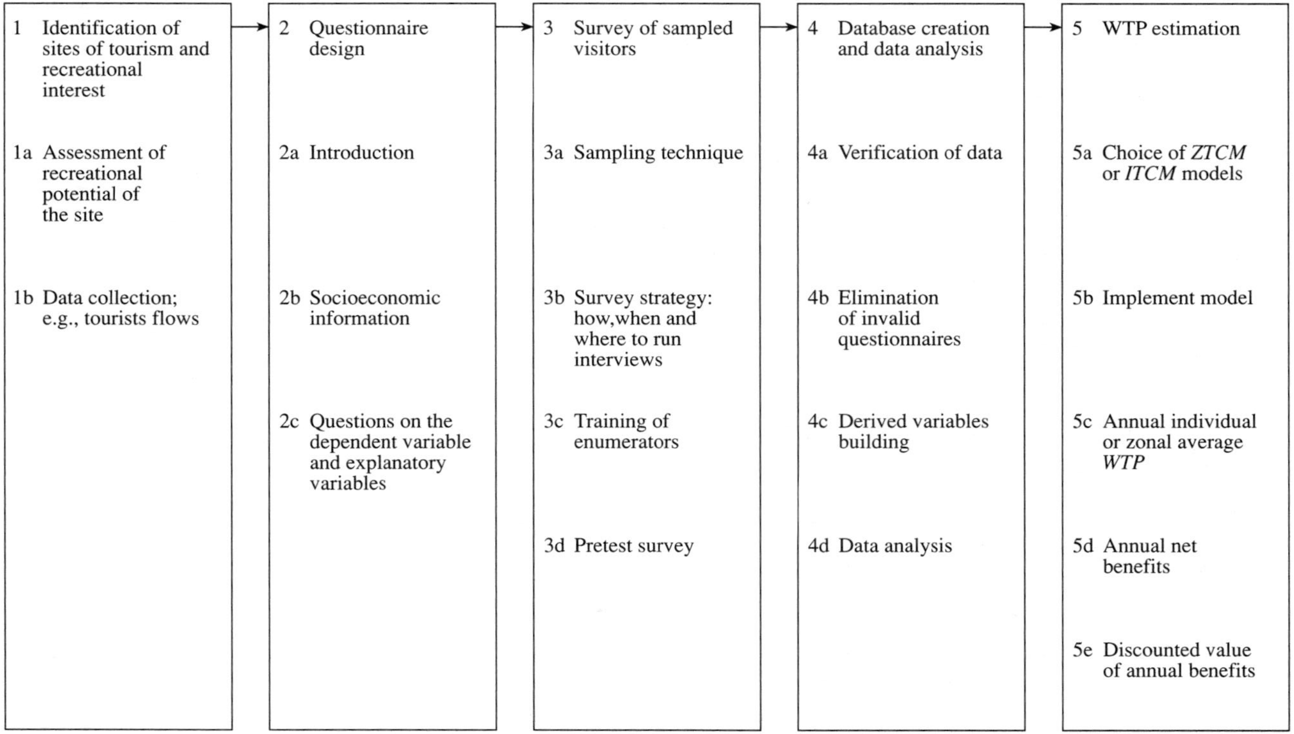

1 Identification of sites of tourism and recreational interest	2 Questionnaire design	3 Survey of sampled visitors	4 Database creation and data analysis	5 WTP estimation
1a Assessment of recreational potential of the site	2a Introduction	3a Sampling technique	4a Verification of data	5a Choice of *ZTCM* or *ITCM* models
1b Data collection; e.g., tourists flows	2b Socioeconomic information	3b Survey strategy: how, when and where to run interviews	4b Elimination of invalid questionnaires	5b Implement model
	2c Questions on the dependent variable and explanatory variables	3c Training of enumerators	4c Derived variables building	5c Annual individual or zonal average *WTP*
		3d Pretest survey	4d Data analysis	5d Annual net benefits
				5e Discounted value of annual benefits

Figure 11.2   Steps of the TCM study

3. *The survey.*   Before the survey is carried out it is suggested that:

   (i)   the enumerators be trained to avoid risks of misinterpretation of the questions and responses and to ensure that the requested information is collected without influencing the respondents' answers;
   (ii)   a pretest be conducted to check the quality of the questionnaire;
   (iii) a plan of action be formulated stating the number of interviews to be undertaken per day, how the interviews should be distributed over the days, the weeks, the months, and where the enumerators should interview the visitors. Often budget constraints do not permit pretesting. In this case one possible alternative would be a simulation exercise with the enumerators acting as both interviewers and interviewees.

   The survey can be carried out in various ways: by mail; by telephone; through on-site face-to-face interviews; or through outside the site face-to-face interviews. Given the characteristics of the goods and services usually valued with this technique, it is recommended that on-site face-to-face interviews be used.

   The sample of respondents can also be determined in many ways. Each visitor should have the same known probability of being selected. To get a random sample of the visitors interviewed on-site, visitor statistics from previous years should be used to determine how many interviews should be conducted during each month of the season. The same proportion of visitors should be interviewed each month.

   Often, however, a random sample of visitors during the peak season is sufficient as it can be considered as representative of the total visits undertaken in one year. The sample size is also a very important point to address for a proper and reliable estimation of the economic value. Usually the number of respondents should increase with the number of variables examined in the questionnaire. In general it is recommended that the number of respondents be at least 200.

4. *Collection of data and validation of the questionnaires.*   At this stage invalid questionnaires are eliminated and a database is created with the data collected. Sometimes new variables can be constructed on the basis of the information collected. There is no need to ask the respondents the cost of travel to reach the site if this can be constructed from known data.[7] Of course, if this information is not available or reliable, specific questions must be included in the questionnaire.

5. *Data analysis.*   The analysis of data is mainly aimed at describing the behaviour of specific variables and checking their consistency through appropriate cross-comparisons.

6. *WTP estimation.* In this phase the selected models of monetary valuation are implemented. The results obtained can be expressed in per capita values (WTP/head) or in terms of total value (total annual value of the environmental service under consideration). The flow of net benefits generated by the environmental service over a period of time can also be calculated, with the use of the appropriate discount rate.

This phase can be broken down further to illustrate the various steps necessary for the calculation of the consumer surplus. A detailed step-by-step approach both for the ZTCM and the ITCM, respectively, is provided in the exercises in the annexes to this chapter.

11.2 HEDONIC PRICE METHOD (HPM): THE CONCEPTUAL FRAMEWORK

The hedonic price method measures the welfare effects of changes in environmental assets and services by estimating the influence of environmental attributes on the value of some marketed goods. This method has been largely applied looking at the influence of environmental attributes on property values, usually houses. In order to obtain a measure of how the environmental attribute affects the welfare of individuals, the HPM attempts to:

1. *identify* how much of a property differential is due to a particular environmental difference between properties; and
2. *infer* how much people are willing to pay for an improvement in the environmental quality and what the social value of the improvement is.

In attempting to isolate the effects of environmental attributes on the price of houses we have to 'explain' the price of a house by means of its characteristics. If we take house price to be a function of all the features of the house, that is, structural (number of rooms, central heating, garage space and so on), neighbourhood characteristics, and environmental characteristics then the following relationship can be identified:

$$P_h = f_h(S_{h1}, ..., S_{hj}; N_{h1}, ..., N_{hk}; E_{h1}, ..., E_{hm}) \text{ for all houses } h,$$

where: P_h represents house price; h represents a unit of housing; f_h represents the function that relates the house characteristics to price; $S_{h1}, ..., S_{hj}$ denote different structural characteristics of the house; $N_{h1}, ..., N_{hk}$ denote different neighbourhood characteristics; and $E_{h1}, ..., E_{hm}$ denote different environmental characteristics.

The function above is the so-called *hedonic price function*. Fixing the level of all the other characteristics of a house, such as number of rooms, central heating and garage space, and any other neighbourhood attributes, we are able to focus on the relationship between the price of the house and the environmental attribute under investigation.

Economic theory does not provide much information on the shape of the hedonic price function, whose only certain characteristic is that its first derivative with respect to an environmental characteristic is positive (negative) if the characteristic is a good (bad). Freeman (1993) suggests that there are a priori reasons to expect the hedonic function for an amenity to be concave from below. The concavity of the hedonic price functions suggests that those individuals with high marginal willingness to pay curves who currently experience high levels of the environmental attribute, would have a low willingness to pay at the margin for additions to the environmental attribute.[8] A possible hedonic price function, all the other independent variables equal, is depicted in Figure 11.3.

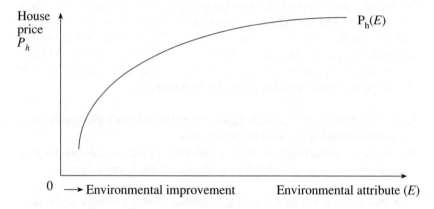

Figure 11.3   Hedonic price function of houses

The estimation of a hedonic price function is usually done using a multivariate regression technique. Data are taken either on a small number of similar residential properties over a period of years (time series), or on a larger number of diverse properties at a point in time (cross-section), or on both (pooled data). In practice almost all property value studies have used cross-section data, as controlling for other influences over time is much more difficult.

In the econometric estimation, the analyst faces the usual issues of choosing the functional form and choosing the variables, both dependent and independent, to be inserted in the model.[9] As has been shown in previous reviews,[10] the choice of functional form can result in significant differences in the estimated benefits, even when the statistical tests cannot distinguish between the forms (that is, both forms are considered acceptable). Following Freeman (1979a, 1979b), Pearce and Turner (1990) and Bateman (1993), an often-used functional form for the hedonic price function is the double log.[11]

$$\mathrm{ln}P_h = a\,\mathrm{ln}S_h + b\,\mathrm{ln}N_h + c\,\mathrm{ln}E_h.$$

Although the double log is often used for the functional form of the hedonic price function, it is considered 'best practice' to test the suitability of alternatives such as Box–Cox transformations[12] and other functional forms. If sensitivity to functional form is important, a range of values for damages resulting from a change in the level of an environmental attribute should be presented to reflect this.

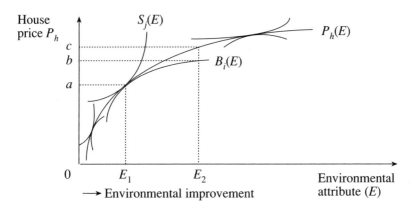

Figure 11.4   Hedonic price function as a locus of individuals' equilibria

For an improvement in the environmental attribute E, say from E_1 to E_2, the individual maximum WTP for the improvement would be correctly reflected by the change in the individual's bid function, say, the distance **ab** in Figure 11.4. Unfortunately, the bid functions are not easy to estimate, because it would require data on the behaviour of the same individuals for different levels of the environmental attributes. A more feasible way of estimating the willingness to pay would be to use the change in the hedonic price function to approximate the maximum WTP for the environmental change. The estimated hedonic equation would give the distance **ac** the measure of the benefit. Hence, the HPM, using the results of the econometric estimation described above, would result in an overestimation of the benefits of an improvement, or an underestimation of the costs of a deterioration.

If all the individuals had the same structure of preferences and the same income, they would also have the same maximum WTP for one additional unit of the environmental attribute and the individual bid curves would coincide with the hedonic price function. In such a case, no underestimation or overestimation of the maximum WTP would occur when using the hedonic price function to approximate the individual bid functions.

The questions that follow are: (a) how serious is the overestimation and (b) can it be corrected by adapting the method? On the issue of the magnitude of the bias, economists have carried out simulation exercises where the utility function representing consumer preferences is specified explicitly, as are the details of the supply of properties with attribute E. Some of these have shown that the hedonic estimate of benefits could be two to three times the true willingness to pay for the benefit depending on the parameters of the problem.

These simulation results are interesting and useful but they also have their limitations. It is also important to look at the results of actual hedonic price studies and compare them to those obtained by other methods on the same data. A few such comparisons have been done for developed countries by Brookshire et al. (1982). They show that, whereas in one study the hedonic estimate was about three times that obtained by the questionnaire approach, in another it was actually less than the questionnaire-based estimate. There is no clear evidence, therefore, from actual empirical studies, to show that the hedonic estimate for environmental improvements is consistently much higher than that obtained by other methods.

The second question posed above was whether this bias could be corrected. Rosen (1974) proposed a 'two-stage procedure' to estimate the marginal maximum WTP functions of individuals, that is, their implicit inverse demand functions, utilizing the results of the estimation of the hedonic price function described above. By partially differentiating the hedonic price function with respect to E, he obtains the 'implicit marginal price function' of the environmental good:

$$P_{\text{impl}.E} = \partial P_h/\partial E.$$

This partial derivative is interpreted as the price paid by the individuals for the last unit of the environmental attribute, purchased by choosing a given house instead of another one with a unit less of the environmental attribute, other things equal. Estimated implicit prices for different houses refer to different individuals. Every estimated implicit price is only one observation of the true individual demand curve and corresponds to the individual WTP for a marginal unit of environmental good only for that specific level of environmental good purchased. Therefore, the implicit marginal price function cannot be viewed as an 'implicit (inverse) demand curve'. Hence, it does not represent the maximum marginal WTP of the individual for one more unit of the environmental attribute, unless we assume that all the individuals have the same structure of preferences and the same income. If this assumption does not hold, the various individuals i will have different implicit (inverse) demand curves of the type $D_i(E)$ in Figure 11.5.[13] As the figure shows, there will be only one point where the marginal WTP for one more unit of E equals the marginal implicit price of E. Nevertheless, in the second stage, the implicit price can be regressed on the observed quantities of the environmental attribute and some socioeconomic characteristics of individuals. This second-stage estimation, under some restrictions,[14] could allow the identification of the implicit inverse individual demand function. When, for example, a double-log inverse demand function is chosen, the functional form is that shown in Annex 11A5.

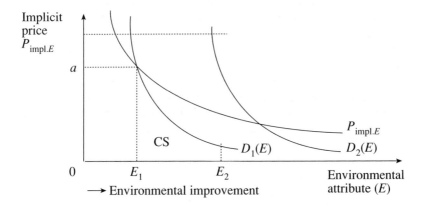

Figure 11.5   Implicit marginal price function of the environmental attribute E

The area under the demand curve $D_1(E)$ in Figure 11.5 between two levels of the environmental attribute, say E_1 and E_2, represents the change in the consumer surplus caused by the change in this attribute. Once the demand function $D_1(E)$ has been estimated, the change in the consumer surplus is calculated as the definite integral of $D_1(E)$ with respect to the quantity of the environmental good between E_1 and E_2. By aggregating all individuals' consumer surpluses we obtain the overall value of the environmental improvement.[15]

In practice, in many studies, especially in developing countries, generally only the first-stage estimation is carried out and the results used to obtain rough values for the impact of the attribute in question. Data and other sources of error are often too great to justify the additional effort of carrying out the second-stage estimation. Virtually all estimation methods, including those identifying simple demand and supply curves, would, if subject to the sort of scrutiny that has been applied here, be found wanting in many respects. However, for many practical applications, even obtaining an order of magnitude of the benefits or costs is worthwhile. In the following Annexes a step-by-step exercise is proposed, following the two-stage procedure mentioned above.

Applications of HPM have been successfully carried out in developed countries, to estimate the costs of air and noise pollution, and of changes in amenities. The use of HPM in developing countries has been more limited; valuation of the benefits of municipal sites and services are among the main applications to be found. There have been a few studies of the costs of air pollution using hedonic methods in Brazil, Korea, Thailand and Mexico. Other applications in developing countries include urban land values on the Ivory Coast (Grootaert and Dubois 1988); tenure security in Manila and piped water in the Bicol region of the Philippines (Friedman et al, 1983, North and Griffin 1993); and rice grain quality in South-East Asia (Unnevehr 1986). The last of these studies does not relate to environmental characteristics, but to how prices of rice vary according to its quality characteristics.

Most of the studies mentioned above are of direct relevance to development projects and could be useful in the context of projects involving sites and services, such as sanitation and agriculture. In these contexts the hedonic price method may be useful in assessing the capitalized benefits of interventions. For example, it is likely that sanitation projects will lead to an increase of the willingness to pay of people for housing land, where there is a well-developed market for housing sites. The increases of WTP can be estimated using the HPM. Similarly in cases where an agricultural project will result in improvements in yields, analysing the increases in land values may be a useful method to check the estimates of yields that are projected in the dose–response functions.

An example of the application of the HPM is provided in Exercise 3 in Annex 11A3.

NOTES

1. Travel cost is the sum of expenditures incurred for gasoline, opportunity cost of time for travelling and for visit on-site.
2. All these variables allow the estimation of different demand functions according to the socioeconomic characteristics of the visitors, thus enabling better estimates of the consumer surplus. In practice they have rarely been used in zonal travel cost studies, being much easier to be exploited in individual travel cost models.
3. A more complete demand function for ITCM in linear form is illustrated in Annex 11A1. A double-log form is presented and utilized in the following step-by-step ITCM numerical example.
4. Following the trend in the literature (McConnell et al. 1981) which maintains that it is necessary to include the opportunity cost of the journey and visit time in the computation of the total travel cost. As pointed out by Bateman (1993), however, the value (utility) of time can be either positive or negative but there is no definite a priori notion about whether travel time utility is positive or negative. Anyway, even assuming the possibility of estimating the sign of the value of time, the problem remains of how to estimate its price. Although various operational approaches have been proposed to place a value on time (Cesario 1976; McConnell

et al. 1981) there is not yet unanimous consensus on their capacity to overcome the risk of over- or underestimation.

5. These may include: the area of origin of the visitor, length of stay at site, number of other possible sites visited in the same trip experience, number of visits/year to the site in question, motive of visit, travel time and so on.

6. These may include: age, sex, educational level, income, member of an environmental organization, possible substitute sites, activities carried out in the site and so forth.

7. If data is available on the zone of origin (provided by the respondent), the distance (provided by maps), the time (provided by the Automobile Club Association or special software such as Autoroute), and the cost per kilometre (provided by the Automobile Club Association) then the cost of travel can be estimated indirectly.

8. 'Low WTP' means in this case lower than those individuals experiencing a low level of the environmental attribute.

9. An issue is whether to use rental or property price data. Usually in empirical work it has been the former.

10. See, for example, Cropper et al. (1988).

11. See Annex 11A5.

12. See Spitzer (1982) or Kennedy (1998) for more on Box–Cox transformations and Cropper et al. (1988) for a more detailed analysis of the choice of functional form of hedonic price functions.

13. The household demand functions may be steeper than the implicit price of the environmental attribute because at low levels of availability of the environmental attribute the marginal WTP for it may be higher than the implicit price and at high levels of availability the marginal WTP may be lower than the implicit price.

14. Problems in the identification of the supply and demand functions arise. A possible assumption is that the system is supply constrained, that is, the supply of the environmental good is fixed irrespective of the price (inelastic supply). This allows the regression of the implicit price P_e on the quantity E and other socioeconomic variables to obtain the inverse demand curve. See Bateman (1993, pp. 70–71) and Maddala (1992, pp. 356ff.).

15. Often the hedonic effect of interest is not a continuous variable but a dichotomous one, for example, either a house has sewerage connection or it does not. When there are such variables as explanatory factors care has to be taken in interpreting the coefficients. There are methods for calculating the relative change in the price. For a discussion of the methods, see Halvorsen and Palmquist (1980) and Blaycock and Smallwood (1983).

CITED BIBLIOGRAPHY

Bateman, I. (1993), Evaluation of the Environment: A Survey of Revealed Preference Techniques, GEC Working Paper 93–06, CSERGE, University of East Anglia, Norwich, and University College, London.

Bellù L. and V. Cistulli (1997), Economic Valuation of Forest Recreation Services in the Liguria Region (Italy), CSERGE Technical Paper 97–08, University of East Anglia, Norwich, and University College, London.

Blaycock, J., and D.M. Smallwood (1983), 'Interpreting the effects of binary variables in transformed models', *Economic Letters*, **12**, pp. 255–59.

Brookshire, D., M.A. Thailer, W.D. Shulze and R.C. d'Arge (1982), 'Valuing public goods: A comparison of survey and hedonic approaches', *American Economic Review*, **72**, pp. 165–78.

Cesario, F.J. (1976), 'Value of time in recreation benefit studies', *Land Economics*, **55**, pp. 32–41.

Cropper, M., L. Deck and K. McConnell (1988), 'On the choice of functional form for hedonic price functions', *Review of Economics and Statistics*, **70**, pp. 668–75.

Freeman, A.M. III (1979a), *The Benefits of Environmental Improvement: Theory and Practice*, Baltimore-London: The John Hopkins University Press.

Freeman, A.M. III (1979b), 'Hedonic prices, property values and measuring environmental benefits: A survey of the issues, *Journal of Environmental Economics and Management*, **11**, pp. 292–95.

Freeman, A.M. III (1993) T*he Measurement of Environmental and Resource Values: Theory and Methods*. Washington DC: Resources for the Future.

Friedman, J., E. Jimenez and S.K. Mayo (1988), 'The Demand for Tenure Security in developing countries', *Journal of Development Economics*, **29** (2), pp. 185–98.

Grootaert. C. and J.-L. Dubois (1988), 'Tenancy choice and the demand for rental housing in the cities of the Ivory Coast', *Journal of Urban Economics*, **24** (1), pp. 44–63.

Halvorsen, R. and R. Palmquist (1980), 'The interpretation of dummy variables in semi-logarithmic equations', *American Economic Review*, **70**, pp. 474–75.

Hanley, N.D., 1990, Valuation of Environmental Effects: Final Report – Stage One, Industry Department of Scotland and the Scottish Development Agency, Edinburgh, UK.

Kennedy, P. (1998), *A Guide to Econometrics*, Oxford: Blackwell.

Maddala, G.S. (1992), *Introduction to Econometrics*, 1992 Maxwell Macmillan International Editions, New York.

McConnell, K.E. and I. Strand (1981), 'Measuring the cost of time in recreation demand analysis: an application to sport fishing', *American Journal of Agricultural Economics*, **63** (1), pp. 153–56.

North, J.H. and C.C. Griffin (1993), 'Water source as a housing characteristic: hedonic property valuation and willingness to pay for water', *Water Resources Research*, **29** (7), pp. 1923–29.

Pearce, D.W. and R.K. Turner (1990), *Economics of Natural Resources and Environment*, New York: Harvester Wheatsheaf.

Rosen, S. (1974), 'Hedonic prices and implicit markets: product differentiation in pure competition', *Journal of Political Economy*, **82**, pp. 34–55.

Spitzer, J. J. (1982), 'A primer on Box-Cox estimation', *Review of Economics and Statistics*, **64**, pp. 307–13.

Unnevehr, L.J. (1986), 'Consumer demand for rice grain quality and returns to research for quality improvement in Southeast Asia', *American Journal of Agricultural Economics*, **68**, pp. 634–41.

ANNEX 11A1   EXERCISE 1: ZONAL TRAVEL COST METHOD (ZTCM): A NUMERICAL EXAMPLE

Background

This exercise is the outcome of a simulation developed with the collaboration of trainees during a training workshop held at the World Bank. The participants were assumed to be travelling to Washington, DC in order to visit the Smithsonian Institute. A questionnaire survey was carried out among the attendants to collect the information necessary to develop a ZTCM. Data have been adjusted for illustrative purposes.

Methodology

To assess the recreational value of a site with the ZTCM, the site must be clearly identified, using maps or other visual aids. Then the analyst must collect the information necessary to estimate the zonal demand function. This is usually done using both existing records and a survey using a specially prepared questionnaire.[1] The procedure for the calculation of the value of a recreational site can be summarized as follows:

1. Conducting of the survey on a sample of p visitors.
2. Collection of the number of visits to the site (V) in a period usually assumed to be one year. Source: statistical records of tickets sold.
3. Subdivision of visitor origins into zones of increasing distance. Source: questionnaire.
4. Determination of the number of visitors by zone (p_j) and the relative shares over the sample size (p_j/p).
5. Calculation of annual visits by zone ($V_j = V*p_j/p$).
6. Collection of data on population by zone (P_j) and zonal socioeconomic features (S_j). Source: statistical records.
7. Calculation of average visit rate in each zone ($R_j = V_j/P_j$).
8. Calculation of the zonal average travel cost to the site (C_j) with reference to the distance. Source: questionnaire or recorded data (for example, Automobile Association).
9. Estimation of the demand function $V/P = f(C,S_j)$.
10. Compute the average visitor consumer surplus by zone (CS).
11. Compute the zonal annual CS by zone (CSZ_j) by multiplying CS_j times the resident population by zone (P_j).
12. Aggregate the zonal annual CS to get the total annual CS ($ACST$).

To summarize, in ZTCM the researcher estimates a demand function using the data from each zone. This derived demand curve is assumed to be the same for each zone. The 'choke point' where demand is 0 is then calculated. The consumer surplus (per visit) for each zone is then calculated in the usual manner; that is, by integrating the curve between the choke point and the travel cost (price) paid by residents of that zone. A schematic illustration of the step-by-step approach is provided in Figure 11A1.1.

Problem Set

The data collected in the survey regarding the origin of visitors, their travel costs and the total population of their countries have been included in a database, shown in Table 11A1.1. The total number of annual visits to the site has been

Table 11A1.1   Zonal travel cost: database

OBSERV	COUNTRY	COUTVO (US$)	POPULA (m.)
1	Guinea	1,029	6
2	Congo	2,650	3
3	Lebanon	900	3.5
4	Seychelles	4,200	7.5
5	Ivory Coast	1,037	13.5
6	Benin	1,064	5
7	Italy	1,000	56
8	Burkina Faso	1,300	10
9	Burkina Faso	1,300	10
10	Mauritius	4,200	100
11	Morocco	1,000	26
12	Ivory Coast	1,037	13.5
13	Ivory Coast	1,037	13.5
14	Benin	1,064	5
15	Togo	1,074	4
16	Italy	1,000	56
17	Madagascar	5,000	100
18	Togo	1,074	4
19	Togo	1,074	4
20	Benin	1,064	5
21	Benin	1,064	5
22	Cameroon	2,600	12
23	Senegal	1,000	10
24	Mali	2,000	8.5
25	Congo	2,650	40
26	Belgium	985	10

| Total annual visits to the site: *TOTVIS* (V) | 30,000 |

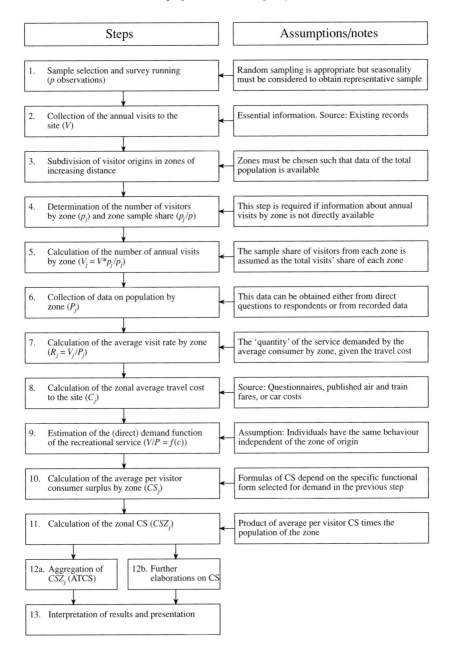

Steps	Assumptions/notes
1. Sample selection and survey running (*p* observations)	Random sampling is appropriate but seasonality must be considered to obtain representative sample
2. Collection of the annual visits to the site (*V*)	Essential information. Source: Existing records
3. Subdivision of visitor origins in zones of increasing distance	Zones must be chosen such that data of the total population is available
4. Determination of the number of visitors by zone (p_j) and zone sample share (p_j/p)	This step is required if information about annual visits by zone is not directly available
5. Calculation of the number of annual visits by zone ($V_j = V*p_j/p_j$)	The sample share of visitors from each zone is assumed as the total visits' share of each zone
6. Collection of data on population by zone (P_j)	This data can be obtained either from direct questions to respondents or from recorded data
7. Calculation of the average visit rate by zone ($R_j = V_j/P_j$)	The 'quantity' of the service demanded by the average consumer by zone, given the travel cost
8. Calculation of the zonal average travel cost to the site (C_j)	Source: Questionnaires, published air and train fares, or car costs
9. Estimation of the (direct) demand function of the recreational service ($V/P = f(c)$)	Assumption: Individuals have the same behaviour independent of the zone of origin
10. Calculation of the average per visitor consumer surplus by zone (CS_j)	Formulas of CS depend on the specific functional form selected for demand in the previous step
11. Calculation of the zonal CS (CSZ_j)	Product of average per visitor CS times the population of the zone
12a. Aggregation of CSZ_j (ATCS) 12b. Further elaborations on CS	
13. Interpretation of results and presentation	

Figure 11A1.1   ZTCM: Step-by-step procedure for consumer surplus calculation

obtained through examination of recorded statistics (steps 1 and 2 of the procedure above).

Problem

Using the data in Table 11A1.1, and following the illustrated step-by-step method, calculate the annual recreational value the national park.[2]

Solution Set

Once the data have been organized in the database, the number of visitors is divided in homogeneous zones of origin (Table 11A1.2) (step 3 of the procedure). Dummy variables (taking a value 1 or 0) are used to codify the different zones.

Table 11A1.2   Classification of data by zone

OBSERV	COUNTRY	COUTVO	POPULA	EURMED	SAHELX	AFRWES	AFRCEN	OCEIND
3	Lebanon	900	3.5	1	0	0	0	0
26	Belgium	985	10	1	0	0	0	0
16	Italy	1,000	56	1	0	0	0	0
7	Italy	1,000	56	1	0	0	0	0
11	Morocco	1,000	26	1	0	0	0	0
23	Senegal	1,000	10	0	1	0	0	0
24	Mali	2,000	8.5	0	1	0	0	0
8	Burkina	1,300	10	0	1	0	0	0
9	Burkina	1,300	10	0	1	0	0	0
1	Guinea	1,029	6	0	0	1	0	0
13	Ivory Coast	1,037	13.5	0	0	1	0	0
12	Ivory Coast	1,037	13.5	0	0	1	0	0
5	Ivory Coast	1,037	13.5	0	0	1	0	0
14	Benin	1,064	5	0	0	1	0	0
20	Benin	1,064	5	0	0	1	0	0
21	Benin	1,064	5	0	0	1	0	0
6	Benin	1,064	5	0	0	1	0	0
18	Togo	1,074	4	0	0	1	0	0
19	Togo	1,074	4	0	0	1	0	0
15	Togo	1,074	4	0	0	1	0	0
22	Cameroon	2,600	12	0	0	0	1	0
2	Congo	2,650	3	0	0	0	1	0
25	Congo	2,650	40	0	0	0	1	0
10	Mauritius Islands	4,200	100	0	0	0	0	1
4	Seychelles	4,200	7.5	0	0	0	0	1
17	Madagascar	5,000	100	0	0	0	0	1
Total		43,403	531	5	4	11	3	3
Mean		1,669	20	0.19	0.15	0.42	0.12	0.12

In Table 11A1.3, the number of visitors by zone has been calculated (*SANUVI*) and the share of visitors from each zone on the sample observations has been obtained (*SASHAR*) using the following formula, as shown in step 4 of the procedure:

$$SASHAR = SANUVI/TOTSAM$$

where *TOTSAM* is the number of sample observations. Subsequently, these shares are used to split the total annual number of visits (*TOTVIS*) and to estimate the number of annual visits zone by zone (*NUMVIS*) using the following equation, as shown in step 5 of the procedure:

$$NUMVIS = TOTVIS * SASHAR.$$

Table 11A1.3   Calculation of annual visits by zone (V_j)

ZONEXX (j)	SANUVI (p_j)	SASHAR (p_j/p) (%)	NUMVIS ($V_j = V*p_j/p$)
EUROPE	5	19.2	5,769
SAHEL	4	15.4	4,615
AFRWES	11	42.3	12,692
AFRCEN	3	11.5	3,462
OCEIND	3	11.5	3,462
TOTSAM	26	100.0	
TOTVIS (p)			30,000

In Table 11A1.4, the population is reported by region (*POPUZO*) (step 6). The visit rate per thousand people (*TAUXVI*) is then obtained as the ratio of the number of visits per year (*NUMVIS*) to the total population by region (*POPUZO*) (step 7):

$$TAUXVI = NUMVIS/POUPZO$$

The average travel costs by zone (*COUTZO*) are calculated (step 8).

Table 11A1.4   Population by zone, zonal visit rates and zonal average travel cost

ZONEXX (j)	NUMVIS ($V_j = V*p_j/p$)	POPUZO (,000) (P_j)	TAUXVI ($R_j = V_j/P_j$)	COUTZO C_j)
EUROPE	5,769	95,500	0.060	977
SAHEL	4,615	28,500	0.162	1,400
AFRWES	12,692	28,500	0.445	1,056
AFRCEN	3,462	55,000	0.063	2,633
OCEIND	3,462	207,500	0.017	4,467
Total (p)	30,000	415,000	0.072	1,669

The (direct) demand function has been estimated by regressing the variable *TAUXVI* (dependent) on the variable *COUTZO* (independent) (step 9 of the procedure).

A linear form is assumed for the demand function, leading to the following regression:

$$TAUXVI = CONSTA + bCOUTZO * COUTZO$$

The estimated parameters (*CONSTA*, a constant term, and *bCOUTZO*, the responsiveness of demand to a change in travel cost) are shown in Table 11A1.5. Also shown are some statistics of the goodness of fit (*t*-ratios, R_2 and *F*-test).

Table 11A1.5   Demand curve estimation

Variables	bCOUTZO	CONSTA
Parameters	−0.000066	0.288998
Std errors	0.000056	0.139565
R^2/Std error $\hat{Y}$	0.317039	0.165798
F-test/DGF	1.392639	3.000000
T-ratios	−1.180	2.071
Choke price (US$)		4,363

The choke price for the linear demand function, that is, the price that leads to zero visits, is calculated by setting the demand function equal to zero:

TAUXVI = 0 implies:
CONSTA + *bCOUTZO* * *COUTZO* = 0
$COUTZO^0$ = −*CONSTA*/*bCOUTZO*
$COUTZO^0$ = *CHOKE*
CHOKE = −*CONSTA*/*bCOUTZO*

The graph in Figure 11A1.2 shows the observations of zonal data (*COUTZO*, *TAUXVI*) and the fitted line, graphed using the estimated parameters.

In Table 11A1.6, the (average individual) consumer surplus is calculated zone by zone by estimating the area under the demand curve between the average travel cost of each zone (*COUTZO*) and the choke price (*CHOKE*) (step 10 of the procedure). This is done by calculating the definite integral between the specific value by zone of *COUTZO*, (*COUTZO*) and the upper bound of integration *CHOKE*, as follows:

$$\int (TAUXVI)\, dCOUTZO = \int [(CONSTA + bCOUTZO * COUTZO)]$$
$$dCOUTZO = CONSTA*COUTZO + 1/2\, bCOUTZO * COUTZO^2 + K,$$

where K is the constant of integration.

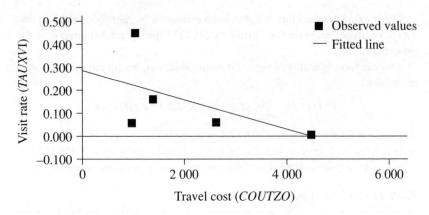

Figure 11A1.2   Zonal travel cost: estimated demand curve and CS

The area between the specific value by zone of *COUTZO*, (*COUTZO*) and the upper bound of integration *CHOKE* is therefore calculated using the following equation:

$$CONSUR = [CONSTA * CHOKE + 1/2\ bCOUTZO * CHOKE^2]$$
$$- [CONSTA* COUTZO + 1/2 * bCOUTZO * COUTZO^2].$$

The consumer surplus (*CONSUR*) per thousand people can then be multiplied by the population of each zone (*POPUZO*). This yields the annual CS by zone, leading to the calculation of the variable *CONZON*, step 11 of the procedure.

Table 11A1.6   Consumer surplus estimation

	CONSUR (US$) (CS_j)	POPULA (,000) (P_j)	CONZON (US$) $(CS_z = CS_j * P_j)$
EUROPE	379.7	95,500	36,264,784
SAHEL	290.8	28,500	8,287,484
AFRWES	362.2	28,500	10,322,252
AFRCEN	99.1	55,000	5,450,553
OCEIND[*]	0.0	207,500	0
Total CS (US$)			60,325,073
Aver. CS per visit (US$)			2.011

Note: [*]Being the choke price lower than the travel cost, the CS is set to 0.

The total consumer surplus is then obtained by aggregating the zonal consumer surpluses (step 12 of the procedure).

The amount of consumer surplus per visit (division of the total consumer surplus by the number of annual visits) can also be estimated. Finally, the present value of the annual recreation benefit can be calculated to find the component of the asset value due to the recreational services supplied by the environmental asset under consideration.

Discussion

For a discussion on both the zonal travel cost and the individual travel cost
methods, see end of Annex 11A2.

Notes

1. The questionnaire should investigate origin of visitors, vehicle used, travel costs, individual
   socioeconomic features and any other attributes which may affect the demand for a site.
2. To run this exercise, use the spreadsheet ZONATCM1.XLS, which contains the database. The
   full solution is contained in the spreadsheet ZONATCM2.XLS. A diskette containing the
   exercise is available on request.

ANNEX 11A2 EXERCISE 2: INDIVIDUAL TRAVEL COST METHOD (ITCM): A NUMERICAL EXAMPLE

Background

This exercise draws on an actual study aimed at estimating the total use-value of forests in the Liguria region, Italy (Bellù and Cistulli 1997). Its purpose is to illustrate the methodology used for assessing the recreational value of the forested areas and to provide some insight on the policy implications of the results obtained.

The Liguria region was an important producer of timber and chestnuts in the past. Over the years, the relative importance of these activities has declined dramatically, thus leading to forest abandonment and the emigration of its population to the urban areas situated on the coast. As a consequence, the coastal areas are now suffering from high and unsustainable population densities that are exacerbated during the summer, when significant flows of tourists add to the local population. Meanwhile the areas of the interior are progressively depopulated and the forests are deteriorating due to a lack of management and maintenance. Furthermore, historic sites within the forested areas are neglected leading to a decline of cultural heritage.

From the financial point of view, revenues from forests in these areas are rather low compared to revenues from other uses of the land. However, the forests provide other important non-valued services such as soil-moisture conservation, open access recreation and hunting, as well as valuable secondary forest products such as berries and mushrooms. Local authorities have therefore undertaken a study to appraise the net social benefits provided by the forested areas, with a view of allocating financial resources for the rehabilitation and development of these areas.

This exercise seeks to estimate the benefits of the recreational use of these forests. In the Liguria region recreation is a non-priced public good, therefore its value could not be assessed using conventional market techniques. The valuation techniques used were the individual travel cost method and the contingent valuation method.

For didactic purposes the original case study has been substantially simplified. The number of observations has been reduced in order to facilitate the handling of the database. Only one of the seven areas surveyed is analysed, and only one of the four functional forms tested in the real study is utilized.

Methodology

The procedure for carrying out a study with the ITCM method is similar to the ZTCM method, at least in the initial stages. The following steps were followed.

   1. *Identification of the site.* A clear description of the site to be surveyed was essential for interviewees and interviewers to know what they are asked to value. It aided the identification of the sites where interviews had to take place. Maps and photographs of the site were used during the interviews. In the particular case of this study, sites were identified on the basis of the following criteria: suitability of the area for tourism; actual flow of tourists; and the plans of the Liguria region for the creation of regional parks.

   2. *Definition of the environmental good/service to be valued.* The good or service to be valued was defined so that no misunderstandings arose. The service or good examined in a forested area could be the whole area of the site or one of the particular services provided by the forest (that is, aesthetics, cycling, fishing and so on), or the change in the supply of one attribute, both in quantity and in quality terms. In the Liguria case, the good selected for valuation was the whole site.

   Five different types of visits have been identified:

i.   visitors who declared a visit of less than one day. These visitors have been considered as if they devoted the whole day to the visit and travel cost and time have been totally allocated to the visit;
ii.   visitors who declared they were spending the whole day for the visit. Here again the trip time and cost were fully attributed to the visit;
iii. visitors who declared they spent more than one day at the site. Here the cost of travel and time have been divided by the number of days spent at the site;
iv.   visitors who had a one day-return trip with multiple destinations. The travel cost and time have been attributed proportionally to the time devoted to the visit; and
v.   visitors who declared they spent more than one day in the site who were planning to visit multiple destinations. Travel costs and time costs were allocated proportionally to the share of the total time spent in the site.

   3. *Questionnaire design.* The questionnaire was aimed at collecting information on consumer behaviour towards the particular environmental good/service to be valued. Information can be subdivided into compulsory and non-compulsory information. Compulsory information included the origin of visitors and the vehicle used for reaching the site, which allows the estimation of the cost of travel. Non-compulsory information included individual socioeconomic features (for example, income, age, education), other attributes such

as, activities carried out on the site, whether interviewee was a member of an environmental association, and the opportunity cost of time. It must be pointed out, however, that these variables can be very important in explaining the behaviour of the visitors.

In this study, the questionnaire was constructed so that it could be used for both the travel cost method and the contingent valuation method evaluation of the value of the forest. In particular it was subdivided in the following sections.

The first section was only for the use of interviewers and was aimed at providing some general information on the interview and interviewers (name of interviewer, location of interview, length of interview and so on).

The second section was devoted to the collection of socioeconomic data. It was assumed here that age, education, income, profession, number of family members and so on are important determinants in visitors' behaviour towards recreational use or visits to forests.

The third section attempted to identify the costs of travel costs faced by individuals to visit the site, by asking them their origin, the vehicle used to reach the site, the time taken to reach the area from their point of origin and the itinerary of their trip.

The fourth section consisted of a few questions aimed at investigating the level of environmental concern and awareness of visitors. It was assumed that the higher the level of awareness of environmental problems, the higher the perceived value of a forest's recreational value.

Two further sections have been included for assessing the WTP with the CVM approach. In particular, the payment vehicle, the elicitation form and the market scenario for recreation have been defined. In this example only the ITCM is analysed. The application of the CVM approach is presented in Chapter 12.

The information provided by the questionnaire will allow the analysts to derive the demand curve for the recreational site (see next section).

4. *Sample Selection.* This step is mainly concerned with the organization and implementation of the survey. Before proceeding with the survey, the type of interview and the sample of interviewees must be defined.

In the Liguria case it was decided that interviews should be carried out on-site. Therefore, for each single area, sites were identified for carrying out on-site face-to-face interviews. Interviewed visitors were selected randomly among the visitors throughout July, August and September 1993 on both weekdays and weekends. The total number of interviews completed was 800.

The behaviour of people visiting the site during the summer is most probably different from that of people visiting the same site in winter and spring (for example, time spent on-site might be shorter). Thus, the total annual value of recreation services provided by the site might be overvalued if the observed behaviour in summer was assumed to be representative of the whole year. This possible bias had to be taken into account in the final interpretation of the results.

5. *Elaboration of calculated variables and statistical description of the sample.*   When the survey had been completed, a database was created using a simple spreadsheet. In order to check consistency of responses and reliability of data, some statistical analysis was carried out.

In the full study, two alternative models were estimated: the first included the *opportunity cost of time* for travelling from the place of origin to the site; the second excluded the opportunity cost of time. Although the opportunity cost of time was estimated to be 1 per cent of the income per hour of the respondents, it was found, as expected, that travel cost, and consequently consumer surplus, is very sensitive to the opportunity cost of time. Given that the sign of the opportunity of time can be in theory either positive or negative, a specific, case-by-case, opportunity cost of time for travel should have been computed. In the particular case of Liguria, it was decided that a zero opportunity cost was realistic, considering that most of the visitors visited the areas during the holiday periods (that is, when it is assumed that the income forgone is zero).

6. *Choice of functional form.*   A functional form relating the dependent variable (visits per year) and independent variables (travel cost, socioeconomic variables) had to be identified to obtain a more accurate demand curve. The choice was among four functional forms: linear, log-dependent, log-independent, double log (also named log-log). In this particular case two functional forms were tried: the double-log form and the linear form.

7. *Estimation of the demand function.*   Once a functional form for the demand curve of the environmental service has been tentatively selected, its parameters are estimated using econometric models. Basic approaches require models to be estimated using the ordinary least squares (OLS) technique. More complex models (for example, truncated demand functions, simultaneous demand systems[1]) require the use of maximum likelihood estimation (MLE) methods, and the use of suitable econometric software packages.

8. *Calculation of the individual consumer surplus (CS).*   Once the most suitable functional form has been estimated, the individual consumer surplus can be calculated. Annex 11A1 to this chapter provides an analytical specification of the consumer surplus calculation for a linear demand function. The step-by-step exercise below supplies the formula of the CS for a double-log demand function.

9. *Calculation of the annual individual average consumer surplus* (averaging within the sample). When applying the ITCM, the consumer surplus is calculated individual by individual, that is, for each observation of the sample. A summary measure of the sample consumer surplus can be obtained taking the sample mean of the consumer surplus. Several mean consumer surpluses can be calculated considering relevant specific socioeconomic features of sample

individuals, such as age, education, gender or visit purposes, in order to obtain different average consumer surpluses for certain socioeconomic groups.

10. *Aggregation and further elaboration.* If the objective of the study is the estimation of the total value of the site, the individual WTP resulting from the analysis has to be multiplied by the total number of visitors to the site during one time period (usually over a period of one year). Once the total value of the area has been computed, the value per hectare can be obtained by dividing the total value by the extension of the area of the site. Although this calculation has been carried out in the real study, it is not presented in this exercise.

11. *Interpretation and presentation of results.* The obtained results need to be explained, interpreted and compared with those of other similar studies. A discussion of issues in the interpretation of results is presented at the end of this annex.

Figure 11A2.1 illustrates the main steps in the calculation of the WTP with the ITCM approach.

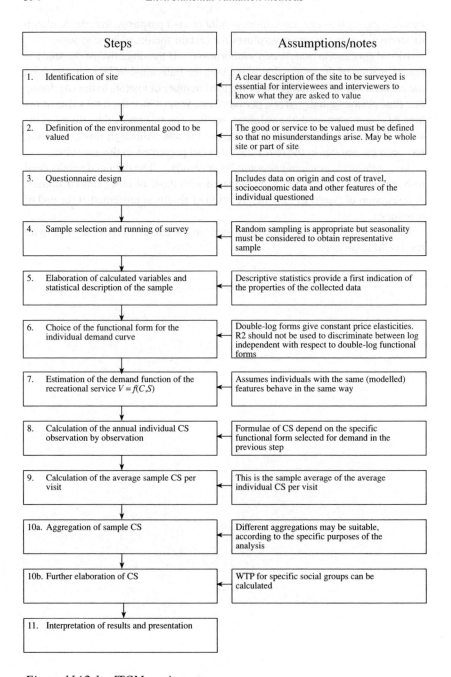

Steps	Assumptions/notes
1. Identification of site	A clear description of the site to be surveyed is essential for interviewees and interviewers to know what they are asked to value
2. Definition of the environmental good to be valued	The good or service to be valued must be defined so that no misunderstandings arise. May be whole site or part of site
3. Questionnaire design	Includes data on origin and cost of travel, socioeconomic data and other features of the individual questioned
4. Sample selection and running of survey	Random sampling is appropriate but seasonality must be considered to obtain representative sample
5. Elaboration of calculated variables and statistical description of the sample	Descriptive statistics provide a first indication of the properties of the collected data
6. Choice of the functional form for the individual demand curve	Double-log forms give constant price elasticities. R2 should not be used to discriminate between log independent with respect to double-log functional forms
7. Estimation of the demand function of the recreational service $V = f(C,S)$	Assumes individuals with the same (modelled) features behave in the same way
8. Calculation of the annual individual CS observation by observation	Formulae of CS depend on the specific functional form selected for demand in the previous step
9. Calculation of the average sample CS per visit	This is the sample average of the average individual CS per visit
10a. Aggregation of sample CS	Different aggregations may be suitable, according to the specific purposes of the analysis
10b. Further elaboration of CS	WTP for specific social groups can be calculated
11. Interpretation of results and presentation	

Figure 11A2.1   ITCM: major steps

Problem Set

Following the methodology outlined above, a survey was carried out and the database has been constructed. The variables listed in Table 11A2.1[2] were considered important and relevant data have been collected.

Table 11A2.1   Observed and calculated variables

	Variables	
1	*AGEXXX*	Age
2	*OTSITE*	Planned visits to other sites
3	*DUAPAR*	Stay in private house
4	*INCOME*	Visitor's income
5	*TRAVCO*	Travel cost of the visit
6	*VISITS*	Number of visits per year

From the observed data, the variables *TRAVCO* and *VISITS* have been calculated. *TRAVCO* excluded the opportunity cost of time. Concerning the variable *VISITS*, visits of less than one day have been considered as daily visits. Visits lasting more than one day were considered to be separate daily visits. All other visits in the year have been considered daily visits. The complete database is presented in Table 11A2.2.

Problem

Using the dataset in Table 11A2.2 and following the procedure from steps 3 to 6 of Figure 11A2.1, calculate the sample average individual consumer surplus.[3]

Table 11A2.2   Individual travel cost method database

NUMREG	AGEXXX	DUAPAR	OTSITE	INCOME	TRAVCO	VISITS
1	70	1	1	75	47,500	32
2	50	1	1	25	1,985	31
3	50	1	0	75	910	26
4	50	1	0	55	4,750	35
5	40	1	1	8	1,049	28
6	50	0	0	15	1,000	11
7	50	0	1	75	9,501	2
8	50	1	0	25	792	70
9	50	1	0	35	9,500	3
10	50	1	1	35	1,351	21
11	60	0	0	15	1,900	16
12	21	0	1	15	1,583	2
13	30	1	0	25	720	2
14	40	0	1	35	2,348	16
15	50	0	1	25	10,512	4
16	30	0	1	15	2,375	2
17	50	0	1	25	3,250	7
18	50	0	1	35	3,250	2
19	40	0	1	35	3,250	2
20	21	0	1	15	2,160	5
21	40	1	1	25	3,250	2
22	60	0	0	25	400	21
23	40	1	1	35	8,540	19
24	50	1	1	35	27,075	2
25	30	0	1	25	6,900	3
26	21	0	0	15	200	21
27	40	0	1	15	637	31
28	50	1	1	45	936	40
29	30	1	0	8	2,167	35
30	21	1	1	15	2,982	41

Solution Set

The solution to the above problem is presented in this section in a systematic format, drawing on the step-by-step approach illustrated in Figure 11A2.1.

Step 3   Choice of the demand function (double log)
After a careful analysis of the data collected, a multiplicative model, linearized by a logarithmic transformation in the double-log (log-log) model, was found to be the most appropriate for this exercise. The demand function was set as follows:

$$VISITS = \exp(CONSTA + bDUAPAR * DUAPAR + bOTSITE * OTSITE) * $$
$$* TRAVCO^{bTRAVCO} * INCOME^{bINCOME} * AGEXXX^{bAGEXXX}$$

Step 4   Estimation of the demand function (double log)
Taking the natural logarithm of both sides of the demand function leads to the following expression:

$$\ln VISITS = CONSTA + bDUAPAR * DUAPAR + bOTSITE * OTSITE +$$
$$bTRAVCO * \ln TRAVCO + bINCOME \ln INCOME +$$
$$bAGEXXX * \ln AGEXXX$$

To estimate the parameters of the demand function, a regression of $\ln VISITS$ (dependent variable) on the logarithm of other variables (independent ones) was run using OLS.[4] Table 11A2.3 summarizes the results.

Table 11A2.3   Demand function parameters

	Variable					
	bTRAVCO	bINCOME	bOTSITE	bDUAPAR	bAGEXXX	CONSTA
Coefficient	−0.460	−0.311	0.040	1.086	1.183	1.925
Std error	0.207	0.430	0.479	0.405	0.724	2.328
R^2/std error $\hat{Y}$	0.395	1.056	—	—	—	—
F-test/DF	3.139	24.000	—	—	—	—
SSReg/SSErr.	17.514	26.778	—	—	—	—
T-ratios	−2.224	−0.724	0.084	2.678	1.635	0.827

Figure 11A2.2 shows the double-log demand function estimated keeping other variables at their sample mean. The plot of the log-independent functional form (estimated outside this exercise) is reported for comparative purposes.

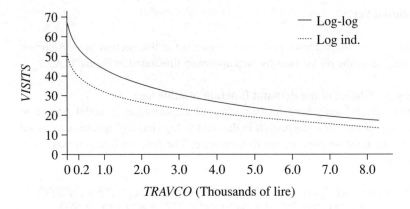

Figure 11A2.2   ITCM: demand curve functions log-log and log-independent OLS: System 3

Step 5   Calculation of the CS with the model double log

For every observation, the annual consumer surplus between the actual travel cost afforded by each individual $TRAVCO_i$ and the upper bound of integration $UPPLIM$ was calculated:

$$CONSUR_i = \int_{TRAVCO_i}^{UPPLIM} (VISITS) dTRAVCO$$

$$= \left[\begin{array}{c} \exp(CONSTA + bDUAPAR * DUAPAR + bOTSITE * OTSITE) * \\ * INCOME^{bINCOME} * AGEXXX^{bAGEXXX} \dfrac{1}{(1+bTRAVCO)} TRAVCO^{(1+bTRAVCO)} \end{array} \right]_{TRAVCO_i}^{UPPLIM}$$

$$= \exp(CONSTA + bDUAPAR * DUAPAR + bOTSITE * OTSITE) * INCOME^{bINCOME}$$

$$* AGEXXX^{bAGEXXX} * \frac{1}{(1+bTRAVCO)} * \left[UPPLIM^{(1+bTRAVCO)} - TRAVCO_i^{(1+bTRAVCO)} \right].$$

The selection of the upper limit of integration within the sample range of $TRAVCO$ (for example, the 99th percentile) leads to some observations having an upper limit of integration lower than the lower limit of integration, which in turn generates negative consumer surpluses. These are excluded from further analysis. The results of the calculation of CS are shown in Table 11A2.4.

Step 6   Calculation of the average consumer surplus per visit and average total WTP per visit

The average consumer surplus per visit is calculated by dividing the total consumer surplus per individual by the annual sample average number of visits. The total average WTP is calculated by summing up the average consumer

Table 11A2.4   ITCM consumer surplus

Upper limit of integration   27,075

Observation NUMREG	Ind.ann.CS CONSUR	Notes
1	=	Upper limit < lower limit
2	275,891	
3	209,095	
4	167,083	
5	330,505	Max sample CS
6	115,379	
7	37,793	
8	298,463	
9	136,360	
10	263,471	
11	131,156	Close to the mean CS
12	40,571	
13	164,485	
14	62,439	
15	49,286	
16	57,707	
17	83,982	
18	75,626	
19	58,074	
20	38,531	
21	191,019	
22	131,754	Close to the mean CS
23	117,014	
24	0	Upper limit = lower limit
25	35,137	Min. CS different from 0
26	46,188	
27	96,266	
28	254,452	
29	203,255	
30	106,686	
Mean	130,264	

surplus per visit and the average travel cost per visit. The results are reported in Table 11A2.5.[5]

Table 11A2.5   ITCM: average individual CS per visit and average total WTP per visit

Sample average visits/year (a)	Sample average trav. cost (b)	Average individual CS (c)	Average CS/visit (d = c/a)	Total WTP per visit (e = b+d)
17.7	5,426	130,264	7,346	12,772

Step 7   Aggregation of results

This step is not reported for the exercise outlined above. However, doing the aggregation is straightforward. The population of visitors is calculated outside the exercise and the annual total benefits from the recreational services of the systems are estimated. Annual values can be discounted to obtain the asset value contribution of the recreational function to the total value of forests.

Discussion

Zonal travel cost method

1. The benefits of the recreational services of the national park can be used in a CBA framework to assess the forgone benefit of an alternative development project. Decision makers will have more information available to decide whether it is worth protecting or developing the site.
2. Hanley (1990) pointed out that there is no consensus in the literature as to which of the two methods (ZTCM or ITCM) is preferable on theoretical grounds. In practice the ITCM is usually preferable for the following reasons:

   a. the dependent variable of the ZTCM does not account for individual explanatory variables that may be highly significant in the determination of the choice of visitors to visit a particular site. In other words, this method assumes that all individuals of the same zone behave in the same way regardless of their social characteristics;
   b. the choice of zones is particularly difficult because living within the same zone does not necessarily correspond to the same time and travel costs. Some variables such as the quality of roads, the morphology of land and so forth may influence both the time and travel cost. It might also be that one point in a given zone offers substitute sites which will influence the number of visits to the site under study;
   c. generally the zones are chosen to reflect similar travel costs. If the identification is done improperly this can lead to substantial differences in the consumers' surpluses; and
   d. as Bateman (1993) remarks, the ZTCM always produces upwardly biased R^2 values which implies that the level of goodness of fit may be overestimated.

Nevertheless, in some circumstances, that is, when zones can be identified precisely and visitors' behaviour can be assumed to be similar because their socioeconomic characteristics are similar, or when the site visited is unique or substitute sites are the same for all visitors coming from different zones, researchers may prefer the ZTCM over the ITCM. In particular, this is true for many of the most interesting cases in developing countries, such as national and historical parks. In practice, there has been a tendency to use the ZTCM for national or international sites of interest (with particular regard for the phenomenon of ecotourism) and ITCM for local sites, such as city parks or recreation areas inside or in proximity to urban areas.

Individual travel cost

Variability of CS among the various areas. In the full study, the consumer surplus per visit varied across the different areas from Lit. 3,467 to Lit. 26,934. This difference can be explained by many factors. In this study, the different results may be attributed to three main causes:

1. statistical reasons;
2. different services provided by the forested areas; and
3. different socioeconomic features of visitors.

In order to check the robustness of these results, a comparison has been made with the results obtained using the CVM approach. The results were consistent in all cases but one, where it was assumed that CVM results were more reliable.

Notes

1. Truncated demand functions are estimated taking into account the fact that the sample excludes observations for which the demand is 0. Simultaneous demand systems are demand functions that are estimated considering the interrelationships between demand of different items.
2. The real questionnaire had 41 observed variables and 10 calculated variables.
3. To aid this exercise, the spreadsheet TCMINDI1.XLS may be used. This contains the database. A copy of this spreadsheet is available on request. The full solution is provided in the spreadsheet TCMINDI2.XLS.
4. In the original study, besides OLS, other methods of estimation, mainly based on the maximum likelihood method were applied to estimate truncated models for zero demand individuals. See Bellù and Cistulli (1997).
5. The whole study was aimed at estimating the recreational value of seven forest areas (systems). This exercise only refers to one area.

ANNEX 11A3   EXERCISE 3: HEDONIC PRICE METHOD (HPM): A NUMERICAL EXAMPLE

Background

This exercise presents an application of the hedonic price method for the valuation of benefits brought about by the improvement of the broadleaf coverage rate in an urban area. The local government decided to improve the quality of urban parks and green spaces near residential areas. Prior to the implementation of the project, a study was undertaken aimed at the assessment of the net benefits of the action. The project consisted of various activities. This study focuses on the valuation of only one of them, namely the increase of broadleaf coverage. To elicit the value assigned to a change in broadleaf coverage, the prices of houses in areas with different coverage rates are observed. The increase in price due to the environmental asset is isolated using econometric techniques.

Methodology

In general, the applications of the HPM include two major actions: the collection of relevant information and data and the calculation of the value of the environmental good. In this section, the methodology for these tasks is presented.

Collection of relevant information and data
When applying the HPM to the value of a house, the collection of data focuses on the price of the house associated with an environmental good, environmental features (for example, the quality of air, level of noise and so on), structural features of the house and the socioeconomic features of their owners. Of course, the HPM can be applied to the value of other assets, but this exercise will focus on houses. Data was collected on prices and houses features, using the following procedure:

- Resident households were randomly selected from the council directory of resident households.
- The broadleaf coverage rate within the range of 300 metres for every house was calculated.
- The price of the house was determined by looking at estate agency bulletins and recent transactions. Expert advice on prices for some properties was also required.
- The collection of information on the socio-economic features of the household was made by looking at recent census data.

An alternative approach that could have been used would have been to draw grids on the area to be analysed and then determine sub-areas. One could then calculate the coverage rate for every area. Following this, one could randomly select a given number of households within every area and look at the house and socioeconomic features.

Calculation of the value of the environmental quality (asset)

Once the data have been collected, the calculation procedure follows the steps listed below:

1. Collection of data.
2. Estimation of the *house price function.*
3. Calculation of the *implicit marginal price* of the environmental good (the responsiveness of the house price function with respect to the environmental quality, that is, the first derivative: $c \times P/Z_m$) for each observation.
4. Estimation of the *implicit inverse demand function* for the environmental good, (implicit price as a function of the environmental good and socioeconomic features of individuals).
5. Calculation of the *consumer surplus* (calculating the area under the demand curve between the observed level of the environmental good and the new level using integration).

A summary of the main steps followed in this exercise for the estimation of the value of an environmental asset using the HPM is provided in Figure 11A3.1.

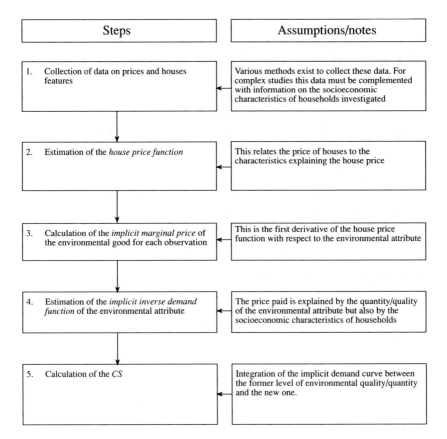

Steps	Assumptions/notes
1. Collection of data on prices and houses features	Various methods exist to collect these data. For complex studies this data must be complemented with information on the socioeconomic characteristics of households investigated
2. Estimation of the *house price function*	This relates the price of houses to the characteristics explaining the house price
3. Calculation of the *implicit marginal price* of the environmental good for each observation	This is the first derivative of the house price function with respect to the environmental attribute
4. Estimation of the *implicit inverse demand function* of the environmental attribute	The price paid is explained by the quantity/quality of the environmental attribute but also by the socioeconomic characteristics of households
5. Calculation of the *CS*	Integration of the implicit demand curve between the former level of environmental quality/quantity and the new one.

Figure 11A3.1   Step-by-step procedure for the calculation of the CS with HPM

Problem Set

The analyst is required to provide the following information to policy makers, so they may make an informed decision on the viability of the project:

1. The average benefit the households receive from an increase of the broadleaf coverage rate of 10 per cent.
2. The relationship between the prices of houses and the broadleaf rate coverage.
3. Policy implications of the results obtained.

To complete the above tasks, the analyst proceeds first with the identification of a sample of households to investigate and with the collection of the relevant data following the procedure described in the previous section (step 1). A database, such as that displayed in Table 11A3.1, must be constructed.

Hints for the Calculation Procedure

Step 2 Estimation of the house price function
The general functional form for the price of houses, given the variables in the database, is:

$$PRICEX = f(BROADL, NUMROO, DISTAN, MURDER, INDEPE).$$

Assuming the multiplicative model, the house price function is specified as:

$$PRICEX1 = e^{(CONSTA+b1INDEPE)} BROADL^{b2} NUMROO^{b3} DISTAN^{b4} MURDER^{b5}$$

Note that when the houses are independent (detached) (that is, dummy *INDEPE* = 1) the model becomes:

$$PRICEX1 = e^{(CONSTA+b1)} BROADL^{b2} NUMROO^{b3} DISTAN^{b4} MURDER^{b5}$$

When the houses are not independent (attached) (that is, dummy *INDEPE* = 0) the model becomes:

$$PRICEX0 = e^{(CONSTA)} BROADL^{b2} NUMROO^{b3} DISTAN^{b4} MURDER^{b5}$$

We can then run the regression of Ln*PRICEX* on ln*BROADL*, ln*MURDER*, ln*DISTAN*, *INDEPE*, plus a constant, to get the related parameters *CONSTA*, $b1$, $b2$, $B3$, $b4$ and $b5$.

Table 11A3.1   Database for HPM exercise

OBSERV	PRICEX	NUMROO	INDEPE	DISTAN	MURDER	BROADL	REDHOU	COMPON
1	50,847	1	0	6	1.8	2	21	2
2	53,593	2	0	44	3.1	4	25	3
3	54,019	2	0	45	4.5	6	23	4
4	59,940	3	0	41	2.5	5	28	5
5	60,849	2	0	7	3.5	8	32	4
6	61,947	3	0	39	2.2	1	34	4
7	75,908	2	0	10	1	6	30	3
8	81,304	4	0	50	4.5	5	36	2
9	85,028	3	0	48	2.1	30	43	2
10	88,484	4	0	35	3	10	38	2
11	98,648	2	1	13	1.5	15	49	3
12	98,920	3	0	9	0.9	13	55	3
13	111,049	3	0	24	1.2	18	72	2
14	121,345	4	0	50	0.5	22	68	3
15	132,049	4	1	6	0.1	11	62	4
16	136,018	4	0	15	0.5	7	78	5
17	142,546	6	0	43	0.1	28	74	4
18	145,584	4	0	3	1.5	5	80	3
19	173,394	4	1	5	1.4	42	92	4
20	173,904	3	0	3	0.9	23	87	5
21	180,394	4	1	4	0.3	11	85	3
22	198,765	3	0	5	0.7	40	93	4
23	212,038	5	1	0.5	0.1	45	96	6
24	234,194	5	1	0.5	0.6	90	80	4
25	241,879	5	1	7	0.4	70	93	5
26	267,944	4	0	0.1	0.1	85	78	4
27	267,975	7	1	24	0.6	80	83	6
28	271,039	6	1	10	0.1	75	98	3
29	294,048	5	1	12	0.4	39	105	4
30	295,536	4	1	1	0.1	80	110	4
Sample average	148,973	3.70	0.37	18.67	1.34	29.20	64.93	3.67

Key

Variable	Description
OBSERV	Number of the observation
PRICEX	Price of house (US$,1995)
NUMROO	Number of rooms in the house
INDEPE	Dummy variable: *INDEPE* =1 Detached house. 0 otherwise
DISTAN	Distance from downtown (km)
MURDER	Murder rate of the area (murders/year/1000 residents)
BROADL	Broadleaf tree coverage rate (covered area/total area)
REDHOU	Annual income of the household (US$, 1995)
COMPON	Number of components in the household

Step 3 Estimation of the implicit price function

Calculate the derivative of the HPF *PRICEX* with respect to the variable *BROADL*, as suggested in step 3 of the methodology, to get the implicit price for one unit of broadleaf tree coverage *IMPLIP*.

$$IMPLIP = \frac{\partial PRICEX}{\partial BROADL} = e^{(CONSTA+b1INDEPE)}b2BROADL^{(b2-1)}NUMROO^{b3}DISTAN^{b4}MURDER^{b5}$$

Multiplying both sides by *BROADL* leads to:

$$IMPLIP\ BROADL = e^{(CONSTA+b1UNDEPE)}\ b2\ BROAD^{b2}\ NUMROO^{b3}$$
$$DISTAN^{b4}\ MURDER^{b5}.$$

Recalling the definition of *PRICEX* and substituting in the right-hand side, leads to:

$$IMPLIP\ BROADL = b2\ PRICEX$$

which implies:

$$IMPLIP = \frac{b2PRICEX}{BROADL}.$$

Calculate the implicit price *IMPLIP* for each observation using the derived formula and insert the variable in the database.

Step 4 Estimation of the implicit inverse demand function

The implicit inverse demand function assumes the form:

$$IMPLIP = e^{d1}\ REDHOU^{d2}\ COMPON^{d3}\ BROADL^{d4}.$$

The estimation of this curve can be made using the OLS method transforming it into a logarithmic form: after calculating the natural logarithm of *IMPLIP*, (ln*IMPLIP*) regress ln*IMPLIP* on a constant and the logarithm of the other variables in the equation above.

Step 5 Calculation of the consumer surplus

Calculate the consumer surplus *CONSUR* for every observation '*i*' supposing an increase in the coverage rate of 10 per cent for every household. Name this new variable *CONSUR* and insert it in the database. To calculate the consumer surplus for each observation use the formula of the CS, derived as follows:

$$CONSUR_i = \int\limits_{BROADL_i}^{UPPLIM} (IMPLIP) dBROADL =$$

$$= \left[\exp(d1)REDHOU^{d2}COMPON^{d3} \frac{1}{(1+d4)} BROADL^{(1+d4)} \right]_{BROADL_i}^{UPPLIM}$$

$$= \exp(d1)REDHOU^{d2}COMPON^{d3} * \frac{1}{(1+d4)} * \left[UPPLIM^{(1+d4)} - BROADL_i^{(1+d4)} \right].$$

Solution Set

After the database has been created (step 1), the following steps need to be taken to provide policy makers with the information necessary for them to make an informed decision on the viability of the project.

Step 2   Estimation of the hedonic house price function
Table 11A3.2 summarizes the result of the regression of the variable ln*PRICEX* on the logarithm of the other variables. Most of the variables included in the model are highly significant from a statistical point of view in explaining the variability of the price of houses. Notably, the coverage rate of broadleaves exhibits a positive relevant relationship with the price, other things equal, that is, after controlling for the other features of the house.

Table11A3.2   Estimation of the hedonic house price function

Variable	ln*BROADL*	ln*MURDER*	ln*DISTAN*	ln*INDEPE*	l n*NUMROO*	*CONSTA*
Coefficient	0.16871	−0.05785	−0.08952	0.13697	0.50855	10.78918
Std error	0.04898	0.04570	0.03133	0.09606	0.13320	0.15815
T-ratios	3.44456	−1.26595	−2.85766	1.42595	3.81788	68.22257

R^2		0.90026	Std error $\hat{Y}$			0.19924
F-test		43.32314	Degrees of freedom			24.00000
Explained sum of squares		8.59852	Sum of squared residuals			0.95268

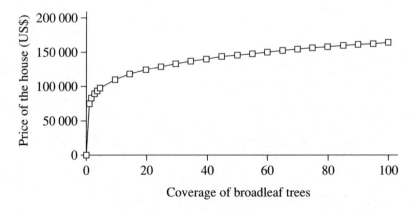

Figure 11A3.2   Estimated hedonic price function of houses for different levels of environmental good (other variables at their mean level)

The estimated price variable (price function) calculated with the estimated parameters reported in Table 11A3.1, is illustrated in Figure 11A3.2. This graph is drawn with the other variables fixed at their sample average level.

From Figure 11A3.2 it can be seen that the change in house price, due to the change in the rate of broadleaf coverage, is not constant. It is indeed increasing but tending to 0 as the coverage rate tends towards 100. This means that a unit increase in the rate of tree crown coverage when the coverage rate is relatively high is not so influential on the price of the houses as the same unit increase when the coverage rate is relatively low.

Step 3   Calculation of the implicit price function of the broadleaf coverage

The considerations above, about the relationship between the broadleaf coverage and the price of houses, are also apparent when looking at the implicit price function derived from the house price function. This function, as described in the methodology, is the first derivative of the house price function with respect to the broadleaf tree rate. The implicit price function is:

$$IMPLIP = (0.16871/BROADL)\ PRICEX.$$

This function is used for estimating, observation by observation, the implicit price of an additional unit of broadleaf coverage. These estimates are summarized in Table 11A3.3.

Note that pre-existing low levels of coverage lead to a high implicit valuation of an additional unit of coverage. Conversely, pre-existing high levels of coverage lead to a low marginal valuation of an incremental unit of coverage. Broadly, these estimates reflect to some extent the willingness to pay of owners for the marginal increase in the coverage rate.

Step 4   Estimation of the inverse demand function

The estimation of the inverse demand function is a second-stage estimation based on the result of the first estimation (that is, the house price function and related first derivative). The estimated implicit price of the broadleaf coverage unit (in this case, the percentage point) is regressed on the observed coverage rate and the socioeconomic features of the owners. Table 11A3.4 summarizes the results of this second-stage estimation.

The inverse demand function is therefore estimated as:

$$IMPLIP = \exp(6.34)\ REDHOU^{0.76}\ COMPON^{0.11}\ ROADL^{-0.85}.$$

Figure 11A3.3 shows the inverse demand function for three different levels of income: the sample first quartile, the sample median and the sample upper

Table 11A3.3   Estimated implicit price of an additional unit of broadleaf tree coverage rate

OBSERV	BROADL	PRICEX	IMPLIP
1	2	50,847	4,289
2	4	53,593	2,260
3	6	54,019	1,519
4	5	59,940	2,022
5	8	60,849	1,283
6	1	61,947	10,451
7	6	75,908	2,134
8	5	81,304	2,743
9	30	85,028	478
10	10	88,484	1,493
11	15	98,648	1,109
12	13	98,920	1,284
13	18	111,049	1,041
14	22	121,345	931
15	11	132,049	2,025
16	7	136,018	3,278
17	28	142,546	859
18	5	145,584	4,912
19	42	173,394	696
20	23	173,904	1,276
21	11	180,394	2,767
22	40	198,765	838
23	45	212,038	795
24	90	234,194	439
25	70	241,879	583
26	85	267,944	532
27	80	267,975	565
28	75	271,039	610
29	39	294,048	1,272
30	80	295,536	623
Sample average	29.20	148,973	1,837

quartile. The variable *COMPON* is fixed at the sample mean level. Notice that lower levels of income imply a lower demand of broadleaf coverage for every level of the price, the demand curve for the first quartile income lies below those of the median and upper quartile income levels. While the difference between the lower quartile and median income demand curve is noticeable, the difference between the median and upper quartile demand curve is more difficult to see in the figure.

Table 11A3.4   Estimation of the inverse demand function

Variable	ln*COMPON*	ln*REDHOU*	ln*BROADL*	ln*CONSTA*
Coefficient	0.1073	0.7619	−0.8530	6.3412
Std errors	0.0991	0.0930	0.0388	0.2950
T-ratios	1.0827	8.1942	−21.9976	21.4966

R^2		0.9620	Std error $\hat{Y}$	0.1581
F-test		219.4173	Degrees of freedom	26.0000
Explained sum of squares	16.4636		Sum squared residuals	0.6503

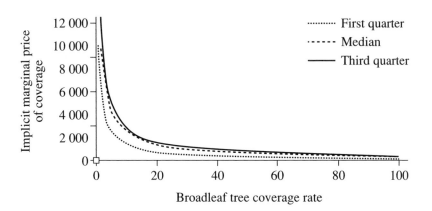

Figure 11A3.3   Inverse demand curve for different income levels

Step 5 Calculation of the consumer surplus
The consumer surplus is calculated by estimating the area under the demand curve. This is done by integrating the inverse demand curve with respect to the implicit price and calculating the definite integral observation by observation (variable *CONSUR*) between the present coverage rate (*E1* = *BROADL*) and the coverage rate (*UPPLIM*) planned by the policy maker:

$$CONSUR = \exp(6.34) * 1/(1{-}0.85) * COMPON^{0.11} * REDHOU^{0.76} *$$
$$[UPPLIM^{(1{-}0.85)} - BROADL^{(1{-}0.85)}]$$

The value of this, observation by observation, the sample mean of the change in the consumer surplus (variable *CONSUR*) and the related planned coverage rate (variable *UPPLIM*) are reported in Table 11A3.5.

Table 11A3.5   Change in the consumer surplus for a 10 per cent increase of broadleaf tree coverage rate

OBSERV	BROADL	UPPLIM	CONSUR
1	2	12	14,113
2	4	14	12,508
3	6	16	9,856
4	5	15	12,902
5	8	18	10,794
6	1	11	27,797
7	6	16	11,700
8	5	15	14,161
9	30	40	5,200
10	10	20	10,000
11	15	25	9,782
12	13	23	11,735
13	18	28	11,098
14	22	32	9,645
15	11	21	14,746
16	7	17	23,520
17	28	38	8,913
18	5	15	27,178
19	42	52	7,757
20	23	33	11,910
21	11	21	18,183
22	40	50	8,119
23	45	55	7,936
24	90	100	3,817
25	70	80	5,367
26	85	95	3,922
27	80	90	4,510
28	75	85	5,004
29	39	49	9,079
30	80	90	5,351
Average	29	39	11,220

Discussion

This information can be used first to calculate the average consumer surplus per household and can be multiplied by the number of households to get a measure of the total benefits which can be compared with the cost of the intervention. On distributional grounds, note that a 10 per cent increase for people living in areas with a high coverage rate does not change the consumer surplus much, compared to those living in low coverage rate areas, which could be lower-income neighbourhoods. The spreadsheet of this exercise can be used for further simulations, for example, for examining the effects in the average consumer surplus when the coverage rate is increased by a different percentage, or for analysing the change in the average sample consumer surplus if the intervention is concentrated in areas with a very low coverage rate rather than being concentrated in areas with high coverage or where broadleaf trees are evenly distributed.

ANNEX 11A4   THE LINEAR MODEL FOR ITCM DEMAND FUNCTIONS

The simplest functional form for demand curves in ITCM valuations is the linear demand function:

$$Q_i = \alpha_0 + \sum_{c=1}^{l} \alpha_c D_{ci} + \sum_{j=1}^{k} \beta_j X_{ji} + \beta_p P_i + \varepsilon_i,$$

where: Q_i represents the number of visits of individual i; D_{ci} are dummy variables referring to individual i; X_{ji} are the socioeconomic features of individual i, and other variables referring to i; P_i is the price paid by individual i (integration variable); α_0 is a constant term; α_c represents the coefficients of the additive dummy variables; β_j represents the coefficients of socioeconomic variables; β_p is the coefficient of the price variable; and ε_i is the error term.

Once estimated, the model is expressed in the following form:

$$Q = a_0 + \sum_{c=1}^{l} a_c D_c + \sum_{j=1}^{k} b_j X_j + bP.$$

Assume $b < 0$ (negative own price elasticity). For each single individual, the consumer surplus is the integral of the demand function Q with respect to the price P between the lower bound P_{Li} and the choke price or the upper bound P_{ui}.[1] The indefinite integral of the demand function is:

$$\int q\,dp = a_0 p + p \sum_{c=1}^{l} a_c D_c + p \sum_{j=1}^{k} b_j X_j + \frac{1}{2} bP^2 + k.$$

The integral between P_L and P_U is:

$$CS = a_0 P_u + P_u \sum_{c=1}^{l} a_c D_c + P_u \sum_{j=1}^{k} b_j X_j + \frac{1}{2} bP_u^2 - a_0 P_L + P_L \sum_{c=1}^{l} a_c D_c + P_L \sum_{j=1}^{k} b_j X_j - \frac{1}{2} bP_L^2,$$

that is:

$$CS = a_0 (P_U - P_L) + (P_U - P_L) \sum_{c=1}^{l} a_c D_c + (P_U - P_L) \sum_{j=1}^{k} b_j X_j + \frac{1}{2} b (P_U^2 - P_L^2).$$

For each individual the consumer surplus is calculated by substituting the values for each individual of the dummy variables D_{ci}, the travel cost P_{Li}, the choke price PU_i and the value of the explanatory variables X_{ji} into the above general formula:

$$CS_i = a_0(P_{Ui} - P_{Li}) + (P_{Ui} - P_{Li})\sum\nolimits_{c=1}^{l} a_c D_{ci} + (P_{Ui} - P_{Li})\sum\nolimits_{j=1}^{k} b_j X_{ji} + \frac{1}{2}b(P_{Ui}^2 - P_{Li}^2).$$

The demand function in Figure 11A4.1 shifts up and down according to the values the additive dummies assume for every individual. The linear demand, if not bounded, assumes negative values for prices greater than the choke price. The own-price elasticity is obtained as:

$$e = b\frac{P}{Q} \text{ being } \frac{\delta q}{\delta p} = b \text{ (partial derivative).}$$

In this case the elasticity is not constant along the curve but depends on the price–quantity set. It is usually calculated assuming average values for the variables.

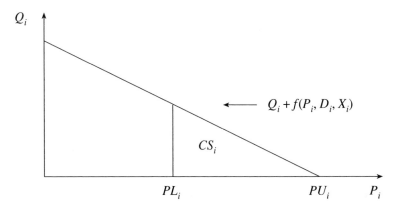

Figure 11A4.1   Estimating consumer surplus using a Linear Demand Function

Note

1. The choke price is the price that 'strangles' the demand, that is, that leads to a demand equal to zero.

ANNEX 11A5   MATHEMATICAL FUNCTIONS FOR HPM

Hedonic Price Function of Houses (Multiplicative Model)

If the relationship between the price of houses and their features is assumed to be multiplicative, the price function is:

$$P_i = aE_i^{\beta_e} \prod_{d=1}^{p} \left(e^{\delta_d D_{di}}\right) \prod_{j=1}^{k} \left(X_{ji}^{\beta_j}\right) e^{u_i},$$

where: P_i is the price of the house i; E_i is the environmental quality of the house (namely, the broadleaf tree concentration); X_{ij} a set of j attributes (location, structure) referring to house i; u_i is the stochastic term referring to observation i; D_d is a set of dummy variables, each of which assumes value 1 when a specific feature is present for observation i and value 0 when the specific feature is absent for observation i; a, β_e and β_j are parameters to be estimated.

This model, taken in logarithmic form becomes:

$$\ln P_i = \ln\left[a \prod_{d=1}^{m} \left(e^{\delta_d D_{di}}\right) E_i^{\beta_e} \prod_{j=1}^{k} \left(X_{ji}^{\beta_j}\right) e^{u_i}\right]$$

$$\ln P_i = \alpha + \sum_{d=1}^{m} \delta_d D_{di} + \beta_e \ln E_i + \sum_{j=1}^{k} \beta_j \ln X_{ji} + u_i,$$

where: $\alpha = \ln a$, that is, $a = e^{\alpha}$. After estimating the parameters α, β and δ, the price relationship is obtained.[1]

The Implicit Price Function (Multiplicative Model)

This is the first derivative of the house price function shown above.

$$\frac{dP_i}{dE_i} = a\beta_e E_i^{(\beta_e - 1)} \prod_{c=1}^{p} \left(e^{\delta_d D_{di}}\right) \prod_{j=1}^{k} \left(X_{ji}^{\beta_j}\right)$$

$$\frac{dP_i}{dE_i} = \frac{\beta_e}{E_i} P_i. \text{ Calling } \frac{dP_i}{dE_i} = Pe_i \Rightarrow Pe_i = \frac{\beta_e}{E_i} P_i$$

The first derivative, when the house price model is multiplicative, is not constant but varies with the price (and the environmental quality) level. Because the first derivative is expected to be positive, in the multiplicative model β_e is expected to be positive, assuming that E is a positive measure of the environmental good.

Inverse Demand Function: The Multiplicative Model

The equation below expresses a multiplicative model for the inverse demand function:

$$P_{ei} = gE_i^{\lambda_e} \prod\nolimits_{f=1}^{q} \left(e^{\chi_f H_{fi}}\right) \prod\nolimits_{r=1}^{s} \left(Z_{ri}^{\lambda_r}\right) e^{h_i}$$

where $i = 1 \dots n$ (index of the observations), $f = 1 \dots q$ (index of multiplicative dummies), $r = 1 \dots s$ (index of socioeconomic variables); P_e is the (estimated) implicit marginal price of the environmental good for observation i; E_i is the quantity of the environmental good for the observation i. H_n is a set of s dummies reflecting the socioeconomic and other individual features of observation i. Z_{ri} is a set of socioeconomic variables referring to observation i; g, λ_s and χ_s are parameters to be estimated; e^u is the random error. λ_e is expected to be negative.

Taking the log form the model becomes:

$$\ln P_{ei} = \ln\left[gE_i^{\lambda_e} \prod\nolimits_{f=1}^{q} \left(e^{\chi_f H_{fi}}\right) \prod\nolimits_{r=1}^{s} \left(Z_{ri}^{\lambda_r}\right) e^{h_i} \right]$$

$$\ln P_i = \gamma + \lambda_e \ln E_i + \sum_{f=1}^{q} \chi_f H_{fi} + \sum_{r=1}^{s} \lambda_r \ln X_{ri} + h_i$$

This can be estimated using OLS regressions.

Consumer Surplus: The Multiplicative Model

The consumer surplus for the multiplicative inverse demand function is:

$$\left[P_e dE\right]_{E_1}^{E_2} = g \frac{1}{\lambda_e + 1} \prod\nolimits_{f=1}^{q} \left(e^{\chi_f H_{fi}}\right) \prod\nolimits_{r=1}^{s} \left(Z_{ri}^{\lambda_r}\right) \left[E_2^{(\lambda_e + 1)} - E_1^{(\lambda_e + 1)}\right].$$

If $\lambda_e < -1$, $E_2^{(\lambda e - 1)}$ goes to 0 as E_2 goes to infinity. The CS assumes therefore finite values even if no upper bound is imposed to the definite integration.

If $-1 < \lambda_e < 1$, and the upper bound of integration is ∞, the CS is infinity unless a finite upper bound is imposed to the integration.

Note

1. To be consistent with the probabilistic structure of the model, we must recall that the u_i are assumed to be random variables normally distributed with 0 mean and common variance: $u_i \sim N(0, \sigma^2)$ and OLS regression analysis enables the estimation of the expected value of the random variables P_i, $E(P_i)$.

12.   Stated preference: contingent valuation methods

OBJECTIVES

This chapter aims to provide an outline to different approaches that may be used for contingent valuation. It provides the reader with a conceptual framework and supporting exercises at different levels of complexity. It also aims to enable the reader to obtain a good understanding of the contingent valuation method and gives practical hints for the application of CVM.

SUMMARY

This chapter focuses on the contingent valuation method (CVM). It provides a detailed and comprehensive analysis of the basic theoretical concepts of the method. It discusses when its use is advisable and how the method should be applied. Several examples and exercises are developed to show the various possible approaches for its use. It offers possible interpretations and policy implications of the results and highlights the advantages and limitations of the method. The chapter concludes that CVM is a valuable and is in some situations the only method available for the estimation of environmental values.

12.1 CONTINGENT VALUATION METHOD: THE CONCEPTUAL FRAMEWORK

The contingent valuation method (CVM) is a technique that allows the value of an environmental good or service to be estimated. Individuals are asked to value their willingness to pay (WTP) or willingness to accept (WTA) for a change in the provision of an environmental good, usually by way of a questionnaire survey.[1] The individual maximum WTP or the minimum WTA compensation for an environmental change is assumed to be the value the individual attaches to such a change.

The major advantage of this approach compared to the proxy methods shown in previous chapters is that the CVM can elicit both use and non-use values, and indeed it is the only possible technique for the evaluation of non-use values. Another attraction of this method is that it may be applied at varying levels of complexity according to the time and financial resources available for the research and according to the mode of survey used to capture the individual's value.

An individual can be asked to express his/her subjective valuation of possible environmental changes in different ways (see also Chapter 9, Figure 9.2 and Table 9.3):

1. *Environmental improvement.* The value of the environmental improvement in such a situation can be measured either by:
   - the individual's maximum willingness to pay (max WTP) to obtain the environmental improvement (estimated by the compensating surplus – CSU); or by
   - the individual's minimum willingness to accept (min WTA) as compensation to forgo the environmental improvement (estimated by the equivalent surplus – ESU).
2. *Environmental damage.* The value of the environmental damage in such a situation can be measured either by:
   - the individual's maximum WTP to avoid the environmental damage (estimated by the ESU); or by
   - the individual's minimum WTA a compensation to agree to the environmental damage (estimated by the CSU).

One basic issue in CVM studies for the estimation of environmental values is the choice of whether to ask individuals their maximum WTP or their minimum WTA for a given environmental change.

To understand the conceptual difference between the maximum WTP and the minimum WTA, let us focus on the case of the valuation of an environmental improvement.[2] With an environmental improvement the individual, currently at the utility level U_0, *ceteris paribus*, is brought to U_1, as shown in Figure 12.1, which is a reproduction of Figure 9.6. The maximum amount of money the individual is willing to pay to secure this improvement is such that after the payment s/he would at most be back to U_0 (s/he should not be prepared to pay any amount of money such that s/he falls below the utility level U_0). This maximum amount of money is the compensating surplus (CSU).

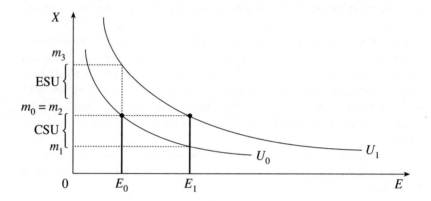

Note: The segments in bold are the budget sets and the points in bold are budget constraints for different levels of environmental good. The good X is money allocated to consumption.

Figure 12.1   Environmental improvement: compensating surplus and equivalent surplus

If, however, the same individual is already enjoying (or has a right to) the improvement, *ceteris paribus*, and has the utility level U_1, then s/he considers it a loss to have to give up the environmental improvement and asks to be compensated for this loss. To calculate how much to ask as minimum compensation s/he looks at the utility level attainable with the environmental damage (that is, without the environmental improvement). This is U_0. S/he will then ask at least a monetary compensation high enough to reach the level of utility U_0 gain back to the level U_1. This is the equivalent surplus (ESU).

It is apparent that the appropriate measure of the value of an environmental asset is related to the property rights of the individual on such an asset. The CSU measure assumes the individual has no consolidated rights in the environmental improvement, assuming therefore as a benchmark the utility level without environmental improvement U_0. The ESU measure assumes instead that the individual somehow deserves, or has a right to, the environmental improvement, and puts the individual at the higher utility level U_1 attained (or attainable) with the environmental improvement.

Randall and Stoll (1980), suggest that the possible differences between the compensating surplus and equivalent surplus are barely significant in most practical situations. However, Hanemann (1991) shows that this is not always the case, especially when the environmental good/service has no close substitutes. In such cases, the minimum WTA can exceed the maximum WTP several times over. Carson (1991) also argues that when individuals are asked to state their minimum WTA, they tend to state their expectation of the maximum they could hope to extract as compensation, rather than their true minimum WTA. On these grounds also Mitchell and Carson (1989), Pearce and Turner (1990) and Knetsch (1990) advise caution on the use of the WTA approach.

A simple but interesting summary of the comparisons between WTP and WTA formats in hypothetical response studies can be found in Freeman (1993). He points out:

> There are reasons to believe that hypothetical WTA questions may result in responses that are not valid. But the observed large differences between WTA and WTP do not prove lack of validity, since large differences are not inconsistent with some forms of value and preference theory. ... If a WTP question is asked when people believe they have a right to the thing being valued (implying a WTA format), there may be a high rate of scenario rejection and a loss of validity of the responses.

He concludes that, fortunately, 'many valuation problems fall naturally in a WTP scenario'. However, he also suggests that ' there is a class of problem for which the WTA format seems appropriate but which can be framed in WTP terms in a plausible way'. Whenever the WTA format is appropriate and unavoidable, the WTA format should be chosen, possibly associated with an appropriate procedure for reducing misleading outcomes.

Over and above the debate regarding the WTP/WTA format, several other issues concerning the accuracy and reliability of valuations based on CVM have been discussed in the literature. The major concerns regard the biases inherent in the technique,[3] mainly the distortions in eliciting the consumer's preferences. Indeed, in order to obtain answers that reflect the true maximum WTP / minimum WTA of the respondent, different formats have been applied. The main formats are: (i) open-ended questions; (ii) bidding games; and (iii) dichotomous choice (referendum) questions. These are briefly discussed below.

Simple CVM exercises can be based on the so-called 'open-ended' elicitation format, where the individual is simply asked to state his/her maximum WTP or minimum WTA for a described environmental change. In this case, simple descriptive statistics (such as means and medians) can be used to obtain rough estimates of values attributed to an environmental asset. However, the main drawback of this approach is the ease with which the respondent can introduce 'strategic bias', that is, to state a WTP/WTA that is lower or higher than the true one in order to influence the decision-making process for the sake of his/her own profit.[4] A second drawback of the open-ended elicitation format is that the individual may not be prepared to express a value judgement starting without a reference point with which to bound his/her value judgement.

To avoid a high rate of misleading or missing answers caused by the lack of bounds typical of the open-ended format, an iterative technique or 'bidding game' can be used. In this case the respondent is asked whether s/he is willing to pay or to accept a given amount of money for a change in the provision of an environmental attribute. If s/he refuses, the proposed amount is reduced (increased) by a given percentage (say, 10 per cent). The procedure is repeated until the respondent provides a positive answer. The penultimate amount proposed is taken as his/her maximum WTP (minimum WTA) for obtaining (to give up) the environmental improvement. If instead the individual accepts the proposed amount, it is increased (reduced) by, say, 10 per cent.

The procedure continues until the individual answers negatively. Again the penultimate amount proposed is taken as his/her maximum WTP (minimum WTA) for obtaining (to give up) the environmental improvement. This technique, however, has the potential to suffer from so-called 'starting-point bias'. It has been observed that the final value judgement is affected by the initial proposed amount. This means that the initial amount somewhat constrains the free expression of the true individual preferences.

To counter starting-point bias and strategic bias, the 'dichotomous choice' (referendum) format is often recommended. Here, a possible range of values for the maximum WTP (minimum WTA) of individuals is pre-set by the analyst.[5] The sample of interviewed individuals is divided into subsamples. A value within the pre-set range is assigned to each subsample. Each individual within a subsample is then asked whether s/he is willing to pay (to accept) the assigned value to obtain (or to compensate for) the environmental improvement (damage). S/he is not allowed therefore to select a figure as in the case of the open-ended format or to play with subsequent acceptance/refusal answers as in the bidding-game format. Besides, s/he does not know the range of values within which the proposed amount is bounded. In this case however, the outcome of the individual answer is not the maximum WTP (minimum WTA) but only the consent or refusal to pay (to accept as compensation) a given amount of money, that is, a WTP (WTA) which is not necessarily the maximum (minimum) one. Specific statistical techniques are therefore required to calculate the individual's valuation of the environmental change.

In order to take account of the possible differences in the results due to the use of one rather than another elicitation format, a combined approach of the three main elicitation formats based on Bateman (1993) can be used. The sample is split as in the dichotomous choice approach. A bidding game is proposed for a fixed maximum number of bids. In case the respondent, during the game, switches from acceptance to refusal (or vice versa), the game is stopped before exhausting the prearranged number of questions and an open-ended question is posed to obtain the maximum WTP (minimum WTA). The same open-ended question is posed at the end of the game to those individuals who never switch

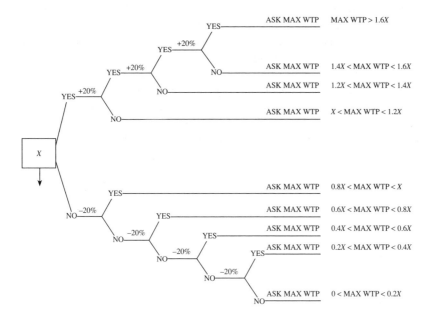

Note: X = initial bid (in Monetary Units)

Figure 12.2   CVM combined elicitation formats (max WTP questions)

from acceptance to refusal (or vice versa) and exhaust the pre-set number of bids.[6] See Figure 12.2 for a representation of this technique.

Despite the efforts to find elicitation formats that allow the controlling of some biases, other biases can occur in CVM studies and must be tackled with appropriate questionnaire design. Among these the most important are: information bias, anchoring bias, vehicle bias and hypothetical bias. The information bias is the mis-statement of the WTP/WTA by the respondent due to a lack of relevant information to state his/her value judgement correctly. Particularly important on these grounds is the 'scenario mis-specification', occurring when the respondent does not correctly understand the choice situation presented by the interviewer.

Anchoring bias is a mis-statement of the WTP/WTA, due to the attempt of the respondent to tie his/her value judgement to some known or presumed reference point, such as existing charges (taxes) for similar public goods or misunderstood hints in the scenario description. Anchoring can also be based on the starting value of the dichotomous choice format, that is, the respondent displays a consenting attitude.

Vehicle bias is a misrepresentation of the WTP/WTA due to the specific payment vehicle hypothesized (for example, increase of income taxes or the introduction of specific charges for each environmental service). Indeed, the way the payment vehicle is designed can affect the individual value judgement.

Hypothetical bias refers to all mis-specifications of the true WTP/WTA due to the fact that the individual is not acting in a real context. Some behavioural tendencies that hold in real life do not hold in a hypothetical context. Among these are seeking for better information, care in comparing alternatives and risk-averting behaviour due to actual risk bearing,[7] and other issues arising in the use of CVM. Methods to address these biases are discussed in the remainder of this chapter.

12.2 CVM METHODOLOGY

Most of the methodology needed to run a CVM exercise is the same as for a travel cost method (TCM) exercise. The difference is that the core of the survey directly focuses on the WTP/WTA for a specific environmental good, instead of the travel costs and number of visits to a specific site. To elicit WTP/WTA using the CVM:

1. a scenario is described and the impacts of the change in the provision of an environmental good/service are explained;
2. the respondents are invited to consider the proposed context within which the choice concerning the environmental good/service will be made; and
3. the respondents are invited to supply their statements concerning their WTP/WTA, from which the value attached to a change in the provision of the good/service in question is inferred.

The general approach to follow for running a CVM survey is outlined in Figure 12.3. In this section the most crucial steps, marked in italics in the diagram, are described briefly.

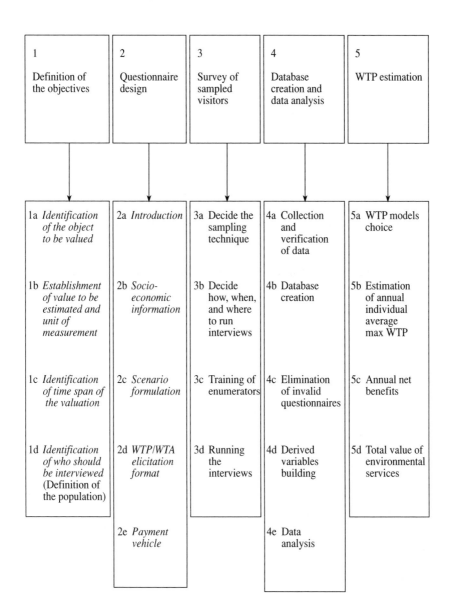

1 Definition of the objectives	2 Questionnaire design	3 Survey of sampled visitors	4 Database creation and data analysis	5 WTP estimation
1a *Identification of the object to be valued*	2a *Introduction*	3a Decide the sampling technique	4a Collection and verification of data	5a WTP models choice
1b *Establishment of value to be estimated and unit of measurement*	2b *Socio-economic information*	3b Decide how, when, and where to run interviews	4b Database creation	5b Estimation of annual individual average max WTP
1c *Identification of time span of the valuation*	2c *Scenario formulation*	3c Training of enumerators	4c Elimination of invalid questionnaires	5c Annual net benefits
1d *Identification of who should be interviewed* (Definition of the population)	2d *WTP/WTA elicitation format*	3d Running the interviews	4d Derived variables building	5d Total value of environmental services
	2e *Payment vehicle*		4e Data analysis	

Figure 12.3   General CVM methodology

The first step identified in Figure 12.3 concerns a definition of the objectives of the survey.

1a. *What to value.*   The purposes of the survey and the object of the valuation exercise has to be identified and stated clearly. What is the environmental good or service we want to place a value on? Are we valuing the whole environmental good, one of its attributes or a specific change in the quality/quantity of the good/service?

1b. *Establishment of the value to be measured and unit of measurement.*   Is the analyst eliciting the marginal value or the average value to the individual of the good/service? What is the unit of measurement?

1c. *Time span of the valuation.*   The analyst must decide whether to collect monthly, annual, multi-period WTP/WTA or lump-sum WTP/WTA.

1d. *Who should be interviewed.*   The relevant economic agents have to be defined, that is, who is affected by the change in the provision of the environmental good or service (individuals, households, production units).

The second step concerns the design of the questionnaire. This activity is of fundamental importance. A well-constructed questionnaire is essential for the success of the whole valuation exercise.

2a. *Introduction.*   Usually the interviewer presents him/herself and explains to the interviewee some, although not necessarily all, of the likely reasons for the survey being carried out. This helps to make the interviewee feel involved.

2b. *Socioeconomic information.*   To enable analysis of answers provided and to facilitate their interpretation in the socioeconomic context of the respondent, data about the interviewee, the household and the social environment are normally collected (for example, age, education, marital status, number of members of the household, annual income of the household and so on).

2c. *Scenario design.*   The scenario description is of course different for each study. However, in general terms, the scenario usually provides a clear and careful description of the environmental good/service that is the object of the valuation. It also provides information on its changes under given conditions, the impacts of the change on the users/consumers, that is, how the respondents will (could) be affected by the change, possibly the type of policies envisaged to secure (prevent) the change and who will pay for these policies. The WTP/WTA question must be phrased so as to present a clear, readily understood and plausible scenario.

2d. *Elicitation format.*   The elicitation procedure establishes the way the question used to elicit the value estimate is posed. Different elicitation formats exist. As noted in the previous section, the main ones are: (i) open ended; (ii) bidding game; and (iii) dichotomous choice.

2e. *Payment vehicle.*   The choice of the payment vehicle is of utmost importance in the design of a CVM questionnaire. One procedure for determining the most appropriate payment vehicle is to carry out a pilot study in which several alternatives are tested. The analysis of the results allows the identification of the payment method with which respondents are most familiar, and the ones most preferred by them. Possible payment vehicles are entrance fees (for example, national parks), taxes (for example, pollution), a one-off contribution to funds (for example, existence values such as protection of endangered species), and charges (for example, water used for agricultural, industrial or domestic purposes).

Steps 3 and 4 relate to practical issues of implementing the questionnaire, and collecting and organizing the results. They are discussed further in the exercises in the annexes at the end of this chapter. Concerning the fifth step, the procedure for estimating the max WTP/min WTA depends upon the elicitation format chosen. This is also elaborated in the exercises in the annexes.

Litigation over natural resources damages has led to an upsurge of interest in the CVM method. Following the Exxon-Valdez oil spill, Exxon commissioned a number of CVM studies criticizing the reliability and validity of CVM as an approach to value environmental impacts. In response, the US government set a blue-ribbon panel under the joint chairmanship of Kenneth Arrow and Robert Solow to advise on the use of CVM in natural resource damage by oil spills. The following are the main guidelines suggested by the panel (Arrow et al. 1993):

- For a single dichotomous question (yes–no type) format, a total sample size of at least 1000 respondents is required. Clustering and stratification issues should be accounted for and random subsampling will be required to obtain a bid curve and to test for interviewer and wording biases.
- High non-response rates would render the survey unreliable.
- Face-to-face interviewing is likely to yield the most reliable results.
- Full reporting of data and questionnaires is required for good practice.
- Pilot surveying and pre-testing are essential elements in any CVM study.
- Underestimation of WTP/WTA is to be preferred to overestimation of WTP/WTA.
- WTP format is preferred.
- The valuation question should be posed as a vote on a referendum, that is, a dichotomous choice question related to the payment of a particular level of taxation.

- Accurate information on the valuation situation must be presented to respondents, particular care is required over the use of photographs.
- Respondents must be reminded of the status of any undamaged possible substitute commodities.
- Time-dependent measurement noise should be reduced by averaging across independently drawn samples taken at different points in time.
- A 'no-answer' option should be explicitly allowed in addition to the 'yes' and 'no' vote options on the main valuation question.
- Yes and no responses should be followed up by the open-ended question: 'Why did you vote yes/no?'.
- Cross-tabulations: the survey should include a variety of other questions that help to interpret the responses to the valuation question, that is, income, distance to the site, prior knowledge of the site and so on.
- Respondents must be reminded of alternative expenditure possibilities, especially when 'warm-glow' effects can be prevalent (that is, purchase of moral satisfaction through the act of charitable giving).

The panel concluded that CVM studies, if founded on the above guidelines, could lead to estimates that would be reliable enough to be a starting point for a determination of natural resources damages, whether by the judiciary or by administrators. Arrow et al. (1993) thus assigned best practice CVM an important place among valuation methods.

In the exercises in the annexes, a step-by-step approach is presented for each procedure that obtains the max WTP/min WTA estimates. The list of proposed exercises is summarized in Figure 12.4.

In the exercises that follow we show how it is possible to elaborate maximum WTP values elicited through a bidding-game questionnaire (Annex 12A1).[8] The subsequent examples illustrate how to deal with dichotomous choice data. The first dichotomous choice exercise outlines how to obtain maximum WTP values by means of fairly simple descriptive statistics (Annex 12A2). The second dichotomous choice exercise is slightly more complex and proposes the application of weighted least square logit models (Annex 12A3). Finally, Appendix 12A5 illustrates how to elicit the maximum WTP from dichotomous choice data by means of maximum likelihood logit models.

Following the exercises we conclude that the contingent valuation method is a powerful technique that may be used to find the individual maximum WTP or minimum WTA. One of its interesting features is that it covers both use and non-use values, which none of the other methods do. Yet the application of the method is not easy and is fraught with many potential biases even when best-practice rules are followed. If it were easy to elicit accurate responses to valuation questions about hypothetical environmental situations, CVM could replace in many practical situations the other valuation methods. However,

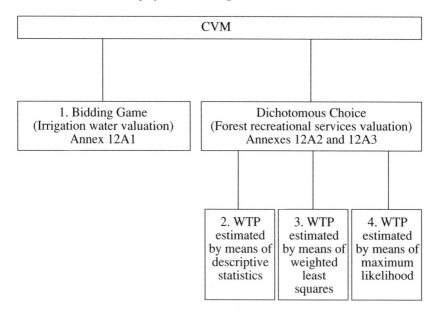

Figure 12.4 CVM: proposed step-by-step exercises

given the possibility of false results and the high costs and time involved in running a sound and reliable CVM survey, policy or project analysts must carefully weigh the pros and cons and the depth of the analysis required, before embarking on a CVM study.

NOTES

1. According to the marginalistic consumer theory, for a rational consumer the maximum willingness to pay or minimum willingness to accept a compensation should be related to the changes in the expenditure function, as illustrated in Chapter 9.
2. Symmetric considerations hold for environmental damages.
3. For a detailed discussion on biases in CVM, see Mitchell and Carson (1989).
4. For example, consider 'free-rider' behaviour. If the individual fears that the interview is run with the purpose of facilitating the setting of charges, s/he could state a maximum WTP to obtain an environmental improvement lower than the true one. Here, s/he would be assuming that other neighbours will state their true (higher) maximum WTP, allowing the public decision maker to go ahead with the provision of the public good. However, in other circumstances, it can be 'strategic' to overstate his/her maximum WTP, to force the public decision maker to implement an improvement.
5. Pre-tests may be used to set the range of values appropriately.
6. Other elicitation formats exist such as, for example, (i) 'payment cards', which report the likely current expenditure of the respondents on other public goods and services such as security, defence, justice, environmental protection and health. The cards are showed to help the

respondent to calibrate his/her reply; (ii) 'contingent ranking' where the respondent is asked to rank alternative policies or projects in order of preference considering different attributes. When at least one of the attributes is expressed in money terms (for example, 'price' to pay), contingent ranking can be considered an extension of the dichotomous choice approach.
7. For a good compendium on biases in CVM see Mitchell and Carson (1989).
8. The procedure proposed in the bidding-game exercise is also applicable to data from open-ended formats.

CITED BIBLIOGRAPHY

Arrow, K., R. Solow, P.R. Portney, E.E. Leamer, R. Radner, and H. Schuman (1993), 'Report of the NOAA panel on contingent valuation', *Federal Register*, **58**, 4601–14.

Bateman, I.J. (1993), 'Evaluation of the environment: a survey of revealed preference techniques', GEC Working Paper 93–06, CSERGE, University of East Anglia, Norwich, and University College, London.

Bellù, L.G. and V. Cistulli (1997), 'Economic valuation of forest recreation services in the Liguria region (Italy)', CSERGE Technical Paper 97–08, University of East Anglia, Norwich, and University College, London.

Cameron, T.A. (1988), 'A new paradigm for valuing non-market goods using referendum data: maximum likelihood estimation by censored logistic regression', *Journal of Environmental Economics and Management*, **15**, 355–79.

Cameron, T.A. (1991), 'Interval estimates of non-market resource values from referendum contingent valuation surveys', *Land Economics*, **67** (4), 413–21.

Carson, R.T. (1991), 'Constructed markets', in John Braden and Charles Kolstad (eds), *Measuring the Demand for Environmental Quality*, Amsterdam: Elsevier, pp. 121–62.

Carson, R.T., M. Hanemann and R.C. Mitchell (1986), 'Determining the demand for public goods by simulating referendums at different tax prices', Department of Economics, University of California, San Diego.

Cooper, J.C. (1994), 'A comparison of approaches to calculating confidence intervals for benefit measures from dichotomous choice contingent valuation surveys', *Land Economics*, **70** (1), 111–22.

Freeman, A.M. (1983), *The Measurement of Environmental and Resource Values: Theory and Methods*, Washington, DC: Resources for the Future, p. 179.

Gibbons, D.C. (1986), *The Economic Value of Water*, Washington, DC: Resources for the Future.

Gujarati, D.N. (1988), *Basic Econometrics*, New York: McGraw-Hill.

Gujarati, D.N. (1999), *Essentials of Econometrics*, 2nd edn, New York: McGraw-Hill.

Hanemann, M. (1984), 'Welfare evaluations in contingent valuation experiments with discrete responses', *American Journal of Agricultural Economics*, **66** (3), 332–41.

Hanemann, M. (1989). 'Welfare evaluations in contingent valuation experiments with discrete responses: reply', *American Journal of Agricultural Economics*, **71**, November, 1057–61.

Hanemann, M. (1991), 'Willingness to pay and willingness to accept: how much can they differ?', *American Economic Review*, **81** (3), 635–47.

Hanemann, M., J.B. Loomis and B.J. Kanninen (1991), 'Statistical efficiency of double bounded dichotomous choice contingent valuation', *American Journal of Agricultural Economics*, **73**, 1255–63.

Hazilla, M. (1999), 'Lecture notes: econometric methods for measurement and valuation of environmental quality', Technical Paper, Environment Division, Sustainable Development Department, Inter-American Development Bank, Washington, DC.

Kanninen, B.J and Sami Khawaja (1995), 'Measuring the goodness of fit for the double bounded logit model', *American Journal of Agricultural Economics*, **77** (November) 885–90.

Knetsch, J.L. (1990), 'Environmental policy implications of disparities between willingness to pay and compensation demanded measures of values', *Journal of Environmental Economics and Management*, **18**, 227–37.

Krinsky, I and A.L. Robb (1986), 'On approximating the statistical properties of elasticities', *Review of Economics and Statistics*, **68**, 715–19.

Le Moigne, G., A. Subramanian, M. Xie and S. Giltner (1994), 'A guide to the formulation of water strategy', World Bank Technical Paper No. 263, World Bank, Washington, DC.

Maddala, G.S. (1983), 'Limited-dependent and qualitative variables in econometrics', Econometric Society Monographs, Cambridge: Cambridge University Press.

McFadden, D. (1976) 'Quantal choice analysis: a survey', *Annals of Economics and Social Measurement*, **5**, 363–90.

Mitchell, R.C. and R.T. Carson (1989), *Using Surveys to Value Public Goods: The Contingent Valuation Method*, Washington, DC: Resources for the Future.

Park, T., J.B. Loomis and M. Creel (1991), 'Confidence intervals for evaluating benefit estimates from dichotomous choice contingent valuation studies', *Land Economics*, **67** (1), 64–73.

Pearce, D.W. and R.K. Turner (1990), *Economics of Natural Resources and the Environment*, Hemel Hempstead: Harvester Wheatsheaf.

Randall, A. and J.R. Stoll (1980), 'Consumer surplus in commodity space', *American Economic Review*, **70** (3), 449–55.

Teerink, J.R. and M. Nakashima (1993), 'Water allocation, rights, and pricing: examples from Japan and the United States', World Bank Technical Paper No. 198, World Bank, Washington, DC.

World Bank (1993), *Water Resource Management*, World Bank Policy Paper, Washington, DC: World Bank.

ANNEX 12A1   CONTINGENT VALUATION METHOD: BIDDING GAME (CVMBG): NUMERICAL EXAMPLES

Background

This exercise draws on a real study conducted for valuing irrigation water in Uzbekistan. Uzbekistan is a Republic of Central Asia with a mostly arid climate, limited natural resources and a large and rapidly growing population, concentrated in densely settled oases. During the Soviet period large irrigation schemes were developed. The vast deserts of the country are of little productive use. Only 10 per cent of the total area of Uzbekistan is presently cultivated. About 95 per cent of the total cultivated area is irrigated, corresponding to about 4.5 million hectares. Irrigated areas in Uzbekistan account for more than 50 per cent of the total irrigated area of Central Asia.

The agriculture sector is the main consumer of water resources in Uzbekistan. Between 80 and 89 per cent of available water resources is absorbed by agriculture, with the largest users being cotton (41 per cent of total irrigated area) and grain crops (32 per cent of total irrigated area). Yields, however, are very low when compared with similar areas of other countries and agriculture productivity is well below its potential.

Water resources of the country are fully utilized and competition for the use of water from other sectors is increasing rapidly, due to population growth, industrial development and environmental degradation. It follows that there is little room for expanding irrigation schemes further in Uzbekistan.

In any case, a new irrigation scheme is not considered to be the most efficient way to increase agricultural productivity. This is for three reasons. The first is that the project undertaken in the 1950s and 1960s for developing irrigated crop production is now considered a major cause of the environmental problems associated with the shrinking of the Aral Sea. These problems have included the loss of fish resources in the Aral Sea, land degradation due to salinization and water-logging, adverse health effects from the poor quality of drinking water, and possible local climatic change. The second reason is that financial constraints have severely limited the funds available not only for constructing new irrigation and drainage systems but also for maintaining, repairing and modernizing the existing ones. The third relates to inefficiencies in the use and management of water resources.

An increase in efficiency in the use and management of already developed water resources, rather than development of new irrigated areas, is required to ensure that a more sustainable developmental path is followed by Uzbekistan's agriculture. This option takes into account financial constraints, increasing competition from other demands for water, and environmental concerns. This entails the introduction of better irrigation, drainage and management techniques, the establishment of a system of water charges, as water in Uzbekistan is presently free of charge, as well as some institutional reforms aimed at developing water markets and water rights.

This analysis is concerned mainly with water-pricing policies. It aims to assess the economic, social and environmental value of irrigation water. It was felt that only if policy makers are aware of the value of water will they be able to design regulatory and institutional systems and policies to allocate water effectively among the competing demands.

In the case of irrigation water, many possible methods exist for deriving its value. Following Gibbons (1986), Teerink and Nakashima (1993), World Bank (1993) and Le Moigne et al. (1994) the methods below may be used.

- *Marginal cost of pumping water.* This method only works if competitive irrigation water supply conditions exist. In this case users will pump to the point where the marginal value of water equals the marginal pumping costs and, hence, the marginal cost of pumping can be used as a proxy for the marginal value of water.
- *Residual return to the crops grown* (gross return minus all costs other than water costs). This provides an estimate of the maximum amount farmers can pay for the water. This can be used as a proxy of the value of water when it is the limiting factor.
- *Value marginal products of water.* By varying the quantity of water applied while holding other inputs constant, a schedule of input/output relationships, and thus the marginal products, can be obtained. These marginal products when multiplied by the product price can provide an estimate of the derived demand for water.

The technique used in this study to assess the value of irrigation water is the contingent valuation method (CVM). CVM is usually suggested for the valuation of goods and services that do not have a market price or cannot be valued with market-price-based (direct proxy) valuation methods such as those mentioned above. In theory CVM can also be applied in valuing marketed goods. The reason why CVM was chosen here is the fact that, although irrigation water is generally considered a traded or tradable good, the direct proxy methods would not be able to capture the total economic value[1] of water. Another reason for the application of CVM in this case is that market-based valuation methods are more likely influenced by ongoing agricultural price policies.

Methodology

The procedure for carrying out the CVM survey considered the steps illustrated in Figure 12.3 of the main chapter.

What to value
The objective of the valuation exercise was to price one cubic metre of water
for irrigation.

Establishment of the value to be measured and unit of measurement
In the context of the survey, the type of value elicited was an annual average
value per cubic metre of irrigation water. The tiyin, the local monetary unit,
was chosen[2] as the unit of measure.

Time span of the valuation
The implicit time horizon of the WTP was taken to be the year of the survey
but, *ceteris paribus*, the elicited WTP can be considered a valid estimation for
subsequent periods as well.

Who should be interviewed
Farmers in Uzbekistan who used water for irrigation were chosen as interviewees.

Scenario design
The following scenario was presented to the interviewees:

> Let us assume now that the government is undertaking a programme for
> improving the services of the water delivery system (punctuality in water
> supplies, provision of adequate quantities of water, etc.) and the quality of
> water delivered in the most critical seasons of the vegetation period. This
> programme would also achieve indirectly a higher productivity of agricul-
> tural production and a more sustainable use of water resources. Since
> irrigation water is not charged in this country it may be helpful for you to
> know that other uses of water (industrial, domestic) as well as other inputs
> (fertilizers, pesticides, etc.) are charged.

Elicitation format
In order to take account of the possible differences in the results due to the use
of one rather than another elicitation format, in this study a combined approach
of the three main elicitation forms has been used. A graphical illustration of
this approach was given in Figure 12.2. The WTP question has been formulated
taking into account the following criteria: clarity, ease of understanding and
plausibility. The starting WTP question was the following:

> Suppose that you were asked to contribute to the programme with the
> payment of the irrigation water you consume. Would you be willing to pay
> ... per m^3 of water?

With the dichotomous choice (DC) method the respondents were asked whether they were willing to pay an amount X with the bid level X being systematically varied across the sample. The possible answers with the DC approach were therefore 'Yes' or 'No'. Twenty-five different bids expressed in monetary units/m^3 were selected. The bid levels were chosen on the basis of the data obtained from other studies conducted in Uzbekistan and the charges currently paid in Kazakhstan. The list of bids is provided in Table 12A1.1.

Table 12A1.1   Bids used for the survey in Uzbekistan (tiyin/m^3)

Subsample number	1	2	3	4	5	6	7	8	9
Bid	0.6	3.1	5.6	8.1	10.6	13.1	15.6	18.1	20.6
Subsample number	10	11	12	13	14	15	16	17	18
Bid	23.1	25.6	28.1	30.6	33.1	35.6	38.1	40.6	43.1
Subsample number	19	20	21	22	23	24	25		
Bid	45.6	48.1	50.6	53.1	55.6	58.1	60.6		

When the reply of respondents to the DC question was positive then the interviewer started iterative bidding, increasing the bid level by 20 per cent and then the WTP question was asked again. When the response was negative, the bid level was decreased by the same amount and the WTP question was asked again. The follow-up question was repeated three times if the starting answer was positive and four times if the starting answer was negative. At the end of the iterative bidding the respondent was asked to reveal his/her maximum WTP using an open-ended question (see Figure 12.2).

Payment vehicle (PV)
Due to financial and time constraints it was not possible to carry out a pilot study to investigate the best payment vehicle. The PV was chosen on the basis of the suggestions of national experts and on the PV currently employed in neighbouring countries where irrigation water is priced. It was therefore decided to use the payment of a price per cubic metre. In order to check whether this payment method was actually the most familiar to the farmers, one final question was included asking the respondents: which would be in their opinion the most appropriate payment vehicle among some proposed alternatives.

Survey strategy
Interviews were conducted by five teams of surveyors, each team consisting of two persons. A training course of two days was given in order to minimize

biases due to misunderstanding of the questions by the interviewers. The training course consisted of a careful explanation of all the questions, simulation of interviews among the surveyors and a pilot interview on a farm in order to check that the respondents were able to understand the questions and that the time required to complete the interview was not excessive. The survey was planned to last 20 days and the target for each team was to carry out five on-site (face-to-face) interviews per day. Each team of interviewers therefore received 100 copies of the questionnaire with an equal sample size for each bid level. The interviewers were asked to mix their questionnaires in order to ensure that the bid level offered to successive respondents was chosen randomly.

Collection, verification of the data, and creation of the database

Every three or four days, the coordinator of the surveyors collected the completed questionnaires and inserted the data into a simple database format prepared with a spreadsheet. Information contained in each questionnaire was organized by row (see Figure 12A1.1).[3] This procedure allowed the completion of the data entry approximately in the same period as the survey.

Answers	A1	...	B1	...	C1	...	D1	...	E1	...	F1	...
Questionnaires												
Questionnaire 1												
Questionnaire 2												
Questionnaire ...												
Questionnaire n												

Figure 12A1.1   Layout of the database for the CVM survey

Estimation of WTP

Calculation and estimation of WTP is described in detail below.

Aggregation

In the particular case of Uzbekistan survey aggregation was not necessary because the objective was to estimate the price of water per cubic metre.

The steps from 4c to 5d of the general CVM procedure illustrated in Figure 12.3, applied in this concrete bidding-game/open-ended context, are summarized in Figure 12A1.2.

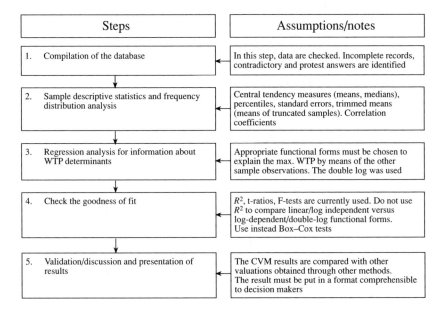

Steps	Assumptions/notes
1. Compilation of the database	In this step, data are checked. Incomplete records, contradictory and protest answers are identified
2. Sample descriptive statistics and frequency distribution analysis	Central tendency measures (means, medians), percentiles, standard errors, trimmed means (means of truncated samples). Correlation coefficients
3. Regression analysis for information about WTP determinants	Appropriate functional forms must be chosen to explain the max. WTP by means of the other sample observations. The double log was used
4. Check the goodness of fit	R^2, t-ratios, F-tests are currently used. Do not use R^2 to compare linear/log independent versus log-dependent/double-log functional forms. Use instead Box–Cox tests
5. Validation/discussion and presentation of results	The CVM results are compared with other valuations obtained through other methods. The result must be put in a format comprehensible to decision makers

Figure 12A1.2   CVMB: step-by-step procedure for WTP/WTA calculation

Problem Set

The first step of the procedure for WTP calculation outlined in Figure 12A1.2 has already been undertaken. Data included in the database of Table 12A1.2 can be considered reliable.

Table 12A1.2 Database for problem set

NUMOBS	WITOPA	ARAIRR	FODYIE	VEGPER (%)	MELPER (%)	VALARE
1	0	0	10	0.3	0.2	2.71
2	0	1	11	0.0	12.5	0.56
3	0	0	10	1.2	0.3	5.51
4	0	1	0	22.2	0.0	43.70
5	0	0	10	0.6	0.8	4.54
6	0	1	10	5.0	5.0	0.50
7	0	0	12	0.1	0.0	1.90
8	1	0	0	3.1	0.0	0.81
9	1	1	17	17.1	28.6	0.43
10	2	0	9	5.0	5.0	1.85
11	3	1	10	0.0	0.0	0.05
12	5	1	2.5	0.0	0.0	2.50
13	5	1	7	6.7	6.7	36.00
14	6	1	0	0.0	0.0	4.78
15	8	1	9	42.9	0.0	12.14
16	10	1	10	0.6	0.3	3.53
17	10	0	10	1.9	0.1	7.69
18	11	0	8	20.0	0.0	5.20
19	15	1	2.5	0.0	0.0	1.55
20	15	0	20	0.7	0.3	4.14
21	19	0	0	0.0	0.0	9.47
22	25	0	11	7.7	0.0	1.62
23	25	0	20	0.0	0.0	0.06
24	31	1	10	13.3	0.0	2.67
25	40	0	18	11.5	0.0	51.72
26	42	1	12	0.8	0.2	4.01
27	46	1	9	20.0	15.0	0.35
28	70	1	10	33.3	13.3	1.07
29	100	1	0	0.0	0.0	51.31
30	145	0	15	25.0	25.0	130.01

The description of the database variables is presented below:

Variable	Description
NUMOBS	Number of the observation
WITOPA	Willingness to pay per additional cubic metre of irrigation water (tiyins)
ARRAIR	Dummy about the question: 'The irrigation water use is the main cause of the shrinking of Aral Sea' (1 = yes, 0 = no)
FODYIE	Yields of fodder (metric tons/hectares)
VEGPER	Share of the irrigated area of the farm allocated to vegetables
MELPER	Share of the irrigated area of the farm allocated to watermelons
VALARE	Gross production value per hectare (thousand)

The problem for the analyst is to select one or more indicators that summarize the observed willingness to pay for an additional cubic metre of irrigation water to provide price policy recommendations. In order to accomplish this task, steps 2 to 5 of the procedure outline in Figure 12A1.2 must be followed, that is:

2. Calculate the sample average and median WTP and graph the WTP frequency distribution.
3. Investigate the effects of truncating the sample by excluding upper tail extreme values of the variable under investigation.
4. Explain the variation across individual responses of the variable *WITOPA*, that is, the willingness to pay for an additional cubic metre of irrigation water, using the additional information provided by the other variables in the sample.
5. Put forward a discussion of the results obtained and formulate the possible price of water to be charged to farmers, supporting it with socioeconomic considerations.

Hints

Box 12A1.1 below provides a summary of the major descriptive statistics that can be used in step 2.

Table 12A1.3 suggests a possible approach for completing step 2.

The description of the variation across individual responses of the variable *WITOPA*, that is, the willingness to pay for an additional cubic metre of irrigation water (step 4) can be obtained by running a regression of *WITOPA* on the other variables in the database.[4]

To complete step 5, consider for instance the effects of selecting a price corresponding to the sample average at different truncation levels. Would you prefer the average of the sample truncated at, say, the 70th percentile, 90th

BOX 12A1.1   DESCRIPTIVE STATISTICS AND FREQUENCY DISTRIBUTIONS

The *mean* of a series of *n* data is the sum of the data divided by *n*:

$$\mu = \frac{\sum_{i=1}^{n} x_i}{n}.$$

The *median* of an ascending (descending) ordered series of *n* data is the value of the data in the middle of the data series, that is, the value of the data that is greater than precisely 50 per cent of the observations. If the number of data is odd, the median is the value of the data in the $[(n-1)/2+1]$th position. For example, if a series contains 31 data, the median is the value of the $[(31-1)/2+1] =$ 16th data. If instead the series contains an even number of data, the median is conventionally assumed to be the mean of the data in the $(n/2)$th and $(n/2+1)$th position, for example, given 30 data, the median is the mean of the 15th and 16th data.

The *xth percentile* ($x = 1 \dots 100$) is the value of the data that is greater than precisely *x* per cent of the data in the series. It is apparent that the median is the 50th percentile.

The *relative frequency* of a value is the ratio between the number of times that a value is observed in the series and the total number of data in the series. For example, if the value of the WTP = 0.3 is observed twice in 30 observations the relative frequency of the value is 2/30 = 0.0666.

The *cumulative relative frequency* of a given value is the sum of the relative frequencies up to that value. For example, if the value of the WTP = 0 is observed four times, WTP = 0.3 twice, WTP = 0.4 is observed once in 30 observations, the cumulated relative frequency of the value 0.4 is 6/30 = 0.20.

percentile, the non-truncated sample? Why? What is the effect of using the median as a summary index of the WTP distribution? What could be the likely socioeconomic effects of setting a relatively high (or low) price for water?

Table 12A1.3   *Percentile analysis of WTP*

Number of observations	WTP	Percentile	Descriptive statistics of the truncated distribution		
			Average WTP	Median	Std dev.
1	0.0	3	0.00	0	=
2	0.0	7	0.00	0.0	0.00
	...	...	...	...	...
6	0.3	20	0.10	0.0	0.15
7	0.4	23	0.14	0.0	0.18
8	1.0	27	0.25	0.2	0.35
	...	...	...	...	...
30	...	...	...	...	...

Solution Set

Step 2   Descriptive statistics
The sample mean (21.15) and median (9.0) are calculated in the last row of
Table 12A1.3. Figure 12A1.3 shows the cumulated relative frequencies for the
WITOPA variable. It allows the determination of the share of sample answers
that declare a willingness to pay below a given value. For example, about 70
per cent of the respondents declare a willingness to pay below 20 tiyin per cubic
metre of irrigation water.

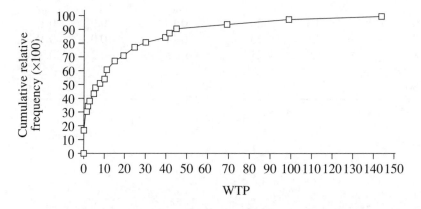

Figure 12A1.3   Cumulative frequency distribution of max WTP

Step 3   Effects of truncation of sample
In Table 12A1.4 the observations are ordered by the willingness to pay value
given. For every observation the respective percentile is calculated. Some
descriptive statistics such as the mean, the median and the standard deviation
are calculated for all the subsamples that can be generated with the truncation
of the sample at different percentiles. For example, truncating the sample at
the 90th percentile, that is, excluding the observations with WTP greater than
45.6, the mean of the truncated sample is 11.84, the median is 6 and the standard
deviation is 14.4.

Figure 12A1.4 shows the mean and median of the truncated samples at
different truncation levels. Both the mean and median show an increasing trend
because observations with increasing values of the variable *WITOPA* are added
to the subsample when the truncation is put forward to the next percentile.

Table 12A1.4   Percentile analysis of max WTP

Number of observations	WTP	Percentile	Descriptive statistics of the truncated distribution		
			Average WTP	Median	Std dev.
1	0.0	3	0.00	0	=
2	0.0	7	0.00	0.0	0.00
3	0.0	10	0.00	0.0	0.00
4	0.0	13	0.00	0.0	0.00
5	0.3	17	0.06	0.0	0.13
6	0.3	20	0.10	0.0	0.15
7	0.4	23	0.14	0.0	0.18
8	1.0	27	0.25	0.2	0.35
9	1.0	30	0.33	0.3	0.41
10	2.0	33	0.50	0.3	0.65
11	3.0	37	0.73	0.3	0.98
12	5.0	40	1.08	0.3	1.55
13	5.0	43	1.38	0.4	1.84
14	6.0	47	1.71	0.7	2.15
15	8.0	50	2.13	1.0	2.63
16	10.0	53	2.62	1.0	3.22
17	10.0	57	3.06	1.0	3.59
18	11.0	60	3.50	1.5	3.96
19	14.6	63	4.08	2.0	4.61
20	15.0	67	4.63	2.5	5.11
21	19.0	70	5.31	3.0	5.88
22	25.0	73	6.21	4.0	7.11
23	25.0	77	7.03	5.0	7.98
24	30.5	80	8.00	5.0	9.16
25	40.0	83	9.28	5.0	11.01
26	42.0	87	10.54	5.5	12.55
27	45.6	90	11.84	6.0	14.04
28	69.7	93	13.91	7.0	17.59
29	100.0	97	16.88	8.0	23.53
30	145.0	100	21.15	9.0	32.89

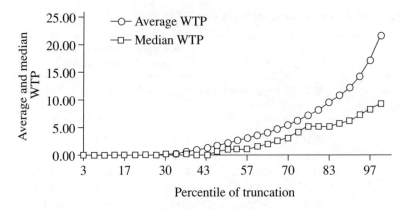

Figure 12A1.4   Sample average and median WTP by percentile of truncation (tiyins)

Step 4   Explanation of WTP values

Table 12A1.5 shows the results of the linear regression of the variable *WITOPA* on all the other sample variables. The explanatory power of the regression model is fairly high, as the coefficient of goodness of fit, R^2, shows. The bulk of the variability of *WITOPA* is captured by the variable *VALARE*, that is, the value of the production per hectare, with a positive relationship between the willingness to pay and this variable. The respective parameter presents a very high *t*-ratio, showing that this is statistically significant.[5]

Table 12A1.5   Regression of max WTP on all other variables

	VALARE	MELPER	VEGPER	FODYIE	ARAIRR	CONSTA
Parameters (b)	0.8512	46.1310	14.6092	0.3763	4.6578	1.1977
Standard error of (b)	0.1843	72.5756	43.8356	0.8843	9.9632	11.6725
t-ratios of (b)	4.619	0.636	0.333	0.426	0.468	0.103

Dependent variable	*WITOPA*	Functional form:	Linear
R^2	0.5802	*F*-test	6.6346
Degree of freedom	24	Sum of sq. resid.	13,172

Step 5   Discussion of results

Some possible ways of using the results of this analysis for policy-making, notes of caution and other comments are presented below.

Discussion

Before proceeding with the discussion it is worth noting that in this particular exercise, CVM has been used to estimate the value of irrigation water, that is the value of an input of the production function. In general, as pointed out in Chapter 10, the values of non-priced inputs are estimated using the productivity change method. The use of the two methods in tandem may be advisable for the following reasons:

1. to cross-check the results;
2. other objectives than allocative efficiency may be being pursued; and
3. the CVM method provides information of WTP by type of farmer, which can be used to design tariffs and other policies which provide poor farmers with minimum amounts of water at affordable rates.

Biases
The use of contingent valuation surveys for valuing goods and services is often criticized on the grounds that many in-built biases hamper the validity and reliability of the results obtained. The first concern in this study has therefore been to minimize, as far as possible, the risk of bias by rigorously following the guidelines suggested for improving the quality of results (Mitchell and Carson 1989; Arrow et al. 1993). Out of the 15 guidelines set up by the recent Blue Ribbon Panel Protocol, 13 have been met in this study.[6] Among the most important are: the choice of the WTP format; the inclusion of a non-response option among the answers; the choice of face-to-face interviewing; formulation of dichotomous choice questions (yes or no answers); providing respondents with accurate information on the valuation situation; complementing yes or no questions with open-ended format questions such as 'why did you vote yes or no?'; and adding questions aimed at interpreting the responses.

Market scenario
Particular attention has also been paid to the construction of a plausible and understandable hypothetical market. A series of questions about respondents' characteristics, their preferences relevant to the good being valued and their use of the good have also been added in order to check whether the predicted relationships between the variables of the underlying theoretical model are consistent with the elicited WTP.

Remarks
Assuming now that the design of the questionnaire conforms to the 'best-practice' standards, some remarks can be made on the validity of this method in the decision-making process.

First, CV surveys are an important tool to aid decision makers in the introduction of economic criteria into the decision-making process for water allocation. They provide decision makers with valuable information on the preferences of consumers and, consequently, allow them to formulate water policies that take into account users' behaviour.

Elicitation of WTP by water users will also help decision makers in the introduction of market mechanisms in the allocation of water among consumers and sectors. There is now widespread acceptance that water provides three types of benefits: (i) benefits to the resource supplier; (ii) benefits to the waste assimilator; and (iii) benefits as a direct source of utility. It is also accepted that competition among the different uses of water is increasing. It follows that WTP is an important indicator for identifying the most desired use of water and for improving the productive and allocative efficiency of water resources.

Finally, in contrast to other economic valuation methods, CV surveys not only address allocative efficiency objectives of water resources among various activities. Other objectives more typical of public actions such as equity and environmental concerns can also be addressed, thus allowing policy makers to meet criteria other than strict economic efficiency.

Policy implications

The policy implications of the Uzbekistan survey results might be as follows. Let us assume first that the main objective of the policy makers is to allocate water efficiently among the various users, both within the agricultural sector and between sectors. It appears that the mean WTP or marginal value of irrigation water for the sample is 21.15 tiyin/m^3. If this WTP minus the costs of production and delivery of water gives a higher value than those obtained in other sectors, it would be more efficient to allocate water to the agricultural sector. The same reasoning holds as regards allocative efficiency within the sector. A water charge of this amount will presumably have the general effect of a reduction in water consumption of those farmers who are not willing to pay that amount in order to raise the marginal value of water to that amount.

There are three categories of farmers who may not be willing to pay that amount:

1. Farmers for whom water consumption on the farm is higher than requirements. In this case an increase in water charges will have the effect of decreasing water consumption, and therefore increasing the efficiency of production. Hence, wastage of water will decrease.
2. Farmers whose water is used efficiently. In this case the farmer will probably reduce water use by replacing it with substitute inputs, or by changing the irrigation or drainage technique, or by changing the cropping pattern.

3. Farmers for whom water is a constraint. The farmer will reduce water consumption by, for example decreasing the cultivated area, or even cease production.

Water resources made available by these farms will be used more efficiently in more productive farms (those who are willing to pay that price) or by other sectors.

The reallocation of water due to the introduction of a charge of 21.15 tiyin/m³ would also have important social impacts. Indeed, as is apparent from Table 12A1.4, more than 70 per cent of the farmers interviewed are not willing to pay this charge. Many of them, as already mentioned, would probably adapt their production function, thus improving efficiency in water use, but many others might also be obliged to leave the agricultural activity. In other words, although the whole society would be better off, some categories of farmers, particularly small farms, would bear the major burden of this measure. Analysts should advise policy makers on the possible social implications of such a choice and evaluate whether it would be more effective to set the charge at a lower level (for example, 8 tiyins) in order to mitigate undesired social impacts.

Technological and environmental impacts of the pricing of water also exist. Higher prices for water will probably lead the farmers to introduce some changes in their production function by, for example, improving irrigation techniques or drainage systems, substituting water with other inputs and so on. Moreover, a reduction in the level of water use in agriculture will free water resources which could be used for environmental purposes, such as recreation or improving fish and wildlife habitats. Finally, it will allow for a more sustainable use of water, with the conservation of water resources for future generations.

Notes

1. Total economic value, as defined in Chapter 8, represents the value which incorporates social and environmental externalities both in the short and long terms.
2. 1 US\$ = 3,250 tiyin. Exchange rate as of June 1995; 1 sum = 100 tiyin.
3. Most of the questions are of the 'yes–no' type. The 'yes' answers were inserted in the database as '1' and the 'no' answers as '0'.
4. To facilitate this exercise, use the spreadsheet CVMBIDD1.XLS. The full set of data plus the solutions is contained in the file CVMBIDD2.XLS.
5. As a rule of thumb, if the *t*-ratio > 2 then the variable is said to be 'statistically significant', that is, it is unlikely that the true value of the coefficient is zero. For a good basic discussion of regression analysis and its interpretation, see Gujarati (1999).
6. Following the Exxon-Valdez oil spill, the US government set up a blue-ribbon panel under the joint chairmanship of Kenneth Arrow and Robert Solow to advise on the use of CVM in natural resource damage for oil spills. Best-practice guidelines, were suggested by the panel (Arrow et al. 1993). They are summarized and reported in Section 12.1.

ANNEX 12A2   CONTINGENT VALUATION METHOD: DICHOTOMOUS CHOICE (CVMD)

Background

This exercise and the next one draw on an actual study aimed at estimating the total use value of forests in the Liguria region of Italy (Bellù and Cistulli 1997), part of which was presented in the previous chapter. Their purpose is to illustrate the methodology used for assessing the recreational value of the forested areas and to provide some insight into the policy implications of the results obtained. A rough-and-ready method for obtaining WTP estimates from dichotomous choice data is presented. The method includes the use of logit models. The original case study has been substantially simplified, with only one of the seven areas originally surveyed being analysed.

The Liguria region was an important producer of timber and chestnuts in the past. Over the years, the relative importance of these activities has declined dramatically, leading to the abandonment of forests and the emigration of its population into the urban areas situated in the coastal zones. As a consequence, coastal areas are now suffering from high and unsustainable population densities, exacerbated during the summer, when significant flows of tourists add to the local population. Meanwhile the areas of the interior are progressively depopulated and the forests are deteriorating due to a lack of management and maintenance. The cultural heritage embodied in the historical sites within the forested areas is also being neglected.

Although from the financial point of view revenues from forests of these areas are rather low compared to revenues from other uses of land, the forests provide important non-valued services such as soil-moisture conservation, open-access recreation and hunting. They also provide valuable secondary forest products such as berries and mushrooms. Local authorities have therefore undertaken a study to appraise the net social benefits provided by the forested areas with a view to allocating financial resources for the rehabilitation and development of these areas.

This exercise seeks to estimate the benefits of the recreational use of these forests. In the Liguria region recreation is a non-priced public good and therefore its value could not be assessed using conventional market techniques. The procedure for applying the CVM method in this context took into account the following specific points (see Figure 12.3 in the chapter).

Identification of the site

In the particular case of this study, the sites were identified on the basis of the following criteria: suitability of the area for tourism; actual flow of tourists;

and the plans of the Liguria region for creating regional parks. Maps and photographs of the area helped inform the interviewees of the object of the survey.

Definition of the environmental good/service to be valued

The good or service to be valued was defined so as to avoid misunderstanding. In general, environmental goods or services of a forested area could be either the whole area of the site or one of the particular services provided by the forest (for example, recreation), or the change in the supply of one attribute, either in terms of quantity and quality. In the case of Liguria, the object to be valued was the whole site.

Questionnaire design

In this study, the questionnaire was aimed at collecting information both for a travel cost method (TCM) exercise, as presented in Chapter 11, and an application of the CVM. In particular it was subdivided into the following sections:

1. the first section was only for the use of interviewers and was aimed at providing some general information on the interview and interviewers (name of interviewer, location of interview, length of interview and so on);
2. the second section was devoted to the collection of socioeconomic data. It was assumed here that age, education, income, profession, number of family members and so on are important determinants in visitors' behaviour towards recreational use or visits to forests;
3. the third section attempted to identify the costs of travel faced by individuals in visiting the site, by asking them their origin, the vehicle used to reach the site, the time employed to reach the area from their origin and the trip plan. This section was therefore relevant to TCM;
4. the fourth section consisted of some questions aimed at investigating the environmental concern and awareness of visitors. It was assumed that the higher the awareness of environmental problems, the higher would be the perception of the value of forests' recreational value; and
5. the fifth section concerned the scenario presentation and the WTP elicitation question.

Scenario design

The hypothetical market was stated as follows:

> The site you are visiting is deteriorating due to lack of management and maintenance. Let us assume that the local government is planning to rehabilitate the area and that, due to budget constraints, it is also considering asking visitors to contribute to investment costs by paying an entrance fee for a day visit. Would you be willing to pay the following fee?

Elicitation form

The elicitation form chosen in this study was the dichotomous choice (DC) format. This means that respondents were asked whether they were willing or not to pay a pre-determined price for entering the park.

Payment vehicle

The payment vehicle (PV) used in this study was the payment of an entrance fee.

Survey strategy

It was decided that interviews should be carried out on-site. Therefore, for each single area, sites were identified for carrying out on-site face-to-face interviews. Interviewed visitors were selected randomly among the visitors throughout July, August and September, on both weekdays and weekends. The total number of interviews completed was 800. Since the behaviour of people visiting the site during the summer is probably different from the behaviour of people visiting the same site in winter and spring (for example, distance and time spent on-site might be shorter), the total annual value of recreation services provided by the site might be overvalued if the observed behaviour in summer was assumed to be representative of the whole year. This possible bias was taken into account in the final interpretation of the results.

Statistical description

When the survey was completed, a database was created using a spreadsheet. In order to check the consistency of responses and reliability of data, some statistical analyses were carried out.

WTP estimation

When using DC approaches, the usual way of estimating WTP measures is to apply logit models. A simplified approach is possible, however, when rough estimates are required or for illustrative purposes. This exercise estimates the WTP from the DC framework using descriptive statistics only. The exercise in Annex 12A3 reports on the WTP estimation using a logit-based method with weighted least squares (WLS). The estimated results using maximum likelihood estimates (MLE) are also reported in that exercise for comparison and discussion.

Aggregation

If the objective of the study is the estimation of the total value of the site, the individual WTP resulting from the analysis has to be multiplied by the total visitors of the site during a particular time period, usually one year. Once the total value of the area has been computed, the value per hectare can be obtained by dividing the total value by the extension of the area of the site.

Methodology

The objective of the dichotomous response approach is to derive a measure of the maximum individual WTP to be used as an estimate of the value individuals attach to a given environmental asset or service. To this end, DC data can be analysed with a descriptive approach based on sample frequencies. Rough-and-ready WTP measures are therefore obtained in a fairly simple way by introducing a few assumptions. As a simple numerical example, suppose that data has been collected about the proposed entrance fee and the related acceptance/refusal answers in the dichotomous format (0,1) as reported in Table 12A2.1 (the names of the variables used in the exercises are reported in brackets).

Table 12A2.1 Example of a (shortened) dichotomous CVM database

Number of questionnaire (NUMOBS)	Proposed entrance fee (TICKET)	Accept(1)/reject(0) answer (ACCEPT)
1	13,000	0
2	3,000	1
3	8,000	1
4	8,000	0
5	13,000	0
6	3,000	1
7	13,000	0
8	3,000	0
9	8,000	0

* In Monetary Units

The following step-by-step procedure allows the individual maximum WTP estimates to be obtained.

1. *Sort the database in increasing order by proposed entrance fee* (TICKET) as shown in Table 12A2.2.

2. *Calculate the acceptance frequencies for each level of the proposed entrance fee*, that is, the conditional acceptance frequencies (*CONFRE*) (for each level of entrance fee, this frequency can be easily obtained as the ratio of the positive answers on the number of questions referring to that level or by taking the mean of the dichotomous variable (*ACCEPT*) for each group of answers) (see Table 12A2.3)

Table 12A2.2   Sorted database for dichotomous CVM

Number of questionnaire (NUMOBS)	Proposed entrance fee (TICKET)	Accept(1)/reject(0) answer (ACCEPT)
2	3,000	1
6	3,000	1
8	3,000	0
3	8,000	1
4	8,000	0
9	8,000	0
1	13,000	0
5	13,000	0
7	13,000	0

3.   *Consider the above frequencies as the cumulative frequencies of acceptance for each level of proposed entrance fee.*   It is necessary to assume that the conditional frequencies above reflect the behaviour of the whole population (that is, each subset of the sample by level of entrance fee is representative of the population).

Table 12A2.3   Relative frequencies of acceptance and refusal

Number of questionnaire (NUMOBS)	Proposed entrance fee (TICKET)	Accept(1)/reject (0) answer (ACCEPT)	Acceptance rel. frequencies (%) (CONFRE)	Relative frequencies of refusal (%)
2	3,000	1		
6	3,000	1	66.6	33.3
8	3,000	0		
3	8,000	1		
4	8,000	0	33.3	66.6
9	8,000	0		
1	13,000	0		
5	13,000	0	0.0	100.0
7	13,000	0		

4.   *Calculate the cumulative frequencies of refusal*, as shown in the last column of Table 12A2.3.

5.   *Calculate the cumulative frequencies of the WTP.*   If an individual refuses to pay a given entrance fee, his/her maximum WTP is lower than that entrance fee. Also, assume that the maximum WTP is equally distributed within each class of values. This allows one to consider the mean of the bounds of each class as the mean maximum WTP within each class. For an example, see Table 12A2.4.

Table 12A2.4   Cumulative frequencies of max WTP

Cumulative frequencies of fee reject	⇒ WTP upper bound	⇒ frequency for WTP classes	Assumption on class mean
33% reject lit. 3,000	33% have WTP < lit. 3,000	33% have 0 ≤ WTP < 3,000	mean WTP of 33%: 1,500
66% reject lit. 8,000	66% have WTP < lit. 8,000	33% have 3,000 ≤ WTP < 8,000	mean WTP of 33%: 5,500
100% reject lit. 13,000	100% have WTP < lit. 1 3,000	33% have 8,000 ≤ WTP < 13,000	mean WTP of 33%: 10,500

Hence, the cumulative frequencies of the maximum WTP are:

Cumulative frequencies (× 100)	0%	33.3%	66.6%	100.0%
Mean WTP of each class (Monetary Units)	0	1,500	5,500	10,500

6a.   *Calculate the mean WTP.*   The mean WTP of the whole distribution is easily calculated by summing up the mean WTP of each WTP class, weighted with the frequency of the class, as shown in Table 12A2.5.

Table 12A2.5   Mean WTP (Monetary Units)

Mean WTP of each class	0	1,500	5,500	10,500
Relative frequency of each class	0%	33.3%	33.3%	33.3%
Mean WTP × Relative freq.	0	500	1,833.3	3,500
Mean WTP	5,833.3			

6b.   *Calculation of the median WTP.*   The median WTP can be estimated graphically by drawing the graph of the cumulative frequencies and finding the value corresponding to the 50 per cent cumulative frequency, or analytically by using the formula for the median of data grouped in classes:

$$Me = L + [(0.5 - FL)/FM]\ W,$$

where: Me = median; L = lower bound of the median class (say, lit. 1,500); U = upper bound of the median class (say lit. 5,500); W = median class width (W = U – L, where, say, 5,500 – 1,500 = 4,000); FL = cumulated frequency at L (say 33%); FU = cumulated frequency at U (say 66%); FM = frequency of median class (FM = FU – FL, say 33.3%).

This gives (in Monetary Units):

$$Me = 1{,}500 + [(0.5 - 0.33)/0.33]\,4{,}000 = 1{,}500 + 2{,}060.61 = 3{,}560.61.$$

When applying descriptive measures for estimating maximum WTP in a dichotomous choice context, points (5a) and (5b) of the general methodology for CVM illustrated in Figure 12.3 are developed according to the steps presented above, which are summarized in Figure 12A2.1.

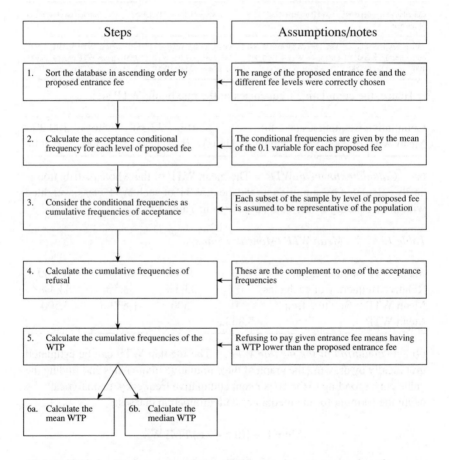

Figure 12A2.1   Dichotomous choice CVM: step-by-step procedure for descriptive measures of individual max WTP

Problem Set

Table 12A2.6 presents the database obtained from the survey at the forest site. Using the information provided and following the procedure for calculating the descriptive statistics of the willingness to pay, carry out the following:[2]

1. Calculate the conditional frequencies of acceptance for each level of the proposed entrance fee.
2. Calculate the cumulative frequencies of acceptance and the cumulative frequencies of refusal to pay the proposed entrance fee, for the different levels of the entrance fee.
3. Plot the cumulated frequencies above on a graph.
4. Work out the cumulative frequency distribution of the maximum WTP.
5. Plot the distribution on a graph.
6. Calculate the median maximum WTP
7. Work out the relative frequency of the different WTP levels and plot them in a graph. Calculate then the mean maximum WTP using the relative frequencies as weights.

Table 12A2.6   Database showing survey at forest site

NUMOBS	TICKET	ACCEPT	NUMOBS	TICKET	ACCEPT
1	3,000	1	16	3,000	1
2	8,000	1	17	3,000	1
3	18,000	0	18	23,000	0
4	13,000	1	19	23,000	0
5	23,000	0	20	13,000	0
6	3,000	1	21	8,000	1
7	3,000	1	22	13,000	0
8	18,000	0	23	13,000	1
9	18,000	0	24	8,000	1
10	13,000	0	25	13,000	0
11	18,000	0	26	18,000	0
12	23,000	0	27	23,000	0
13	18,000	1	28	3,000	1
14	23,000	0	29	8,000	0
15	8,000	0	30	8,000	1

Solution Set

The solutions to questions 1 to 7 are provided here.

Question 1

Question 1 is answered by sorting the database in ascending order by the variable *TICKET* and calculating the conditional relative frequencies for every group of observations (see Table 12A2.7). Note that the observations are grouped according to the proposed entrance fee.

Table 12A2.7   Conditional relative frequencies

NUMOBS	TICKET	ACCEPT	Conditional frequency
16	3,000	1	
6	3,000	1	
28	3,000	1	
1	3,000	1	
7	3,000	1	
17	3,000	1	1.00
2	8,000	1	
21	8,000	1	
29	8,000	0	
15	8,000	0	
24	8,000	1	
30	8,000	1	0.67
23	13,000	1	
22	13,000	0	
10	13,000	0	
25	13,000	0	
4	13,000	1	
20	13,000	0	0.33
3	18,000	0	
11	18,000	0	
13	18,000	1	
8	18,000	0	
26	18,000	0	
9	18,000	0	0.17
27	23,000	0	
18	23,000	0	
19	23,000	0	
12	23,000	0	
5	23,000	0	
14	23,000	0	0.00

Question 2
Table 12A2.8 shows the cumulated frequencies of acceptance and refusal to
pay the proposed entrance fee. Note that the relative frequencies of refusal are
the complement to one of the acceptance relative frequencies.

Table 12A2.8 Relative frequencies of acceptance and refusal

Entrance fee (Monetary Units)	0	3,000	8,000	13,000	18,000	23,000
Accept answers (%)	100.0	100.0	66.7	33.3	16.7	0.0
Reject answers (%)	0.0	0.0	33.3	66.7	83.3	100.0

Question 3
Figure 12.A2.2 plots the cumulative frequencies of acceptance and refusal to
pay the proposed entrance fee.

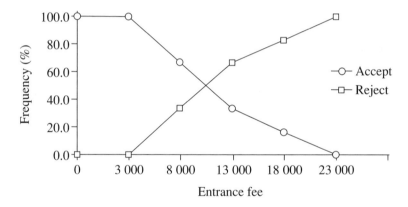

Figure 12A2.2 Relative frequencies of acceptance

Question 4
Table 12A2.9 reports the frequency distribution of the maximum WTP. Note
that it is assumed that the maximum WTP is uniformly distributed within each
interval of the proposed entrance fee. The narrower are the intervals, the less
important is this assumption.

Table 12A2.9 Cumulative frequency distribution of max WTP

Max WTP (Monetary Units)	0	1,500	5,500	10,500	15,500	20,500
Cumulative frequency (%)	0.0	0.0	33.3	66.7	83.3	100.0

Question 5

Figure 12A2.3 graphs the cumulative frequency distribution of the maximum WTP.

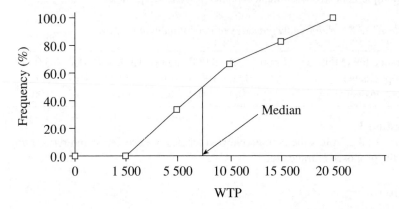

Figure 12A2.3   Cumulative frequency distribution of the max WTP

Question 6

Table 12A2.10 shows the calculation of the median WTP. The formula for the median calculates the share of the median class frequency below the 0.5 cumulated frequency; it uses this proportion to split the median class width and adds to the lower bound of the median class the same proportion of the class width. The calculation is based on the assumption that the maximum WTP is distributed equally within the median class.

Table 12A2.10   Median of max WTP (Monetary Units)

Lower bound of the median class (L)	5,500
Upper bound of the median class (U)	10,500
Median class width (W = U − L)	5,000
Cumulated frequency at L (FL) (%)	33.3
Cumulated frequency at U (FU) (%)	66.7
Frequency of median class (FM = FU − FL) (%)	33.3
Median (Me = L + [(0.5 − FL)/FM] × W)**	8,000

Question 7

Figure 12A2.4 illustrates the relative frequencies of the maximum WTP. Table 12A2.11 shows the calculation of the relative frequencies and the calculation of the mean maximum WTP. Note that the mean is obtained as the weighted sum of the maximum WTP data, where the weights are the relative frequencies.

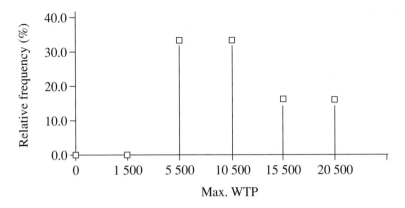

Figure 12A2.4   Relative frequency of maximum WTP

Table 12A2.11   Relative frequencies and mean of max WTP (Monetary Units)

Max. WTP	0	1,500	5,500	10,500	15,500	20,500
Relative frequencies (%)	0.0	0.0	33.3	33.3	16.7	16.7
Max. WTP × freq.	0	0	1,833	3,500	2,583	3,417
Mean max. WTP	11,333					

Discussion

This method of using dichotomous choice data is simple and can be carried out without using an econometric software package. In practice, given the easy availability of such packages, the analysis of actual data is rarely done in this way. Instead, methods described in the exercise in Annex 12A3 are employed.

Notes

1. Names in brackets refer to variables used in the spreadsheet.
2. For running this exercise, use the spreadsheet CVMDICH1.XLS which contains the data set. The answers are shown on the spreadsheet CVMDICH2.XLS.

ANNEX 12A3   DICHOTOMOUS CVM USING THE LOGIT MODEL: A NUMERICAL EXAMPLE

The exercise developed in this section follows the approach suggested by Hanemann (1984, 1989), and is based on a random utility model, which is theoretically grounded in neoclassical consumer theory.[1] The welfare foundation of this approach is briefly outlined in the next section. The step-by-step procedure for running the exercise is then presented with the support of a numerical example. Some of the complexities of the estimation of the logit model by maximum likelihood estimation (MLE) have been removed by using the weighted least squares (WLS) method, as outlined in Gujarati (1988).[2] The conceptual and analytical structure of the logit model is described in Annex 12A1.

The Dichotomous Choice Approach and its Welfare Foundations

The objective of the dichotomous choice approach is to derive a measure of the maximum individual willingness to pay (WTP) to be used as an estimate of the value individuals attach to a given environmental asset or service. To obtain this measure, a probability distribution of the WTP is estimated. The mean and/or median of the estimated WTP probability distribution is usually considered as an estimate of the value that an average individual attaches to the specific good or service under analysis.

To start with, it is necessary to consider the welfare implications of the acceptance or refusal to pay a proposed amount for, for example, the entrance fee to a park. When the individual agrees to pay for a ticket, his/her utility with the ticket but with less money to spend on other goods (U_1) is greater than, or at least equal to, his/her utility without the ticket but with the ticket price in hand (U_0). That is if:

$(U_1 - U_0) \geq 0$, the individual will accept to pay the entrance fee t.

(12A3.1a)

$(U_1 - U_0) < 0$, the individual will refuse to pay the entrance fee t.

(12A3.1b)

This utility difference is, unfortunately, not directly observable, but may be considered as a variable expressing the propensity to accept the payment of the entrance fee.[3] We can therefore use the analytical framework described in the annex for modelling the behaviour of the individual faced with the alternative accept/reject to pay the proposed entrance fee.

Even if the utility U of the individual is not directly observable, its determinants are observable, and a model for U can be assumed. Under the two scenarios above, the following specifications of the utility function have been proposed:

$$U_1(1, y - t; s) = v(1, y - t; s) + e_1 \qquad (12A3.2a)$$

$$U_0(0, y; s) = v(0, y; s) + e_0, \qquad (12A3.2b)$$

where: y represents income; 1 shows that the individual is in possession of the ticket; 0 shows that the individual is not in possession of the ticket; s represents other socioeconomic features; and e is a random error term due to the limited knowledge of the individual's actual utility model.

The above functions are, respectively, the utility of the individual with the ticket and the reduced income after paying the ticket price, and the utility of the individual without the ticket but with the price available for other expenditures.

The utility difference becomes:

$$(U_1 - U_0) = v(1, y - t; s) - v(0, y; s) - (e_0 - e_1). \qquad (12A3.3)$$

Calling $(U_1 - U_0) = \Delta U$, $(e_0 - e_1) = e$, and $[v(1, y - t; s) - v(0, y; s)] = \Delta V$, equation (12A.3) can be rewritten as:

$$\Delta U = \Delta V - e. \qquad (12A3.4)$$

Given (12A3.4), the inequalities (12A3.1a) and (12A3.1b) can be written as:

$$\Delta V \geq e \qquad \Rightarrow e \leq \Delta V \qquad \text{accept } t \qquad (12A3.5a)$$

$$\Delta V < e \qquad \Rightarrow e > \Delta V \qquad \text{accept } t. \qquad (12A3.5b)$$

Given the random nature of the component e, it is possible to model the individual choice in a probabilistic framework. The probability that the individual agrees to pay the entrance fee is therefore:

$$P(\text{accept } t) \equiv P(Y = 1) \equiv P(e \leq \Delta V) = F(\Delta V),$$

where Y is the observed dichotomous variable, with acceptance represented by the figure '1', and refusal by the figure '0'.

Note that, given a utility function, the larger the observable component of the utility difference, ΔV, the greater is the likelihood that the random variable e will be smaller than ΔV, implying therefore a greater likelihood of payment. The probability of the (continuous) random variable e being smaller or equal to a given value ΔV is expressed by its distribution function: $F(\Delta V)$.

Assuming that the random variable e follows a logistic probability distribution we can write:

$$P(\text{accept } t) \equiv F(\Delta V) = 1/[1 + \exp(-\Delta V)]. \qquad (12A3.6)$$

When the individual agrees to pay the proposed entrance fee t, it means that the maximum WTP is greater than the proposed entrance fee t. The probability of acceptance, given a fee t, is the probability that the individual WTP is greater than t. Therefore, we can write:

$$P(\text{accept } t) \equiv P(WTP > t) = 1/[1 + \exp(-\Delta V)]. \qquad (12A3.7)$$

This implies that the probability that the WTP is less than or equal to t is:

$$P\,(WTP \leq t) \equiv G(t) = 1 - 1/[1 + \exp(-\Delta V)], \qquad (12A3.8)$$

where $G(t)$ is the probability distribution of the WTP. The mean and the median of the WTP distribution ($G(t)$) are commonly assumed to be indicators of the individual WTP.

In empirical work a functional form for the utility difference must be specified. Subsequently, the parameters that appear in the utility difference function, that is, the parameters of the WTP probability distribution $G(t)$, can be estimated using either ordinary (weighted) least squares methods or maximum likelihood estimation using a suitable econometric package which includes logit estimation routines.[4] On the left-hand side of the logit model there is the dichotomous variable $(0,1)$ reflecting the reject/accept answer. The right-hand side usually includes a constant plus a set of explanatory variables, including the proposed entrance fee.

The utility difference to be used in dichotomous approach models should respect the constraints on the shape of the utility function imposed by the theory. In Box 12A3.1 the linear utility difference model is presented in a detailed way.

Much empirical work has used utility difference specifications that are not grounded in theory but are empirically effective. Notably, the income of the individual, which in the linear utility difference is not present (see Box 12A3.1), is usually included due to the good explanatory power of the acceptance or refusal to pay. The proposed entrance fee is sometimes included in the model in logarithmic form, to rule out the theoretical possibility of having a negative individual WTP and the likelihood of having negative measures of the average WTP.

BOX 12A3.1   LINEAR UTILITY DIFFERENCE FUNCTION

The linear utility function of the type: $U = \alpha + \beta y + e$, where y is income, α is a composite parameter of all the other explanatory variables, (β is the coefficient of income and e is a random component, is a simple functional form that can be used for modelling utility differences.

Using the same notation as above, the linear utility in the scenarios with and without the entrance fee are, respectively:

$$U_1 = \alpha_1 + \beta(y - t) + e_1 \quad (\alpha_1 \text{ includes the utility of the visit}) \qquad (1a)$$

$$U_0 = \alpha_0 + \beta y + e_0 \qquad (1b)$$

$$(U_1 - U_0) = \alpha_1 + \beta y - \beta t + e_1 - \alpha_0 - \beta y - e_0 \qquad (2)$$

$$\Delta U = (\alpha_1 - \alpha_0) - \beta t - (e_0 - e_1) \qquad (3)$$

Calling $(\alpha_1 - \alpha_0) = c$ and $(e_0 - e_1) = e$

$$\Delta U = c - \beta t - e \qquad (4)$$

recalling that $\Delta U = \Delta V - e$ (see (12A3.4) in the text, and substituting in (4) we get:

$$\Delta V = c - \beta t \qquad (5)$$

This utility difference is expected to be negatively correlated with the entrance fee:

$$\frac{\delta \Delta V}{\delta t} < 0 \Rightarrow -\beta < 0 \Rightarrow \beta > 0.$$

The probability distribution of the WTP, assuming the linear utility model, and assuming that the random variable e follows a logistic probability distribution, becomes:

$$P(\text{WTP} \le t) \equiv G(t) = 1 - \frac{1}{1 + \exp\left[-(c - \beta t)\right]}. \qquad (6)$$

Note that, if the proposed entrance fee is entered in the database with the positive sign, the sign of β is expected to be negative. Other variables are usually included for improving the adaptation of the model to data.

The calculation of the formulae of the median and mean maximum WTP is outlined in Annex 12A2.

Methodology of CVMD with Logit

The procedure below summarizes the practical steps to be followed in order to obtain maximum WTP estimates using LOGIT models.

Suppose a database as shown in Table 12A3.1 is built. To estimate measures of the maximum WTP for the environmental services provided by the asset under valuation, follow the steps outlined hereafter.

Table 12A3.1   Example of a (shortened) dichotomous CVM database

Number of questionnaire (*NUMOBS*)	Proposed entrance fee (*TICKET*) (Monetary Units)	Response 1 = Accept 0 = Reject (*ACCEPT*)
1	13,000	0
2	3,000	1
3	8,000	1
4	8,000	0
5	13,000	0
6	3,000	1
7	13,000	0
8	3,000	0
9	8,000	0

1.   *Choice of a utility difference model.*   The linear model is the most straightforward (but gives rise to the possibility of negative WTP) (see Box 12A3.1).

The linear model is of the type:

$$\Delta U = CONSTA - \beta TICKET * TICKET - e,$$

where: ΔU is the utility difference, *CONSTA* is a constant of the model, *TICKET* is the proposed entrance fee, $\beta TICKET$ is the slope of the variable *TICKET*.

2.   *Choice of the probability distribution of the random component* of the utility difference model (logit, normal, other). The logit format is the simplest and in most cases no advantage arises from the use of other models. This implies that:

$$P(\text{accept } TICKET) \ \dots \ P(\text{max.WTP} > TICKET) = \frac{1}{1 + \exp\left[-(CONSTA - \beta TICKET * TICKET)\right]}.$$

3. *Transform the probability model to make it linear in the parameters* CONSTA *and* βTICKET.   The parameters *CONSTA* and *βTICKET* need to be estimated in order to work out the probability distribution of the maximum WTP and to calculate its mean or median. To ease the estimation of the two parameters, avoiding the need for the application of non-linear maximum likelihood estimations, the probability model in the previous step can be made linear. After weighting the variables to take heteroscedasticity into account, the parameters can be estimated by OLS.

The probability that a person accepts to pay a given entrance fee, say $TICKET_i$ is given by:

$$P(\text{accept } TICKET_i) \equiv P\left(ACCEPT = 1\,|_{TICKET_i}\right) \equiv P_i = \frac{1}{1 + \exp\left[-(CONSTA - \beta TICKET * TICKET_i)\right]}.$$

This implies that:[5]

$$\frac{P_i}{1 - P_i} = \exp\left(CONSTA - \beta TICKET * TICKET_i\right).$$

$P_i/(1 - P_i)$ is called the 'odds ratio' for the proposed entrance fee $TICKET_i$.
Taking the natural logarithm of both sides gives:

$$\ln \frac{P_i}{1 - P_i} = \ln\left[\exp\left(CONSTA - \beta TICKET * TICKET_i\right)\right] \Rightarrow \ln \frac{P_i}{1 - P_i} = CONSTA - \beta TICKET * TICKET_i,$$

which is called 'log odds ratio' and it is linear in the parameters *CONSTA* and *βTICKET*.

Note that, if the proposed entrance fee is entered in the database with a positive sign, the sign of β is expected to be negative and for estimation purposes the model can be written with the positive sign. Moreover, for estimation purposes, a random component must be added to the model. The model therefore becomes:

$$\ln \frac{P_i}{1 - P_i} = CONSTA - \beta TICKET * TICKET_i + u_i.$$

4. *Obtain estimates for the probability of accepting to pay a given the entrance fee* P_i.   Recall that the probability is the limit of the relative frequency when the number of observations tends to infinity. Provided that the number of observations for every proposed level of entrance fee are large enough (say, more than

5), the relative frequencies for every entrance fee ($CONFRE_i$) can be assumed as estimates of P_i. To calculate the relative frequencies, sort the database in increasing order by proposed entrance fee (*TICKET*), as in Table 12A3.2.

Table 12A3.2   Sorted database for dichotomous CVM

Number of questionnaire (*NUMOBS*)	Proposed entrance fee (*TICKET*) (Monetary Units)	Response Accept = 1 Reject = 0 (*ACCEPT*)
2	3,000	1
6	3,000	1
8	3,000	0
3	8,000	1
4	8,000	0
9	8,000	0
1	13,000	0
5	13,000	0
7	13,000	0

For each level of entrance fee i, the relative frequency $CONFRE_i$ (shown in Table 12A3.3, column d) is the ratio of the positive answers $NACCEP_i$ (column c) on the number of questions referring to that level $OBSERV_i$ (column b), that is,

$$CONFRE_i = \frac{NACCEP_i}{OBSERV_i}.$$

For example, the entrance fee is proposed to three people and is accepted by two of them. The conditional relative frequency for the entrance fee 3,000 is therefore 2/3 = 0,666 or 66.6 per cent.

5.   *Calculation of the 'odd ratios' for every entrance fee* i.   The odd ratios $ODDRAT_i$ (Table 12A3.3, column e) are obtained with the formula:

$$ODDRAT_i = \frac{CONFRE_i}{1 - CONFRE_i}.$$

For example, the odd ratio for the entrance fee 3,000 is: $ODDRAT_i = 0.666/(1-0.666) = 2$.

Table 12A3.3   Calculation of variables for the estimation of parameters

			Calculation of the log odd ratios and weighting of the variables					
			Estimated probab.	Odd ratios	Logs of the odd ratios	Weights	Weighted ticket	Weighted log odd ratios
TICKET	OBSERV	NACCEP	CONFRE	ODDRAT	LNODDS	WEIGHT	TIKEWE	LNODWE
a	b	c	d = c/b	e = d/(1–d)	f = ln(e)	g = [cd(1–d)]^0.5	h = a*g	i = f*g
3,000.00	3.00	2.00	0.67	2.00	0.69	0.82	2,449.49	0.57
8,000.00	3.00	1.00	0.33	0.50	–0.69	0.82	6,531.97	-0.57
13,000.00	3.00	0.00	0.00	0.00	–23.03	0.00	0.00	0.00

6.   *Calculation of the 'log odd ratios' for every entrance fee i.*   The log odd ratios $LNODDS_i$ (Table 12A3.3, column f) are obtained with the formula:

$$LNODDS_i = \ln (ODDRAT_i).$$

For example, the odd ratio for the entrance fee 3,000 is:

$$LNODDS_i = \ln(2) = 0.6931472.$$

The model to be estimated is therefore:

$$LNODDS_i = CONSTA + \beta TICKET * TICKET_i + u_i.$$

7.   *Calculation of the 'weights' to weight the variables*, in order to improve the efficiency of the estimators by eliminating heteroscedasticity.[6] The application of the OLS to the model illustrated in the previous step should be correct if all the random components u_i $(i = 1, ..., n)$ have the same variance. Unfortunately, this is not the case.

> It can be shown that if the number of observations [for every entrance fee] N_i is fairly large and if each observation [in a given entrance fee group] is distributed independently as a binomial variable, then $U_i \sim N [0, (1/N_i P_i(1 - P_i))$ that is, each u_i follows a normal distribution with zero mean and variance equal to $1/N_i P_i(1 - P_i)$. (Gujarati 1988)

Instead of using OLS the WLS must be used. For empirical purposes P_i is replaced by $CONFRE_i$ and the estimated variance of each u_i is therefore:

$$\hat{\sigma}_i^2 = \left[\frac{1}{OBSERV_i \, CONFRE_i \, (1 - CONFRE_i)} \right].$$

This implies that to eliminate the heteroscedasticity, both the left-hand side (LHS) and right-hand side (RHS) of the model must be multiplied by a weight that offsets the heteroscedasticity. The weight is calculated with the formula below (see, for example, Table 12A3.3, column g):

$$WEIGHT_i = \sqrt{OBSERV_i \, CONFRE_i \, (1 - CONFRE_i)} \ .$$

For example, the weight for the entrance fee 3,000 is:

$$WEIGHT_i = \sqrt{3 \ \ 0.666(1 - 0.666)} = 0.8165.$$

8. *Weighting of the model by multiplying all the variables with the weights.* The weighted model becomes:

$$WEIGHT_i \, LNODDS_i = WEIGHT_i \, CONSTA$$
$$+ \beta TICKET * WEIGHT_i \, TICKET_i + WEIGH_i u_i$$

It can be easily shown that this model is homoscedastic.

The transformed dependent variable (LHS) is therefore calculated as:

$$LNODWE_i = WEIGHT_i \, LNODDS_i \text{ (see Table 12A3.3 column i)}$$

and the transformed independent variable (RHS) is:

$$TIKEWE_i = WEIGHT_i \, TICKET_i \text{ (see Table 12A3.3, column h).}$$

For example, for the entrance fee 3,000, the transformed dependent variable becomes:

$$LNODWE_i = 0.8165 * 0.693147 = 0.565952,$$

and the transformed independent variable is:

$$TIKEWE_i = 0.8165 * 3000 = 2449.49.$$

9. *Running the OLS regression on the transformed model to estimate the parameters* CONSTA *and* βTICKET.   The transformed model is:

$$LNODWE_i = CONSTA\ WEIGHT_i + \beta TICKET * TIKEWE_i + WEIGHT_i u_i.$$

Note that this is a regression through the origin, without a true constant. Indeed, in the transformed model, the constant of the original model *CONSTA* plays the role of the slope of the variable $WEIGHT_i$. The results of the OLS regression of the variable *LNODWE* on the variables *WEIGHT* and *TIKEWE* using Table 12A3.3, are reported in Table 12A3.4.

Table 12A3.4   Estimated parameters by OLS regression

Variables	bTICKET	CONSTA
Parameters	–2.77E–04	1.52E+00
Std errors	2.31E–19	1.39E–15
R^2/ Std error $\hat{Y}$	1.00E+00	6.66E–16
F-test/DGF	7.22E+29	1.00E+00
Regr. SS/Resid. SS	6.41E–01	4.44E–31
T-ratios	–1.20E+15	1.09E+15

Note that, as expected, the parameter *bTICKET* is negative because the variable *TICKET* in the database is introduced with a positive sign.

10. *Calculation of the mean maximum WTP.*   For the linear utility model, the mean, (truncated for negative values of the WTP) is given by the following formula (see Annex 12A2):

$$E(\text{WTP}) \approx \frac{1}{-bTICKET} * \ln[\exp(CONSTA) + 1],$$

where *CONSTA* and *bTICKET* are the estimated regression parameters.
  In the example under consideration, the mean maximum WTP is:

$$E(\max \text{WTP}) \approx \frac{1}{0.000277259} * \ln[\exp(1.524923749) + 1] = 6210.21.$$

11.   *Calculation of the median WTP.*   For the linear utility model, the median becomes (see Annex 12A2):

$$\text{Me(max WTP)} = CONSTA/(-bTICKET)$$

In the example under consideration, the median maximum WTP is:

$$\text{Me(max WTP)} = 1.524923749/0.000277259 = 5499.99.$$

The 11 steps outlined above are summarized in Figure 12A3.1.

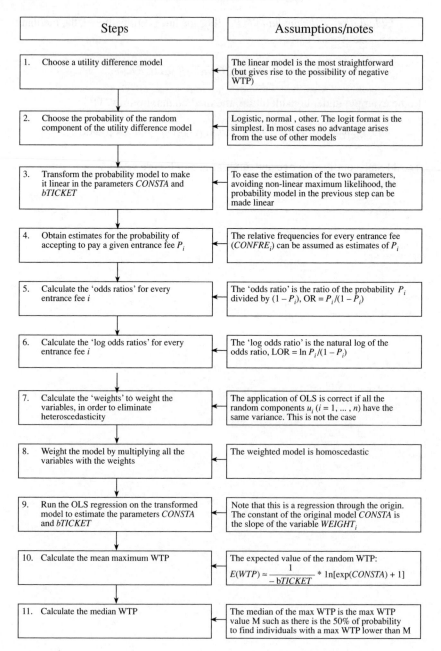

Steps	Assumptions/notes
1. Choose a utility difference model	The linear model is the most straightforward (but gives rise to the possibility of negative WTP)
2. Choose the probability of the random component of the utility difference model	Logistic, normal , other. The logit format is the simplest. In most cases no advantage arises from the use of other models
3. Transform the probability model to make it linear in the parameters *CONSTA* and *bTICKET*	To ease the estimation of the two parameters, avoiding non-linear maximum likelihood, the probability model in the previous step can be made linear
4. Obtain estimates for the probability of accepting to pay a given entrance fee P_i	The relative frequencies for every entrance fee ($CONFRE_i$) can be assumed as estimates of P_i
5. Calculate the 'odds ratios' for every entrance fee i	The 'odds ratio' is the ratio of the probability P_i divided by $(1 - P_i)$, OR $= P_i/(1 - P_i)$
6. Calculate the 'log odds ratios' for every entrance fee i	The 'log odds ratio' is the natural log of the odds ratio, LOR $= \ln P_i/(1 - P_i)$
7. Calculate the 'weights' to weight the variables, in order to eliminate heteroscedasticity	The application of OLS is correct if all the random components u_i ($i = 1, \dots , n$) have the same variance. This is not the case
8. Weight the model by multiplying all the variables with the weights	The weighted model is homoscedastic
9. Run the OLS regression on the transformed model to estimate the parameters *CONSTA* and *bTICKET*	Note that this is a regression through the origin. The constant of the original model *CONSTA* is the slope of the variable $WEIGHT_i$
10. Calculate the mean maximum WTP	The expected value of the random WTP: $$E(WTP) \approx \frac{1}{-bTICKET} * \ln[\exp(CONSTA) + 1]$$
11. Calculate the median WTP	The median of the max WTP is the max WTP value M such as there is the 50% of probability to find individuals with a max WTP lower than M

Figure 12A3.1   Step-by-step procedure for probabilistic measures of max WTP with logit estimated by weighted least squares

Problem Set

Table 12A3.5 shows the database obtained running the survey at the forest site. Using the information provided in the table and following the procedure for calculating the maximum WTP with the linear utility difference model and the logit estimates, answer the following questions:[7]

1. Calculate the estimate for the probability of accepting to pay for each of the proposed entrance fees (variable *CONFRE*, see step 4 of the procedure).
2. Calculate the odds ratio for each of the proposed entrance fees (variable *ODDRAT*, see step 5 of the procedure).
3. Calculate the log odds ratio for each of the proposed entrance fees (variable *LNODDS*, see step 6 of the procedure).
4. Calculate the weights for each of the proposed entrance fee (variable *WEIGHT*, see step 7 of the procedure).
5. Calculate the weighted dependent and independent variables (variables *LNODWE* and *TIKEWE*, respectively, see step 8 of the procedure).
6. Run the OLS regression of the weighted log odds ratios (variable *LNODWE*) on the weights and on the weighted entrance fees (variables *WEIGHT* and *TIKEWE*, respectively, see step 9 of the procedure).
7. Calculate the mean maximum WTP (see step 10 of the procedure).
8. Calculate the median maximum WTP (see step 11 of the procedure).

Table 12A3.5   Database for dichotomous choice CVM

NUMOBS	TICKET	ACCEPT	NUMOBS	TICKET	ACCEPT
1	3,000	1	16	3,000	1
2	8,000	1	17	3,000	1
3	18,000	0	18	23,000	0
4	13,000	1	19	23,000	0
5	23,000	0	20	13,000	0
6	3,000	1	21	8,000	1
7	3,000	1	22	13,000	0
8	18,000	0	23	13,000	1
9	18,000	0	24	8,000	1
10	13,000	0	25	13,000	0
11	18,000	0	26	18,000	0
12	23,000	0	27	23,000	0
13	18,000	1	28	3,000	1
14	23,000	0	29	8,000	0
15	8,000	0	30	8,000	1

Solution Set

The solutions to questions 1 to 5 are given in Table 12A3.6.

Table 12A3.6   Calculation of variables for the estimation of max WTP probability distribution function

			Estimated probab *	Odd ratios	Logs of the odd ratios	Weights	Weighted ticket	Weighted log odd ratios
TICKET	OBSERV	NACCEP	CONFRE	ODDRAT	LNODDS	WEIGHT	TIKEWE	LNODWE
a	b	c	d = c/b	e = d/(1–d)	f = ln(e)	g = [cd(1–d)]^0.5	h = a*g	i = f*g
3,000	6	6	1.00	999999.00	13.82	0.00	7.35	0.03
8,000	6	4	0.67	2.00	0.69	1.15	9237.60	0.80
13,000	6	2	0.33	0.50	–0.69	1.15	15011.11	–0.80
18,000	6	1	0.17	0.20	–1.61	0.91	16431.68	–1.47
23,000	6	0	0.00	0.00	–13.82	0.00	56.34	–0.03
* Approximation coefficient APPROX				0.000001				

Note: * To allow the calculation of the odd ratio when the estimated frequency is 1 and the log odd ratio *LNODDS* when the estimated frequency is 0, the frequency *CONFRE* has been fixed arbitrarily close to 1 and to 0, respectively, subtracting and adding, respectively, the approximation coefficient *APPROX*.

The solution to Question 6 is given in Table 12A3.7.

12A3.7   Estimated parameters of max WTP probability function by OLS

Variables	bTICKET	CONSTA
Parameters	–0.000235	2.498185
Std errors	0.000017	0.217060
R^2/ Std error$\hat{Y}$	0.985164	0.121966
F-test /DGF	99.607117	3.000000
Regr. SS/Resid. SS	2.963441	0.044627
T-ratios	–13.917	11.509

The solutions to Questions 7 and 8 are reported in Table 12A3.8.

Table 12A3.8   Mean and median max WTP

Mean max WTP	10,989
Median max WTP	10,652

Having obtained the point estimates of the maximum WTP of individuals, the analysis is usually extended by calculating confidence intervals for those measures, to gain some insight into the reliability of the estimates. Attempts have been made to derive confidence intervals analytically (Cameron 1991), but the usual practice is to apply Monte Carlo based approaches and bootstrapping techniques, which basically amount to generating repeated random samples using the available data and calculating the measures of WTP for each sample to obtain an empirical distribution of the WTP estimate.[8] A good review and comparison of approaches for the calculation of confidence intervals for WTP from dichotomous choice CVM can be found in Cooper (1994).

Discussion and Comparison with Another Estimating Technique

The data utilized for the previous exercises, reported in Table 12A3.9, have also been used to estimate the logit model by maximizing the logarithm of the likelihood function. This is frequently done in practical work where suitable econometric packages are commonly available.[9] To be more consistent with economic theory, income has been added as an explanatory variable of the probability of obtaining a positive answer.

Table 12A3.9   Database for dichotomous choice contingent valuation

NUMOBS	INCOME (Monetary Units – millions)	TICKET (Monetary Units)	ACCEPT
1	75	3,000	1
2	25	8,000	1
3	75	18,000	0
4	55	13,000	1
5	8	23,000	0
6	15	3,000	1
7	75	3,000	1
8	25	18,000	0
9	35	18,000	0
10	35	13,000	0
11	15	18,000	0
12	15	23,000	0
13	25	18,000	1
14	35	23,000	0
15	25	8,000	0
16	15	3,000	1
17	25	3,000	1
18	35	23,000	0
19	35	23,000	0
20	15	13,000	0
21	25	8,000	1
22	25	13,000	0
23	35	13,000	1
24	35	8,000	1
25	25	13,000	0
26	15	18,000	0
27	15	23,000	0
28	45	3,000	1
29	8	8,000	0
30	15	8,000	1
Sample mean	30.200	13,000	0.43

The results of the logit estimation of the linear utility model by maximum likelihood are reported in Table 12A3.10. The *t*-ratio on the variable *TICKET*, the price of the ticket, is very high, showing a high explanatory power of this variable with respect to the decision whether to pay the entrance fee or not. To improve the adaptation of the model the explanatory variable *INCOME* is added. However, as shown by the *t*-ratio, this does not appear to be statistically significant. Notice that the sign of *bTICKET* is negative because the variable *TICKET* was introduced in the database with a positive sign.

Table 12A3.10   Estimated parameters of the linear utility model by maximum likelihood

	CONSTA	*bTICKET*	*bINCOME*
Parameters	2.92555	–0.000389	0.049838
t-ratios	1.838	–2.619	1.333

The mean maximum WTP is calculated with the formula illustrated in Annex 12A2. For the calculation of the mean maximum WTP, the income is set at the sample mean value.

$$E(\max\ \text{WTP}) \approx \frac{1}{-bTICKET} * \ln\left[\exp(CONSTA + bINCOME * \mu INCOME) + 1\right],$$

where *bTICKET* and *bINCOME* are the estimated parameters referring, respectively, to the variables *TICKET* and *INCOME* and $\mu INCOME$ is the sample mean of the variable *INCOME*. Therefore:

$$E(\max \text{WTP}) \approx \frac{1}{0.000389} * \ln\left[\exp(2.92555 + 0.049838 * 30.2) + 1\right] = 11,420.$$

The median, for the linear utility model (see Annex 12A2), is:

$$\text{Me(WTP)} = (CONSTA + bINCOME * \mu INCOME)/-bTICKET$$

Therefore:

$$\text{Me(WTP)} = (2.92555 + 0.049838 * 30.2)/0.000389 = 11,390.$$

Note that the estimated mean and median maximum WTP are not far from those obtained in the previous exercise, where the logit model was estimated by weighted least squares.

As mentioned in the introduction, this exercise is based largely on the approach suggested by Hanemann (1984, 1989), the so-called single bounded approach based on a random utility model.[10] A slightly different approach, introduced by Cameron (1988) bypasses the utility function entirely. It claims that the estimation of the parameters of the inverse Hicksian demand function is directly and much simply obtainable by the referendum data. This approach somehow bypasses the practical limitations in computation, which arise by directly dealing with utility functions for inferring welfare measures. The results, however, are not materially different from those presented above.

In addition to these attempts to simplify the theoretical framework of CVM, some significant improvements have been introduced in CVM with the use of the so-called 'double bounded' approach, introduced by Carson et al.(1986). In a double bounded approach, respondents are asked a two-step question concerning their WTP. After the initial usual question regarding their willingness to pay a given amount of money, a follow-up question is introduced. If the answer to the first question is positive, the amount proposed is increased to a higher value and the question is asked again. If the answer to the first question is negative, the amount is reduced to a lower value and the question is asked again. The analyst is therefore able to put each respondent in one of the following categories: (i) Yes–Yes; (ii) Yes–No; (iii) No–No; (iv) No–Yes. The second question enables the analyst to narrow the interval of the true WTP. As shown in Hanemann et al. (1991), this approach improves the efficiency of the estimated parameters of the WTP, leading to more reliable estimates of the true WTP of individuals.[11]

The individual WTP estimates elicited with the dichotomous choice format CVM for the sample can be extrapolated across the whole population. If the WTP/WTA models include some socioeconomic characteristics of the individuals, it is possible to estimate the maximum WTP or minimum WTA for different social groups and to use this information also when calculating the aggregate WTP or WTA. In some cases, the values obtained by CVM studies can be compared with estimates obtained using different techniques. If a capital value is required, the total annual values obtained can be discounted and aggregated.

Notes

1. The reader is advised to go through the previous exercise before starting the present one, in order to understand the welfare implications of dichotomous response models and the usefulness of estimating a probability distribution of the maximum WTP.
2. In practice most studies apply MLE for logit models. The present exercise can be seen as an introduction to the use of such models. The results of the estimation by MLE are also reported for comparison and discussion. An interesting review of the main econometric issues in dichotomous CVM can be found in Hazilla (1999).
3. This is denoted by the variable Z described in Annex 12A4.

4. For example, LIMDEP is a useful tool for logit analysis.
5. The full algebra of this step is as follows:

$$1 - P_i = \frac{1}{1 + \exp\left[(CONSTA - \beta TICKET * TICKET_i)\right]} \Rightarrow \frac{P_i}{1 - P_i} = \frac{1 + \exp(CONSTA - \beta TICKET * TICKET_i)}{1 + \exp\left[-(CONSTA - \beta TICKET * TICKET_i)\right]}$$

$$= \frac{1 + \exp(CONSTA - \beta TICKET * TICKET_i)}{1 + \dfrac{1}{\exp(CONSTA - \beta TICKET * TICKET_i)}} = \frac{1 + \exp(CONSTA - \beta TICKET * TICKET_i)}{\dfrac{\exp(CONSTA - \beta TICKET * TICKET_i) + 1}{\exp(CONSTA - \beta TICKET * TICKET_i)}}$$

$$= 1 + \exp(CONSTA - \beta TICKET * TICKET_i) \frac{\exp\left[(CONSTA - \beta TICKET * TICKET_i)\right]}{\exp\left[(CONSTA - \beta TICKET * TICKET_i)\right] + 1} \Rightarrow$$

$$\frac{P_i}{1 - P_i} = \exp(CONSTA - \beta TICKET * TICKET_i).$$

6. Heteroscedasticity is a case where the variance of the random term is not independent of one or more of the explanatory variables. In such cases the estimates of the parameters are not efficient – they are larger variances than can be obtained by other methods. In this case there is heteroscedasticity and so a WLS estimate is used to provide efficient estimators.
7. To aid this exercise, the spreadsheet CVMDICH1.XLS contains the data set. The answers are shown on the spreadsheet CVMDICH2.XLS.
8. Some of these are extensions and adaptations of the Krinsky and Robb (1986) method for calculating confidence intervals of estimated elasticities, which can be complex non-linear functions of estimated parameters (see, for example, Park et al. 1991).
9. An example of a package that can be used for this type of model is LIMDEP.
10. Random utility models were originally established by McFadden (1976).
11. An approach for measuring the goodness of fit of double bounded logit models can be found in Kanninen and Khawaja (1995).

ANNEX 12A4   DICHOTOMOUS AND POLICHOTOMOUS LOGIT MODELS

Individuals have attitudes that cannot be directly observed and measured. The basic idea underlying logit models is that there is an unobservable (latent) variable, say Z, which expresses the intensity of these attitudes. This latent variable can be explained by a vector of independent variables, say $\mathbf{X}$, weighted by a vector of parameters, say b, plus a random component e with a given probability distribution, that is, by the model:

$$Z_i = b'X_i + e_i.$$

What is observable, besides the realizations of the independent variables, is a dichotomous or polichotomous variable, say Y, that is somehow linked to the latent variable and assumes different values when the unobserved variable falls in different ranges. The different responses that individuals give to specific questions allow the effects of this dichotomous/polichotomous variable to be observed.[1]

Box 12A4.1 gives the specification of the model in the case of a four-category polichotomous variable, and the expression of the probabilities of every category, given the distribution function of the random component of the underlying response model.

Consider a dichotomous choice or a 'take it or leave it' question, for example, whether one is willing or not to pay an entrance fee for a visit to a natural park. Suppose Z is the latent variable reflecting the propensity of the individual to accept paying for the entrance fee. Z_i is specified as above, as a function of some observable variables $\mathbf{X}$ plus a random component U: $Z_i = b'X_i + e_i$. Among the right-hand-side variables, the most important variable that explains the propensity to accept is the amount of the entrance fee. Income, socioeconomic features and site features can also play an important role. The dichotomous choice model becomes: $Z_i \leq 0$, then $Y_i = 0$ (the refusal of payment is observed, the dichotomous variable Y takes value 0); $Z_i > 0$, then $Y_i = 1$ (the acceptance of payment is observed, the dichotomous variable Y takes value 1). When $Z_i \leq 0$, $bX_i + e_i \leq 0$, that is, $e_i \leq -bX_i$; when $Z_i > 0$, $bX_i + e_i > 0$, that is, $e_i > bX_i$.

The probability that a negative occurs, that is, the probability of $Y = 0$, is the probability $e_i \leq -bX_i$, that is:

$$p(Y = 0) = p(U_i \leq -bX_i).$$

If we assume that U_i is a random variable with a logistic cumulative probability, the probability distribution of a refusal is given by the formula below, that is, the logistic distribution function:

BOX 12A4.1 EXAMPLE OF SPECIFICATION OF MODEL WITH FOUR-CATEGORY POLICHOTOMOUS VARIABLES

Observed polichotomous variable	Ranges for latent variable	Substitution of the model	Ranges for the error term
$Y = 0$	$Z < = 0$	$b''X + e < = 0$	$e < = b'X$
$Y = 1$	$0 < Z < = m1$	$0 < (b'X + e) < m1$	$-b'X < e < = m1 - b'X$
$Y = 2$	$m1 < Z < = m2$	$m1 < (b'X + e) < m2$	$m1 - b'X < e < = m2 - b'X$
$Y = 3$	$m2 < Z$	$m2 < b'X + e$	$-e < (b'X - m2),$ i.e.: $e > (m2 - b'X)$

Probability of the observable variable intervals	Probability of error term	Cumulative probability distribution functi
$P(Y = 0) =$	$P(u < -b'X) =$	$F(-b'X)$
$P(Y = 1) =$	$P[-b'X < u < = (m1 - b'X)] =$	$F(m1 - b'X) - F(-b'X)$
$P(Y = 2) =$	$P[m1 - b'X) < u < = (m2 - b'X)] =$	$F(m2 - b'X) - F(m1 - b'X)$
$P(Y = 3) =$	$P[u > (m2 - b'X)] =$	$1 - F(m2 - b'X)$

Logistic cumulative distribution function for u.

$$F(-b'X) = \exp(-b'X) / [1 + \exp(-b'X)] = 1/[1 + \exp(b'X)])$$

$$p(e_i \le -b'X_i) = 1/[1 + \exp(b'X_i)].$$

The probability that the individual accepts, that is, $p(Y_i = 1)$ is given by:

$$p(e_i > -b'X_i) = 1 - 1/[1 + \exp(b'X_i)].$$

The coefficients b' can be estimated with the maximum likelihood method using suitable software, for example, LIMDEP. Once these parameters have been estimated it is possible to describe how the probability of acceptance varies with respect to the level of the entrance fee required and measures of the maximum individual WTP for the good under analysis can be estimated.

Note

1. For a complete and exhaustive treatment of qualitative dependent variable models, see, for example, Maddala (1983).

ANNEX 12A5   MEAN AND MEDIAN MAXIMUM WTP IN THE LINEAR UTILITY DIFFERENCE MODEL

The mean of the maximum WTP can be calculated using the formula that relates the mean of a random variable to its probability distribution:

$$E(WTP) = \int_0^\infty [1 - G(t)]\,dt - \int_{-\infty}^0 G(t)\,dt.$$

Where the second term of the right-hand side is relatively small, it may be ignored. In such circumstances, the expected maximum WTP is:

$$E(WTP) = \int_0^\infty [1 - G(t)]\,dt = \int_0^\infty \left[1 - 1 + \frac{1}{1 + \exp[-(c - \beta t)]}\right] dt = \int_0^\infty \left[\frac{1}{1 + \exp[-(c - \beta t)]}\right] dt.$$

This integral can be solved by substitution, calling $\exp[-(c - \beta t)] = z$:

$$-(c - \beta t) = \ln(z) \Rightarrow t = 1/\beta \ln(z) + c/\beta \Rightarrow dt/dz = 1/\beta z \Rightarrow dt = dz/\beta z.$$

Therefore , the indefinite integral becomes:

$$\int \frac{1}{1 + \exp[-(c - \beta t)]}\,dt = \frac{1}{\beta} \int \frac{1}{z(1 + z)}\,dz = \int \left[\frac{1}{z} - \frac{1}{1 + z}\right] dz$$

$$= \frac{1}{\beta} \int \frac{1}{z}\,dz - \frac{1}{\beta} \int \frac{1}{1 + z}\,dz$$

$$= \frac{1}{\beta} \ln(z) - \frac{1}{\beta} \ln \frac{1}{1 + z} = \frac{1}{\beta} \ln \frac{z}{1 + z}.$$

Substituting back $\exp[-(c - bt)]$ to z leads to:

$$\frac{1}{\beta} \ln \frac{\exp[-(c - \beta t)]}{1 + \exp[-(c - \beta t)]} = \frac{1}{\beta} \ln \frac{1}{\exp(c - \beta t + 1)}.$$

The integral above becomes therefore:

$$\frac{1}{\beta}\left[\ln\frac{1}{\exp(c-\beta t)+1}\right]_0^\infty = \frac{1}{\beta}\lim_{k\to\infty}\left[\ln\frac{1}{\exp(c-\beta t)+1}\right]_0^k$$

$$= \frac{1}{\beta}\lim_{k\to\infty}\left[\ln\frac{1}{\exp(c-\beta k)+1} - \ln\frac{1}{\exp(c)+1}\right]$$

$$\Rightarrow E(WTP) = \frac{1}{\beta}\ln[\exp(c)+1].$$

Note that, when the upper bound of integration is set at the maximum entrance fee asked in the survey, and this upper bound is 'sufficiently' high, the mean WTP is approximated by the formula below:

$$E(WTP) \approx \frac{1}{\beta}\left[\ln\frac{1}{\exp(c-\beta t)+1}\right]_0^{t_{max}} = \frac{1}{\beta}\ln\frac{\exp(c)+1}{\exp(c-\beta t_{max})+1}.$$

An alternative measure of the WTP is the median (Me) of the distribution, that is, the value of the WTP such that there is a 50 per cent probability of finding an individual with a maximum WTP lower than it. The median is worked out by imposing the probability distribution equal to 0.5 and solving for Me.

$$P(\max WTP \le Me) \equiv G(Me) = 1 - \frac{1}{1+\exp[-(c-\beta Me)]} = 0.5 \Rightarrow \frac{1}{1+\exp[-(c-\beta Me)]}$$

$$= 0.5 \Rightarrow \frac{1}{1+\exp[-(c-\beta t)]} = 0.5 \Rightarrow 1+\exp[-(c-\beta Me)] = 2 \Rightarrow \exp[-(c-\beta Me)] = 1 \Rightarrow [-(c-\beta Me)]$$

$$= 0 \Rightarrow -c+\beta Me = 0 \Rightarrow Me = \frac{c}{\beta}.$$

13. Use of monetary values of environmental and natural resources for benefit–cost analysis: an application to a soil moisture conservation project in Tunisia

OBJECTIVE

This chapter develops a step-by-step exercise using benefit–cost analysis (BCA), extended to environmental externalities (positive and negative). It encourages the reader to apply all the steps of a financial and economic BCA by supplying a working framework that can be used as a reference point in more complex actual analysis.

SUMMARY

A simplified version of a real project analysis carried out in Tunisia is used. After a presentation of the context of the project, the data set and issues to be addressed are supplied. The questions are designed to guide the reader through the process of calculation. The solution set shows the methods of presenting cash flows of environmental costs and benefits and techniques to calculate profitability indicators. It points out the usefulness of economic valuation techniques in incorporating environmental externalities in project analysis. The productivity change method and the contingent valuation method are used to place an economic value on environmental impacts. Finally the exercise highlights the contribution of extended cost–benefit analysis towards enhancing the decision-making process.

13. Use of monetary values of environmental and natural resources for benefit-cost analysis: an application to a soil moisture conservation project in Tunisia

13.1 BACKGROUND

This exercise is a simplified version of a soil moisture conservation project in Tunisia,[1] as illustrated in Figure 13.1. It is based on one of the watersheds considered in the original study, and has been freely adapted for illustrative purposes. Two valuation techniques have been used to show how environmental impacts can be accounted for in project appraisals: (i) the productivity change method (PCM); and (ii) the contingent valuation method (CVM). The first method has been used to estimate the value of the soil moisture conservation effect of the contour-ditches action; the second in the estimation of the value of reduced risk of floods due to the implementation of the project.

The watershed analysed in this exercise covers about 154,000 hectares and is closed in the lower part by a dam, creating a reservoir of about 78 million m^3. Sedimentation of the reservoirs is one of the most pressing problems of the watershed. Erosive processes, similar to those in many other parts of Tunisia, are widespread. More than 75 per cent of the soils in the watershed have physical characteristics and slopes that make them subject to a high rate of erosion. Agricultural lands must therefore be carefully protected, and this explains why most of the corrective action consists of soil and water conservation, as shown in Table 13.1.

Table 13.1 Actions and related quantities (1 TD = 1 US$)

Actions	Investment period (years)	Quantities involved per year	Unit investment cost (TD)	Total cost per year (TD)
1 Terracing	10	750 ha	373 TD/ha	279,750
2 Retaining walls	10	400 ha	500 TD/ha	200,000
3 Contour ditches	10	300 ha	140 TD/ha	42,000
4 Fruit trees plantations	10	296 ha	780 TD/ha	230,880
5 Forage trees plantations	10	600 ha	790 TD/ha	402,000
6 Range improvement	10	1,000 ha	196 TD/ha	670,000
7 Protective plantations	10	600 ha	670 TD/ha	402,000
8 Small reservoirs	4	1 unit	150,000 TD/unit	150,000
9 Landslide fixation	10	17,200 m^3	18 TD/m^3	309,600
10 Watercourse management works	10	7,000 m^3	63 TD/m^3	441,000

Note: TD = Tunisian dynars.

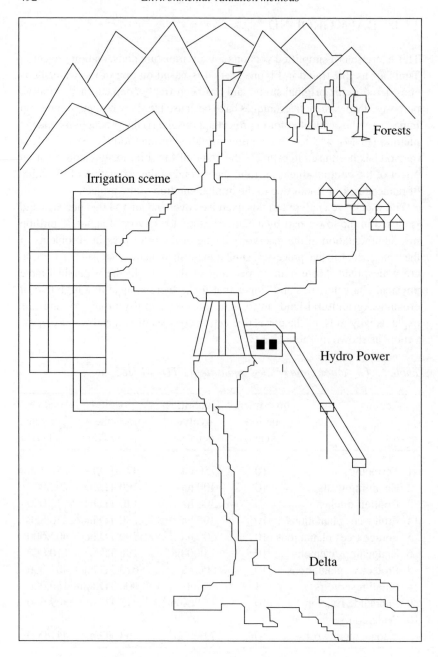

*Figure 13.1   Schematic view of the soil moisture conservation project in
            Tunisia*

The project area covers 40,000 hectares *of highly erodible lands*, and represents about 25 per cent of the total watershed area.

13.2   METHODOLOGY

In order to develop the BCA of this project, the following steps have been considered:

1. *Identifying environmental impacts of each component of the project.*   This activity required the cooperation of experts of various disciplines, both local and international, and ended with the preparation of a check-list of first-order and higher-order impacts.[2] These impacts were then subdivided into on-site and off-site effects.
2. *Quantifying impacts.*   Much of the study was devoted to gathering data and measuring the environmental impacts in physical terms. Both activities encountered some difficulty because of lack of data and, sometimes, lack of sufficient scientific knowledge and methodologies for measuring environmental impacts. Where data and methodologies were missing, proxies were used based on the specialized literature or on studies carried out in countries with similar conditions.
3. *Evaluating environmental impacts.*   The impacts were subdivided into market and non-market effects. Market effects were taken to be impacts that give rise to goods and/or services for which values could be obtained by the observation of market prices. Non-market effects were taken to be impacts that give rise to goods/services for which no market prices are observable; the most appropriate valuation techniques were selected for placing a monetary value on these.
4. *Creating cash flow statements.*   Once the environmental impacts and the other cost and benefits component of the project were measured in monetary terms, the cash flow statements were created taking account of the accrual time of each monetary cost or benefit.
5. *Discounting.*   In BCA the analyst must consider the different value of money accruing at different points in time. This aspect was taken into account by discounting the monetary flows[3] and calculating indicators of project viability.

The main purpose of this exercise is to demonstrate the techniques used in developing a cash flow for a project and the methods used in estimating the main profitability indicators in project analysis. Therefore, only one component has been considered – the creation of contour ditches. The benefits of this component accruing to farmers as a result of the increased availability of water and the increased soil fertility have been measured applying the productivity change method.[4] However, as such intervention also leads to a reduced risk of downstream floods, the flows of such positive externalities have been included in the analysis. These were estimated using the contingent valuation method using the dichotomous choice approach.

13.2.1   Productivity Change

As far as the productivity changes induced by the project are concerned, the following assumptions were made:

- Changes in the output of fruit trees will not affect output prices. Thus the welfare effects of the change in environmental service can be captured as the change in the producer surplus (see Chapter 9).
- It has been assumed that contour ditches would allow for an increase in water availability in the soil of 13 per cent and at the same time they would allow for an increase in the natural fertility of the soil.

Then, the increased benefits due to the intervention were estimated in five steps:

1. A functional relationship was defined for each fruit tree between the yields of fruit trees, the supply of water and natural fertility. The functional relationship is of the form:

$$Y = f(W, NF),$$

   where Y represents the yields; W represents the amount of water available; and NF represents the natural fertility of soil.
2. Subsequently, the elasticity of yields with respect to increased water availability were estimated using regression analysis on observed data. The responsiveness of crop yields to increases in natural fertility was also estimated using dummy variables associated with three different levels of observed soil fertility.
3. The estimated elasticities were then used to calculate the cumulative effect of water availability and natural fertility increases on yields, by multiplying the yields of fruit trees observed in the situation without contour ditches by the percentage level of water change and changes in natural fertility.
4. On the assumption that contour ditches would also have a beneficial impact on soil conservation and therefore on soil fertility, the yields of the second and third years have been increased by applying the estimated coefficients of soil fertility. Figure 13.2 illustrates the approach followed.

5. The value of the beneficial effects of the construction of contour ditches on soil and moisture conservation is calculated by measuring the value of the increased output of fruit trees due to increased water availability and natural fertility.

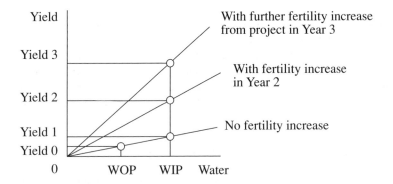

Legend: WOP   = Quantity of water available without project
         WIP   = Quantity of water available with project
         Yield 0 = Yield without project
         Yield 1 = Yield in year 1 (with no fertility increase)
         Yield 2 = Yield in year 2 (with fertilty increase)
         Yield 3 = Yield in year 3 (with further fertility increase)

Figure 13.2   Production function of fruit trees versus water for different levels of soil fertility

13.2.2   Contingent Valuation

It was assumed that without the implementation of the project, erosion and silti-fication would be responsible for floods occurring on average every ten years, as has happened in the past. The damages due to floods were substantial both in terms of destruction of crops and houses, and loss of human life. With the implementation of the project, it was assumed that floods would be eliminated.

To estimate these benefits, the analysts used the CVM approach with a dichotomous choice elicitation format, to avoid strategic biases. They selected a sample of households living in the area subject to floods and asked them if they were willing to pay a proposed amount of money to prevent floods from occurring. The payment vehicle chosen was a lump-sum annual tax paid by individuals.

Given this basic information the following exercise takes the reader through the BCA, in stages, and provides some discussion of the results.

13.3 EXERCISE: CASE STUDY OF THE BCA FOR THE TUNISIA SOIL MOISTURE CONSERVATION PROJECT

13.3.1 Data and Questions for Financial Analysis

The data, as presented in Tables 13.2 and 13.3, have been collected by the analyst in order to run the financial analysis of the project. The building of contour ditches will occur at the beginning of the project (Year 0) over the entire project area. The project is assumed to have a life span of five years. It is assumed that after such a period no residual benefits and costs are left. At the end of the project, in order to replicate the same stream of net benefits, the whole project must be replicated.

Table 13.2   Per hectare quantities of inputs and unit cost of inputs

Description	Unskilled labour (man/day)	Skilled labour (man/day)	Tractors and equipment (hours)	Plant (number)	Other materials
(a) Physical quantities of input per ha	40	8	1	5	1
(b) Unit prices of inputs (TD)	4	6	80	9	40

Using the information provided answer the following questions:[5]

1. Calculate the yields for the different trees in Years 1 to 5. (Hints: use the percentage change in water supply and the elasticities of yields to water provided in Table 13.2 for calculating the yields of Year 1. Apply the natural fertility increase factor to the yields of Year 1 to obtain yields in Year 2. Apply again this factor to the yields in Year 2 to obtain those of Year 3. From Year 3 to Year 5 the yields are assumed to be constant.)
2. Calculate the cost per hectare of contour ditches building and the total cost of the investment in Year 0.
3. Calculate the value of the output of the agricultural activities in Years 1 to 5 and their operating costs in the situation *with* project (Hint: work out the physical output for the project area using the appropriate yields and apply the prices provided in the data set.)
4. Calculate the value of the output of the agricultural activities in Years 1 to 5 and their operational costs in the situation *without* project.
5. Estimate the annual net cash flow *with* project from Years 0 to 5 (Hint: include both the cost of contour ditches building, and the operating costs and

Table 13.3 Yields, prices and operational costs (dynamic) of agricultural products on areas affected by the building of contour ditches

Species of tree	Area (ha) (a)	Yields Y0 (kg/ha) (b)	Yields Y1 (kg/ha) (c)	Yields Y2 (kg/ha) (d)	Yields Y3 to 5 (kg/ha) (e)	Unit price of output (TD/kg). (f)	Per hectare op. charges (g)
Olive	2,000	1,660	1,743	1,830	2,000	0.24	160
Almond	400	2,500	2,625	2,756	3,000	0.45	260
Apricot	300	416	437	459	500	1.50	150
Pistachio nut	300	290	305	320	500	4.00	150
Total hectares	3,000						

revenues of the agricultural activities. Assume the costs and revenues as accruing at the end of every period.)

6. Estimate the annual net cash flow *without* project from Years 0 to 5.
7. Determine the net incremental cash flow of the project.
8. Discount the net incremental cash flow of the project, calculate the Financial Net Present Value (FNPV) at 10 per cent discount rate, the Financial Internal Rate of Return (FIRR) and the Financial Benefit–Cost atio (FBCR).

13.3.2   Data and Questions for Economic Analysis

To run the economic analysis of the project the following shadow project conversion factors have been collected and are shown in Table 13.4.

Table 13.4   Conversion factors for economic analysis

Items	Conversion factor
Olive trees	1.02
Almond trees	1.02
Apricot trees	1.02
Pistachio nut trees	1.02
Unskilled labour	0.85
Skilled labour	0.90
Tractors/equipment services	0.98
Seedlings	0.95
Other agricultural materials	0.95
Other agricultural operating charges	0.95

Using the data provided in Tables 13.2, 13.3 and 13.4, answer the following questions:

9. Calculate the economic prices of the inputs, factors and outputs of the project.
10. Using the economic prices and following the same path indicated by the questions for the financial analysis, calculate the Economic Net Present Value (ENPV), the Economic Internal Rate of Return (EIRR) and the Economic Benefit–Cost Ratio (EBCR).

13.3.3   Data and Questions for Extended Economic Analysis

The existence of positive externalities of the project to downstream populations, in terms of eliminated risks of floods, led the analysts to extend the economic analysis including externalities. To evaluate them in monetary terms a Dichotomous Choice Contingent Valuation Method (CVMDC) had to be applied. To this extent the data on the annual individual willingness to pay (WTP) to avoid floods have been collected through a survey. The payment vehicle suggested was an annual tax. The results are reported in Table 13.5.

Table 13.5   Database for dichotomous choice contingent valuation

NUMOBS	ANNTAX	ACCEPT
1	1.00	1
2	2.67	1
3	6.00	0
4	4.33	1
5	7.67	0
6	1.00	1
7	1.00	1
8	6.00	0
9	6.00	0
10	4.33	0
11	6.00	0
12	7.67	0
13	6.00	1
14	7.67	0
15	2.67	0
16	1.00	1
17	1.00	1
18	7.67	0
19	7.67	0
20	4.33	0
21	2.67	1
22	4.33	0
23	4.33	1
24	2.67	1
25	4.33	0
26	6.00	0
27	7.67	0
28	1.00	1
29	2.67	0
30	2.67	1

Individuals affected by floods 68,000

The variable *NUMOBS* refers to the number of the observation; the variable *ANNTAX* is the annual payment asked of the interviewee; the variable *ACCEPT* is a dichotomous variable reporting the acceptance (*ACCEPT* = 1) or refusal (*ACCEPT* = 0) to pay the proposed annual charge. Table 13.5 also indicates the number of individuals likely to be affected by a flood.

Using data provided in Tables 13.2 to 13.5, answer the following questions:

11. Calculate the median individual annual maximum WTP to avoid the floods. (Hint: follow the procedure applying descriptive statistics outlined in Chapter 11.)
12. Estimate the total annual external benefits of the project. (Hint: they are measured by the median individual annual maximum WTP times the number of individuals affected by floods.)
13. Calculate the extended economic net present value (EENPV), the extended economic internal rate of return (EEIRR) and the extended economic benefit–cost ratio (EEBCR). (Hints: Add the flow of the annual external benefits to the economic cash flow statement and rework the above project indicators as done in the financial and economic analysis.)

13.4 SOLUTION SET

13.4.1 Solutions for the Financial Analysis

This section presents the answers to questions 1 to 8 above, with a step-by-step guide to the method used.

Question 1

The yields for the different fruit trees are reported in Table 13.6. Notice that the yields in Year 1 are calculated as follows:

$$Y_{i1} = E(Y, w) * \Delta W/W * Y_{i0},$$

where:

y_{i1}	=	Yield in year 1
$E(Y, w)$	=	Elasticity of the yield with respect to water
$\Delta W/W$	=	Percentage change in the availability of water
Y_{i0}	=	Yield in year 0 (without project).

The yields in Year 2 are calculated as follows:

$$Y_{i2} = Y_{i1} * FF,$$

where:

Y_{i2}	=	Yield in year 2
Y_{i1}	=	Yield in year 1
FF	=	Fertility factor

The yields in Year 3 are calculated as for Year 2 and those for Years 3 to 5 are assumed equal to those in Year 3.

Table 13.6   Estimated yields for different fruit-trees

Species of tree	Area (hectares) (a)	Yields Y0 (kg/ha) (b)	Yields Y1 (kg/ha) (c)	Yields Y2 (kg/ha) (d)	Yields Y2 to 5 (kg/ha) (e)
Olive	2 000	1 660	1 930	1 968	2 008
Almond	400	2 500	2 809	2 865	2 922
Apricot	300	416	475	485	495
Pistachio nuts	300	290	322	328	335
Total hectares	3 000				

Question 2

The cost per hectare of contour ditches and the total cost of the investment in Year 0 is calculated and reported in Table 13.7.

Table 13.7   Cost per hectare of contour ditches and the total cost of investment in Year 0

Description	Unskilled labour (man/day)	Skilled labour (man/day)	Tractors and equipment (hours)	Seedlings (number)	Other materials	Total
(a) Physical quantities of input per ha	40	8	1	5	1	
(b) Unit prices of inputs (TD)	5	7	80	9	40	
(c) Cost per ha (a*b) (TD)	200	56	80	45	40	421
(d) Total ha						3,000
(e) Total cost of the investment (thousand TD) (c*d/1000)						1,263

Question 3

The output in physical terms, the output value and the total operating costs *with* project are then calculated. These are reported in Table 13.8.

Question 4

The output in physical terms, the output value and the total operating costs *without* project are calculated and reported in Table 13.9.

Question 5

Table 13.10 reports the net financial cash flows *with* the project. Note that both the investment costs and the operating costs are compared with the operating benefits.

Question 6

The net financial cash flows *without* project are calculated and reported in Table 13.11.

Question 7

The incremental net financial cash flows are calculated as the difference between the net financial cash flows *with* project and the net financial cash flows *without* project. The incremental net financial cash flows are reported in Table 13.12.

Table 13.8 Output in physical terms, output value and total operating costs with project

Species of tree	Area (ha) (a)	Yields Y0 (kg/ha) (b)	Yields Y1 (kg/ha) (c)	Yields Y2 (kg/ha) (d)	Yields Y3 to 5 (kg/ha) (e)	Unit price of the product (f)	Per ha operating cost (g)
Olive	2,000	1,660	1,930	1,968	2,008	0.19	160
Almond	400	2,500	2,809	2,865	2,922	0.40	260
Apricot	300	416	475	485	495	1.30	150
Pistachio nuts	300	290	322	328	335	3.50	150

Species of tree	Physical output (metric tons)			Output value (thousand TD)			Operating cost (th.TD)
	$Y1$ $(h = a*c)$	$Y2$ $(i = a*d)$	$Y3\text{–}5$ $(j = a*e)$	$Y1$ $(k = f*h)$	$Y2$ $(l = f*i)$	$Y3\text{–}5$ $(m = f*j)$	$Y1\text{–}5$ $(n = a*g)$
Olive	3,860	3,937	4,015	733	748	763	320
Almond	1,124	1,146	1,169	449	458	468	104
Apricot	143	145	148	185	189	193	45
Pistachio nuts	97	99	101	338	345	352	45
Total output value and operating costs *with* project				1,706	1,740	1,775	514

Table 13.9 Output in physical terms, output value and total operating costs without project

Species of tree	Area (ha) (a)	Yields Y0 (kg/ha) (b)	Unit price of output (c)	Physical output (m. tons) (e = a*b)	Per ha operating cost (d)	Output value (th.TD) (f = d *c)	Operating costs (th.TD) (g = a * d)
Olive	2,000	1,660	0.19	3,320	160	631	320
Almond	400	2,500	0.40	1,000	260	400	104
Apricot	300	416	1.30	125	150	162	45
Pistachio nut	300	290	3.50	87	150	305	45
Total output value and operating costs *without* project						1,498	514

Table 13.10   Net financial cash flows with project (thousand TD)

Item	Year					
	0	1	2	3	4	5
Contour ditches building	−1,263	0	0	0	0	0
Output value of agricultural activities	0	1,706	1,740	1,775	1,775	1,775
Operating costs of agricultural activities	0	−514	−514	−514	−514	−514
Net cash flows *with* project	−1,263	1,192	1,226	1,261	1,261	1,261

Table 13.11   Net financial cash flows without project (thousands TD)

Item	Year					
	0	1	2	3	4	5
Contour ditches building	0	0	0	0	0	0
Output value of agricultural activities	0	1,498	1,498	1,498	1,498	1,498
Operating costs of agricultural activities	0	−514	−514	−514	−514	−514
Net flows *without* project	0	984	984	984	984	984

Table 13.12   Incremental net financial cash flows (thousands TD)

Item	Year					
	0	1	2	3	4	5
(a) Net cash flows *with* project	−1,263	1,192	1,226	1,261	1,261	1,261
(b) Net cash flows *without* project	0	984	984	984	984	984
(c = a − b) Incremental net cash flows	−1,263	209	243	278	278	278

Question 8

In Table 13.13 the incremental net financial cash flow is discounted using a discount rate of 10 per cent. A negative Financial Net present Value (FNPV) is obtained. This means that, for this opportunity cost of capital, the project is not worthwhile from a financial point of view. This view is confirmed by the Financial Internal Rate of Return (FIRR) which is found to be 0.5 per cent, much lower than the discount rate. Also, note that, as expected, the Financial Benefit Cost Ratio (FBCR), reported in Table 13.14, is below unity.

Table 13.13   Discounted incremental net financial cash flow, financial net present value and financial internal rate of return (thousands TD)

Item	Year					
	0	1	2	3	4	5
(a) Incremental net cash flow	−1,263	209	243	278	278	278
(b) Discount factors	1.00	0.909	0.826	0.751	0.683	0.621
(c) Discounted incremental net cash flow (a*b)	−1,263	190	201	209	190	172
Discount rate (%)	10.0					
Net present value	−302					
Internal rate of return (FIRR) (%)	0.5					

Table 13.14   Financial benefit–cost ratio (thousands TD)

Item	Year					
	0	1	2	3	4	5
(a) Incremental benefits	0	209	243	278	278	278
(b) Discount factors	1.00	0.91	0.83	0.75	0.68	0.62
(c) Discounted incremental benefits (c = a*b)	0	189.8	200.7	208.6	189.7	172.4
(d) Present value of incremental benefits	961.2					
(e) Incremental costs	−1,263.0	0	0	0	0	0
(f) Discount factors	1.00	0.91	0.83	0.75	0.68	0.62
(g) Discounted incremental costs (g = e*f)	−1,263.0	0	0	0	0	0
(h) Present value of incremental costs	−1,263.0					
(i) Benefit–cost ratio (BCR) (i = d/(−h))	0.761					

13.4.2   Solutions for Economic Analysis

Question 9
The economic prices of the inputs, factors and outputs of the project are reported in Table 13.15.

Question 10
The use of economic prices rather than financial ones changes the flows of benefits and costs of the project. In Table 13.16, the investment costs are based on economic prices. Comparing them with those in Table 13.7 shows them to be lower, due to the conversion factors of costs which are all below unity. The operating costs and benefits in Table 13.17 are based on economic prices.

Comparing these values with those of Table 13.8 shows that the value of output is greater and the costs are lower than those calculated using the financial analysis.

Table 13.15   Economic prices of inputs, factors and outputs of the project

Items	Financial prices (a)	Conversion factors (b)	Economic prices (c = a*b)
Olives (TD/kg)	0.19	1.02	0.19
Almonds (TD/kg)	0.40	1.02	0.41
Apricots (TD/kg)	1.30	1.02	1.33
Pistachio nuts (TD/kg)	3.50	1.02	3.57
Unskilled labour (TD/man/day)	5.0	0.85	4.25
Skilled labour (TD/man/day)	7.0	0.90	6.30
Tractors/equipment services (TD/hour)	80.0	0.88	70.40
Seedlings (TD/unit)	9.0	0.95	8.55
Other materials for contour ditches (TD/ha)	40.0	0.95	38.00
Other operating costs for olives (TD/ha)	160.0	0.95	152.00
Other operating costs for almonds (TD/ha)	260.0	0.95	247.00
Other operating costs for apricots (TD/ha)	150.0	0.95	142.50
Other operating costs for pistachio nuts (TD/ha)	150.0	0.95	142.50

Obviously, the flows without project also change when using economic prices, as shown in Table 13.18, compared with Table 13.9.

Tables 13.19 to 13.23 show the calculation of the economic project indicators, following the path already discussed for the financial analysis. Note that the project performance is increased when looked at from an economy-wide point of view. However, despite this, the project is still not viable, with an EIRR of 9.3 per cent against a cut-off value of 10 per cent.

13.4.3   Solutions for the 'Extended' Economic Analysis

Question 11

To run the 'extended' economic analysis the flows of the externalities of the project must be included. The median annual maximum WTP to avoid floods

Table 13.16 *Economic cost per hectare of contour ditches and the total economic costs of investment in year 0*

Description	Unskilled labour (man/day)	Skilled labour (man/day)	Tractors/equip (hours)	Seedlings (number)	Other materials	Totals
(a) Physical quantities of items per ha	40.00	8.00	1.00	5.00	1.00	
(b) Unit economic prices of items (TD)	4.25	6.30	70.40	8.55	38.00	
(c) Economic cost/ha Contour ditches (TD) = (a * b)	170	50	70	43	38	372
(d) Total hectares						3,000
(e) Total economic cost of the investment (thousand TD) = (c * d/1000)						1,115

Table 13.17 *Output in physical terms, economic value of output and total economic operating costs with project*

Species of tree	Area (ha) (a)	Yields Y0 (kg/ha) (b)	Yields Y1 (kg/ha) (c)	Yields Y2 (kg/ha) (d)	Yields Y3–5 (kg/ha) (e)	Unit economic price of the product (f)	Per ha economic operating cost (g)
Olive	2,000	1,660	1,930	1,968	2,008	0.194	152.0
Almond	400	2,500	2,809	2,865	2,922	0.408	247.0
Apricot	300	416	475	485	495	1.326	142.5
Pistachio nut	300	290	322	328	335	3.570	142.5

Species of tree	Physical output (metric tons)			Economic value of output (thousand TD)			Operating cost (th.TD)
	Y1 (h = a*c)	Y2 (i = a*d)	Y3–5 (j = a*e)	Y1 (k = f*h)	Y2 (l = f*i)	Y3 to 5 (m = f*j)	(Y1–5) (n = a*g)
Olive	3,860	3,937	4,015	748	763	778	304
Almond	1,124	1,146	1,169	458	468	477	99
Apricot	143	145	148	189	193	197	43
Pistachio nut	97	99	101	345	352	359	43
Total economic value of output and economic operating costs *with* project				1,740	1,775	1,811	488

Table 13.18 Output in physical terms: economic value of output and total economic operating costs without project

Species of tree	Area (ha) (a)	Yields Y0 (kg/ha) (b)	Unit price of output (c)	Per ha operating cost (d)	Physical output (m. tons) (e = a * b)	Output value (th.TD) (f = d * c)	Operating costs (th.TD) (g = a * d)
Olive	2,000	1,660	0.19	160	3,320	631	320
Almond	400	2,500	0.40	260	1,000	400	104
Apricot	300	416	1.30	150	125	162	45
Pistachio nut	300	290	3.50	150	87	305	45
Total economic value of output and economic operating costs *without* project						1,498	514

Table 13.19   Net Economic cash flows with project (thousands TD)

Item	Year					
	0	1	2	3	4	5
Contour ditches building (investment costs)	–1,115	0	0	0	0	0
Economic value of output	0	1,740	1,775	1,811	1,811	1,811
Operating costs of agricultural activities	0	–488	–488	–488	–488	–488
Net cash flows with project	–1,115	1,252	1,287	1,322	1,322	1,322

Table 13.20   Net economic cash flows without project (thousand TD)

Item	Year					
	0	1	2	3	4	5
Contour ditches building (investment costs)	0	0	0	0	0	0
Economic value of output	0	1,498	1,498	1,498	1,498	1,498
Operating costs of agricultural activities	0	–488	–488	–488	–488	–488
Net economic flows without project	0	1,009	1,009	1,009	1,009	1,009

Table 13.21   Incremental net economic cash flows (thousand TD)

Item	Year					
	0	1	2	3	4	5
(a) Net cash flows with project	–1,115	1,252	1,287	1,322	1,322	1,322
(b) Net cash flows without project	0	1,009	1,009	1,009	1,009	1,009
(c) Incremental net cash flow = (a–b)	–1,115	243	278	313	313	313

Table 13.22   Discounted incremental net economic cash flow, economic net present value and economic internal rate of return (thousands TD)

Item	Years					
	0	1	2	3	4	5
(a) Incremental net cash flow	–1,115	243	278	313	313	313
(b) Discount factors	1.00	0.909	0.826	0.751	0.683	0.621
(c) Discounted incremental net cash flow (=a * b)	–1,115	221	229	235	214	194
Discount rate (%)	10.0					
ENPV	–21					
EIRR (%)	9.3					

Table 13.23   Economic benefit–cost ratio (thousands TD)

Item		Years					
		0	1	2	3	4	5
(a) Incremental benefits		0	243	278	313	313	313
(b) Discount factors		1.00	0.91	0.83	0.75	0.68	0.62
(c) Discounted incremental benefits							
(c = a*b)		0	220.8	229.5	235.3	213.9	194.5
(d) Present value of incremental benefits	1,094.0						
(e) Incremental costs	−1,114.7	0	0	0	0	0	
(f) Discount factors	1.00	0.91	0.83	0.75	0.68	0.62	
(g) Discounted incremental costs (g = e*f)	−1,114.7	0	0	0	0	0	
(h) Present value of incremental costs	−1,114.7						
(i) EBCR (i = d/(−h))	0.981						

of individuals likely to be affected by them is assumed to be a measure of the annual benefit of flood avoidance accruing to an individual. The median annual individual maximum WTP has been calculated using data in Table 13.5, following the dichotomous choice CVM with descriptive statistics outlined in Chapter 12. It amounts to 2,666 Tunisian dynars per person.[6]

Question 12
To obtain the total benefits, this average individual measure has to be multiplied by the number of individuals likely to be affected by floods. Table 13.24 displays the calculation.

Table 13.24   Calculation of total annual benefits of flood prevention

(a) Individual annual max WTP for flood prevention (median, TD)	2.67
(b) Affected population by risk of floods	68,000
(c) Total annual benefits of flood prevention (Th. TD) (=a*b)	181.3

Question 13
Table 13.25 shows the cash flow statement *with* project with an additional positive flow of benefits due to the valuation of the elimination of the risk of floods.

Tables 13.26 to 13.29 present the calculation of extended economic project indicators, following the same path of the financial and economic analysis. Note that including the externalities in the project analysis means that the project becomes worthwhile.

Table 13.25 Annual net extended economic cash flows with project (thousand TD)

Item	Year					
	0	1	2	3	4	5
Contour ditches building (investment costs)	–1,115	0	0	0	0	0
Economic value of output	0	1,740	1,775	1,811	1,811	1,811
Operating costs of agricultural activities	0	–488	–488	–488	–488	–488
Total annual benefits of flood prevention	0	181	181	181	181	181
Net extended economic cash flows with project	–1,115	1,433	1,468	1,504	1,504	1,504

Table 13.26 Net extended economic cash flows without project (thousand TD)

Item	Year					
	0	1	2	3	4	5
Contour ditches building (investment costs)	0	0	0	0	0	0
Economic value of output	0	1,498	1,498	1,498	1,498	1,498
Operating costs of agricultural activities	0	–488	–488	–488	–488	–488
Net economic flows without project	0	1,009	1,009	1,009	1,009	1,009

Table 13.27 Incremental net extended economic cash flows (thousand TD)

Item	Year					
	0	1	2	3	4	5
(a) Net ext. ec. cash flows with project	–1,115	1,433	1,468	1,504	1,504	1,504
(b) Net ext. ec. cash flows without project	0	1,009	1,009	1,009	1,009	1,009
(c) Incremental net ext. ec. cash flow (= a–b)	–1,115	424	459	495	495	495

Table 13.28 Discounted incremental net extended economic cash flow, extended economic net present value and extended economic internal rate of return (thousand TD)

Item	Year					
	0	1	2	3	4	5
(a) Incremental net ext. ec. cash flow	–1,115	424	459	495	495	495
(b) Discount factors	1.00	0.909	0.826	0.751	0.683	0.621
(c) Discounted Incr. net ext. ec. cash flow (= a*b)	–1,115	386	379	372	338	307
Discount rate (%)	10.0					
EENPV	667					
EEIRR (%)	30.7					

Table 13.29   Extended economic benefit–cost ratio (thousand TD)

Item	Year					
	0	1	2	3	4	5
(a) Extended economic incremental benefits	0	424	459	495	495	495
(b) Discount factors	1.00	0.91	0.83	0.75	0.68	0.62
(c = a*b) Discounted ext. ec. increm. benefits		0	385.6	379.4	371.5	337.8	307.1
(d) Ext. ec. present value of increm. benefits	1,781.4					
(e) Extended economic incremental costs	–1,114.7	0	0	0	0	0
(f) Discount factors	1.00	0.91	0.83	0.75	0.68	0.62
(g = e*f) Discounted ext. ec. incremental costs	–1,114.7	0	0	0	0	0
(h) Ext. ec. present value of incremental costs	-1,114.7					
(i) EEBCR (i = d/(–h))	1.598					

13.5   DISCUSSION

The exercise above illustrates the case of a project appraisal, extended to include environmental impacts. A three-step framework has been used, consisting of financial analysis, economic analysis and extended economic analysis. In theory, the economic analysis should take account of all the possible adjustments for price distortions due to policy and market failures, including environmental externalities. However, the framework described above helps provide a better understanding of the difference between what is often named 'conventional' economic analysis and the 'extended' economic analysis. Conventional analysis accounts only for on-site effects and marketed goods and services, whereas the extended analysis also accounts for off-farm impacts and non-marketed goods and services.

From the various steps of the project appraisal, it can be concluded that from the financial point of view, it is not profitable to farmers to build contour ditches since the costs of undertaking this action are higher than the financial benefits obtained.

Although the economic analysis shows some improvement in the profitability of the action, the values of indicators remain very low and it is highly probable that alternative actions or projects would ensure a more efficient allocation of resources. The extended economic analysis provides more definitive answers to the decision makers in so far as the profitability indicators clearly show that the project would make the whole society better off.

The results obtained using CVM can be compared with those obtained with the damage costs technique. The damages to materials due to floods are estimated at about TD 1 million. We also know that the floods occur on average every ten years. Assuming that there is 100 per cent probability that they actually occur within ten years, we can calculate the present value of a such a cost accruing in one of the ten subsequent years, and compare it with the present value of the annuity flow of annual maximum WTP in the same time span. The CVM estimate of the annual value is TD 181.3 thousand. Hence, over ten years it would amount to TD 1.8 million, other things being equal. This is 80 per cent higher than the damage estimates, but that is quite plausible as the CVM includes a risk-aversion factor, not built into the damage estimates.

The possible policy implications of these results are that decision makers might consider some form of transfer of benefits from the social groups that benefit from the positive environmental externalities provided by way of flood eradication to the farmers who would bear the costs. In other words a subsidy may be envisaged to compensate the farmers for the service they provide to the whole community.

NOTES

1. Cesaro et al. (1997).
2. Assuming, for example, an action of landslide fixation, one possible first impact is the reduction of dam siltation which in turn (as a second-order impact) will have beneficial effects on yield and area increases in the irrigation scheme downstream, and subsequently third-order impacts on farmers' income.
3. The technique of discounting is illustrated in Section 8.7.
4. The productivity change method is outlined in Chapter 10.
5. For this exercise, the spreadsheet ANALPRO1.XLS can be used. Solutions are contained in the file ANALPRO2.XLS. A disk containing these files is available on request.
6. For the details of the calculation, see Chapter 12, Exercise 2, Annex 12A2.

CITED BIBLIOGRAPHY

Cesaro, L., V. Cistulli, M. Merlo and D. Pettenella (1997), 'Extended cost–benefit analysis: an application to the second forestry development and soil moisture conservation project in Tunisia', *Rivista di Economia Agraria*, **1–2**, pp. 61–89.

14. Use of monetary values of environmental and natural resources in the framework of national accounts: an application to Costa Rica

OBJECTIVE

This chapter aims to show how the valuation techniques presented in the previous chapters can be applied in a macroeconomic context. The utilization of the 'residual value' and 'travel cost' valuation techniques for macroeconomic adjustments is presented using a stepwise approach.

SUMMARY

The chapter starts with a review of some theoretical considerations regarding the measurement of the wealth produced by an economy. Some of the critical issues in this field are highlighted and basic macroeconomic identities presented. The necessity of adjusting the GDP for depreciation of both man-made capital and natural assets is pointed out. A case study concerning the above GDP adjustments in Costa Rica is presented.

14.1   THEORETICAL BACKGROUND

National accounts give systematic empirical form to an economy's structure, patterns and performance (Young and Tice 1985). The modern system of national accounts is a set of interrelated accounts that attempt to cover different aspects of the functioning of market economies. The most fundamental of these are the production accounts (national income and product (NIP) and input–output accounts (I/O)) which attempt to measure the creation of national welfare and how it is used.

NIP is concerned only with the final use of the product, therefore it focuses only on the net product. Indeed NIP excludes the portion of total product which is the equivalent of inputs used up in the year's production, as to do otherwise would lead to double counting.[1]

The proper measure of net product is net national product (NNP), but since depreciation measures are often unreliable, production accounts commonly do not deduct depreciation in the measure of the national product. This measure, gross of depreciation but net of intermediate consumption, is called gross national product (GNP) if it refers to the net production of the nationals of a country, including the return on assets held abroad. This is called gross domestic product (GDP) if it refers to production within the nation.

GDP (or GNP) can be viewed from the perspective of: (i) uses; or (ii) revenues. Uses include of personal consumption, government purchases, private investment and net exports. Revenues can be split into wages, profits and taxes.

GDP focuses only on production-related flows.[2] It thus has two major limitations:

1. it does not inform the policy maker about transactions that are not directly related to production (financial flows); and
2. it does not inform the policy maker about the status of stocks of real and financial wealth.

To overcome these limitations, the UN System of National Accounts (UN-SNA) (United Nations 1992) introduced two *additional* accounts:

1. financial accounts, which attempt to correct for the first limitation by reporting on financial flows beyond those directly tied to production, that is, sources and uses of funds for capital transactions (transactions which affect stocks of financial and real assets); and
2. national balance sheets, which attempt to correct the second limitation by linking flows to changes in stocks. For example, positive investment adds to the stock of fixed capital, and positive household savings add to the stock

of household financial assets. Balance sheets also allow the accounting for of unreproducible assets such as natural resources.

To fulfil their potential, the production, financial and balance sheet accounts should be integrated into one another, as more or less accomplished in the UN-SNA.

In 1993 the United Nations issued the 'System of Integrated Environmental and Economic Accounting' guidelines, containing indications for the consideration of environmental issues in the system of national accounts. Until that time the changes in environmental assets were not accounted for as components of national welfare.

In practice, the degradation of the environment is rarely counted as a reduction of income or wealth. For example, if industry cleans up its own pollution, the expenditure is counted as an intermediate input, and hence output is not affected. But if the government cleans it up, this expands the measure of net output because government expenditures are considered to be purchases of final goods and services. Likewise, if households incur medical expenses as a consequence of environmental problems, the expenditure raises the measure of consumption and hence the measure of the final product.[3]

Although there is widespread recognition that these issues need to be addressed in national accounts, there is no consensus yet on the appropriate treatment of them within any system of accounts. However, one environmental issue that can be considered is the use of natural resources, stocks of which can be treated as being on a par with any other capital stock. Economic activities that increase the value of land or natural resources would be counted as investment; activities that exhaust them would be counted as depreciation. Following the scheme proposed by Repetto et al. (1989), a case study is presented here in which the change in the physical stock of resources, valued at average prices over the period, is added to net national product as net investment or disinvestment. The exercise is freely adapted and integrated from a real case study on natural resource depreciation in Costa Rica (Solorzano 1991).

14.2 METHODOLOGY

This exercise makes use of some basic macroeconomic relationships that are defined below.

1. *Gross Domestic Product and Net Domestic Product.* In standard national accounts the value of GDP is usually adjusted downward to reflect the depreciation of man-made capital in the period:

$$NDP = GDP - CCA, \tag{14.1}$$

where: GDP is gross domestic product and CCA is Conventional Capital Consumption Adjustment.

2. *Net Domestic Product and Natural Resource Depreciation.* In general, and for a variety of reasons, standard national accounts do not reflect the loss of value of national environmental assets. Therefore it is necessary to further adjust the domestic product in order to yield meaningful information on the net wealth produced in a period.

$$ANDP = NDP - NRD, \tag{14.2}$$

where: *ANDP* is adjusted net domestic product and *NRD* is natural resource depreciation.

3. *Natural resource depreciation assessment.* Common components entering computations of natural resource depreciation include: forests; soils, for the depreciation due to erosion; fish stocks, which lose value when overfishing practices occur; and other natural assets, including oil stocks, mines and other exhaustible (non-renewable) resources.

$$NRD = DEF + DSE + DFO + ODE, \tag{14.3}$$

where: *DEF* is depreciation of forests, *DSE* is depreciation of soil due to erosion, *DFO* is depreciation of fish stock due to overfishing and *ODE* is other environmental depreciation.[4]

4. *Forest depreciation assessment.* In assessing forest depreciation due to land clearing, the main components considered are:

- The value of extracted timber that is no longer available for future uses.
- The loss of growing timber that could have been available in future years.
- The value of secondary forest, that is, the forest that naturally grows after primary forest is cleared if no other use of the land is made. This has a positive effect on to the economy that partially covers other losses.
- Other valuable services of forests lost due to deforestation, such as biodiversity, recreational use, and protection of soils.

$$DEF = LST + LFH + LOV - GSF, \tag{14.4}$$

where: *LST* is loss of value of standing timber, *LFH* is loss of value of future harvests, *LOV* is loss of other forest values and *GSF* is growth in value of secondary forest.

5. *Unit values and total loss of the standing timber.* The overall loss of value of standing timber is calculated by multiplying the loss of stumpage value per hectare by the number of hectares deforested.

$$LST = STU/\text{ha} \times \text{DEA}, \tag{14.5}$$

where: *DEA* is deforested area, *STU* is stumpage value and *LST* and *DEA* refer to a period of one year.

6. *The rent of timber (stumpage value): an application of the residual value technique.* The value of extracted timber that is no longer available for future use is calculated by considering the rent included into the overall timber value. This rent is called 'stumpage value' (*STU*). To calculate the stumpage value the valuation technique usually known as the residual value technique is applied. The rent that can be extracted by one unit of timber, assuming perfectly competitive markets, is the market price of one unit of timber minus all costs required in the extraction and processing of the timber. This unit rent times the units of timber obtainable from one hectare of forest gives the stumpage value of timber per hectare of forest.

$$STU = MAV - ETM, \tag{14.6}$$

where: *STU* is stumpage value, *MAV* is market value and *ETM* is extraction, transport and milling costs.[5]

7. *The loss of other forest values: an application of the travel cost method.* It is assumed that the only component of the *LOV* item (loss of other forest values) in the identity (14.4) is the loss of recreational services provided by the forests to visitors. To assess this value, the travel cost method can be applied to determine peoples' willingness to pay for the recreational services of forests.

$$LOV = DEA * SHA * VAL/RAT, \tag{14.7}$$

where: *LOV* is loss of other forest values, *DEA* is deforested area (in hectares), *SHA* is share of the deforested area of recreational interest, *VAL* is willingness to pay for recreational services per hectare and *RAT* is discount rate.

The estimate of adjusted national income is illustrated in the following exercise, which uses the methodologies outlined above.

14.3 EXERCISE: CASE STUDY OF ENVIRONMENTAL ACCOUNTS FOR COSTA RICA

14.3.1 Problem Set

To assess the adjusted net domestic product (ANDP) of Costa Rica data on forests, data on other environmental assets, and standard macroeconomic data have been collected. These are supplied in Tables 14.1 to 14.4 below. Values are expressed in colones at 1984 constant prices (colones/US$ = 44.5).

Data on forests
Table 14.1 provides data on total deforested areas (*DEA*) in the period from 1986 to 1989, the estimated 'stumpage value' per hectare (*STU*) and the overall national loss due to the loss of future harvests (*LFH*). Some positive effects of forest clearing, the value of secondary forest (GSF), have been recorded and have been included in the evaluation process.

Table 14.1   Data on forests

Year	*DEA*(ha)	*STU*/ha (col.)	*LFH* (m. col.)	*GSF* (m. col.)
1986	20,979	439,678	2,575	128
1987	20,697	312,267	1,414	212
1988	20,818	680,901	4,003	288
1989	20,659	693,451	3,000	355

To calculate the loss of other forest values (*LOV*) the analysts, owing to a lack of time, focused only on those of 1989. They found that the main component of *LOV* was the loss of recreational services supplied by forested areas. The zonal travel cost method (ZTCM) was chosen to assess this value component.

An on-site survey was run in a well-defined forested area of recreational interest, with a sample size of one hundred visitors. The area visited was 400 hectares. They were asked their country of origin, the cost of travel, the number of daily visits to the forested area during their trip and the total population of their country of origin. The 100 observations have then been grouped into five homogeneous zones of origin on travel cost grounds: (i) Central America (CENAME); (ii) North America (NORAME); (iii) South America (SOUAME); (iv) Central Europe (CENEUR); and (v) Mediterranean Europe (MEDEUR). For each homogeneous zone the following variables have been recorded: the sample number of visitors (*SANUVI*); the average travel cost per daily visit to the forested area in colones (1984 prices) (*COUTZO*); and total population (*POPUZO*). The total surface in hectares of the forested area, the long-term real discount rate and the total number of daily visits to the site per year have been calculated. This information is reported in Table 14.2.

Table 14.2   Data for travel cost valuation

ZONEXX (j)	SANUVI (n_j)	COUTZO (C_j)	POPUZO (,000) (n_j)
CENAME	32	3,000	120,000
NORAME	44	4,600	275,000
SOUAME	13	5,000	240,000
CENEUR	7	6,900	200,000
MEDEUR	4	7,600	100,000
Total (*n*)	100		935,000

Total number of visits (*n*) (*TOTVIS*)	7,000
Total hectares of the site	400
Real long-term discount rate (*RAT*)	3%
Estimated share of tourist forest (*SHA*)	5%

Data on other environmental assets

To add information on natural resource depreciation, data on depreciation of soils due to erosion (*DSE*) and depreciation of fish stocks due to overfishing (*DFO*) were calculated and are reported in Table 14.3. Depreciation of other environmental assets (*ODE*) was not assessed due to a lack of time and funds.

Table 14.3   Data on other environmental assets

Year	DSE (m. col.)	DFO (m. col.)	ODE (m. col.)
1986	2,497	386	n.a.
1987	2,295	562	n.a.
1988	2,623	650	n.a.
1989	2,576	n.a.	n.a.

Other macroeconomic data

Other standard macroeconomic data (GDP and conventional capital adjustment (CCA)) have been collected and are reported in Table 14.4.

Table 14.4 Other macroeconomic data

Year	GDP (m. col.)	CCA (m. col.)
1986	177,327	4,408
1987	186,019	4,651
1988	207,816	5,301
1989	231,289	5,323

14.3.2 Questions

Question 1

On the basis of the supplied data, using the 'residual value' technique by applying the relevant relationships above, calculate the loss of value of standing timber (*LST*) for the years 1986 to 1989.

Question 2

Using the zonal travel cost method, calculate the loss of other forest values (*LOV*).

Hints:

a. Calculate the sample share of visitors (variable *SASHAR*) for each zone as the ratio of the sample number of visitors from each zone (variable *SANUVI*) on the total sample observations (*TOTSAM*):

$$SASHAR = SANUVI/TOTSAM \ (TOTSAM = n)$$

b. Use these shares for splitting the total annual number of visits (*TOTVIS*) and estimating the number of annual visits zone by zone, (variable *NUMVIS*):

$$NUMVIS = TOTVIS * SASHAR$$

c. Calculate the visit rate (variable *TAUXVI*) as the ratio of the number of visits per year (*NUMVIS*) and the total population by region (variable *POPUZO*):

$$TAUXVI = NUMVIS/POPUZO$$

d. Estimate the (direct) demand function regressing the variable *TAUXVI* (dependent) on the variable *COUTZO* (independent). The linear form for the demand function can be chosen:

$$TAUXVI = CONSTA + bCOUTZO * COUTZO$$

e. Calculate the choke price (variable $CHOKE$) for the linear demand function, that is, the price that lead to zero visits, by setting the demand function equal to zero:

$$TAUXVI = 0 \text{ implies: } CONSTA + bCOUTZO * COUTZO = 0$$

$$COUTZO^0 = - CONSTA/bCOUTZO \quad COUTZO^0 = CHOKE$$

$$CHOKE = - CONSTA/bCOUTZO$$

f. The average individual consumer surplus zone by zone ($CONSUR$) is calculated by integrating under the demand curve between the average travel cost of each zone ($COUTZO$) and the choke price ($CHOKE$). This is shown in Table 14.5.

Table 14.5   Consumer surplus by zone

Zone	CONSUR (US$)
CENAME	37.7
NORAME	16.5
SOUAME	12.5
CENEUR	1.1
MEDEUR	0.0

g. The consumer surplus ($CONSUR$) referring to a population unit (in this case, per one thousand people) has to be multiplied by the population of each zone ($POPUZO$), to obtain the annual consumer surplus by zone (variable $CONZON$).

h. The total consumer surplus (variable $TOTACS$) is then obtained by taking the sum of the zonal consumer surpluses.

i. The annual consumer surplus per hectare (VAL) is then calculated by dividing the total consumer surplus ($TOTACS$) by the number of hectares of the site.

j. The loss of other forest values is then calculated as described in the identity (14.7) above, using the fact that the share of tourist sites is 5 per cent.

Question 3
a. Calculate the depreciation of forests (*DEF*).
b. Can you think of any other source of value for forests?

Question 4
Considering also the depreciation of other natural assets (fisheries and soils), calculate the total natural resource depreciation (*NRD*) for years 1986 to 1989.

Question 5
a. Calculate the net domestic product (*NDP*) and the adjusted net domestic product (*ANDP*).
b. Work out a table showing the percent composition of GDP by *ANDP*, conventional capital depreciation (*CCA*) and *NRD*.
c. Give a graphic illustration of the above data.
d. Do you think that the difference between *NDP* and *ANDP* is large enough to justify calculations for this adjustment?

14.3.3   Solution Set

Solution to question 1

The loss of standing timber value is obtained from equation (14.5) as the product of hectares of deforested area (*DEA*) and the stumpage value per hectare (*STU*/ha), as shown in Table 14.6. Values are expressed in colones at 1984 constant prices (colones/US$ = 44.5).

Table 14.6   Calculation of loss of standing timber (variable LST)

	DEA (ha)	STU/ha (col.)	LST (m. col.)
1986	20,979	439,678	9,224
1987	20,697	312,267	6,463
1988	20,818	680,901	14,175
1989	20,659	693,451	14,326

Solution to question 2

Table 14.7 reports the calculations of the variables *SHASAR* and *NUMVIS* (steps a and b of the hints).

Table 14.7   Calculation of sample shares by zone and annual visits by zone

ZONEXX (*i*)	SASHAR (n_i/n) (%)	NUMVIS ($V_i = V*n_i/n$)
CENAME	32.0	2.240
NORAME	44.0	3.080
SOUAME	13.0	910
CENEUR	7.0	490
MEDEUR	4.0	280
Total (*n*)	100.0	7.000

Table 14.8 reports the calculation of the visit rates by zone (variable *TAUXVI*, step c of the hints).

The demand function of visits per year is estimated by running a linear regression of the visit rate on the travel cost per visit. The estimated parameters of the function are then utilized for calculating the choke price. The results are reported in Table 14.9 (steps d and e of the hints).

Table 14.8   Calculation of the visit rates by zone

ZONEXX (j)	NUMVIS $(V_j = V*n_j/n)$	POPUZO (,000) (N_j)	TAUXVI $(R_j = V_j/N_j)$
CENAME	2,240	120,000	0.019
NORAME	3,080	275,000	0.011
SOUAME	910	240,000	0.004
CENEUR	490	200,000	0.002
MEDEUR	280	100,000	0.003
Total (n)	7,000	935,000	0.039

Table 14.9   Estimated parameters of the demand function and choke price

Variables	bCOUTZO	CONSTA
Parameters	–0.000003	0.026536
Std errors	0.000001	0.005854
R^2/Std error $\hat{Y}$	0.788670	0.003817
F-test/DGF	11.195900	3.000000
T-ratios	–3.346	4.533
Choke price (col.)		7,676

Figure 14.1 illustrates the estimated demand curve of daily visits.

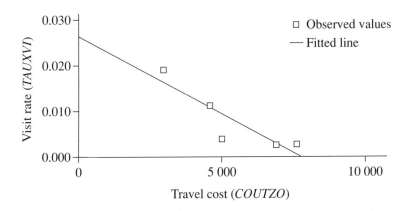

Figure 14.1   Estimated demand curve of daily visits

The integration of the estimated demand function between the choke price and the average travel cost of each zone gives the average consumer surplus for a population unit of a thousand people, in this case, of each zone (variable *CONSUR*, step f of the hints). The product of the average unit consumer surplus and the population of each zone gives the consumer surplus of each zone (variable *CONZON*, step g of the hints). The aggregation across zones gives the total annual consumer surplus (variable *TOTACS*, step h of the hints). The results of the steps f, g and h are reported in Table 14.10.

Table 14.10   Estimated unit CS, CS by zone, total CS and CS per hectare

Zone	CONSUR (US$)	POPULA (,000) (N_j)	CONSZON (US$) ($CSz = CS_j * N_j$)
CENAME	37.7	120,000	4,522,626
NORAME	16.5	275,000	4,526,475
SOUAME	12.5	240,000	3,001,770
CENEUR	1.1	200,000	226,495
MEDEUR	0.0	100,000	2,350
Total CS (col. 84)			12,279,716
Total area (ha)			400
Total CS/ha site (*VAL*)			30,699

The loss of other forest values (*LOV*) is then calculated according to the formula (14.7) reported above, using the value of the CS per hectare (variable *VAL*, step i of the hints). The result is reported in Table 14.11.

Table 14.11   Calculation of loss of other forest values (LOV)

Deforested area (ha) (*DEA*)	20,659
Share of tourist sites (*SHA*)	5%
WTP (col./ha) (*VAL*)	30,699
Annual loss of value (col.)	31.7
Discount rate (*RAT*)	3%
Loss of other forest values (*LOV* 1990, m. col.)	1,057

Solution to question 3
The loss value of forest stock (*DEF*) is obtained from equation (14.4), as the sum of the loss of value of standing timber (*LST*), the loss of value of future harvests (*LFH*), the loss of other forest values (*LOV*) minus the growth of value of secondary forests (*GSF*). This is shown in Table 14.12.

Table 14.12   Calculation of loss value of forest stock (variable DEF)

	LST (m. col.)	LFH (m. col.)	LOV (m. col.)	GSF (m. col.)	DEF(*) (m. col.)
1986	9,224	2,575	n.a.	128	11,671
1987	6,463	1,414	n.a.	212	7,665
1988	14,175	4,003	n.a.	288	17,890
1989	14,326	3,000	1,057	355	18,028

Solution to question 4

The natural resource depreciation (*NRD*) is obtained by equation (14.3) as a sum of depreciation of forests (*DEF*), depreciation of soils (*DSE*), depreciation of fish stocks (*DFO*) and other environmental assets depreciation (ODE). The absence of the last item contributes to further lowering the estimate of *NRD*. See Table 14.13.

Table 14.13   Calculation of natural resource depreciation (variable NRD)

Year	DEF (m. col.)	DSE (m. col.)	DFO (m. col.)	ODE (m. col.)	NRD (m. col.)
1986	11,671	2,497	386	n.a.	14,554
1987	7,665	2,295	562	n.a.	10,522
1988	17,890	2,623	650	n.a.	21,163
1989	18,028	2,576	n.a.	n.a.	20,604

Solution to question 5

(a) The net domestic product (*NDP*) is obtained from identity (14.1) as the difference between the gross domestic product (*GDP*) and the conventional capital adjustment (*CCA*).[6] The adjusted net domestic product (*ANDP*) is obtained from the identity (14.2) as the difference between *NDP* and natural resource depreciation (*NRD*). The results are shown in Table 14.14.

Table 14.14   Calculation of net domestic product (variable NDP) and adjusted net domestic product (ANDP)

Year	GDP (m. col.)	CCA (m. col.)	NDP (m. col.)	NRD (m. col.)	ANDP (m. col.)
1986	177,327	4,408	172,919	14,554	158,365
1987	186,019	4,651	181,368	10,522	170,846
1988	207,816	5,301	202,515	21,163	181,352
1989	231,289	5,323	225,966	20,604	205,362

(b) Table 14.15 shows the percentage composition of *GDP* by adjusted net domestic product (*ANDP*), conventional capital depreciation (*CCA*) and natural resource depreciation (*NRD*).

*Table 14.15   Percentage composition of GDP made by adjusted net domestic product (*ANDP*), conventional capital depreciation (*CCA*) and natural resource depreciation (*NRD*)*

Year	ANDP (m. col.)	CCA (m. col.)	NRD (m. col.)	GDP (m. col.)
1986	89.3	2.5	8.2	100.0
1987	91.8	2.5	5.7	100.0
1988	87.3	2.6	10.2	100.0
1989	88.8	2.3	8.9	100.0

(c) Figure 14.2 gives a graphic illustration of the above data.
(d) The difference between *NDP* and *ANDP* is large enough to justify calculations for this adjustment, because:

- It is a non-negligible share of the GDP (about 10 per cent).
- It is, at least in the analysed years, from three to four times the conventional adjustment for man-made capital depreciation included in standard national accounts.

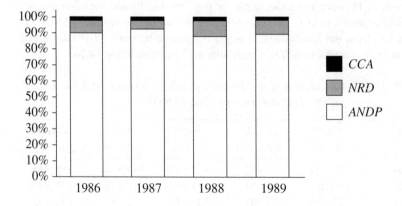

Figure 14.2   Percentage composition of GDP

14.3.3 Discussion

The Costa Rican case study highlights the importance of adjusting national product measures for depreciation of both man-made and natural capital. The case study shows how measures of natural resource depletion can be added in to the national accounting framework, and shows the level to which they are important. Such measures need to be taken into account in assessing moves towards sustainable development. The case study focussed mainly on the impact of forests, but other resources may be assessed using the same framework. The methods for making the adjustments are not always straightforward (e.g. the use of the travel cost method in this exercise) and are not, as yet, part of the statistical procedures in any country when preparing regular national income accounts The World Bank is currently working on extending its wealth accounts and estimating on a consistent basis as many of these impacts as possible.

Questions for further discussion

- What environmental assets are important in your country?
- How could you assess impacts on these assets?

NOTES

1. Shaikh and Tonak note that 'there is nothing sacrosanct about the net product as a measure'. It depends on the objective of the exercise in measuring what the economy produces. For example, if the aim is to assess total product in input–output accounts, undercounting would result if input use was ignored.
2. Similar to the I/O approach.
3. These issues are also discussed in Chapter 3 of this book.
4. In this illustrative framework the *ODE* component can be seen as consisting of two items: other renewable resources depreciation (*ORD*) and non-renewable resources depreciation (*NRR*): *ODE = ORD + NRR*. For the sake of simplicity we shall concentrate on renewable resources only.
5. These costs include profit, considered a 'normal' return on investment for financing capital assets required for operations of harvesting milling and transporting. In this case study the 'normal' profit was assumed to be 6 per cent of the total investment.
6. This measures depreciation of the capital stock.

CITED BIBLIOGRAPHY

Repetto, R., W. McGrath, M. Wells, C. Beer and F. Rossini (1989), *Wasting Assets: Natural Resources in National Income Accounts*, Washington, DC: World Resources Institute.

Shaikh, A.M. and E.A. Tonak. (1994), *Measuring the Wealth of Nations: The Political Economy of National Accounts*, Cambridge: Cambridge University Press.

Solorzano, R. (1991), *Accounts Overdue: Natural Resource Depreciation in Costa Rica*, Washington, DC: World Resources Institute, December.
United Nations (1992), *Revised System of National Accounts*, New York: United Nations.
Young, A.H. and H.S. Tice (1985), 'An introduction to national economic accounting', *Survey of Current Business*, **65**, 59–76.

15. Valuing health impacts: a case study of air pollution in New Delhi, India

OBJECTIVE

The aim of this chapter is to provide the reader with a brief overview of the conceptual aspects underlying health impact valuation and to give an example of the application of these in practice drawing on a stepwise exercise based on a case study in India.

SUMMARY

This chapter reviews the approaches commonly used in the monetization of health benefits due to air pollution reduction. These approaches can be divided into the human capital approach, cost of illness approach and the willingness to pay approach. The theory behind each approach and the methods used to obtain empirical estimates of willingness to pay for health benefits are outlined briefly. A practical exercise, freely adapted from an actual case study, presented and solved step by step, analyses the valuation of changes in health associated with changes in air quality in New Delhi, India.

15.1 INTRODUCTION

The health benefits arising from reduced pollution levels or improved quality of life are often a large part of the benefits of projects with an environmental impact. Advances have been made in recent years in the development of methodologies to value these impacts (see, in particular, Markandya 1999; ExternE 1999). This chapter provides a broad overview of this topic, including a case study to compute the value of reduction in air pollution in New Delhi, India.

15.2 CONCEPTUAL FRAMEWORK

The impacts on health of environmental damage take a variety of forms. The following impacts are often investigated:

- *Health impacts of common air pollutants.* This category of pollutants includes particulate matter, lead, sulphur dioxide, nitrogen oxides, carbon monoxide and ground-level ozone. These substances are normally present in all urban areas.
- *Health impacts of hazardous or toxic air pollutants.* This category of pollutants includes arsenic, asbestos and vinyl-chloride. The effects of these are more localized in nature.
- *Health impacts of a lack of water and sanitation.* This problem is spread across the world, and is often associated with poverty.

This chapter focuses on the health impacts of common air pollutants.

To implement a health impact valuation it is crucial to *identify* and *quantify* specific links between pollutants and health impacts. The health impacts commonly investigated can be classified as: acute and chronic *premature mortality*,[1] and acute and chronic *morbidity* (or reduced life quality).

The valuation of the health effects of an environmental change requires the establishment of two links:

1. the link between the environmental change and the change in health status (changes in mortality, morbidity, minor diseases and so on). Establishing this link consists of estimating functions, which relate specific health impacts with the level of exposure to a pollutant or to a set of pollutants and to other control variables (for example, socioeconomic or geographic variables); and
2. the link between the impact on health and its monetary equivalent, using different approaches to elicit the economic value of the impact on health.

Table 15.1   Common air pollutants and related health effects

Pollutant	Quantified health effects	Unquantified health effects	Other possible effects
Ozone	Acute mortality Respiratory symptoms Minor restricted activity days Respiratory restricted activity days Hospital admissions Asthma attacks Changes in pulmonary function Chronic sinusitis and hay fever	Increased airway responsive- ness to stimuli Centroacinar fibrosis Inflammation in the lung	Immunological changes Chronic respiratory diseases Extrapulmonary effects (e.g., changes in the structure, function of the organs)
Particulate Matter/TP/Sulphates	Acute and possibly chronic mortality Bronchitis – chronic and acute Hospital admissions Lower respiratory illness Upper respiratory illness Chest illness Respiratory symptoms Minor restricted activity days All restricted activity days Days of work loss Moderate or worse asthma status (asthmatics)	Changes in pulmonary function	Chronic respiratory diseases other than chronic bronchitis Inflammation of the lung

Pollutant			
Carbon monoxide	Hospital admissions – congestive heart failure	Behavioural effects Other hospital admissions	Other cardiovascular effects
Nitrogen oxides	Decreased time to onset of angina Respiratory illness	Increased airway responsiveness	Developmental effects Decreased pulmonary function Inflammation of the lung Immunological changes Respiratory symptoms in non-asthmatics Hospital admissions
Sulphur dioxide	In exercising asthmatics: Changes in pulmonary function Respiratory symptoms Combines responses of respiratory symptoms and pulmonary function changes		
Lead	Mortality Hypertension Non-fatal coronary heart disease Non-fatal strokes IQ loss effect on lifetime earnings IQ loss effects on special education needs	Health effects for individuals in age ranges other than those studied Neurobehavioural function Other cardiovascular diseases Reproductive effects Fetal effects from maternal exposure Delinquent and anti-social behaviour in children	

Source: USEPA (1997).

Several models, referred to in Freeman (1993, p. 315) as 'Comprehensive Models of Individual Behaviour', have been formulated, both for premature mortality and morbidity.

For example, for premature mortality, life-cycle consumption/saving models with uncertain lifetime have been applied. These models are usually based on a multiperiod utility function, whose arguments are utilities in each period t, $U_t(X_t)$, which are in turn assumed to be functions of the consumption X_t in period t. After discounting with the time preference rate of consumption and weighting with the conditional probability of dying later than in each period t, these annual utilities are aggregated. It is assumed that the individual maximizes the multiperiod expected utility under a budget constraint, which reflects current wealth plus discounted weighted lifetime earnings. The maximum willingness to pay (WTP) for a reduction in the probability of dying in period t, following an environmental improvement, is measured by the wealth that must be taken away from a person to keep his/her expected utility constant whenever the environmental improvement occurs.

Also for morbidity several 'comprehensive models of individual behaviour', such as health production function models, have been formulated. These are based on the assumption that an individual has some control over his/her health through choices of life-style, level of medication and so on. The model then considers the days of sickness as a function of the exposure to pollution, some variables, which describe averting behaviour to avoid sickness, and medical treatments to mitigate the severity of the sickness. The individual is assumed to maximize utility under a given budget constraint. Utility is positively affected by the level of consumption and the days of leisure, and negatively affected by days of sickness. The budget constraint is in turn negatively affected by the days of sickness due to the lack of wages earned for such days. As before, the maximum WTP for a reduction in exposure to pollutants is calculated as the wealth that must be taken away from a person to keep expected utility constant whenever a reduction in exposure to the pollutant concerned occurs.

In addition to these comprehensive models of individual behaviour, other approaches that do not deal explicitly with optimization have been developed. To obtain monetary estimations of premature mortality, contingent valuation methods (CVMs), wage differential methods or human capital methods are usually used. To obtain monetary estimations of changes in morbidity, CVMs, the cost of illness approach or defensive/averting expenditure methods are used.

This chapter will focus on the health impacts of common air pollutants, because they are of direct relevance for the proposed exercise. For a more complete and general review of concepts and models on health impact valuation, see Freeman (1993). Table 15.1 provides a list of possible health effects of common air pollutants, some are quantifiable in physical terms, whilst others remain more difficult to quantify.

15.2.1   Estimating Changes in Premature Mortality

Various types of studies exist for the investigation of the impact of air pollution on mortality. The following have been applied:

- *Time series studies* allow the study of the impact of short-term exposures on mortality rates by correlating the daily variation in major air pollutants (PM_{10}, $PM_{2.5}$, SO_2 and so on) on day $(t - s)$ with deaths in day (t). Separate equations are often estimated for different causes of death (respiratory, cardiac and so on) controlling also for different weather conditions and seasons (Ostro 1994; Schwartz 1993). Such studies focus on the acute effects.
- *Episodic studies* capture the impact of short-term peaks in exposure on mortality. A frequent concern is that the people affected by short-term exposure would have died anyway in a few days or weeks from other causes. There is no way to measure exactly the average number of life-years lost in such studies.
- *Cross-sectional studies* are used to examine the impact of the variation in air pollution levels across cities. They identify both acute and chronic effects. Early studies of the impacts of air pollution on mortality rates correlated mortality rates by county or city with average air pollution levels in the county or city. Cross-sectional studies that use individual data can, however, better control for factors other than air pollution that affect mortality. The ideal study is a prospective cohort study, that is, a study of groups of the same age, in which a cross-section of individuals living in different cities is followed for several years. This study records the health outcome of interest for each subject and air pollution levels in the city involved. The study also measures other factors that may affect the probability that the subject dies, such as whether the subject is a smoker, has access to medical care or has a family history of disease, (For a survey, see Pope et al. 1995; ExternE 1999.)

An important question is whether the effects of short- and long-term exposures can be aggregated when estimating the damages associated with air pollution. In the case of premature mortality, it is not appropriate to add together deaths associated with particulate matter (PM) based on a time-series study with deaths from PM calculated using a prospective cohort study. The latter study should capture both effects.[2]

The basic mathematical model used to relate mortality to pollution is typically a semi-logarithmic one, of the type:

$$E(deaths) = \exp[\beta(pollution) + X'\gamma],$$

where: E is the expectation operator; (*deaths*) is the number of deaths in a given period per unit of population (for example, one hundred thousand people); (*pollution*) is a variable reflecting the level of pollution; β is a coefficient associated to the pollution level; X represents a vector of other variables; and γ is a vector of coefficients associated to the other variables.

This model implies that:

$$(\Delta deaths)/deaths = \beta(\Delta pollution).$$

That is, the percentage change in deaths is a linear function of the change in pollution.[3] Assuming this model holds, it is useful to note that a given change in pollution (for example, 10 micrograms per cubic metre of particulate matter with diameter less than 10 microns, or PM_{10}) has the same percentage impact on mortality regardless of the level of pollution. This is a limitation of the model.

The above function, once estimated, yields the number of lives that would be saved by an environmental programme, for example, a project which aims to bring about a reduction in the level of air pollution, given the baseline number of deaths. These lives saved can be interpreted as statistical lives in the sense that there is no direct association with any specific person. Each person experiences a reduction in the probability (risk) of dying in a given period $Pd(t)$.

More analytically, the probability of dying without the envisaged environmental programme in the period (t), $P_{d(t)(wo)}$, is the ratio of expected deaths in period t, $E(D)_{(t)(wo)}$ divided by the number of the exposed persons N. Analogously for the probability of dying with the programme is $P_{d(t)(wi)}$. Both probabilities are written as follows:

$$P_{d(t)(wo)} = \frac{E(D)_{(t)(wo)}}{N}; \quad P_{d(t)(wi)} = \frac{E(D)_{(t)(wi)}}{N}.$$

The reduction in the risk of dying in period t, $R_{rd(t)}$ is given by:

$$R_{rd(t)} = \left[P_{d(t)(wi)} - P_{d(t)(wo)} \right] = \frac{\left[E(D)_{(t)(wi)} - E(D)_{(t)(wo)} \right]}{N} = \frac{lives\ saved}{N}.$$

15.2.2 Valuing Changes in Premature Mortality

The mortality approach in the valuation literature has been based mainly on the estimation of the willingness to pay for a change in the risk of death. This is converted into the 'value of a statistical life' (VSL) by dividing the WTP by the change in risk. So, for example, if the estimated WTP is $100 for a reduction in the risk of death of 1/10,000, the value of a statistical life is estimated at 100*10,000, which equals $1 million. This way of conceptualizing the willingness to pay for a change in the risk of death has many assumptions, primary among them being the 'linearity' between risk and payment. For example, a risk of death of 1/1000 would then be valued at $1m./1000, or $1000 using the VSL approach. Within a small range of the risk of death at which the VSL is established this may not be a bad assumption, but it is clearly indefensible for risk levels very different from the one used in obtaining the original estimate.

Estimates of the WTP for a reduction in risk or the willingness to accept an increase in risk have been made by three methods. First, there are studies that look at the increased compensation individuals need, other things being equal, to work in occupations where the risk of death at work is higher. This provides an estimate of the WTA. Second, there are studies based on the CVM method, where individuals are questioned about their WTP and WTA for measures that reduce the risk of death from certain activities (for example, driving); or their WTA for measures that, conceivably, increase it (for example, increased road traffic in a given area). Third, researchers have looked at actual voluntary expenditures on items that reduce death risk from certain activities, such as cigarette smoking, or purchasing air bags for cars.

In the environmental economics literature, mortality impacts are valued by multiplying the change in risk of death by a VSL. This methodology has been extensively surveyed (for a recent review, see ExternE 1999). Although there are good reasons for thinking that alternative methods of valuation may be preferable (for example, based on the value of life years lost), the VSL method of valuation has been widely used and has some general acceptance. For the European Union countries, Markandya (1996) estimated a central VSL in 1990 prices at ECU 2.6 million ($3.1m.), which is broadly consistent with figures used for the United States.

Although much of the valuation of mortality has been based on VSL, the method has not been fully accepted, and there are alternatives that have been used. One is to value life years lost (VLYL), rather than VSL. The argument in favour of VLYL is that it allows the researcher to take account of factors such as the age of the person affected by pollution. There is considerable evidence, for example, that particles formed from pollutants such as PM, SO_X and NO_X affect older and sick persons disproportionately. Hence VSL values based on a 'typical' health population may not apply to them.

Another method of valuation is the human capital method (HCM). The basic idea underlying this approach is that a lower bound to the value of a statistical life can be found by looking at the value of goods and services an individual is able to produce in his/her remaining years of life. Usually earnings before taxes are assumed as a measure of the value produced by an individual from the point of view of the society. Although the economic rationale for such a valuation is weak (it gives no value to saving the lives of retired people, for example), it has been used quite frequently in developing countries. The justification given is that, when applied on average, to a cross-section of society, HCM provides a lower-bound estimate of the total value of a saved life, because it does not include the value of the individual well-being, the satisfaction and the right to live of all the individuals and the value of that individual to his/her family.

The human capital method can be summarized as follows:

1. estimating the remaining productive years of an individual, deriving this from the age of the individual;
2. estimating an average wage (before taxes) of the socioeconomic category the individual belongs to for all the productive years remaining; and
3. calculating the present value of the stream of wages by discounting using an appropriate discount rate and aggregating this stream.

The valuation of the impact of a reduction in pollution on premature mortality using a dose–response model plus human capital approach or WTP approach is summarized in Figure 15.1. If the WTP approach is to be pursued, the researcher will need values of VSL or VLYL that are appropriate for the country concerned. Frequently studies are not available, and so the choice is either to make a benefit transfer, or to use a simpler method such as HCM. A benefit transfer involves taking a value calculated in another country and applying it to the situation of interest.

15.2.3 Estimating Changes in Morbidity

Morbidity can be defined as a departure from a state of physical or psychological well-being resulting from disease or injury. It can be classified as *chronic*, of indefinite duration, or *acute*, lasting a defined number of days. The degree of impairment is also an important indicator for classifying the morbidity status. Different degrees of impairment can be defined: 'restricted activity days' (RADs) are those where an individual can carry on only some of the ordinary activities; 'bed disability days' are those where the individual has to stay in bed all day. An important classification is that of whether the individual retains the ability to carry on ordinary working activities: 'work loss days' are those in which an individual cannot carry on the work s/he is usually paid for. Note that the listed indicators reflect the behavioural response of the individual as a result of sickness, rather than the actual sickness itself. The units used to measure the occurrence of such behavioural responses can be of the type days per period for

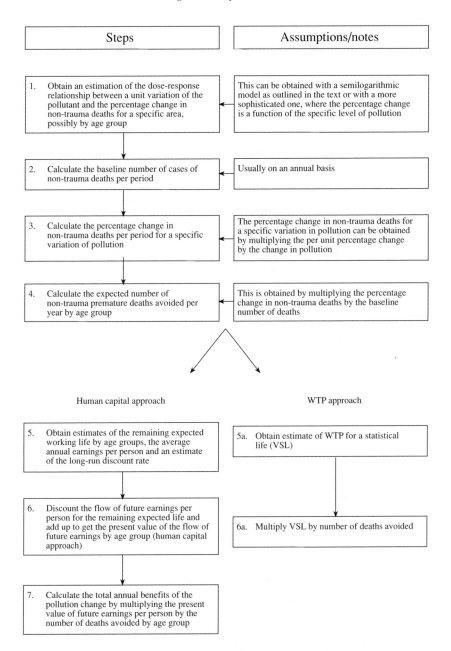

Figure 15.1   Procedure for valuing impacts of environmental changes on premature mortality using number of deaths avoided

a given population unit, for example 3.4 work loss days per year per thousand people.

A rather different but related approach is to look at the 'symptom days' which is used to quantify the morbidity status of a given illness.

An issue in measuring morbidity arises due to the fact that morbidity occurs over a period, and may take time to develop. Four possible scenarios might be evaluated:

1. morbidity begins before the observation period and ends within the period;
2. morbidity begins before the observation period and ends after the period;
3. morbidity begins and ends within the observation period; and
4. morbidity begins within the observation period and ends after observation period.

Some studies use the number of cases of morbidity per period over a given population as a measure. If only morbidity cases beginning in the observation period are recorded, that is, cases 3 and 4, the resulting indicator is the so-called 'incidence rate'. It is appropriate to measure the response of morbidity to changes in the exposure. Another indicator that may be applied is one that records all the four categories provided above, known as the 'prevalence rate'. In many cases this rate is more appropriate as it captures the time dimension of morbidity.

In any case, an appropriate measure of morbidity to be used to test the WTP of people should reflect both the severity of the symptoms and the duration of the morbidity status. Once the appropriate measure of the morbidity status is chosen, the dose–response model has to be estimated. As for the case of mortality, the dose–response model supplies the percentage change in the chosen morbidity indicator per unit change in the environmental pollutant.

15.2.4   Valuing Changes in Morbidity

The value of reducing morbidity by means of a reduction in pollution can be estimated at least in part through application of the contingent valuation method (stated WTP for the environmental change). This approach allows the estimation of the total costs or benefits accruing to an individual as a result of an environmental change impacting on health conditions, including the discomfort of illness and/or disutility of averting behaviour. However, if some of the costs of illness or the defensive measures against pollution are not borne by the individual but are carried by the provider of health care, which may be the state or a private company, the stated WTP might underestimate the social benefits resulting from a reduction in pollution. In so far as these costs are not borne by the individual, they are 'additional to any stated WTP and should be added to the latter.

Other complementary approaches, simpler and less expensive, but partial, are market-based techniques such as (i) the cost of illness approach, which considers the costs of lost productivity and medical care and (ii) the estimation of defensive or averting expenditures, for example, the cost of installing double-glazed windows or air conditioning.

The cost of illness approach does not include a subjective valuation of the discomfort of the illness status. It represents therefore a lower bound of the social value of the improvement in the level of the environmental asset that causes the illness. Defensive and averting expenditure methods also provide a lower bound of the WTP for the environmental improvement (or to avoid the environmental damage) as the benefits derived from preservation or damage prevention are at least as high as the costs involved in abatement. Figure 15.2 sets out the methodology to be used in valuing morbidity impacts.

15.3   CASE STUDY: VALUING HEALTH IMPACTS IN DELHI

15.3.1   Background

The exercise aims to illustrate the valuation of the benefits of reducing air pollution in Delhi from 1991 levels to the levels indicated in World Health Organization (WHO) standards. Because total suspended particulate (TSP) matter is the only common air pollutant in Delhi that is above WHO standards, this example focuses upon the impact of reducing the TSP levels from the 1991 average of 375 micrograms per cubic metre to 75 micrograms per cubic metre, the WHO standard. A reduction of 300 $\mu g/m^3$ of TSP is therefore envisaged.

Three basic steps are involved in this process:

1. computing the difference in pollution concentrations between 1991 concentrations and WHO standards;
2. evaluating the health impacts of these differences using dose–response functions, considering both reduced morbidity and reduced premature non trauma mortality;
3. monetizing the health impacts computed in step 2.

Both for mortality and morbidity impacts the procedures outlined in the diagrams above are applied step by step.

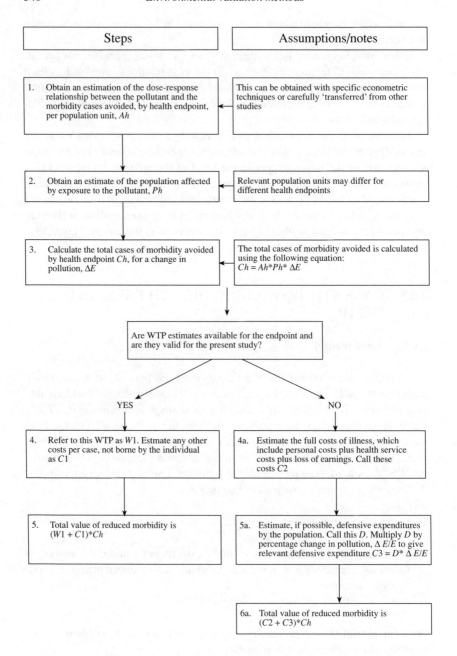

Figure 15.2   Method for valuing impacts of environmental changes on reduced morbidity

15.3.2 Problem Set

To calculate the value of health impacts of reduced TSP from 375 to 75 μg/m^3, both data on morbidity and mortality are required. Data are provided in Tables 15.2 and 15.3, respectively.[4]

Table 15.2   Data for valuation of reduction in morbidity[*]

Health endpoint	Relevant population (a)	Pop. units (1,000pers.) (b)	Cases avoided pop. unit/year[**] (c)	Value per case avoided (d)
Respiratory hospital admissions	All	8,375	0.66	147.00
Emergency room visits	All	8,375	12.95	4.15
Restricted activity days	Over 18	4,690	3,163.33	2.00
Respiratory symptom days	All	8,375	10,066.67	0.12
Chronic bronchitis	Over 25	4,188	3.37	542.00

Notes:
[*]   Estimated and freely adapted from Cropper et al. (1997 a and b).
[**]   Cases avoided in morbidity per thousand relevant population per 100 μg/m^3 reduction.

Table 15.3   Data for valuation of decrease of non-trauma deaths by age for reduction of TSP in Delhi[*]

Age group	Var. % deaths[**]	Non-trauma deaths/year	Remaining life expectancy	Remaining working days
0–4	2.4	11,583	60	50
5–14	2.6	2,423	57	50
15–44	4.3	15,140	40	40
45–64	2.0	13,400	19	19
65 and up	0.8	7,292	7	7
Total		49,838		
TSP reduction envisaged (μg/m^3)		300		
Average annual wage (1991) of a manufacturing worker in Delhi (US$)		500		
Annual (risk-free) discount rate		3%		

Notes:
[*]   Estimated and freely adapted from Cropper et al. (1997 a and b).
[**]   Percentage decrease of non-trauma deaths per 100 micrograms reduction of TSP.

Using the information in the tables above and the methodology illustrated in the previous sections of this chapter, answer the following questions:

Estimation of benefits from changes in morbidity

1. Calculate the expected morbidity cases avoided per year by health endpoint.
2. Estimate the total annual value of morbidity cases avoided by health endpoint.

Estimation of benefits from changes in premature mortality

3. Calculate the percentage reduction in death envisaged as a result of the programme per year by age group.
4. Calculate the expected total number non-trauma deaths per year avoided by age group.
5. Calculate the present value of earnings gained by age group.
6. Estimate the value of expected deaths avoided.

Estimation of overall health benefits

7. Calculate the total annual benefits of the TSP reduction programme.

15.3.3 Solution Set

Question 1: Calculation of expected morbidity cases avoided per year
Using the dose–response information provided in Table 15.2, the expected number of cases avoided with the reduction of 300 micrograms are shown in Table 15.4, column (d).

Table 15.4 Morbidity: calculation of expected cases avoided per year

Health endpoint	Pop. units (1,000 pers.)	Cases avoided pop. unit/year/ 100 μgm^3	μgm^3 reduction envisaged	Total cases avoided/year
	(a)	(b)	(c)	(d = a * b*c/100)
Respiratory hospital admissions	8,375	0.66	300	16,583
Emergency room visits	8,375	12.95	300	325,285
Restricted activity days	4,690	3,163.33	300	44,508,100
Respiratory symptom days	8,375	10,066.67	300	252,925,000
Chronic bronchitis	4,188	3.37	300	42,299

Question 2: Total annual value of morbidity cases avoided per year
Using the cost of illness approach, the values per case of morbidity avoided by health endpoint has been calculated and reported in Table 15.5, column (b). They are then used to calculate the total value of morbidity cases avoided per year (column (c)).

Table 15.5 Total annual value of morbidity cases avoided

Health endpoint	Total cases avoided/year (a)	Value per case avoided (US$) (b)	Total value of cases avoided (c = a * b)
Respiratory hospital admissions	16,583	147.00	2,437,628
Emergency room visits	325,285	4.15	1,349,933
Restricted activity days	44,508,100	2.00	89,016,200
Respiratory symptom days	252,925,000	0.12	30,351,000
Chronic bronchitis	42,299	542.00	22,925,950
Total (US$)			146,080,710

Question 3: Expected death percentage reduction by the programme
The expected non-trauma death percentage reduction envisaged by the programme is calculated by multiplying the percentage reduction in non-trauma deaths per 100 micrograms as given in Table 15.3 times the reduction in TSP programmed. The calculation is reported in Table 15.6, column (c).

Table 15.6   Mortality: total death percentage reduction envisaged

Age group	Death reduction year/ 100 μg/m³ (%) (a)	μg/m³ reduction of programme (b)	Expected death reduct./year with programme (%) (c = a*b/100)
0–4	2.4	300	7.2
5–14	2.6	300	7.8
15–44	4.3	300	12.9
45–64	2.0	300	6.0
65 and up	0.8	300	2.4

Question 4: Calculation of the expected non-trauma number of deaths avoided per year

The percentage obtained in the previous step is used to calculate the non-trauma number of deaths avoided per year expected with the programme in Table 15.7, column (c).

Table 15.7   Total non-trauma deaths per year avoided

Age group	Expected death reduct./year with programme (%) (a)	Current non-trauma deaths/ year (b)	Expected deaths avoided/year with programme (c = a*b)
0–4	7.2	11,583	834
5–14	7.8	2,423	189
15–44	12.9	15,140	1,953
45–64	6.0	13,400	804
65 and up	2.4	7,292	175
Total		49,838	3,955

Question 5: Present value of earnings gained, by age group

To answer question 5, the human capital approach is applied. Using the residual working life by age group (Table 15.8, column (a)), an estimate of the average wage rate per year (column (b)) and an estimate of the long-run real discount rate (column (c)) provided in the database, the present value of earnings gained per person by age group can be calculated (column (d)).

Table 15.8 Present value of earnings gained by age group

Age group	Remaining expected working life (a)	Average wage per year (US$) 1991 (b)	Annual discount rate (%) (c)	Present value of future earnings (US$)
0–4	50	500	3	9,573
5–14	50	500	3	11,430
15–44	40	500	3	11,557
45–64	19	500	3	7,162
65 and up	7	500	3	3,115

Note that the earnings of age-group 0–4 are additionally discounted for ten years because they are assumed to occur in ten years time. Those for age-group 5–14 are additionally discounted for four years for the same reason.

Question 6: Value of expected deaths avoided with the programme
Multiplying the present value of future earnings per person by age group calculated in the previous step times the number of deaths expected to be avoided with the programme, the total value of premature deaths avoided is calculated (Table 15.9, column (c)).

Table 15.9 Value of expected deaths avoided

Age group	Expected deaths avoided/year with programme (a)	Present value of future earnings (US$) (b)	Total value of premature deaths avoided (c = a*b)
0–4	834	9,573	7,983,615
5–14	189	11,430	2,160,323
15–44	1,953	11,557	22,571,575
45–64	804	7,162	5,758,167
65 and up	175	3,115	545,150
Total			39,018,830

Question 7: Total annual benefits of the TSP reduction programme
Adding up the annual benefits from reduced morbidity (from Table 15.5) and those from reduced premature mortality (from Table 15.9), the total annual benefits of the TSP reduction programme are obtained and are presented in Table 15.10.

Table 15.10　Total annual benefits of the TSP reduction programme (US$, 1991)

	Value	Share (%)
Benefits of reduced morbidity	146,080,710	78.9
Benefits of reduced premature mortality	39,018,830	21.1
Total	185,099,540	100.0

15.3.4 Discussion

In many cases, due to lack of data for specific locations or pollutant, dose–response results for both mortality and morbidity are transferred from locations where thorough studies have been conducted. Nevertheless, caution must be used in implementing these transfers. Table 15.11 contrasts the dose–response results used in the exercise, which were taken from Cropper et al. (1997b) for Delhi, with results of a similar study conducted in Philadelphia by Schwartz and Dockery (1992). Clear differences can be seen. The reason for these differences lies in differences in the distribution of deaths by age and by cause. The impact of TSP on total non-trauma deaths is lower in Delhi than in the United States because a smaller fraction of deaths in Delhi are attributable to cardio-vascular and respiratory disease, the main categories of disease affected by air pollution. In the United States about half of all deaths are attributable to respiratory or cardio-vascular causes. In Delhi the figure is 20–25 per cent. The difference in impacts by age reflects the fact that, in the United States, three-quarters of all deaths occur after age 65. In Delhi three-quarters of all deaths occur before age 65.

Table 15.11   Comparison of Delhi and Philadelphia estimates of impacts of TSP

Mortality endpoint	Increase in mortality per $100\mu g/m^3$ increase in TSP (%)	
	Delhi (Cropper et al.)	Philadelphia (Schwartz and Dockery)
By selected cause		
Total deaths	2.3[*]	6.7[*]
Cardio-vascular disease	4.3[*]	9.2[*]
Respiratory	3.1[*]	Pneumonia: 10.2
		Chronic obstructive lung disease: 17.8[*]
By age group		
Ages 0–4	2.4	2.7
Ages 5–14	2.6[*]	
Ages 15–44	4.3[*]	
Ages 45–64	2.0[*]	
Ages 65 and up	0.8	9.1[*]

Note: [*] Indicates significance at 95% confidence level.

Sources: Schwartz and Dockery (1992) and Cropper et al. (1997b).

The fact that TSP has a smaller impact on cardio-vascular and respiratory deaths in Delhi is, in part, explained by differences in the composition of deaths within these categories. A smaller proportion of respiratory deaths in Delhi is attributable to chronic obstructive lung disease and a larger fraction to pneumonia and tuberculosis, which are affected less by particulates. Some of the differences in impacts by cause may be attributable to differences in the chemical composition and size distribution of particles between the United States and Delhi. While the ratio of particles less than 10 microns in diameter (PM_{10}) to TSP is about 0.55 in both locations, little is known about the ratio of fine particles ($PM_{2.5}$) to TSP in Delhi.

The valuation of mortality can also have a major impact on the estimated damages. In this example a value based on the HCM was used. This provides a much lower value than most estimates of VSL. Hence any estimate based on the latter must be regarded as a lower bound to the true cost of mortality. More work is being done to provide better estimates of VSL, or the value of life years lost, based on WTP methods.

In the case of morbidity, there is no choice but to use dose–response functions from other countries, since the collection of studies completed in the United States and other industrialized countries did not exist for Delhi. In the exercise, calculations are made for the following morbidity endpoints: respiratory hospital admissions, emergency room visits, restricted activity days (for adults), respiratory symptom days and chronic bronchitis. While this list is not exhaustive, it captures the health endpoints that are likely to have the largest monetary impact on total damages.

In valuing morbidity, one could use either cost of illness estimates, ideally based on Indian data, or estimates of willingness to pay to avoid morbidity transferred from US studies, with adjustment for income. In estimating total damages from air pollution in 36 Indian cities, Brandon and Homman (1995) follow the cost of illness approach. The values provided in Table 15.2 represent an average of their 'low' and 'high' estimates, with the exception of the value of chronic bronchitis. Their value for a case of chronic bronchitis vastly understates the seriousness of this disease. The US$542 figure is obtained by multiplying the human capital estimate for mortality (US$10,000) by the ratio of the value of a case of chronic bronchitis to the value of a statistical life in USEPA (1997).

The numbers in Table 15.2 must be interpreted with caution. Indeed, morbidity endpoints depend on cultural and economic factors that differ significantly between Delhi and the United States. Respiratory hospital admissions and emergency room visits, for example, depend on the price and availability of health care. What constitutes a restricted activity day depends on cultural factors, as well on the availability of paid sick leave. Besides, the coefficients in Ostro (1994) reflect the baseline incidence of each health endpoint in the city where the original study was conducted, not baseline incidence in Delhi.

Furthermore, the magnitude of the change in air pollution considered in the exercise 300 micrograms of TSP is much larger than the variation in the original Ostro study (1987).

NOTES

1. Pollutants such as particulate matter can give rise to acute and chronic effects. Acute effects are those that take place immediately after an increase in the pollution levels. Chronic effects also arise as a result of the increase in pollution, but occur over a much longer period of time (theoretically they are of indefinite duration).
2. In case of morbidity, however, the aggregation is allowed if the exposures affect different health endpoints. For example, in computing total health damages, it is appropriate to add cases of acute respiratory illness associated with short-term exposures to PM to cases of chronic bronchitis associated with long-term exposures to PM.
3. Assuming the simplified model is: $death = e^{\beta pollution}$, differentiate with respect to the pollution level: $(d\,deaths)/(d\,pollution) = \beta e^{\beta pollution}$. Recalling $e^{\beta pollution} = death$, substituting: $(d\,deaths)/(d\,pollution) = \beta\,death$, and rearranging $(d\,deaths)/(death) = \beta^{d pollution}$.
4. Calculations for morbidity are based on unit values in Ostro (1994) for PM_{10}. For mortality, they are based on Cropper et al. (1997). The relevant population is all persons in Delhi, except for restricted activity days (persons over 18) and chronic bronchitis (persons over 25).

CITED BIBLIOGRAPHY

Brandon, C. and K. Homman (1995), 'Valuing environmental costs in India: the economy-wide impact of environmental degradation', Mimeo, October.

Cropper, M., N. Simon, A. Alberini, S. Arora and P.K. Sharma (1997b) 'The health benefit of air pollution control in Delhi', *American Journal of Agricultural Economics*, **79**, 1625–9.

Cropper, M., N. Simon, A. Alberini and P.K. Sharma (1997a), 'The health effects of air pollution in Delhi, India', Policy Research Working Paper No. 1860, World Bank, Washington, DC.

ExternE (1999), *Externalities of Energy, Volume 7, Methodological Update*, Luxembourg: European Commission.

Freeman, A.M., III (1993), *The Measurement of Environmental and Resource Values: Theory and Methods*, Washington, DC: Resources for the Future.

Markandya, A. (1996), 'External costs of electricity: valuation of health impacts', in *Electricity, Health and the Environment: Comparative Assessment in Support of Decision-Making*, Vienna: International Atomic Energy Agency, pp. 199–214.

Markandya, A. (1999), 'The valuation of health impacts in developing countries', *Planejamento e Politicas Publicas*, **18**, 119–54.

Ostro, B. (1987), 'Air pollution and morbidity revisited: a specification test', *Journal of Environmental Economics and Management*, **14**, 87–98.

Ostro, B. (1994), 'Estimating the health effects of air pollutants. A method with an application to Jakarta', Policy Research Working Paper No. 1301, World Bank, Washington, DC.

Pope, C.A., M.J. Thun, M.M. Namboodiri, D.W. Dockery, J.S. Evans, F.E. Speizer and C.W. Heath (1995), 'Particulate air pollution as a predictor of mortality in a prospective study of US adults', *American Journal of Respiratory and Critical Care Medicine*, **151**, pp. 669–74.

Schwartz, J. (1993), 'Particulate air pollution and chronic respiratory disease', *Environmental Resources*, **62**, 7–73.

Schwartz, J. and D. Dockery (1992), 'Increased mortality in Philadelphia associated with daily air pollution concentrations', *American Review of Respiratory Disease*, **145**, 600–604.

United States Environmental Protection Agency (USEPA) (1997), *The Benefits and Costs of the Clean Air Act, 1970 to 1990*, Washington, DC: EPA.

Index